DATE			

The Gifted Group
in Later Maturity

* * *

THE GIFTED GROUP
IN LATER MATURITY

Carole K. Holahan and Robert R. Sears
in association with Lee J. Cronbach

Stanford University Press
Stanford, California

Stanford University Press, Stanford, California
© 1995 by the Board of Trustees of the
Leland Stanford Junior University
Printed in the United States of America

CIP data appear at the end of the book

Stanford University Press publications are distributed exclusively by
Stanford University Press within the United States, Canada, and Mexico;
they are distributed exclusively by Cambridge University Press
throughout the rest of the world.

This is the sixth volume of a series on intellectual giftedness published by Stanford University Press. All but the second volume are based on the Terman Study of the Gifted. The other volumes in the series, formerly known as Genetic Studies of Genius, are:

1. Mental and Physical Traits of a Thousand Gifted Children
   by Lewis M. Terman and others

2. The Early Mental Traits of Three Hundred Geniuses
   by Catharine M. Cox

3. The Promise of Youth: Follow-up Studies of a Thousand
   Gifted Children
   by Barbara S. Burks, Dortha W. Jensen, and Lewis M. Terman

4. The Gifted Child Grows Up: Twenty-five Years' Follow-up
   of a Superior Group
   by Lewis M. Terman and Melita H. Oden

5. The Gifted Group at Mid-Life: Thirty-five Years' Follow-up
   of the Superior Child
   by Lewis M. Terman and Melita H. Oden

This book is dedicated to the gifted men and women, whose generous sharing of their rich lives for over 70 years has made the Terman Study of the human life cycle possible.

Foreword

by Ernest R. Hilgard and Albert H. Hastorf

During the last three decades of his life, prior to his death on May 22, 1989, Dr. Robert R. Sears had been deeply involved in the follow-up studies of the group of children of superior intelligence initially studied by Dr. Lewis M. Terman in 1921. Dr. Terman had a long history of interest in the characteristics of intellectually gifted individuals. In 1921 he organized a study of a group of intellectually gifted youngsters, all of whom resided in California. His original interest focused on the psychological, behavioral, and physical characteristics of this group who were in the top 1 percent of measured intelligence. Dr. Terman benefited from the capable colleagueship of Dr. Melita Oden, who was associated with the study for over 30 years and with whom he authored several of the earlier volumes in the series of works on the Terman subjects.

Before his death in 1956, Dr. Terman designated those to be responsible for carrying on the work, including his son, Dr. Frederick E. Terman, Provost of Stanford University, and Dr. Quinn McNemar of the Department of Psychology, as custodians. Dr. Sears was to have the responsibility for planning and carrying out the continuing research operations. Faithful to the charge, Dr. Sears was responsible for five surveys of these cooperative subjects carried out between 1960 and 1986. The latter four of these surveys — carried out in 1972, 1976, 1982, and 1986 — are reported in this volume, the sixth in the series. The previous volume, published in 1959, was based on data gathered while Dr. Terman was still alive, but was published after his death. The 1960 survey was reported in a monograph by Dr. Oden.

In the course of these studies, Dr. Sears also had the advice and assistance of a number of professional psychologists at Stanford, including his wife, Dr. Pauline S. Sears, and Dr. Lee J. Cronbach of the School of Education, and

Dr. Albert H. Hastorf of the Department of Psychology. After 1972 the study's focus was altered from the characteristics and achievements of the gifted to how this group of individuals dealt with occupational retirement, the health issues of later maturity, and psychological adaptation to these later years.

Dr. Sears was particularly fortunate to have had the collaboration of Dr. Carole K. Holahan of the University of Texas at Austin. For a number of years she was a visiting scholar at Stanford — at the Institute for the Study of Women and Gender during 1978–80, and regularly in the Psychology Department in later years. During this time, she worked with Dr. Sears in conducting the later surveys and published several papers based on the data. Dr. Sears invited her collaboration on this volume in 1987.

The present volume was jointly planned and much of the data analysis carried out before Dr. Sears's death. He had written initial drafts of chapters on the study's background, attrition, the men's occupational history, marital patterns, and social networks. With one exception, Dr. Holahan wrote the other chapters and revised the entire manuscript. Dr. Cronbach analyzed and wrote most of the chapter on life satisfactions, and also updated the attrition analyses.

The second author of this foreword had been a colleague of Dr. Sears since 1961, and has now taken over responsibility for the Terman archive and the continuation of the study. The first author of this foreword was never directly involved with the study but was closely associated with Dr. Terman as a member of the Psychology Department from 1933 until the time of Dr. Terman's death. He can attest to Dr. Terman's deep interest in the participants in this study as individuals — thought of as "his children." The present volume is important not only because it reports a longitudinal study — we have in essence scientific biographies of this large sample — but because through it we learn a great deal about the life satisfactions, goals, and disappointments of gifted individuals in the later years of life. With the present interest in the status of women, much of the evidence bears on the ways in which the opportunities of gifted women were constrained in their generation. Were he alive today, Dr. Terman would be pleased with this volume that has so well carried out his plan for a lifetime study — and he would hope for more to come.

Preface

This volume traces the progress of the men and women in the Terman Study of the Gifted through the years of later maturity, when on average they were in their 60's and early 70's. The study was begun in 1921 by Dr. Lewis M. Terman, when the subjects averaged eleven years of age. It has continued for over 70 years and has become the longest life-cycle study in the history of the social sciences. This is the sixth in a series of books and monographs that document the lives of these gifted individuals at various points in the life cycle. The last comprehensive summary presented the results of the 1960 survey (Oden, 1968), when the subjects were well into mid-life, and averaged 50 years of age.

Begun at a time when little was known about the associated characteristics and long-term outcomes of intellectual giftedness, the Terman Study amassed a vast store of data on these individuals. Seeing the intellectual gifts of these subjects as a precious resource for our society, Dr. Terman was interested in knowing whether their intellectual superiority would be matched by superiorities in other domains or whether, as was commonly believed, they would be lacking in other positive characteristics, such as physical and mental health, social adjustment, and breadth of interests. He also wanted to know if the intellectual gifts the subjects demonstrated in childhood would be maintained into their adulthood years, or would be hopelessly lost, as was widely assumed.

The earlier work by Dr. Terman and his colleagues, tracing these lives from childhood to mid-life, has laid to rest these negative stereotypes about the lives of gifted individuals in childhood and adulthood. Now the Terman subjects have reached the years of later maturity, years that carry special challenges — physically, psychologically, and socially — after the highly productive years of mid-life. Thus it is appropriate now to see if the pattern of positive findings Dr.

xi

Terman reported for these individuals in earlier years persisted into their later years.

The Terman subjects came to later maturity at a fortunate time for the fields of life-span development and gerontology. In recent years, life-span developmental researchers have looked beyond childhood and adolescence, to study the entire life cycle. At the same time, earlier assumptions of broad decline in the process of aging are being replaced in the gerontological field by a more optimistic vision that searches for the determinants of successful aging. The study of the Terman subjects — a group that is advantaged in many respects — can provide invaluable insights into the prospects for successful aging, suggesting a benchmark against which to judge the process of aging more generally.

We have approached the book with several objectives. First, we have pursued one of the goals of Dr. Terman and his colleagues — that of providing rich and complete descriptive data on the subjects' lives — by extending the description of their lives into the years of later maturity. In so doing, we have maintained thematic continuity with earlier reports by including topics such as educational and career history, avocational pursuits, and physical and mental health. At the same time, however, we have supplemented these earlier themes with topics that are unique to later maturity, such as retirement and retrospective life satisfactions. Moreover, with the vast store of data in the Terman archives, we can begin to answer questions concerning the precursors of successful aging. We therefore also include analyses of antecedents of later-life outcomes in our presentation. We compare these subjects with the general population, and the subjects of other available life-cycle studies, whenever possible.

The book is intended for scholars and professionals in diverse disciplines who are interested in intellectual giftedness, the study of the life cycle, and gerontological studies. However, we have also endeavored to present the study's findings in a form that is accessible to the general reader. For example, to capture the uniqueness and rich variety in these subjects' life patterns, we have included a number of case studies along the way.

When Lewis Terman began this study in 1921, he was in his mid-40's. He died in 1956, and at his request Dr. Robert R. Sears assumed the research directorship of the study. Dr. Melita Oden continued as de facto manager and chief investigator through the analysis and publication of the 1960 data. In 1972 Dr. Pauline S. Sears and Dr. Lee J. Cronbach joined Dr. Sears in preparing the follow-up questionnaire. They, with the collaboration of Dr. Carole K. Holahan in 1982 and 1986, and Dr. Albert H. Hastorf in 1986, were responsible for the follow-ups which cover the years of later maturity, 1972–86.

Dr. Sears, joined by Dr. Cronbach, undertook the ambitious project of constructing a computerized data bank covering the 65 years of data collection, with over 4,000 variables. The coding and transfer to computer of the data from the many questionnaires took more than 10 years. In addition to the coding of the basic questionnaires, comprehensive specialized files were created, including a file on marital history and parental deaths and divorces constructed by Dr. Sears, and a file on educational history created by Dr. Cronbach. Completion of the data bank has received financial support from the National Institute of Aging, the Spencer Foundation, and the Ford Foundation. These data will be available to generations of scholars, and will provide the basis for continuing research into the nature of the human life cycle.

My own involvement with the study began when I was a visiting scholar at Stanford University from 1978 to 1980. I had the opportunity to join Dr. Sears in the work on the completion of the computerized data base, and to begin studies of my own with the gifted sample. In 1987 Dr. Sears invited me to join him in the work on this volume. Sadly, he did not live to see the volume completed. With his death in 1989, I have felt the deep loss of a colleague and a friend. I have been inspired through the sometimes lonely process of the completion of the book by his deep enthusiasm for and commitment to the project.

The book has received the support of many individuals. Lee J. Cronbach deserves special thanks. He graciously agreed to draft the major portion of the chapter on life satisfactions, and completed the updating of the analyses of attrition. In addition, he has served as a reader and statistical consultant for the manuscript. I would also like to thank Albert H. Hastorf, who has assumed the directorship of the Study, for his continuing support of the project, for his hospitality as I worked on the book at Stanford, and for making funds from the Terman Fund available to facilitate the book's completion. Historians Carl Degler and Hamilton Cravens also read chapters. John Loehlin and Bill Koch provided statistical advice.

The study could not have been completed without the able assistance of Eleanor Walker, research assistant for the Terman Study. Her cheerfulness and willingness to help were important at every point. At Stanford Press Muriel Bell offered continuing encouragement and constructive suggestions while the manuscript was being completed; Ellen F. Smith carried the project through the editing and production process. I would also like to thank Marilyn Yalom and the Institute for the Study of Women and Gender at Stanford for providing me with a home during my first two-year visit to Stanford.

Many others also contributed to the completion of the project. The Spencer Foundation provided research funds for the book, financing much of the data analysis, and enabling me to visit Stanford to consult the study files. The Hogg Foundation for Mental Health provided funds for the analysis of the women's data. Several graduate students were involved in the data analysis: Sul-Ri Bai, Hugh Crean, Deborah Duncan, Kate Mackie, Gloria Ramalho, and David Valentiner. A number of undergraduates also helped with the study: Margaret Bezmalinovic, Elizabeth Bruch, Erin Everett, Tracey Fowler, Dietland Hernandez, Xochil Montez, and Jennifer Svoboda. Jo Schneider provided helpful editorial advice, as well as typing parts of the first draft. Keri Trudeau, Kathleen Keeley, and Dean Garrett provided clerical assistance. I also greatly appreciate the continuing support of H. Paul Kelley, director of the Measurement and Evaluation Center at the University of Texas at Austin.

Finally, I am grateful to my family, whose encouragement and support helped make this book possible. I was heartened by my daughter, Alisa Holahan, who gave me continuing joy during my work on the manuscript, a time which coincided almost exactly with her first six years of development. My husband, Charles J. Holahan, was always available to offer support, both personal and professional, as the book progressed. His contributions and thoughtful advice are reflected throughout.

C.K.H.

Contents

PART V. OVERALL ADJUSTMENT

Figures

Tables

The Gifted Group
in Later Maturity

* * *

Introduction

In this volume we examine the later-life experience of the men and women in Dr. Lewis M. Terman's landmark study of gifted children. The individuals originally included in this (longitudinal) study now have reached the years of later maturity. After having participated for over 60 years in psychology's longest life-cycle study, by 1986 the subjects were on average in their mid-70's, and many remained active participants in the study.

This study of gifted children began in 1921, just three years after the close of World War I. The timing was auspicious. The war had revealed a rather surprising amount of illiteracy among young American men, and it had called attention to the need for articulate and intellectual leadership wherever groups of individuals worked together. With the more sophisticated military equipment and tactics of the early twentieth century, illiteracy and lack of intelligence were liabilities. Quickness of apprehension, capacious and accurate memory, and the ability to read and understand orders as well as instructions for the use of equipment were assets — provided they were associated with courage, leadership, and other qualities required for effective group productivity.

Identical qualities were needed in the rapidly growing industrial empires of the following decades. The massive organizations that were growing up in the steel, automobile, drug, and retail industries could no longer be managed by individual entrepreneurs; they needed many bright and sophisticated leaders.

The development of group intelligence tests during the war had provided an efficient means of selecting candidates for officer training and for other military tasks requiring intellectual ability, and industrial psychologists immediately began applying similar tests to personnel selection. But there remained the nagging question whether there was some lurking weakness of character or physique in people who were school-bright, and whether the brightness of youth might burn out later, reducing their long-term productivity in civilian occupations.

Some humanists, and not a few philosophers, were skeptical of psychologists' ability to measure such an intangible mental quality as intelligence. The notion of mental measurement apparently challenged some unspoken dualistic assumption about the relation of mind and body. However, practical educators and industrial personnel officers wanted solid answers to the above questions. Hence, Terman's plan to study the development of a group of gifted children was welcomed by those who were more interested in solving problems than in maintaining outworn philosophical assumptions.

Terman had published the Stanford-Binet intelligence test (his adaptation of the test devised in France by Binet and Simon) in 1916. The Stanford-Binet and the group tests developed by the U.S. Army had provided reliable measuring instruments for selecting a group of children with high intellectual potential. Two questions were on Terman's mind. First, were these school-bright children superior in other ways, too? Or were they, as common lore had it, physically weak and socially incompetent? Second, was their intellectual superiority a stable quality, permitting them to provide continuing leadership into adult life in business and the professions, or would they burn out, become deviant and perhaps even mad? The public at the time took comfort in the saying, "Early ripe, early rot."

Terman suspected that these negative assumptions about gifted individuals not only were false but also had for too long guided educational practice, to the clear detriment of society's potentially greatest human assets. Thus he began his study of gifted children to discover, first, whether they had other associated superiorities — motivational and other qualities needed for lifetime productivity, leadership, and success — and second, whether they would retain their intellectual superiority over the years.

Provisional answers to Terman's first question were not long in coming. Comparison of the study's gifted children with groups of unselected children showed clearly that these bright children were, on the average, superior in a number of other ways. They had more social as well as intellectual accomplishments in school; they were healthier, bigger, and stronger; and their conduct was more acceptable by the standards of the times. They were high achievers, not only in schoolwork but in many extracurricular activities as well. Terman's second question, whether the gifted would retain their superiority, could be answered only by following their progress through their later lives. This was why Terman's study of gifted children became a longitudinal one — the first and longest in human history.

Lest this recitation of the first findings from the 1920's suggest that this book is an antiquarian report from dusty archives, let us say at once that the archives are far from dusty, the research is contemporary and ongoing, and the main findings reported here are based on data collected between 1972 and 1986. We will be reporting some of the early data as antecedents to contemporary outcomes, however, and therefore some history will be in order in Chapter 2. There has been no major report of the study's results for nearly twenty years, and the details of the study — its origins, methods, and findings at intervening points in time — have somewhat dropped from the common knowledge of scholars.

Toward Understanding Successful Aging

The Terman Study could not have developed an emphasis on aging at a more opportune time for the field of gerontology. With the steady and dramatic increase of the elderly as a proportion of the general population, the attention of scholars and policymakers has turned to understanding successful aging and to optimizing the later years. Both individuals and society are searching for knowledge that will contribute to better physical, psychological, and social well-being during the years of later maturity.

In recent years, the tone of gerontological studies has become more positive and optimistic (e.g., Baltes & Baltes, 1990b; Perlmutter, 1990). In the early years of gerontology, a belief in unavoidable biological decline dominated approaches to the field. More recently, researchers have begun to question the inevitability of some of the losses commonly observed in aging (Rowe & Kahn, 1987). There is enormous variability among older individuals, and what is usual during the aging years is not necessarily linked to biological processes of aging. Many controllable risk factors can contribute to losses commonly attributed to aging. For example, the etiologies of cardiovascular disease and osteoporosis are dramatically affected by external risk factors. Moreover, psychosocial factors, such as social support and feelings of autonomy and control, interact with physical factors and can mitigate some of the undesirable outcomes of aging (Rowe & Kahn, 1987). Thus although recent approaches to gerontology do not deny the physical realities of aging, they encourage careful study to differentiate among normal, pathological, and optimal aging (Baltes & Baltes, 1990a).

Contemporary gerontology, while recognizing the realities of age-associated declines, is therefore increasingly the study of the possible. Successful aging was a theme of only a few earlier theorists, notably Jung (1933) and Erikson (1959; recently extended in Erikson, Erikson, & Kivnick, 1986), but today the possibilities for continued development and fulfillment through the aging years are emphasized throughout the field of gerontological studies (Baltes & Baltes, 1990b; Perlmutter, 1990). Inherent in this emphasis on successful aging is an awareness that human beings have much latent reserve. The tapping of that reserve and the delineation of its limits are important agendas for contemporary research on aging and offer potential for positive interventions.

For example, biological and medical researchers have noted the variability of physical aging and the benefits of preventative factors such as exercise and nutrition in minimizing disabilities (e.g., Ericsson, 1990; Fries, 1990; Kozma & Stones, 1990). Cognitive researchers, while documenting declines related to aging, are also investigating individual and environmental conditions that mitigate declines or minimize their impact on everyday life (Salthouse, 1991; Schaie,

1990; Willis, 1990). There is also an emerging interest in the untapped cognitive potential of aging people, as evidenced in studies of wisdom and creativity (Baltes, Smith, Staudinger, & Sowarka, 1990; Labouvie-Vief, 1985; Simonton, 1990). Investigators have explored the active efforts of aging individuals to shape their well-being and to maintain a sense of control and selfhood by manipulating goals and aspirations and interpreting their life experiences (Brandtstadter & Baltes-Gotz, 1990; George & Clipp, 1991). Finally, studies have shown the potential for social relationships to contribute to well-being in aging (Antonucci & Akiyama, 1990; Antonucci & Jackson, 1987).

Thus current research on aging emphasizes the maintenance of positive functioning through an understanding of the overall needs of older persons. This maintenance often involves providing needed supports for the older person, while at the same time building on individual capabilities. For example, Baltes and Baltes (1990a) advocate the fostering of healthy lifestyles that may prevent pathology and build physical and psychological reserves. At the same time, however, they recognize that aging typically involves more losses than gains, and they suggest a strategy of selection, optimization, and compensation to deal with increasing losses during the later years. In their view, both the individual and society must recognize and deal with the limitations of aging in a manner that maximizes the individual's functioning in areas of priority and that involves "a convergence of environmental demands, and individual motivations, skills, and biological capacity" (Baltes & Baltes, 1990a: 21).

Plan of This Book

These reflections bring us to our purposes in the study of the Terman subjects in later maturity. First, of course, this study provides information on the outcomes and correlates of intellectual giftedness in the later years, completing the knowledge base created by Terman and his colleagues. Do the subjects on average continue to exhibit the same high levels of adaptive skills they demonstrated earlier? Have their attitudes and behaviors in central realms of life changed from those exhibited earlier in the life cycle?

The data presented here are invaluable in answering such questions about the nature of later life for gifted individuals. We describe how this group of individuals has aged, how they have handled the inevitable changes in frequently exciting and fruitful lives, what they did with themselves as they relinquished some of the exacting tasks of middle age, and how they have felt about their past and present lives. Terman and his colleagues provided a rich and full record of these subjects' lives through middle age. No other data base of this size presently exists that can tell us how intellectually gifted individuals approach the aging years. Moreover, we will implicitly and explicitly be asking what an understanding of these individuals' lives contributes to the understanding of successful aging. We will pay particular attention to what the Terman subjects may be able to teach us about the potential for optimizing the later years. On average, their earlier personal and external life circumstances augured favorable outcomes. Have these individuals set an exceptional standard for the later years, as so many of them have done with respect to earlier achievement? How do they compare with individuals unselected for high intelligence in their approach to aging and in the favorability of outcomes? Because gender is a powerful shaper of lives, especially for this cohort, we will pay particular attention to the different ways that women and men may approach the challenge of aging well.

Finally, taking advantage of the vast store of data in the Terman archives, we will ask what early experiences shaped our subjects' responses to these later years and what factors differentiate between those with more and less favorable outcomes. We will search for antecedents of certain life outcomes, trying to find precursors of satisfaction or regret, of stability or instability, of different styles of working and mating. Because statistical summaries cannot fully capture the richness and variety of individual lives, or the interactions between personal characteristics and idiosyncratic events and circumstances, we will provide many case vignettes along the way to bring this study to life.

*   *   *

Part I provides basic background information about the study and the sample. Chapter 2 describes the contents and major conclusions of previous surveys. It gives the age-distribution and sex-composition of the later maturity group and the kinds of information available on the group. Chapter 3 outlines the sometimes dramatic historical context that surely influenced our subjects' lives and analyzes the attrition that occurred over the years in the original Terman sample. (A more detailed analysis of this attrition is presented in Appendix B).

In Part II, Chapters 4 and 5 review the occupational histories of the men and women in the later-maturity group. This history is explored in depth because of its central role. The experiences of the men and the women are dealt with in separate chapters because their occupational histories differed so greatly. These chapters conclude with descriptions of the retirement process.

Part III provides a comprehensive view of interpersonal relationships in the subjects' lives. Chapter 6 examines the variety of marital outcomes in the study, along with predictors of divorced and always-single status. The effectiveness of Terman's Marriage Questionnaire in predicting marital outcomes is also considered. Chapter 7 emphasizes the role of relationships in the subjects' lives in later maturity.

Part IV focuses on our subjects' personal involvements. Chapter 8 presents their interests and activities in later maturity, and Chapter 9 examines their orientations toward self and others, as reflected in their contemporary goals and values. These chapters delineate major areas of meaning for the subjects in the process of aging and examine the ways in which the subjects have changed over the years in these areas.

Part V presents different perspectives on overall adjustment. Chapter 10 first examines mortality patterns in the sample. It next considers health and well-being in 1986 and searches for antecedents of favorable outcomes. Chapter 11 assesses the subjects' retrospective views of their lives. In this important part of the aging process, individuals look back over their lives to integrate and evaluate them.

Chapter 12 brings the major findings from earlier chapters together to make a coherent picture. The chapter also reflects on what the findings from the lives of these gifted individuals can tell us about successful aging.

PART I

Background

Nature of the Study

Lewis M. Terman was born in 1877 on an Indiana farm. After the customary country schooling, at which he excelled, he began teaching at a school in a nearby town, interspersing teaching with attendance at a normal school in order to prepare himself for graduate work in psychology. He went to Indiana University in 1902, and transferred to Clark University the following year to work with G. Stanley Hall. At Clark he began a serious exploration of the literature on education of gifted students, and completed his doctoral work in 1905 with a dissertation project in which he compared seven bright and seven dull boys on a 48-hour battery of individual tests. He found wide individual differences among the boys, and some differences between the two groups, but the research left him with no solid conclusions about the nature of intellectual giftedness or how to measure it reliably.

Never sturdy, and suffering from tuberculosis, Terman took a teaching job in Los Angeles in order to have a favorable environment for his health. He had little time or opportunity to pursue his interest in the gifted, but the 1908 publication of Binet and Simon's intelligence test in France rearoused his interest. He resolved at once to construct an American version of the test, an opportunity ensured him when he received an appointment in Stanford University's Department of Education in 1910.

During the next six years, while he was constructing and standardizing the intelligence test that became known as the Stanford-Binet, he kept a persistent lookout for children of unusually high intelligence quotient (IQ). By 1916 he had located well over 100 with IQs of 140 or higher. His studies of them, and his interviews with their parents and teachers, suggested that they by no means fit the common stereotype of one-sidedness, physical weakness, and social incompetence—quite the contrary. It was then that he began planning for the large scale systematic investigation that has come to be known as the Terman Gifted Children Study.

World War I delayed its start, as it did another famous child research enterprise at the State University of Iowa. In 1917 both Terman and Bird Baldwin, who had just been appointed director of the new state-supported Iowa Child Welfare Research Station, joined the Army task force assigned to construct the group tests to be used for officer selection and personnel placement in the armed forces. This experience was valuable, for it enabled Terman quickly to construct the Terman Group Test after his return to Stanford, and this instrument proved to be of major assistance in selecting high school students for the gifted group. (The Stanford-Binet was useful only with younger children, for older children with high IQs bumped up against the ceiling of the test.)

The Study's Beginning, 1921–28

Early in 1921, the Commonwealth Fund awarded Terman a $20,300 grant to begin his study, and by September he had constructed a massive questionnaire for parents, a briefer one for teachers, and an interest blank for the children. He had secured and trained four very able young women to serve as field-workers to conduct the search for subjects, and he was ready to go. His aim was to locate 1,000 children with IQs of 140 and over, to make a detailed study of their physical, social, and psychological qualities, and to compare them with samples of children unselected for intellectual brilliance.

Selection

Field-workers visited grades three to eight in all the elementary schools of San Francisco, Oakland, and Los Angeles, and in some of those in a dozen smaller cities and towns. They secured teachers' nominations of the brightest and youngest children in each class.* These nominees were given the National Intelligence Test B, and those who secured high scores were then tested with an abbreviated form of the Stanford-Binet. After this second seeding, the highest-scoring children were tested with the full Stanford-Binet test. Those achieving IQs of 135 or over were selected for the research group (see Burks, Jensen, & Terman, 1930; Terman et al., 1925).

A similar procedure was used for selecting high school students, from the same communities, but in this case Terman relied on a single testing with the Terman Group Test. About two-thirds of the high school students selected were located in a cooperative effort by a number of Californian high school principals,

---

* In California schools of the 1920s, skipping or repeating half-grades was common. It was a standard procedure for equalizing the abilities of the children in a class. The youngest children in a class would often be the brightest. In recent years "tracking" has been substituted to help in the education of both retarded and gifted children, with "enrichment" sometimes added for the latter.

a process only loosely supervised by Terman. Altogether, 309 high school students were added to the research group.

These search procedures were not totally haphazard, but they certainly did not yield a random selection of Californian children with high IQs. In the three large cities, the field-workers made a conscientious effort to locate every child who fit the IQ criterion, but a careful test of their effectiveness in two large elementary schools suggested that perhaps 20 percent of the suitable subjects were missed. The search in the other communities was less intensive and much less systematic, and in only one southern Californian county was there any attempt to examine rural schools. No private, parochial, or Chinese schools were included in the search. In the final selection, 67 percent of the children were from the large cities, 26 percent were from towns of less than 20,000 population, and 7 percent were from rural areas. Terman had originally wished to get all the children with IQs that placed them in the upper 1 percent of the population of the three metropolitan areas. He gave up this effort when it became evident that the cost would far exceed his resources. Since he wanted a large number of cases, he settled for the less expensive alternative of collecting those who could be found easily rather than the smaller number who would constitute a total of all possible cases from a specifiable population sample. Publicity about the study made it easy to discover additional cases during the years just after 1922. Some school systems undertook searches on their own initiative, and school psychologists throughout the state, and even a few from other states, occasionally brought bright children to Terman's attention. A substantial number of siblings of the originally selected children were tested too, and this added to the size of the group. Forty of these were added in 1923 and 58 more in 1928. When Terman stopped adding new cases in 1928, he had established a research group of 1,528 children who constituted a nonrandom sample of mainly Californian children, chiefly from urban schools, with IQs of 135 or over. The median IQ was 147.

Demographic Characteristics

The unsystematic selection of this group of children makes impossible its comparison with other samples for any purpose that would lead to inferences about the relative frequency of secondary qualities in the gifted and comparison groups. In order to make an inference about the relative frequency of males and females in a high IQ sample, for instance, that sample would have to be either a total population which could be compared with some other total population, such as all the children in a particular city or state, or it would have to be a genuinely random sample of them. We do know the relative frequency of males and females in California in 1920, and we know that each sex had an average IQ of 100. Our gifted group, however, is neither the total population of gifted Californian children nor a random sample of them. Therefore, the relative frequency of the two sexes or of any of the other demographic qualities discussed below tells us nothing about the correlation of these qualities with giftedness. They are related to many other characteristics of children, however, and it is important to be aware of the group's characteristics in these respects.

Gender. When additions to the group were discontinued in 1928, it contained 856 boys and 672 girls. Terman was unable to give a satisfactory explanation for this disparity in number. There was ample evidence that the selection tests were nondiscriminatory. There were at that time slightly more boys than girls in elementary school, but the difference was not large enough to account for the relative number of cases located. The gender difference among the high school students was even greater than among the elementary school children, but no data were reported for total high school enrollment by sex. Terman rejected the notion that teachers would nominate more boys than girls; most of the elementary school teachers were women, and therefore he assumed that if they had any bias it would favor girls. We now know that this assumption was false, and that there very likely may have been a bias toward boys in teachers' nominations, but we have no direct evidence for this. Terman hazarded a suggestion that perhaps males are more variable in intelligence than females and that had he made a search for the lowest 1 percent of IQs, he would have found more males also. Our own conclusion is that the method of search and selection was too unsystematic to warrant trust in the sex difference figures as a stable finding worthy of explanation.

Age. The mean birthdate for boys was January 1910; for the girls it was October 1910. The respective Standard Deviations (S.D.'s) were 3 years, 9 months, and 3 years, 7 months. The total range of birthdates for boys was 1900 to 1925; for girls it was 1903 to 1924.

This wide range makes for a little awkwardness in some kinds of data analysis, but the difficulty is minor. There were very few extreme cases, and the effective range was about 18 years rather than 25. In any case, two-thirds of the children were within a range of seven and a half years (one S.D. on either side of the mean). With few exceptions they all belong to the generation that experienced World War I while they were children, that had reached later adolescence or young adulthood at the onset of the Great Depression, that was reasonably mature at the onset of World War II, and that was in young middle age at the beginning of the postwar economic lushness. Most of them were a little too old to participate as parents in the postwar Baby Boom, and none of them was young enough to belong to the rebellious youth movement of the 1960's.

Parents' national and racial origin. Eighty percent of the fathers and 83 percent of the mothers were born in the United States. The preponderance of these were from California (17 and 23 percent, respectively), the middle western farming states (36 and 35 percent), and the North Atlantic seaboard (12 and 11 percent). Only Texas contributed as much as 1 percent of the remainder. The foreign-born parents were from many countries, but three areas or nationalities contributed most of them: Great Britain and the Commonwealth (6 percent and 6 percent respectively), Northern Europe (4 percent and 4 percent), and Russia and Eastern Europe (6 percent and 4 percent).

The family culture in which a child develops is determined by more generations than just the parental. Terman et al. (1925, ch. 3) calculated the percentage of contribution by nationality of the two preceding generations also — grandparents and great-grandparents — and found that Britain and the Commonwealth, Northern and Eastern Europe contributed 54 percent, 30 percent, and 6.5 percent respectively. The predominant immigration during the preceding century had been from Britain and Northern Europe, and this is clearly reflected in these figures. The Russian and East European immigration was just beginning in the parental generation that spawned the sample of gifted children. Those immigrant parents were almost all of Jewish religion and descent. America's intellectual wealth continued to increase by Jewish immigration through two more generations after that one, though it was always a bitter wind that blew them westward. Since World War II the wind has shifted to the south, and Israel has been the beneficiary of the flight from Eastern Europe. In the meantime, that first wave of Jewish immigrants, together with several American, French, and German families of Jewish heritage, provided 10.5 percent of the children in the gifted group.

Racially, the group was almost entirely white, about 90 percent of various North European stocks, with only a tiny representation of the Mediterranean or its Latin American derivative. Asia was represented by a few Japanese-American children, and there was only one black child.

The chief significance of national origin is in respect of language. English had been the family language of about 86 percent of the children for three or more generations, and only a tiny fraction — perhaps 3 or 4 percent — grew up in bilingual homes. In connection with the problem of bias in selection of the children, these figures suggest one further factor that deserves mention. The selection tests depended heavily on the skillful use of language, and bilingualism or even recent family adoption of English may have handicapped some children in their test performance. Language may also have had an unconscious influence on teachers' nominations.

Parents' education. Both the fathers and mothers of the gifted group were better educated than the average of their generation. The median grade completed was tenth for the fathers and eleventh for the mothers, a gender-difference characteristic of that generation. At the upper end of the educational ladder, 29 percent of the fathers and 20 percent of the mothers had a bachelor's degree, or higher, from a four-year college or university. Their professional training was also relatively extensive. Among the fathers there were 23 Ph.D.'s, 47 M.D.'s, and 52 law degrees. Among the mothers, there were 4 Ph.D.'s, 3 M.D.'s, and 1 law degree. Doubtless this heavy weighting of graduate degrees was partly a product of Terman's occasional recruiting from his colleagues' families. None of the parents was still a student at the time of the children's selection, so these figures probably represent a final statement about parental education.

Parents' occupations. At the time of the children's selection, 17 percent of the mothers were employed, and almost half of these were in occupations listed by the U.S. Census as professional, semiprofessional, and higher level of business (Classes I and II). The remainder classified themselves as housewives. In 1900 less than 5 percent of married women in the general population were employed, and even in 1940 the figure was 15 percent. All the living fathers were employed, 50 percent in the first two Census classes. With respect to the remaining occupational categories, almost 9 percent were in some aspect of ranching or farming, mainly in owner or management positions. Only 10 percent were judged to be in skilled trades, minor business, and semi-skilled or sales occupations. The fathers averaged 45 and the mothers 40 at the time these data were obtained, so probably the percentage of Classes I and II did not change much thereafter.

Family composition. The family of origin for these children was commonly intact — that is, with a father, a mother, and their child or children living in the same household. The single-parent household was by no means rare, but in contrast with today, single parenting was much more often caused by death than divorce. Almost 8 percent of the children lost their fathers before they reached age twelve, and as many more did so during adolescence. About 4 percent lost their mothers during these same two periods. Divorce broke up the families of about 6 percent of the boys and 5 percent of the girls. Not all these losses resulted in single-parenting; if the remaining parent was the father, he usually remarried. But 11.5 percent of the boys and 7.6 percent of the girls grew up with a single parent; this was the mother in all but two cases of boys who were already in mid-adolescence at the time of their mothers' deaths.

Most of the children had siblings, but about 17 percent had none. Another 32 percent were the oldest in a multichild family, and 21 percent were the middle children in a family of three or more. Youngest children comprised 30 percent of the sample. There were no sex differences in these ordinal position frequencies.

Early Measurement

The great bulk of the data collected in the first wave of the study focused on contemporary matters and may be relied upon to whatever extent any reports and judgments of current events can be considered accurate. However, because the children ranged in age from 2 to 22 years at the time they were selected, information about the early childhood of many of them had to be retrospective. Reports on the younger children were probably fairly accurate, for most of what the parents and teachers reported was based on contemporary observation. For the older children, those in high school, the retrospective reports are suspect. By the time a youngster has reached the teenage years, the mother's recollection of the age when he or she had measles is likely to be a bit cloudy.

The field-workers were responsible for final selection of nearly all the younger children (except siblings added by Terman himself between 1923 and 1928) and many of the high school students. A field-worker would interview a child, give a Stanford-Binet, and interview the mother (only occasionally the father) and the teacher. She would leave a questionnaire with the mother and teacher and ask that it be mailed to Terman. She also filled out a brief questionnaire herself, the Whittier Environmental Data blank, which was an objective appraisal of the home and the neighborhood, providing the basis for a useful estimate of socio-economic status.

Parent questionnaire. This 16-page questionnaire was usually filled out by the mother, though many fathers evidently assisted. The areas covered most intensively were health history and current health status, the child's intellectual interests, amount and kind of preschool age tutorial assistance, school experience, extracurricular interests, and family background. Terman's interest in achievement and talent was nowhere more evident than in the sections asking about parental and grandparental accomplishments and honors. The children's character and personality were examined by a set of rating scales of 25 traits and a number of questions concerning peer relationships and minor personality deviance.

Teacher questionnaire. Questions to the teachers were appropriate to their vantage point. Queries about the health of the children were limited to those aspects a teacher might notice, and emphasis was placed on intellectual qualities and interests, school achievements, social adjustment, and peer relations. The teachers rated the same 25 dimensions of personality and social behavior as the parents.

Medical and anthropometric examinations. About half the subjects were given a careful medical examination and were measured anthropometrically by two assistants from Baldwin's laboratory at the Iowa Child Welfare Research Station. The medical reports seem to have had questionable value for the developmental study of individual children; there were too few negative findings to offer assistance in understanding any one child. The anthropometric measures were — and remain — state-of-the-art, but since the children varied so widely in age around the crucial pivot of puberty, the use of the measures is laborious because they must be referred constantly to different age norms.

Children's questionnaire and tests. The children's first data contributions, other than their intelligence tests, were obtained from an interest test distributed by the field-worker at the time of her home visit. The questions were mainly about intellectual interests — reading and school subject preferences — career anticipations, and extracurricular interests — collections, recreation, and things made, invented, or constructed (e.g., artistic or mechanical creations).

In the late spring of 1922, the children of elementary school age and a few of those in high school were brought together in groups of 20 to 50 to take a large battery of school achievement tests and several personality tests which measured gender role, over- and under- self-estimation, sociability, and knowledge and preferences about games. Some of the personality tests were situational tests with surprisingly high reliability and validity coefficients, a few high enough to provide meaningful measures for individual children, and all high enough to permit significant comparisons between the gifted group means and the means for control groups.

Initial Findings

The hundreds of questionnaire items, listings, and ratings, together with the children's test scores, permitted an enormous number of such comparisons. Terman directed his initial efforts toward the question of how the gifted group differed from unselected groups. They differed substantially in some respects and very little in others. Some generalizations from the dozens of findings can help to provide a kind of "psychological demography" of the group. This is comparable to the list of demographic characteristics we gave above in one sense: it characterizes this group of subjects with respect to certain qualities that are important in understanding what kind of people they were. It is quite different in another respect, however. The demographic characteristics described earlier were highly dependent on the selection process, while the psychological demographics are based on comparisons with fully appropriate control groups, usually either normative samples or else the other children in the same school classes. Thus we can say not only that these qualities characterize our present group of gifted children but that, *in general,* they differentiate gifted from unselected children. Three such generalizations, with some examples to pinpoint their limits and flesh out their behavioral substance, can serve to summarize the findings of the first wave of this longitudinal study.

Precocity. The gifted children were precocious in many ways, the most extreme being with respect to the use of language. They talked in sentences earlier than most children, and they learned to read much earlier, the majority by four years of age, most of them self-taught. They were also precocious in arithmetic and music, though less spectacularly so, but not at all in painting or common motor skills. Leisure and play interests paralleled their skills. Reading was the favorite occupation for spare time, and at preschool age many of the children were already fascinated by atlases and encyclopedias. It is to be remembered, of course, that the group was selected by the Stanford-Binet and the Terman Group Test, both of which are highly dependent on language and much less so on mathematical reasoning. This group of children can be labeled most accurately as language-gifted, or Stanford-Binet gifted.

Mental age as behavior determinant. Through the school years and into adolescence, these children's interests, attitudes, and knowledge developed in correspondence with their mental age rather than with their chronological age. Their academic achievement as measured by tests, their interest and liking for various future occupational careers, their knowledge about and interest in games, their choice of recreational reading materials, and their moral judgments about hypothetical conduct were all characteristic of older non-gifted children whose mental age range was approximated by this much younger and brighter group. Even the intellectual level of their collections was more mature than that of their chronological age-mates.

Variability. Both the initial and continuing precocity were qualities of the gifted group. The mean maturity level of the children's interests, knowledge, and behavior was significantly greater in many ways than that of unselected control children measured with the same instruments in the same schools at the same time. The variability within the gifted group was substantially less on all measures involving knowledge or other intellectual matters such as maturity of occupational expectations. Nevertheless, there was substantial variability within the gifted group, even on achievement tests. On such non-intellectual matters as activity level of preferred games and social interaction, the variability among individuals was as great as it was in the comparison groups. To put it another way, the Terman group was most homogeneous in those aspects of intellect and behavior that were most nearly related to the qualities of mind measured by the selection tests. The farther removed a behavior aspect or an interest was from that domain, the more heterogeneous the group was.

The significance of this generalization is somewhat hidden in the early measurements of these children because Terman emphasized matters of intellect so strongly in his choice of things to measure. It will become evident as we glance quickly at the later years — young adulthood and middle age, when matters of intellect are crowded into their proper corner by friendships, marriage, careers, children, economics, community service, politics, religion, and the unending fight to keep life on an even keel — that the Terman gifted group provided quite sufficient variability and heterogeneity of developmental patterns to permit a useful search for causes and consequences in the psychological and social aspects of the human life course, whether the subjects be Binet-gifted or not.

Follow-up Surveys Through Mid-life: 1928–60

By 1928, three-fourths of the subjects were in high school, college, or graduate school, or had finished their education altogether; 39 percent of the men and 43 percent of the women had completed all the formal education they would ever get. That year marked the beginning of the wave of follow-ups that have continued at approximately five-year intervals through 1986. Terman secured information by several means: questionnaires and rating scales were answered by parents, teachers, and the subjects themselves, and, later, by spouses. At three follow-up dates — 1928, 1940, and 1950 — field-workers who went to the subjects' homes reported their interviews with not only the subjects but also their parents, when available, and often their spouses. In both 1940 and 1950, hundreds of the subjects, with their spouses, were brought together in small groups for the administration of a high-level intelligence test, the Concept Mastery Test, and extensive questionnaires about their family lives, marriages, and the presence or absence of children. Since Terman's death in 1956, there have been five follow-ups, all by mail questionnaires. A brief review of the methods used and the kinds of information obtained by each of these follow-ups since 1928 will be useful as background for an understanding of the life-history variables to which we will refer in later chapters.

1928 Follow-up

In 1928 the field-workers interviewed about three-fourths of the subjects and submitted reports on their then current educational status, changes in family situation, health, salient personality qualities, and significant events that might be expected to influence future development. A parent (usually the mother) answered a 4-page questionnaire covering these same areas, and rated the subject on twelve dimensions of behavior. Teachers' responses to a questionnaire similar to that of 1922 provided information on educational status and several personality variables. An interest and information blank from the subject emphasized both academic and extracurricular interests as well as career and educational intentions and preferences.

1936 Follow-up

There were two mail questionnaires in 1936, one an 8-page "Information Blank" sent to the subjects, and the other a 4-page questionnaire sent to the parents. The former established a format and pattern of inquiries that was repeated, in substance, in each follow-up questionnaire through 1986. The domains covered were education, occupation, avocation and interests, health, emotional status and adjustment, social affiliations, marital status, family development and children, bereavements, disappointments, good fortune, and achievements. This list need not be repeated for each subsequent follow-up, though in the years of later maturity there has been some variation in the detail with which some domains have been explored. We will comment on these matters as well as describe the additional domains examined in the appropriate paragraphs.

The parents' questionnaire of 1936 was devoted to a quite detailed exploration of the subject's personality, motivation, and social behavior, especially in the domains of achievement, sociability, leadership, and sexual orientation. It also updated the basic demographic information about parents and siblings, especially their health, marital, and occupational status.

1940 Follow-up

The 1940 survey was the most intensive of all the follow-ups. It included a parents' questionnaire, modeled after the one used in 1936 but containing in addition thirteen graphic rating scales relating to dimensions of personality and social behavior that had been rated by parents in 1922 and 1928.

The subjects' information blank was twice as long as that of 1936, covering all the same domains but in more detail, and with what seems in retrospect a more searching demand for information and self-judgments. There were questions also on political and public service activities and, for the first time, on the use of alcohol.

This was the first year of the marriage study of the gifted group. By 1940, 68 percent of the men and 70 percent of the women were married, and 37 percent and 39 percent, respectively, had children. The subjects came together in small groups, with spouses if they had them, to fill out an elaborate questionnaire called "Personality and Temperament" and a briefer one designed to discover the favorable and unfavorable aspects of their marriages. As mentioned above, they also took Form A of the Concept Mastery Test.

In this same year the field-workers visited many of the subjects' homes and reported independently on most of the same domains that had been included in the subjects' and parents' questionnaires. They also rated both subject and spouse on a dozen behavioral dimensions as these were displayed during the visit.

1945 Follow-up

The 1945 addition to the usual domains in this questionnaire was the record of military service or war-related work. The mailing was poorly timed, for many of the men (and spouses of the women) were still in military service, and they were unable to report on their completed war experiences because they had not, in fact, completed them.

1950–55 Follow-up

The regular information blank administered in 1950 was half as long as the 1940 one, but it covered all the same domains; in 1955 an even briefer general information blank was administered. Again most of the scales were ones that had been used in previous years. In addition, the subjects answered a "Supplementary Biographical Data" questionnaire in 1950, an eight-page set of queries and self-rating scales that went exhaustively into feelings about parents, spouse, children, and many external events having to do with career and peer relationships.

This was the other intensive period for the marriage study. As part of the continuing detailed attention to marital matters, Terman included a questionnaire on "Rate of Reproduction" in 1950 which investigated contraceptive practices, feelings about child-bearing, continence, fertility, and other aspects of the biology and social psychology of marriage.

In the decade since 1940, Terman had constructed Form B of the Concept Mastery Test, and in small-group meetings many hundreds of the subjects took it. Four field-workers performed the same kinds of visits and interviews in 1950–52, and made the same kinds of reports, that they had performed in 1940.

By 1950, 75 percent of the men and 74 percent of the women had children. The subjects answered a 4-page questionnaire about each of their offspring, providing (more briefly) much the same kind of information that their parents had provided about them in 1922. A very brief questionnaire covered the usual domains in more or less skeletal fashion.

1960 Follow-up

An information blank very similar to that of 1950 was sent to the subjects in 1960. No other data were secured, but as these from the 1960 questionnaire were tabulated, it became clear that sufficient information had been collected to answer Terman's question about the staying power and the relative effectiveness of these gifted "children." They were now 50 years old, on the average, and even the youngest ones had demonstrated beyond doubt that their careers, on average, were already highly successful. What further research was called for? A costly pro forma extension of the evidence with this vigorous (and busy) middle-aged group seemed unnecessary, and they were not old enough to begin a more gerontologically oriented study. It was decided to wait until they were old enough and then begin investigating the ways in which a gifted group grew into later maturity. This decision created a 12-year gap in the stream of follow-up studies.

Findings Through Mid-life

By 1972 an unequivocal answer had been obtained to Terman's second question, namely, whether these originally school-bright children would retain their academic and intellectual superiority in adulthood, and whether they would show comparable competence in other domains, such as the occupational, economic, marital, moral, and whether they would show social leadership. The general results can be summarized under but two headings.

Maintenance. In those aspects of living and behavior that rely heavily on language, abstract thinking, and other intellectual skills, the gifted children retained or even enhanced their superiority. On the Concept Mastery Test, for example, they were clearly in the top 1 percent of the population when they took the two forms of the test at average ages of 30 and 40 years, respectively (see Bayley & Oden, 1955). Their academic performance was almost (but not quite) equally superior. In high school and college their grades were consistently high, and approximately eight times as many continued for doctoral degrees as was common at that time among college graduates.

Education is so closely linked with occupation that, not surprisingly, 70 percent of the men entered occupations in the top two classifications of the U.S. Census (professional and high-level business) and 95 percent ended their careers at that level. The proportion was less for the income-working women, but the circumstances of their entering employment were often so different from those of the men that comparison is not very meaningful. This matter will be discussed further in Chapter 5. Income, in turn, is so linked with occupation that, as would be expected, the average income of the men subjects by 1972 was about four times that of the general population. The women lagged behind somewhat, because fewer of the income workers were at the professional level. The homemakers' husbands, however, had average incomes at least as high as those of the men subjects. Membership in organizations and volunteer work were both high on the average, but it is difficult to find data for comparison with an unselected sample; in any case, these activities are related rather closely to occupation and income.

Variability. In childhood, nearly all of the subjects had parents or guardians to cope with exigencies of life in the outer world. These caretakers were themselves competent people and most of them provided the children with a stable, supportive environment. Hence in childhood the children's homogeneity of intelligence led to a relative homogeneity in the other main performance domains: schoolwork and leisuretime activities, in which intellectual level plays an important role. As the children grew into adolescence, young adulthood, and middle age, and as new developmental tasks faced them without the support of parents, other aspects of their personality and the nature of the events of the outer world began to weigh more heavily in determining the kinds of lives they would live and the success with which they themselves would cope with exigencies.

For example, the incidence of divorce, alcoholism, and suicide illustrate the existence within the group of wide variability in areas apparently unconnected with the intellectual capacity for which the subjects were selected. Their rate of divorce through mid-life was identical with that for the nation as a whole. The frequency of suicide did not differ, nor did the apparent frequency of homosexuality; for neither of these items, however, can great confidence be placed in the complete accuracy of the data of the study or those of other investigators. Comparative figures on alcoholism at late middle age suggested that the gifted had no special facility for avoiding that fate. In sum, it must be concluded that, whatever the averages may show, and however the group as a whole even in later life may cluster toward the favorable end of any distribution related to intelligence, there is still variability in the outcomes of their lives in their occupational and marital success, their health, their effectiveness as people relating to other people, and in their personal happiness.

The Present Focus on Later Maturity, 1972–86

The present study reports on 569 men and 494 women, referred to here as "the later-maturity group." These persons filled out a follow-up questionnaire in any of the years 1972, 1977, 1982, or 1986. Because not all respondents answered all questions, the N's in tables may be less than 569 and 494, for the men and women respectively. The data on the later-maturity group are drawn from all the information gathered about them since they entered the original sample (referred to in this book as "the Terman group" or "the Terman sample"). Following are descriptions of the age-distributions of the men and women in the later-maturity group, the follow-ups from 1972 to 1986, and the kinds of data in the data bank.

Age-distributions of Later-maturity Group

The average birth year of the total original Terman group was 1910. The averages in the later-maturity group were July 1910 (men) and June 1911 (women). The standard deviations were 3.8 and 3.5 years respectively, essentially the same as in the original sample. To show the age-distribution of the later-maturity group, we have divided the total group into three subgroups by age. Tables 2.1 and 2.2 present the age-breakdowns for the men and women respectively. The

TABLE 2.1

Age-Groups of Men in Later-Maturity Group by Follow-up Year and for Total Group

| | Age-group of respondents | | | | | | Total | |
| | Youngest | | Middle | | Oldest | | | |
Follow-up year	N	Pct.	N	Pct.	N	Pct.	N	Pct. of original Terman group
1972	127	25.7%	246	49.7%	122	24.6%	495	57.8%
1977	106	24.9	213	50.0	107	25.1	426	49.8
1982	116	27.8	205	49.0	97	23.2	418	48.8
1986	108	28.3	194	50.9	79	20.7	381[a]	44.5
Total later-maturity group	149	26.2	289	50.8	131	23.0	569	65.0

SOURCE: Questionnaires from indicated years.

NOTE: The "total late-maturity group" consists of all the men in the original Terman group who answered a questionnaire in any of the four follow-up years. As a result, numbers in the bottom row exceed the number answering the questionnaire in any particular year.

[a]This figure includes ten men whose questionnaires were filled out by relatives after the subjects' death.

divisions were made on the basis of birth dates for the entire Terman group of 856 men and 672 women. The subgroups are composed of the youngest quarter of the group, the middle 50 percent, and the oldest quarter.

The average ages of the men in these three groups in 1972 were 57, 62, and 67 years respectively. We find no differential effects of attrition on the three age-groups in 1972 and 1977 for the men. As can be seen in Table 2.1, however, by 1982 the percentage in the oldest group had shrunk a little in favor of the youngest group, and by 1986 the percentage in the youngest group was 7 percent higher than that in the oldest. The middle group retained the 50 percent with which it started at birth. The number of available cases in the later-maturity group, given in the last column, dropped from 58 percent of the original group in 1972 to 44.5 percent in 1986. The numbers of returned questionnaires for each follow-up year and for the later maturity group as a whole are also shown in Table 2.1. The bottom line shows the numbers and percentages of the three age-subgroups in the total later-maturity group. It is to be remembered that this latter is composed of subjects who returned any one or more of the four questionnaires. That is why the bottom-line numbers are larger than those of any single follow-up year.

For the women, the average age of the youngest group in 1972 was almost 57, and the average ages of the middle and oldest groups were 61 and 65 respectively. The participation rates in 1972, 1977, and 1982 were remarkably similar, with differential attrition in the oldest group beginning to occur in 1986. The available proportion of the original Terman study group dropped from 66 percent in 1972 to 50 percent in 1986. In general, the women have maintained a slightly higher rate of participation in the study than the men through their aging years, but have shown the same reduction in the size of the sample over the years from 1972 to 1986. The last line of Table 2.2 includes the number and percentage of the women in the total later-maturity group who were in each age-group. As with the men, the later-maturity group of women has a slightly greater proportion of younger subjects in comparison to older subjects.

1972 Follow-up

By 1972 the subjects were in their early sixties, on average, and for nearly all of them education had become a less important domain for current report. Marriage, family, and career had replaced it. Furthermore, the differentiation between men's and women's lives — the responsibilities and opportunities of family life, career, and service to society — had become more and more salient in the thinking and research planning of social scientists. For the first time, separate questionnaires were prepared for the men and women. They both covered the same ground but there were additional questions for the women and these were also asked of the men respecting their spouses. Added areas of inquiry were retirement and plans or expectancy about future activities. The questionnaire was only four pages but was comparable to that of 1940 in detail and self-ratings. This questionnaire, as well as the three succeeding ones, are reproduced in Appendix A. When there is occasion to refer in the text to a specific question from one of them, the year and question number will often be given rather than the full question.

1977 Follow-up

The emphasis on aging was increased substantially in the 1977 8-page questionnaire, which was again slightly different for the men and women. Formal education disappeared altogether and was replaced by such matters as living arrangements, social networks, retrospective reports on work style and intensity, retirement preferences and experiences, avocational and daily activities, and measures of life satisfaction.

TABLE 2.2
Age-Groups of Women in Later-Maturity Group by Follow-up Year and for Total Group

| Follow-up year | Age-group of respondents | | | | | | Total | |
| | Youngest | | Middle | | Oldest | | | |
	N	Pct.	N	Pct.	N	Pct.	N	Pct. of original Terman group
1972	113	25.7%	222	50.5%	105	23.9%	440	65.5%
1977	94	24.4	200	51.8	92	23.8	386	57.4
1982	102	25.6	202	50.6	94	23.6	398	59.4
1986	93	27.4	172	50.7	74	21.8	339[a]	50.4
Total later-maturity group	125	25.3	254	51.4	115	23.3	494	73.5

SOURCE: Questionnaires from indicated years.

NOTE: The "total later-maturity group" consists of all the women in the original Terman group who answered a questionnaire in any of the four follow-up years. As a result, the numbers in the bottom row exceed the number answering the questionnaire in any particular year.

[a]This figure includes seven women whose questionnaires were filled out by relatives after the subjects' death.

1982 Follow-up

By 1982 with the subjects in their late sixties and early seventies, careers and occupation lost some of their importance, and took a back seat, along with education. There was no further need for separate questionnaires for men and women. The increasing importance of health and adjustment to reduced capacities brought questions on these matters to the fore, along with goals for the immediate future. Measures of depression and anxiety supplemented the usual motivational, personality, and satisfaction measures.

1986 Follow-up

In 1986 an eight-page questionnaire quite similar to the preceding one contained additional questions on religion, activities in retirement, and problems associated with aging. In an attempt to make up for the bad timing of the 1945 questionnaire, two full pages were devoted to the effects of World War II on the subjects' life course through the subsequent four decades.

The Data Bank

For our examination of how these gifted people have developed into their later maturity we have two general kinds of information. Primary is the body of codable answers to the questionnaires collected between 1972 and 1986, along with antecedent data from the earlier questionnaires. In addition, there is the idiosyncratic and uncodable material contained in subjects' personal files. This includes correspondence, informal reports, newspaper clippings, curricula vitae, photographs, book notices, magazine articles by or about subjects, and other ephemera. For some subjects the file is thick with these things; for others it is not. The thick ones are very useful for illustrative case material, but they cannot contribute to the data provided by the standardized format of the tests and questionnaires.

The data obtained from these are of four kinds. First, there are scores from intelligence, achievement, and personality tests. Second, there are graphic or other kinds of rating scales in the questionnaires and in field-workers' reports. Third, there are listings, such as collections made (e.g. stamps, rocks) or occupations held during a sequence of years. Fourth, there are open-ended questions; for example, "Have any disappointments or failures over the last few years exerted a prolonged influence on you? Describe."

Of the four types of information, only the last presents any significant problems in coding for computer storage and analysis. From the beginning, the investigators used simple scales or multiple-choice answers whenever possible; about 50 percent of the codes are of this kind. The third type, listings, are tedious to code and to work with on the computer, but they present no problems of coder reliability or ambiguity. The open-ended questions do — and they also arouse the always-to-be-resisted challenge to code according to schemes that will have value to contemporary theoretical formulations. So far as the basic data bank is concerned, this challenge has been resisted, however, and all of the data from the many instruments have been coded to reflect as accurately as possible the actual responses written on the questionnaires. The details of this process, all of which has been performed during the last ten years, have been reported elsewhere (Sears, 1984). Suffice it to say that a careful verification process has revealed fewer than half of 1 percent errors in any of the 68 computer files into which the data have been placed.

There are approximately 3,900 nonredundant variables in this data bank. Of these, about 900 are obtained from the questionnaires used in the four follow-ups from 1972 through 1986, which is the period comprising our view of the subjects' later maturity.

Summary

The Terman subjects as children were precocious in many ways, the most extreme being with respect to the use of language. They talked in sentences before most children do and they learned to read much earlier. The mean maturity level of their interests, knowledge, and behavior was significantly greater in many ways than that of unselected control children. Moreover, both initial and continuing precocity were qualities of the gifted group. In those aspects of living and behavior that rely heavily on language, abstract thinking, and other intellectual skills, the gifted children retained or even enhanced their superiority. Their academic performance was superior in high school and college, and eight times as many continued on for doctoral degrees as was common at that time among college graduates. Occupational attainments for the men were also superior. In matters less related to intellect, however, greater variability was present in the sample. Four follow-up surveys conducted from 1972 to 1986 explored the course of the subjects' lives in later maturity and are the principal focus of the present volume.

＊ 3

Historical Context and Attrition

To understand our subjects' lives in later maturity, two kinds of contextual information are necessary. The first is the historical context in which the subjects lived. If we are to understand their reactions and behavior in aging, we must know something about the times that helped shape their earlier lives. Such historical forces, in combination with age, help distinguish one generation from the next, and often have profound influence on the hopes and dreams, opportunities and obstacles, that characterize individual lives. Second, in a longitudinal study of over 60 years' duration, it is inevitable that some subjects should no longer remain in the sample. In order to interpret the findings concerning our subjects in later maturity, the reader must know something about the kinds of individuals who remained to be studied in their later years. Accordingly, after a discussion of the historical context of our subjects' lives, this chapter proceeds to summarize the amount and kind of attrition in the sample.

The Historical Context

Obviously, many aspects of personality and intellectual ability are responsible for behavioral outcomes. Quite a few of these qualities can be traced and measured in the data at hand — evaluations by self, parents, teachers, and spouses. But another major class of determinants is equally important — the external events that provide the structure of the world in which a person grows up. This world not only limits and enhances the opportunities for behavioral outcomes but also provides a matrix within which learning occurs, and new facets to the personality develop. Our data provide many indications of these events as well as of the personalities that encountered them.

Many of the local events that occurred in the immediate family or neighbor-hood environment of each of these children were idiosyncratic to that particular child. Family illness or death, a real estate development, a father's lost job, or inheritance of property could have monumental effects on the child's develop-ment, providing opportunities or creating burdens, but such events can be con-sidered only in the context of that child's own life.

There are, however, other, broader, aspects of history, that influenced all of the subjects. Developments such as wars, economic depressions, periods of boom, and social tensions over human rights affected everyone — not necessarily in the same way, but they were universals that every child heard discussed, every adult thought about, and everyone, whether child or adult, adapted to in one way or another. In our research analyses we cannot easily examine the effects of these universals because we have no comparison group that escaped their influence entirely. We can compare children who were faced with certain events at dif-ferent ages — economic depression striking before or after college, for exam-ple — but we have no one to look at who never experienced an economic depres-sion (see Elder, Pavalko, & Hastings, 1991, for a discussion of cohort influences in the study). As we examine the ways in which these people have developed into the years of later maturity, it is well to keep in mind what events they have lived through, what opportunities they have had and what ones they have lacked, what adversities they have suffered and what ones they have escaped, what feelings have been aroused more or less continuously through their lifetimes, what values have been highly regarded and what ones have been derogated. These need summary here because, like the idiosyncratic events, they are poorly represented by any direct measures in our data bank.

Roughly speaking, the time frame of reference for the lives of these individ-uals has been the twentieth century. Two-thirds of them were born between 1906 and 1914, but family memories and the time frames of children usually go back a little further than their date of birth. They were Californian children, and the things that happened nearest home or that characterized the immediate environ-ment were the things that counted.

First there was the community and the neighborhood. Although San Fran-cisco, Oakland, and Los Angeles were all called cities, only San Francisco had the kind of population density that is associated with the label along the Atlantic seaboard or in Europe. Even it, in the early part of the century, was divided clearly into neighborhoods, and the neighborhoods of both Oakland and Los Angeles were more like clusters of small towns than "real" cities. California was sparsely settled, with a population less than a tenth the size it has become in the century since. Vacant lots and dusty — or muddy-rutted — unpaved streets were common in all the Californian population centers except San Francisco.

Second in importance to a young child were the schools, a very pervasive part of a child's environment. In the 1910's there were two kinds of public schools, elementary and high. They divided after the eighth grade. In the mid-1920's junior high schools began to appear. Most town and city children lived a few blocks from their elementary school, and walked or rode bicycles to them. High schools were beginning to be consolidated into larger districts; hence some children took street cars to school, and there were a few school buses in rural areas. There was, however, no legal requirement at that time to bus children from one school or district to another in the interests of desegregation. The school population was quite homogeneous, white in the main; in 1910 blacks were 2 percent of the population of California, and there was only a scattering of Asians. There were more Hispanics than other minorities, located largely in Southern California. In the urban centers, the clustering of races or nationalities in neighborhoods provided little heterogeneity in the schools from which the gifted group was selected.

In the political sphere, the first three decades of the century were a time of turmoil, mainly about the role of government in business, public morality, and America's place in the world. The latter issue had been exacerbated by the Spanish-American War, and the questions of government and political morality had been focused by President Theodore Roosevelt. In California the early years of the century were spiced with Senator Hiram Johnson's battles against the conservative domination of the railroads and public utilities. His attacks were successful and he himself achieved power as he reconstructed the Republican Party toward a new liberalism.

By 1914 the war in Europe had become a dominant theme, even in faraway California. President Woodrow Wilson had already demonstrated his internationalist and interventionist impulses by sending General Pershing to chase Pancho Villa in Mexico. However, in two years' time, the agrarian middle west would help to reelect him on a keep-out-of-the-war platform. In California sympathy for the Allies was widespread and outspoken. Nevertheless, opinion was divided. Johnson, for example, vigorously opposed intervention.

Then came the first in a series of incidents raising the specter of political radicalism. There was a bombing of the *Los Angeles Times*, and during a 1916 Preparedness Day parade in San Francisco, someone also exploded a bomb. The names of radicals such as Mooney and Billings were repeatedly in the headlines and they became somehow symbolic of a left-wing radicalism that many Americans feared as much as the monarchical right-wing power of Germany's Kaiser Wilhelm.

Less than a year after Wilson's reelection, the United States declared war. A vocal minority expressed resistance at first, but prowar propaganda was everywhere. Schools developed nearby vacant lots into Victory Gardens; they recruited children to go from house to house selling war savings stamps, and collecting tin foil for recycling into something useful for the war. Posters hung on school walls, store fronts, railway stations, everywhere they could be effective in rousing the people to a patriotic fervor toward the war that would "make the world safe for democracy." A strong element in this propaganda was the highly publicized cruelty of the "Huns" and their alleged killing of Belgian children. Hatred of Germany and everything German was pervasive and sometimes violent in its outcomes. People of identifiable German origin were ostracized and harassed. One prominent architect changed his name; a young assistant professor of German committed suicide; and almost universally German language courses in high school were discontinued, most of them not reappearing until several years after the war. World War I marked the United States' first experience with a genuine universal draft of young men for military service.

The war ended in late 1918. It had been strongly supported but now it was a bad dream. A few epidemics took half a million lives. The U.S. Senate revolted against Wilson's internationalist policies and rejected his plans for the future. Two do-nothing presidents, Harding and Coolidge, were elected, one after the other, and an able Californian conservative, Herbert Hoover, followed them. Early in the decade, radicalism again became a foe. U.S. Attorney General Palmer and a number of state officials attacked the Industrial Workers of the World (IWW) with the syndicalist laws. Then, only a decade after Mooney and Billings had dominated the headlines, two new names replaced them — Sacco and Vanzetti — who were likewise accused of terrorist activities although in fact they were only self-styled anarchists and were convicted of killing a guard during a payroll robbery.

Most of the Terman group entered the 1920's at the transition to adolescence. Still quite young, they experienced a period of severe inflation in the first couple of years, and then several years of economic advance. They lived through the era of mah-jongg, flappers, and sheiks, the popularization of intercollegiate football, Prohibition, bootlegging, the coming of *Time, The New Yorker, Readers Digest*, and *College Humor*, the omnipresent Model T Ford, and finally the fantastic runaway stock market at the end of the decade.

More important in the long run, of course, was the radical modernization in the 1920's of many serious aspects of life. Communication expanded enormously with the development of commercial radio. Entertainment was revolutionized by the technical improvements in motion picture production. The automobile was responsible not only for huge increments in mobility of the people in general but for the widespread financial effects of great new manufacturing empires and the essential expansion of paved road systems — together with explosive growth of bond issues to pay for them. Suburbs changed quickly from convenient *loci* of summer cottages (which could be reached once a year by horse and buggy) to the normal residence centers for many middle-class business and professional families. The automobile also added a huge new market for petroleum products, and hence increased still more the size and complexity of the business world and the banking industry. The airplane was just beginning to play a role in communication by the end of the 1920's; air mail — like the radio and long distance telephone — speeded the interchange for both individuals and businesses. And along came electrical engineering with its discovery of an economical way to transport great quantities of high-voltage electricity without substantial loss, thus broadening the opportunity for dispersion of heavy industry. The decade of the 1920's was not the beginning of the explosion by science and technology; that had occurred in the second half of the nineteenth century. But it was the time when the earlier developments were maximized by a species of fine tuning that changed the impact of these new things from experimental oddities to deeply ingrained physical, social, and economic forces.

The bubble burst in October 1929, just as the younger members of the gifted group were finishing high school or entering college, and the older ones were getting their first start on a career. The economic depression worsened rapidly. Businesses closed, jobs disappeared, stocks and bonds dropped to a fraction of their former value, real estate was unsalable. Hitherto comfortably off families found themselves without resources to send their children to college or to graduate school. By 1932, a political revolution was brewing. Franklin D. Roosevelt replaced Hoover. The New Deal optimism replaced the conservative gloom. A government relief program replaced private charity breadlines. The times certainly felt better, but true jobs and truly profitable businesses remained in short supply until the end of the 1930's and the entry of the United States into World War II in 1941.

Politics, both national and international, were as much a focus for the 1930's as they had been during the two preceding decades. The rise of Nazism in Germany coincided in time with the New Deal reforms in the United States, but had a very different flavor. While a vigorous but ineffectual minority of American conservatives were grimacing as they spoke of "that man in the White House," German conservatives were successfully supporting the anti-unionism, suppression of free speech, violence, and anti-semitism of the Nazis. In America, just the opposite was occurring; unions were supported, and freedom of speech and press were not only tolerated but encouraged. Left-wing politics, including communism, was looked upon with some tolerance and even favor, especially among the young intellectuals and artists, while in Germany it was bitterly suppressed. The battle between isolationists and interventionists lined up in the same way.

In certain psychological aspects, World War II was similar to World War I. There were two years of sympathetic build-up of feelings for the Allies and then an incident — this time the bombing of Pearl Harbor — to cause a declaration of war. On the West Coast the Japanese replaced the Germans as the treacherous enemy, and the internment of 112,000 Japanese-Americans followed. The Yellow Peril had been a staple of Californian journalism from the beginning of the century, and at least for the duration of actual hostilities, the fear of the Japanese was very real. (This racist hysteria was felt with a special strength by the half-dozen members of our research group of Japanese ancestry, who suffered internment.) The period following World War II resembled that following World War I. Again there was a brief inflation and a prolonged period of antiradicalism, this time under the aegis of then Representative Richard Nixon and Senator Joseph McCarthy.

In the quarter-century since the end of World War I, levels of education had risen generally. By 1950 a high school education was taken for granted, and college was a normal expectation for almost all middle-class children and many lower-class as well. A prominent feature of life after World War II was the return to college of those who had served in the military forces. About half the men in our group had been in uniform and some benefited from the government educational support. The colleges and universities were jammed with students, research funding was lavish, business prospered, and there were jobs galore for all professionals. The wartime interruption of marriage and child-bearing led to a "baby boom" in the postwar period, a boom accompanied by a briefly developed ideology supporting large families. Most of the research group were a little too old to join in this movement, but they were of the right age to benefit from the business and professional opportunities induced by the favorable economic scene during the 1950's.

The next decade brought some different and less comfortable influences to bear on them, however. The 1960's were a time of revolt, a revolt by women and ethnic minorities who found ready allies in the generation of children some of whose parents were our "children." The war had improved the economic status of many black Americans and there was ferment for better political status for blacks. The human and civil rights struggle began in the southern states, but it quickly spread to the north and west. Tension among the young was building up from their hatred of the new war in Vietnam, and some of this hostility was channeled first into the "free speech" and then the human rights movements. By the mid-1960's, however, this hostility turned more directly against the government and other authority figures such as universities, banks, and big business.

Simultaneously, women were demanding better treatment in the workplace, equal opportunities for employment, and pay scales equivalent to men's. Feminism had largely disappeared after the 1920 passage of the women's suffrage amendment to the Constitution, both from exhaustion after the long fight and the assumption that full equality would follow the right to vote. The depression of the 1930's brought so much male unemployment and consequent family distress that women's right to work was severely challenged. Iowa, for example, adopted a law preventing two members of the same family from holding positions on the state payroll. Many girls were denied money for college expenses so that a brother might go to college. It was a time of social regression to traditional men's and women's roles (see Chapter 5). World War II made a radical change in that situation. The millions of women who replaced the men drawn into military service provided a necessary increase in workers for war-essential industry. Many women beyond the childrearing years remained in the work force after the war. When the younger women had raised families, they turned to paid employment and the search for careers.

College-aged youth revolted against the highly unpopular Vietnam war, but their revolt did not stop there. It became a revolt against the authoritarianism, or at least the authority, of the parental generation. The convenient development of reliable contraception permitted a new sexual freedom, and along with this came the exploration of "mind-freeing" drugs. Came, too, the uncloseting of homosexuality, and a highly increased divorce rate. By the end of the 1960's the Terman group was 50 years old, on average, and they experienced these events not only from an older generation's position but through the eyes of their own children and, for quite a few, through those of their grandchildren.

The 1970's brought some respite from the expression of the revolt, but economic changes that did not rival the Depression in their impact nevertheless led to various adjustments in both living and earning. The recession of the early and mid-1970's was followed by severe inflation—just as some of the group were reaching retirement. For those who had liquid capital, the accompanying high interest rates gave them an opportunity to resolve financial problems, but others were faced with genuine difficulty. It was a period of "stagflation" in which prices rose radically but the economy did not improve. Job opportunities became fewer and fewer; age became a handicap, and older people who lost their jobs found it difficult to obtain another. In the late 1970's jobs in the manufacturing sector began to erode, the foreign trade balance deteriorated, and by 1986 the United States, after 70 years as a creditor nation, had become a debtor nation.

Some of these historical events had little influence on some of the group. Some unquestionably left their mark. Sadly, not all subjects lived through the complete cycle; increasingly there have been deaths along the way. Increasingly, too, subjects have been lost or have withdrawn from the study. What we can report is the experience of the still-participating members. In the next section we will summarize the attrition that has taken place over the years, and try to define what kinds of people have left the sample and what kind have remained to provide the data for the later chapters. The interested reader will find a fuller treatment of attrition in Appendix B, where the analyses which form the basis of the conclusions to follow are presented in detail.

Attrition

The managers of all longitudinal studies have to wage an incessant battle against the loss of subjects. No matter how hard they try, their samples grow smaller and smaller as the years pass. The causes of this attrition are many, some inescapable, some partially controllable. No life-cycle study can be continuous. Data collection must come in waves, months or even years apart.

Categories of Attrition

The causes of attrition can be summarized in three categories. First, and most obviously, people die, and others, incapacitated by illness or age, become unable to respond and for our purposes are equivalent to those who died. The second category includes those who, disenchanted with the research or irritated by questions posed to them, ask to be dropped from the study. Here we also place those who simply ignore requests for information or who, giving priority to other concerns, set questionnaires aside for later attention—a time that never comes.

The third category consists of persons who move, leave no forwarding address, and cannot be traced. (We have spent much energy in tracing subjects, sometimes through the record of a driver's license, and not infrequently we were able to locate them or to learn about their deaths.)

Accompanied as this research was in the early years by much attention to the subjects (and by some acclaim), many participants had the study sufficiently in mind to notify us of their moves or marriages. As the years passed, and with follow-ups five years or more apart, these notifications gradually became less frequent. In recent years, too, the fabled automation of the postal service has led to an almost total failure of the forwarding process for first class mail. Even recent changes of address — in one of our cases, to next door — can derail delivery of questionnaires.

Attrition by choice is another matter altogether. We have found in our study that non-cooperation can be accompanied by many kinds of feelings, ranging from marked irritation and exasperation (which subjects tell us about) to mere boredom (which they usually do not). Some of our subjects, as they aged and perhaps became less interested in the academic type of competence for which they had been selected, said they wished not to be bothered further. Some deprecated their own talents, and thought they should withdraw. In recent years, a few became resentful of the change in emphasis from achievement to aging. One unmarried woman refused further cooperation in 1972 because she perceived the questionnaires to be too much concerned with marital experience. For the great majority of cases classed as attrition by choice, however, we know only that, despite repeated urgings and mailings, the subjects withdrew from the research. Neither they nor the post office returned our questionnaires.

The damage from attrition is not so much the reduced number of subjects as the possible change in the makeup of the sample. If attrition is selective — if the attriters differ in any significant way from those who remain in the study — the final sample no longer corresponds to the group recruited. The group becomes less variable — and variability is the lifeblood of antecedent-consequent research. Furthermore, reducing the range of some personality or motivation measures would change correlations from the values to be expected if death, the post office, and withdrawal by choice had not intervened. It is important, therefore, to check whether the subjects who did not contribute data in the later years differed from those who remained in the study.

Attrition does not occur all at once. It is a gradual erosion of the sample that is most definitely noted by the total cessation of a subject's response to the questionnaires. One person after another fails to respond to a next and then succeeding questionnaires. In our analysis of this process, we use the year of the final response as the criterion of both the fact and the approximate date of attrition. Thus, if a subject responded to some (not necessarily all) of the questionnaires between 1921 and 1955, and did not respond in 1960 or thereafter, he or she is counted in the 1955–60 decrease. Before looking at data, we say more about the categories for the analysis.

Attriters are placed in the three categories introduced earlier, to which we assign brief and not entirely descriptive labels: death, choice, and loss.

Death. If a subject died after he or she last returned a questionnaire and before we mailed the next one, the attrition is charged to death. If a questionnaire went unanswered prior to death — the subject answered in 1955, missed in 1960, died in 1964 — this is counted as choice. Subjects who became incapacitated were also placed in the death group. Because the incapacitated were so few, we shall speak of the group simply as the "death" group.

Choice. During the 65 years of the study, 15 men and 21 women asked that their names be removed from the mailing list. The request was fully respected — after our best persuasive efforts failed to reverse the decision. (Some latterday follow-up to check on date of death or survival did approach the subjects.) Nonresponders make up the rest of the "choice" category.

Loss. The "loss" group is distinguished from the "choice" group because we doubt that these subjects received our mailings. Some of them probably were silent withdrawals like most cases labeled attrition by choice. No doubt, however, many in the "loss" group were lost merely because of moves or name changes.

Cases of attrition by death are generally well documented, but some of the loss cases may have been lost because of death or disability. Some we have labeled as attrition by choice also may have died before response to a questionnaire was completed and we failed to trace the death.

The numbers of subjects who dropped out and who remained active participants at the various stages of the study between its inception in 1921 and the follow-up in 1986 are reported in Tables 3.1 and 3.2. Each dated row reports the number of subjects still participating at each point and the number of attriters in the preceding interval.* The number of participants stated for a year prior to 1986 is greater than the number of respondents for that year, because some subjects came back into the fold after missing one or more surveys.

The first row of Tables 3.1 and 3.2 counts all children, identified as suitable for the study, whose parents were asked to cooperate. Early data are available on some of the children counted as initial attrition, but the children themselves never sent in responses. Some did take the Stanford-Binet and some took the group-administered achievement tests in 1922. For about half these cases, the parents returned the 1922 Home Information Blank, but they did not return the child's interest blank. There were several causes of this initial attrition, including the death of several children, withdrawal of children from the study by parents, and early changes in residence. One 1986 "participant" made his first return in that year, although his parents had sent in some 1922 information.

---

* For four women and nine men, the factual questions in the 1986 information blank were filled out by a spouse or sibling, the subject having died or become incapacitated. These cases are counted in the death group in Tables 3.1 and 3.2 (and in Table B.1 if the subject was unable to respond in 1982). The "1986 responses" in the data file include the surrogate returns.

TABLE 3.1
Classification of Men Leaving Terman Sample in Each Time Interval

Year	Number participating[a]	Decrease	Classification Death[b]	Choice[c]	Loss[d]
Invited	856	—	—	—	—
Initial attrition	848	8	3	5	0
1928	834	14	6	2	6
1936	815	19	11	4	4
1940	805	10	8	1	1
1945	794	11	7	3	1
1950	776	18	11	5	2
1955	749	27	7	16	4
1960	673	76	22	45	9
1972	567	106	68	27	11
1977	501	66	37	24	5
1982	449	52	39	11	2
1986	371	78	46	26	6

SOURCE: Questionnaires and information gathered by research staff.

[a]Responded to a survey in this or a later year; thus numbers in this column may exceed number of respondents in any given year. Persons treated as initial attrition did not fill out the 1922 interest blank or, if recruited after 1922, did not respond to any later instrument.

[b]Includes persons not responding because they became incapacitated.

[c]Subject (or parent) asked to be removed from mailing list or responded to none of the questionnaires presumably delivered after the last year of response.

[d]Presumably failed to receive questionnaires after the last year of response.

Under the ground rules for the analysis, he is counted as a nonattriter in Table 3.1 and he is included in the later-maturity sample.

Once the study was in full swing, attrition was slight until after World War II. Figure 3.1 displays the cumulative percentage attrition by choice and by death. Percentages for "loss" are too small to merit plotting, remaining below 7 percent in 1986. Through 1945 (when the average age of the subjects was 35 years), there was about as much attrition from death as from choice and loss combined. Death was the cause of attrition for a greater proportion of men at almost every period. From 1945 to 1986, death continued its preponderant role among men. For women, from 1960 through 1982, cumulative loss by choice ran slightly ahead of attrition by death. "Loss" cases were a little more numerous among the women. This is understandable; a substantial number of women change their names by marriage or divorce, and some of them become virtually untraceable after a few years.

After 1955 the curves for choice rise much more steeply than they did earlier. What happened? Nothing in the historical setting suggests an obvious cause, but two matters connected with the study itself may have been relevant. First, Terman died in 1956. This was widely known to the subjects through news reports, a special mailing from Oden, the cover letter for the 1960 questionnaire, and the foreword to volume 5 of Genetic Studies of Genius (Terman & Oden, 1959). Terman had been personally close to the research subjects, and highly support-ive; in the years after his death many have written of their warm memories and

TABLE 3.2

Classification of Women Leaving Terman Sample in Each Time Interval

Year	Number participating[a]	Decrease	Classification		
			Death[b]	Choice[c]	Loss[d]
Invited	672	—	—	—	—
Initial attrition	664	8	2	4	2
1928	652	12	1	4	7
1936	635	17	11	1	5
1940	628	7	6	1	0
1945	621	7	4	2	1
1950	609	12	3	5	4
1955	596	13	6	7	0
1960	558	38	5	23	10
1972	493	65	32	26	7
1977	459	34	14	16	4
1982	421	38	19	18	1
1986	332	89	44	33	12

SOURCE: Questionnaires and information gathered by research staff.

[a]Responded to a survey in this or a later year; thus numbers in this column may exceed number of respondents in any given year. Persons treated as initial attrition did not fill out the 1922 interest blank or, if recruited after 1922, did not respond to any later instrument.

[b]Includes persons not responding because they became incapacitated.

[c]Subject (or parent) asked to be removed from mailing list or responded to none of the questionnaires presumably delivered after the last year of response.

[d]Presumably failed to receive questionnaires after the last year of response.

appreciation for his help in one matter or another. It is likely that for some participants the research was essentially an interaction with a respected mentor; when he was gone, motivation to respond was reduced. Second, there was a 12-year gap between the 1960 survey and the next follow-up. That long interval could have caused some loss of interest, though the choice curves, reflecting change per-year, are not especially steep in that interval.

The comparatively large attrition in the long 1960–72 interval (Tables 3.1 and 3.2) is easy to understand. The rise in attrition was also great between 1955 and 1960, which matches the choice curves and may be related to Terman's death.

Steepness of the choice curves at the right end is artifactual, since persons who failed to respond to the 1986 blank are counted as attriters. Judging by past experience, in the next survey, a number of these "attriters" will respond.

Correlates of Attrition

The emphasis in our discussion is on attrition in the sample at the time of the 1982 survey. Nearly all our analyses on attrition were carried out before 1986 questionnaires were coded. Attrition is defined by the information in the file at the time of analysis; persons who had not responded to the 1982 survey were counted as attriters, along with those who had dropped out earlier. In fact, attrition is never-ending; it is a continuous process. Our 1982 date, however, marks 61 years of the study and such a span provides data on attrition quite sufficient to answer the questions of interest to us.

Our initial expectation was that subjects who had suffered some developmental handicaps and who reacted somewhat ineffectually would be the ones most likely to drop out. Most of the evidence supports this view. Poor health and education, mental disturbance or illness, and (among men) lack of occupational success and lack of self-esteem show up more often in the history of attriters by choice than among the 1982 participants. Such differences tended to be greater in the period close to withdrawal than in earlier periods.

This temporal trend has a corollary. None of the early childhood measures we examined predicted attrition by choice. This was true for ratings by parents or teachers of self-confidence, inferiority feelings, and conscientiousness, for childhood socioeconomic status, and even for death or divorce of the parents. Indeed, the earliest life event found to predict eventual attrition was nearness of age at first marriage to age of puberty — and this relation appears only among men. It seems that withdrawal in adult life stemmed from events that occurred or feelings that developed in adulthood. Dropping out was not a behavioral product of some limitation that existed from childhood, but was a response to events nearer the time of withdrawal.

The subjects' marital histories were a little more in line with the norms of their times as compared with the marital histories of the full sample; intact

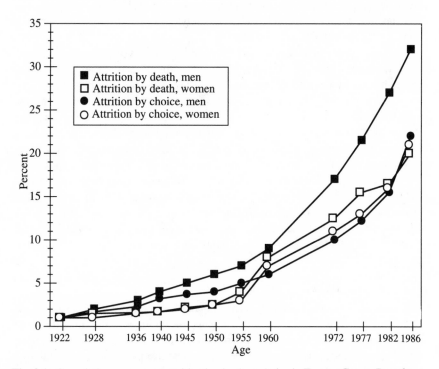

Fig. 3.1. Cumulative percentage attrition by death or choice in Terman Group. Data from questionnaires in various years and information gathered by research staff.

marriages and widows and widowers were a bit overrepresented among them, whereas divorced and always-single persons were underrepresented. Perhaps the across-sex similarity of effects of marital history on attrition reveals an important point. For most women in this generation, occupation was a sometime thing. Marriage and family were more central in young adulthood. The single woman, like the single man, was atypical, and possibly in some cases was less satisfied than her married counterparts. Divorce was as disruptive for women as for men. Widowhood left the sexes with similar need for continuity of meaningful experiences, and participation in research may have been one of these.

Except for poor physical health and nonnormative marital history, correlates of attrition tended to be substantially more predictive of attrition of men than of women. Part of the reason is the greater salience of occupation in the men's lives than the women's. We see this especially in connection with the measures of self-esteem, which did not predict women's withdrawal but did predict withdrawal by men.

Finally, we must consider what attrition has done to the subject sample. Since the subjects were never a representative sample of any larger population, not even of the gifted Californian children of a certain cohort, the fact that the remaining participants do not match the original research group perfectly is of no great moment. It is worth briefly summarizing how they differ, however, because this may help the reader decide just how widely or in what directions generalizations to other populations can be pressed.

First and most obviously, the 1982 remainder consists of those whose genes, life experiences, and life styles kept them alive. In adulthood they remained in somewhat better health than the attriters. They were initially no brighter nor scholastically more efficient than others of the gifted group, but they became somewhat better educated. The men achieved greater occupational success. The men by and large reported higher self-esteem and self-confidence than did the entire mid-life sample. The attriters over the years did not differ from the survivors with respect to several indicators or reports of achievement motivation. The subjects remaining in the study tended to have more normative marital histories. Attriters did not have an unusual incidence of alcoholism, nor did they express unusual lack of feelings of achievement motivation. The persons we follow into the vicissitudes of later maturity, then, have been somewhat more successful in several aspects of life than those who no longer remain in the group.

Sources of Data on Later Maturity

The present report is based chiefly on data obtained from the questionnaires of 1972, 1977, 1982, and 1986. The subjects for whom we have some data — at least one of the four questionnaires — include not only those whom we have called the remainder group but also persons whose last participation was in 1972 or 1977. The sample also includes some persons counted as choice withdrawals in this chapter who "returned" in 1986.

The average birth year of the total original group was 1910. The averages in the later maturity sample were July 1910 (men) and June 1911 (women). The standard deviations were 3.8 and 3.5 years respectively, essentially the same as in the original sample.

The following tabulation shows the number (among 569 men and 494 women in the later-maturity sample) for whom we have questionnaires in the years indicated:

Year	Men	Women	Year	Men	Women
1972	497	440	1982	417	398
1977	426	386	1986	381	339

This counts 1986 returns for a few persons classified in the "death" attrition group for analysis, whose questionnaire was filled out by a spouse, sibling, or offspring after the subject's death or disability. Because many questions were left unanswered, these cases contribute little to the data.

Including the late attriters as part of the later-maturity sample has two beneficial side-effects: It decreases moderately the difference distinguishing the later-maturity sample from the original group, and it increases the number of cases supplying 1972 and 1977 data. Surprisingly, after nearly 66 years, in spite of defection, death, and inadvertent loss, we are able to use 67 percent of the men and 73 percent of the women from the original group to study later maturity.

Summary

It is impossible to understand the course of our subjects' lives fully without an appreciation for the remarkable historical developments they experienced. Their youth and young adulthood were influenced by World War I, radical modernization, and the Great Depression. They experienced World War II and then benefited from postwar prosperity. At mid-life they experienced the social revolutions of the 1960s.

Despite attrition, it is remarkable that over the 66-year-span of the study, over two-thirds of the sample provided data in at least one of the four surveys in later maturity. The individuals remaining to be studied showed several trends. On average the 1982 participants remained in somewhat better health than those who had chosen to leave the study. They were initially no brighter than the attriters, but they became somewhat better educated. The continuing men achieved greater occupational success, and had greater self-confidence and self-esteem. In addition, the remaining subjects' marital histories were more in line with the norms of their times; those with intact marriages and widows and widowers were somewhat overrepresented, whereas divorced and always-single persons were underrepresented.

PART II

Occupations

4

Men's Work History

Although men will be considered here and women in the next chapter, the differential influences on the two groups will help to introduce the occupational themes. For our subjects' generation, occupational choice and performance were much simpler for men than for women. Most of these Californian boys were heritors of a centuries-old traditional male role of which gainful employment was a major feature. In temporal sequence, seeking, finding, securing, and supporting a mate were secondary goals, and their accomplishment waited on the successful choice and entry into an income-producing vocation. In contrast, the women of this generation were reared in a world that still had a traditional female role to which girls were exposed from birth. This role was, however, beginning to evoke conflict in increasing numbers of young women. On the one hand there was the vocation of childbearing, childrearing, and homemaking; but on the other there was the possible choice of work for money, a professional, or business career. The two roles were not totally incompatible, but the latter sufficiently threatened the former to create a classic conflict — instigation toward two positive goals, the relinquishing of either of which would be dissatisfying.

For women, work outside the family was not a thing prescribed by centuries of tradition as it was for men. In western Europe and America, it had come with the industrial revolution. Then the last half of the nineteenth century had seen such work glorified as a means of permitting women independence, an opportunity for them to actualize their own intellectual potential, to have freedom of choice in many respects that they had not had through centuries as wives and mothers. During the first two decades of the twentieth century women pressed increasingly for occupational freedom as well as for many others. This conflict between the new and the traditional had only a pale comparison in the world to which the men came. They experienced the conflict as spectators of the changing lives of their mothers, sisters, wives, and daughters. But this was a change outside themselves, and simply something to be coped with. It did not involve conflict within, as it did for women.

That these differential pressures existed pervasively in the lives and experiences of children is illustrated in a minor way by the first questionnaire Terman submitted to the gifted children, in 1922. One of the four pages contained a checklist of 125 occupations with the instruction "Put an X before each occupation you may possibly decide to follow." Of this list, 89 occupations were traditionally male (such as section hand, soldier) and twelve were traditionally female (such as nurse, secretary). The remaining 24 were conceivably available for either sex (teacher, physician, waiter, or waitress). Most of the world's income work — in California, at least — appears to have been masculine, an undoubted fact of life accepted even in psychological research.

More telling however, was a question placed at the bottom of the page: "If you are a girl, do you prefer the duties of housewife to any other occupation?" Of the 534 girls who answered the questionnaire, 16.1 percent said "yes," 48.3 percent said "no," 4.3 percent were "uncertain," and 31.3 percent simply did not answer. It seems not unlikely that this numerical split within the group was a fair reflection of the ambivalence in many of the girls' minds.

That 1922 questionnaire did not reveal the single-mindedness of the boys. But in 1936, when most of the subjects were in their twenties, there was evidence that is quite unambiguous. After a question orienting the respondent to occupational matters, an open-ended question was asked: "Describe your ultimate goals as fully as you can at this time." Of the 689 men who answered, 94.9 percent mentioned a goal related to occupation. Of the 516 women who answered, only 62.4 percent mentioned occupation, while 40.3 percent mentioned family roles (wife, mother). Among the men, only 1.3 percent mentioned the latter (husband, father) (see also Holahan, 1984–85).

The early single-mindedness of men in this generation and the conflictual status of women had consequences in later life that make it difficult to prepare a single report on the occupational domain. Hence we have devoted a chapter to each sex, and gender differences will be discussed wherever they seem most appropriate to an understanding of the experiences of both sexes in later maturity, mainly in Chapter 5.

Educational Preparation

While a high level of education — college or even graduate school — may prove valuable for many occupations, it is truly essential only for those professions for which much specialized knowledge is required. For occupations such as law, medicine, pharmacy, engineering, scientific research, and teaching at all levels from grade school to university, advanced education is a necessary, if not suffi-

cient, prerequisite. Increasingly in recent decades various types of business practice have begun to depend on training in law, accounting, engineering, or psychology, but this is a relatively recent development. At the time our subjects were
starting their careers formal educational preparation had not yet begun to exert
rigid control over entry into even the highest levels of business or banking.
Hence some who did not graduate from college were able to reach substantial
heights of accomplishment in these areas by practical experience, in-service
training, and independent study. This was even more the case with literary,
artistic, musical, and cinematic career development. Although the most successful practitioners of these creative activities did have specialized training, especially in art and music, others relied on self-education.

The formal education of the subjects had been pretty well completed before
later maturity began; the last degree earned by a man was a Ph.D. received in
1960 at 49 years of age. The latest bachelor's degree was obtained by a man of 54
in 1958. Sufficient details about the educational history of the group have been
presented in previous volumes (Terman and Oden, 1959; Oden, 1968) so that
only a summary is needed here.

All but two of the 569 men in the later-maturity group finished high school; 39
ended their education with high school; 98 had some college work but did not
obtain a college degree. The 430 other men (76 percent of the later-maturity
group) finished college; 113 (20 percent) secured terminal master's degrees,
mainly in engineering and education, and 151 (26 percent) obtained doctoral or
major professional degrees, Ph.D., M.D., and LL.B. Thus 46 percent of the group
were prepared educationally for a professional occupation. This generally high
level of education contrasts dramatically with the educational preparation of the
general population for this cohort, only 8 percent of whom obtained as much as a
bachelor's degree (Terman & Oden, 1947).

Doubtless more would have taken advanced degrees, especially doctorates, if
the Depression and World War II had not supervened. Table 4.1 shows the effects
of these historical events. Among those boys who graduated from high school in
1929 or earlier, 30 percent secured doctorates, while among those who graduated
between 1930 and 1939, only 15 percent did. A similar diminishing effect is
found when pre-Depression college graduates are compared with graduates of
the Depression years: 43 percent of those who graduated before the Depression
secured doctorates, while only 32 percent of those graduating during the Depression obtained them. The war reduced the proportion of advanced degrees even
more than the Depression. All but one of the boys had completed high school
before the war. Only 22 graduated from college between 1940 and 1945, and
only 23 percent of them secured doctorates. The percentage who obtained master's degrees was only two-thirds as great as the percentage among the Depression graduates.

Age of completing education was not, however, much influenced by these
events. The men who graduated from high school before the Depression started

TABLE 4.1

Effect of the Depression and World War II on Educational Level of Men

Educational level achieved	High school graduates				College graduates					
	1916–29		1930–39		1920–29		1930–39		1940–45	
	N	Pct.	N	Pct.	N	Pct.	N	Pct.	N	Pct.
High school, some college	98	22.5%	36	28.1%	—	—	—	—	—	—
A.B. or B.S. degree	94	21.6	35	27.3	23	22.5%	86	30.3%	12	54.5%
M.A. degree or some graduate work	111	25.5	38	29.7	35	34.3	108	38.0	5	22.7
Doctoral or major professional degree	132	30.3	19	14.8	44	43.1	90	31.7	5	22.7
Total	435		128		102		284		22	
Significance (p) by chi square			.05					.05		

SOURCE: Cumulative education data.

NOTE: Two men who did not finish high school are omitted from the table, as are those who completed college after 1945.

did not get their bachelor's degrees any younger than those who graduated during the Depression. There was a slight tendency ($p < .10$) for those who received their bachelor's degrees before the Depression to obtain the doctorate earlier, but the difference was only 2.3 years. The war was more influential in this respect. Men who were caught up in military service were delayed in getting their bachelor's degrees on the average by 5.6 years compared with their older comrades who finished their bachelor's degrees during the Depression, and 6.0 years as compared with the comparable pre-Depression cohort.

This first report of statistical analyses is a suitable place for a comment that applies throughout the book. When dozens of analyses are made in a research project, one can make some judgment from p values of the extent to which equally strong relations would *as a set* be likely to arise from sampling variation alone. But one cannot infer that a relation reaching (say) the .01 level is stronger in the population than one reaching the .05 level, or even that in a replication the same relations would be nominally significant. The p values we present are not, then, a proper statistical inference. To avoid overdramatizing, we report p values at only two levels, even though, in our large sample, some calculations do yield $p < .001$. The importance of a difference should be judged primarily by the size of that difference, unless it comes from a small subgroup.

It is worth noting that the federal government did not provide much assistance to young people seeking graduate training during the Depression, and the result was a one-third reduction in the number of advanced research and professional degrees obtained by the population as a whole. The GI Bill of Rights after World War II did provide good support, but even so, only a quarter of the college graduates went on to higher degrees. After three or more lost years in military service, most graduates were anxious for economic independence and family life. Many felt that time was running out, and that they had to get to work, even though a possibly more attractive career had to be forgone.

Occupational Levels

About a quarter of the men began full-time work in late teenage, when they graduated from high school. The remainder began some years later, after completion of the bachelor's degree or of graduate or professional training. For many of our subjects, regular part-time employment was a seemingly natural accompaniment of adolescence — paper routes, pumping gasoline, gardening, clerking, janitoring, etc. Quite a few of those who graduated from high school or college during the Depression had to take brief part-time employment for a while, sometimes two jobs at once, until their schooling could be resumed or they could locate work that promised continued employment and career development.

Occupational Choices

The kinds of work the men ultimately chose were listed by Oden (1968). She found that in 1960, 88 percent were employed in positions in the top two categories of the U.S. Census occupational classification. This compares with 20 percent of men at these levels in the general population (Hauser, 1964). By 1972/77, nearly half the group had retired or died, but 95 percent of the 399 still occupied in paid work, at least part-time, were in these top categories. The percentage of men in these categories had risen from 71 in 1940. Among those at these top levels, the distribution between professional and business occupations had not changed since 1940 (Terman and Oden, 1947).

Table 4.2 shows the occupational status of employed men in the later-maturity group in terms of the categories of the U.S. Bureau of the Census in 1940, 1960, and 1972 or 1977. For 1972 and 1977, occupational categories were based on the most recent questionnaire on which relevant employment data were reported. Only one subject was in the unskilled category in 1940, and none thereafter. From 1940 to 1960 there was a substantial shift from Class III to Class II, and by 1972 or 1977 a few more of the Class III workers had moved into higher categories. The decrease in the percentage in lower-level occupations after 1940 was, however, mainly caused by death or other selective attrition.

Satisfactions and Goals

As they approached the end of their careers, we asked the men to look back and describe the aspects of their work that had given them the greatest satisfaction (1972, Question A6; 1977, Question 18). The 1972 question was open-ended; the 1977 one was multiple-choice, but the judgments of 1977 exactly replicated those of 1972. The men with business and professional careers differed considerably in what they reported. The professionals mostly gave answers such as "a helping and teaching relationship with associates" and "the opportunity for creativity and growth." The businessmen mentioned "financial gain," "administrative or organizational pleasure," and "securing recognition." In 1977, the difference between the two groups on each of these choices was significant

TABLE 4.2
*Occupational Categories of Employed Men in Later-Maturity Group
in 1940, 1960, and 1972 or 1977*

Occupational category	1940		1960		1972/1977	
	N	Pct.	N	Pct.	N	Pct.
I Professional	230	47.8%	243	47.8%	204	51.1%
II Business	149	31.0	207	40.7	174	43.6
III Clerical, sales	88	18.3	49	9.6	14	3.5
IV Agriculture	1	0	4	0.8	1	0.2
V Semi-skilled	12	2.5	5	1.0	6	1.5
VI Unskilled	1	0	—	—	—	—
Total	481		508		399	

SOURCE: Questionnaires from indicated years.
NOTE: Percentages are based on the total numbers of men in the group who were employed, not the total later-maturity group. For 1972 and 1977, occupational categories were based on the most recent questionnaire on which relevant employment data were reported.

($p < .01$), as was a chi-square determination of the difference between the distributions for the two groups for all five codings in 1972 ($p < .01$).

In 1982 (Question 26) and 1986 (Question 29), we asked the men to specify which of many goals they had for their lives, and to indicate the three most important. In 1982 the professionals chose the goal of "continue to work" more frequently than the businessmen. As will be seen in a later section, this verbal attitudinal difference reflected a very real difference in actual occupational behavior. By 1986, two of the earlier sources of satisfaction in work became reflected in more general goals for the future. The businessmen more frequently mentioned "financial security" ($p < .01$) and the professional men mentioned "continue work" ($p < .01$) and "grow and be creative" ($p < .01$). (Chapter 9 will cover later maturity goals in greater detail.)

It appears that the professional men got more intrinsic satisfaction from their work than the businessmen — and enjoyed it more — and this same distinction was reflected in their broader goals for the future.

Change of Career

The apparent stability of career levels, as measured by the gross Census categories, hides a great deal of occupational change in the men's earlier work histories. As mentioned earlier in connection with education, the Depression was responsible for much of the turmoil. For some of the younger men the war continued this instability, but most of them had finally settled on an occupation by the 1950's, and the data for 1960 represent a reasonable estimate of the group's life-time occupational achievements.

Overall, the group's career lines were fairly stable once established. Nonetheless, in 1977, about 40 percent of the 390 men who answered a question about this matter (Question 21) still recalled changes they had had to make at one time or another. Such changes are thought to be common in the early stages of careers but also appear later, even in the professions (Evans & Lauman, 1983; Treiman, 1985). Of the 41 percent of the group mentioning changes, 5 percent made them in the earlier period of seeking and choosing, and 14 percent had made relatively minor changes (minor from our standpoint, at least; e.g., from writing and directing motion pictures to directing and producing TV shows). However, a residue of cases are of special interest in connection with later maturity: 16 percent because the new occupation was adopted in later mid-life and involved entirely different fields of activity — with different aims, organizational setting, and type of required training; and 3 percent because they occurred after normal retirement from the man's original occupation. Several of the latter group of men went into real estate brokerage or college teaching after lifetime careers in teaching and business management, respectively.

The great variety of occupations of these men, both before and after such changes, makes any kind of summary impossible. A few brief examples will be more revealing than artificial categorizations.

Bernard started as a newspaper reporter but did not enjoy the work, and after a three-year tour of army duty during World War II he went into farming for ten years. Feeling dissatisfied again, he quit at age 47, went to law school, and in due course was admitted to the bar. At age 50 he began practice, developed a small firm, and was highly successful until his retirement in his late 60's.

Carl secured a doctorate and taught economics at a large state college. He was invited to become chairman of the board of a local bank. He had relatively heavy financial needs, and at age 58 he took early retirement from his college position and became a full-time banker, a career that provided a very satisfactory income for another fifteen years.

Eric grew up in the Depression, had a little college training, and then got a non-technical job in a chemical plant. He went into farming during the war and then became a lumberjack. After a few years he bought and operated the sawmill, and began playing contract bridge as a serious hobby. Within five years he became a professional bridge player, and finished his occupational life with a 22-year stint as a highly successful duplicate bridge player, teacher, and official.

Fred began his first career as a low-level railroad employee, worked his way up to a good management position, and at 54 retired out of sheer boredom. For three years he was essentially unemployed, and in considerable financial want, but then found a job in a bookstore and was still working there, with pleasure, in his middle 60's.

Irwin was the son of a very successful sports writer. In 1929 after college, where he had majored in psychology, he became a sports cartoonist, working as a partner with his father. He served for four years in World War II, and after discharge returned to the university for a Ph.D. in his old department. This provided a channel to a college teaching position from which he was mandatorily retired at age 65. He then extended his hobby of oil painting into a serious endeavor, and during the remaining ten years of his life "sold enough paintings to warrant the effort."

John was a small-scale Renaissance man. After college he was a candy manufacturer for a year, an employed actor for the next, and a professional photographer for the next. He returned to college for two years of graduate work in art and music. He worked at several technical jobs in Hollywood for three years, and finally went into college teaching in music, publishing a number of well-regarded compositions during the next few years. At age 40 he became an art teacher in a high school, a position he retained until his retirement at 60. He began devoting nearly full time to water-color painting, selling nearly 250 works during the next dozen years. He had published two books of poetry along the way, had been a life-long prospector in the southern Sierras, and had discovered a hitherto unknown gemstone and several important lower Cambrian fossils, one of which was named for him.

Kenneth was trained in economics and became a highly successful investment analyst. His life-long hobby was the history of science, a field in which he published widely. At age 61 he retired to become a full professor in the History of Science department of a prestigious university, where he was still continuing his technical publications at age 70.

The many case histories of men who changed careers at some time give the impression that failure and success in the first career were about equally common. Those who were fired before they were ready to quit usually sought new work, but the level at which they sought it varied considerably. Some continued a vigorous competitive role in business or a profession, but not all. Several looked for and found work that provided nothing more than a minimally adequate income. Some of these were quite happy, satisfied to be out of the rat race and away from a job they had never liked anyway. The others were depressed and felt themselves failures.

The men who changed careers after a marked and satisfying success differed considerably from those whose first careers were more troubled. In most instances their change came in their late 40's and early 50's rather than in their late 50's and 60's. They were almost all well-to-do, some quite wealthy, and they were seeking a new experience or an opportunity to maximize some interest that had been submerged by a primary occupation.

The Lower Occupational Level

It is evident that the intellectual level of the group permitted the vast majority of the men to achieve positions at the top rungs of the occupational ladder. All of them had the intellectual ability to do so, given the opportunity. Since success and achievement were such widespread goals for this generation of American men, we may question why some of the men failed to end their careers at the same high level as their peers. We will examine differences between men employed in lower-level occupations in 1972 or 1977, and those who were working in higher-level jobs at these times. The three variables of family background, ability and opportunity, and motivation seem appropriate for examination as possible correlates and antecedents of continuing employment in lower-level occupations such as sales, service, and trade.

Family background. The life-style, accomplishments, and values of a child's family of origin provide models and standards for him to pursue. They also set limits on his expectations for his own life and for the horizons he can see for his possible accomplishments (Alexander, Eckland, & Griffin, 1975; Duncan, Featherman, & Duncan, 1972; Farmer, 1985; Featherman, 1980; Gottfredson, 1981; Sewell & Hauser, 1975). We have some of these elements, but they were obtained at various times and from different sources. Not all are available for all cases. For example, only 7 of the 21 families of the men in lower-level occupations were evaluated on the Whittier Environmental Scale by the field-workers in 1922. Hence our information about neighborhood, housing, and family attitudes at that early time is too limited to provide a satisfactory statistical measure of differences between the lower- and the higher-level groups. What comparisons can be made show uniformly that the boys who went into lower-level occupations had mostly grown up in poor neighborhoods, in badly cared-for or slovenly homes, in families where language usage was poor, where attitudes toward the child were negligent and the fact of his inclusion in a gifted group was a matter of indifference. We do have adequate information for all the boys on the size of community in which they grew up. The youngsters who later went into lower-level occupations came mainly from small towns or rural areas. Also, in 1928 another six boys were seen by the field-workers, and we have evaluations of their neighborhoods at that time; four of the six neighborhoods were rated "below average," while only 35 percent of the professional and managerial boys' neighborhoods were so rated.

Adequate data are available on the parents' occupations and education in 1922, but there was no difference in the level of occupations of fathers or mothers of the higher- and the lower-level sons, although the educational achievements of both parents of the higher-level subjects tended to be better (but not significantly).

Parent-child interactions play a crucial role in the development of the skills and attitudes requisite for later achievement (Albert & Runco, 1986; Block, 1971; Crandall & Battle, 1970; Henderson, 1981; Janos & Robinson, 1985; Spaeth, 1976; Williams, 1976). With respect to parent-child interactions, however, our variables did not discriminate between the two groups of boys. The 1922 Home Information Blank reported a number of measures of parental achievement-related activities with the child that might be considered as both reinforcement and modeling: number of hours devoted to teaching the child to read or to work with numbers or nature study, at various preschool and early school ages; amount of outside tutorial help provided in music, drawing, and dancing, again at various ages; amount of encouragement in schoolwork. None of these many measures distinguished between the boys who would go on to professional or high-level business careers and those who would be content with more modest work.

These reports from field-workers and parents tell us nothing of how the children perceived their family background. Only later, when they had grown to adulthood, can we get a retrospective view of two aspects of these perceptions. In 1950, the subjects were asked to estimate their families' financial position on a 4-point scale, and their families' social position on a 5-point scale, in both cases when they themselves were children. The men in lower-level occupations recalled financially poorer and less stable family circumstances and poorer parental social position than did the higher-level men. On both scales these differences were significant ($p < .05$ by chi-square).

Since parental attitudes, occupations, and education did not differ, it is not surprising that twice as large a proportion of the men in lower-level occupations admitted, in 1950, that they had not followed parental advice in selecting an occupation, and more of them acknowledged, also, that this had led to some conflict with their parents.

Ability and opportunity. Obviously there are many individual and idiosyncratic circumstances that can facilitate or interfere with vocational choice, but initial intelligence (and aptitude for schooling) are important determinants of where a person will end up vocationally (Sewell & Hauser, 1975; Featherman, 1980).

Although the whole Terman group was high on initial intelligence, it did have a range of more than four standard deviations on the IQ scale. The boys who were later to be in lower-level occupations were slightly less bright as measured by IQ. Their mean IQ was 142, compared with a mean of 152 for the boys who went into higher-level occupations; the difference was significant at the .05 level. Not surprisingly, the mean scores of the two groups on the Concept Mastery Test (CM) in 1940 and 1950 also differed significantly on both occasions ($p < .01$). Careers and personal variables are interactive (Kohn & Schooler, 1973, 1978), so it is logical to ask whether the professional and managerial men were getting brighter or the men in lower-level occupations were losing some of their brightness — or if perhaps both these developments were occurring.

There is no clear answer to this question. For the entire sample of men who took the Concept Mastery Test at average ages of 30 and 40 years, the Pearson correlations between intra-group ranked positions on these tests and on initial IQ were .27 and .35 respectively; the two measures of Concept Mastery obtained a decade apart correlated .85. Perhaps the most direct way of determining whether the higher and lower occupational groups differed in the way they changed from childhood to young adulthood and then to middle age is to compare the average rank order of the members of the higher and lower groups within the total group at these three stages of life (Sears and Sears, 1978). There was no difference in the amount of change in intellectual performance from childhood (IQ) to young or middle adulthood (CM 1940, CM 1950), or in Concept Mastery score over the decade from early to later middle age. We must conclude that while there was some difference in intellectual ability both in childhood and adulthood, favoring the men whose careers were to end at the higher levels, there was no greater tendency for the lower-level occupation group to slip downward during their careers.

Education has been consistently found to be a determinant of occupational achievement (Featherman, 1980; Featherman & Hauser, 1978; Sewell & Hauser, 1975). In the present comparison, there was no doubt of its influence. The difference between the two occupational-level groups was enormous. A third of the men in lower-level occupations did not go beyond high school, and only a quarter of them completed an A.B. or a B.S. Only one obtained an M.A., and none earned a doctorate. In contrast, 54 percent of the men in higher-level occupations obtained advanced degrees. On our 8-point scale of amount of education completed, ranging from "did not finish 8th grade" to "doctorate or advanced professional degree," the difference between the distributions of the two groups was significant by chi-square ($p < .01$).

The question to be answered is why the men in lower-level occupations did not progress further in their education. Early marriage, with its attendant responsibilities, was a probable cause in two cases of men who married before they were 21. Physical health may have played a part in two other cases, one being a man who lost his hand in an accident and seems never to have recovered his vocational directedness thereafter, and the other a man whose deteriorated vision following an illness led him to select a vocation requiring manual dexterity rather than reading. A more telling set of circumstances was revealed in the 1940 questionnaire in response to a question asking for "reason for leaving school." This retrospective report indicated that eight of the men in lower-level occupations (42 percent of the nineteen who answered) had lost interest, been ill, had marital responsibilities (or other dependents), had "had to go to work," or had failed in college. This contrasted with only 15 percent of the men in higher-level occupations who gave these same reasons, a difference significant by chi-square ($p < .01$).

Since only a third of the men in lower-level occupations completed college, it is difficult to get any measure of the effect of either the Depression or World War II; of those who finished high school in the Depression slightly more fell into the lower-level group than into the higher-level, but the difference is not significant. It appears that lack of education was partly a direct cause and partly an indirect effect of other circumstances that may have been equally responsible for a lifestyle that led to modest occupational accomplishments.

Motivation. Achievement motivation is an important intervening variable to examine in differentiating between our occupational groups (Atkinson, 1978; Clausen, 1981; Elder, 1969, 1974; Helmreich, Spence, Beane, Lucker, & Matthews, 1980; McClelland, 1971; Sewell & Hauser, 1975). It is represented by a multitude of measures in the data that on both theoretical and empirical (factor-analytic) grounds hang together and provide indexes of its strength. These include a variety of reports on both feelings and behavior that seem to be alternative reflectors of the operation of achievement motivation: (1) ratings on traits of perseverance, desire to excel, and the apparent possession of good integration toward goals (by parents, teachers, field-workers, spouses, and the subjects themselves); (2) parental reports on the subjects' liking for school in childhood, self-reports on liking of occupation in young adulthood, and desire to change the latter; and (3) behavioral indexes of accomplishment, school achievement test scores, such as high-school and college grades, amount of extracurricular activity, including reading, collecting, construction, and other activities that might be alternatives to scholastic dedication, and honors in such activities.

The first two groups of variables provided better prediction than the last one. In both 1922 and 1928 the parents were asked to rate their children on a 4-point scale of "how well they liked school." In both years, the professional and managerial boys were rated somewhat (though not significantly) higher than those at the lower occupational level ($p = .14, .08$ respectively, by chi-square). Parental ratings of "perseverance" on a 13-point scale were in the same direction. The difference was not significant in 1922, but was distinctly higher for the professional and managerial boys in 1928 ($p < .01$ by t-test). A similar rating on "desire to excel" provided a somewhat weaker finding ($p = .11$ by t-test). By 1940 the parental rating of perseverance was highly predictive; the difference between the two groups was significant ($p < .01$) and the comparison for a similar scale for "integration toward goals" was also significant ($p < .05$).

Perhaps more objective than parental ratings were those of the field-workers. Although in 1922 they saw and evaluated only seven of the lower-level boys, their judgments of "amount of achievement motivation" on a 3-point scale provided a difference between the groups, favoring the professional and managerial boys ($p < .01$ by chi-square).

The subjects' self-ratings on several related variables showed significant differences between the men in higher- and lower-level occupations. In 1940, self-confidence was measured by summing two scales tapping self-confidence and lack of inferiority feelings. Instrumentality was similarly measured by self-ratings of perseverance and definite purpose in life. Both of these measures discriminated between the two groups ($p < .01$ by t-test). In 1960 a retrospective measure of ambition in four aspects of work from age 30 to 40 showed significant differences between the two groups, with the men in lower-level occupations scoring lower ($p < .01$ by t-test).

The subjects' feelings about their occupational status in 1940 were expressed in response to three questions. The first asked whether the subject had "definitely chosen" or "just drifted into" his current occupation. Of the men in lower-level occupations, 55 percent replied "drifted into," while only 22 percent of the professional and managerial men gave that answer ($p < .01$ by chi-square). The second question asked whether the subject would prefer other work. The percentages of affirmative answers were 59 and 22 percent for the lower-level and higher-level groups, respectively ($p < .01$ by chi-square). Moreover, a question

TABLE 4.3

*Results of a Discriminant Analysis Predicting Level
of Final Occupation of Men in Later-Maturity Group
(Professional or Higher-Level Business versus Lower-Level)*

Year reported	Variable	Standardized discriminant function coefficient
1922	IQ	.33
Cumulative[a]	Educational level	.58
1940	Definitely chosen life's work	.33
1940	Self-confidence	.16
1940	Instrumentality	−.01
1940	Ambition from age 30 to 40	.42
1950	Parents' financial and social position	.45

Wilks's lambda = .73; df = 1,245; $p < .01$

SOURCE: Questionnaires and test scores from indicated years.
[a]Cumulative educational level indicates highest educational level attained.

asking whether the subject had by now definitely chosen his life's work was answered either negatively or ambiguously by 67 percent of the lower-level group but by only 30 percent of the higher-level group ($p < .01$ by chi-square).

The various possible measures of the behavioral outcomes of high achievement motivation did not provide any predictive power whatever for this ultimate occupational-level variable. Early measures of school achievement on the Stanford Achievement Test and on a parallel series of information tests revealed no group differences in 1922. High-school grades and college grades, as reported in 1928, 1936, and 1940, were equally non-discriminative, and the number of extra-curricular activities and the honors obtained in them in both high school and college were also valueless as predictors.

Integrative analysis. Because the variables we have discussed combine in the overall prediction of occupational outcome, we performed an integrative descriptive discriminant analysis to determine the relative predictive power of each type of variable, while controlling for the other variables. We used representative variables from each set to avoid possible statistical problems arising from multicollinearity of similar variables. The variables chosen were: parents' financial and social position as measured retrospectively in 1950, IQ, educational level, 1940 self-ratings of self-confidence, instrumentality (perseverance and purpose in life), having definitely chosen life's work, and 1960 self-ratings on ambition from age 30 to 40.

Table 4.3 presents the results of the discriminant analysis.* The analysis shows the importance of all three types of variables: family background, ability

* Because of the small size of the lower-level occupational group, missing data from a few subjects on each variable resulted in an extremely small number of subjects. To make the multivariate analysis possible, we substituted the subgroup mean for missing data in this subgroup. This strategy will also be followed in Chapters 5 and 6 where the same circumstance is encountered.

and opportunity, and motivation. The most heavily weighted variables were educational level, parents' financial and social position, and ambition from age 30 to 40. IQ and having definitely chosen life's work at an average age of 30 were the next most heavily weighted variables. Self-confidence made a smaller independent contribution to the prediction, and instrumentality was nonpredictive in the context of the other variables.

Summary. The factors determining occupational choice are obviously complex, especially so in men whose intellectual potential is so high that they could succeed at almost any type of work. It is doubtful that any one variable or even any small group of variables could completely account for such men's adoption of low-prestige occupations. The variables that seem to have contributed to such choice in the small group of men whose occupational level remained very modest throughout life are listed here for such contribution as they may make to our understanding.

1. A limited and non-demanding family background. This includes rural and small town origins, relatively poor neighborhood and housing, lack of parental interest in child's activities, and the subjects' retrospective memories of financial and social status in childhood as being rather on the low side.

2. Less education. The reasons for this appear to have varied considerably from one subject to another, including early marriage, too many financial responsibilities, poor health, and lack of financial support. Within the narrowly limited intellectual level of the group, the men in lower-level occupations had slightly lower initial IQ and lower Concept Mastery scores in young middle age, but the difference in IQ, at least, seems irrelevant in the light of equal school achievement in the early years.

3. Poor motivation, little directedness of effort, and low occupational initiative. Parents rated the boys who were to remain in lower-level occupations as less persevering, with less desire to excel, and as liking school less, both at elementary and high-school age. The field-workers' early estimates of lower achievement motivation were clearly predictive, as were the parents' ratings of lower perseverance in the subjects' early middle age. The subjects' lower self-ratings of self-confidence, instrumentality, and ambition were also suggestive. The subjects in lower-level occupations reported less initiative in selecting an occupation and were less satisfied with what they got. They were also less likely, in young adulthood, to feel that they had found a permanent occupation.

Case summaries of the occupational histories of three of the low-achieving men whose records were most complete illustrate the difficulty of untangling causative factors in their early lives that may have contributed to the modesty of their occupational achievement.

Albert was born in a small mining town in the Northern Sierra during the first decade of the century. His father had been a carpenter, a miner, and at the time of Albert's birth had become a farmer. His mother had been a mother's helper before marriage and was a housewife thereafter. The father's health gave out as

Albert finished high school, and Albert took on responsibility for the farm. Shortly thereafter he had a severe attack of influenza which left his eyes too weak for college work. Relinquishing plans for college did not appear to distress him. He got a job as a miller, married at age 27, and had a first child four years later. During the remainder of the Depression, he had a number of brief low-level jobs until he reached his mid-forties, when he became a professional carpenter. This work appealed to him strongly, partly because of its nature and partly because he liked working on his own. On the Strong Vocational Interest Test, filled out at age 37, Albert received A's on several individual professional occupations (physician, architect, chemist, mathematician) and C's on several that involved social interaction (personnel work, YMCA secretary, social science teacher, sales manager). By age 50 he owned a small farm and was building houses on it for sale. At that time, too, he began providing carpentry service to his church as a community service. As he turned 60, he climbed a challenging mountain peak with one of his sons and repeated this feat annually through 1986, gaining national attention for his vigor and skill. This activity was essentially a hobby that replaced his occupation in retirement.

Charles was born in a small midwestern town where his father was vice-president of a regional bottling company that prepared chocolate drinks for dairy distribution. Charles loved astronomy as a child, reading and star-gazing extensively. His other reading preferences were adventure and detective stories. In high school he was active in dramatics and writing. He attended a small liberal arts college, joined a fraternity (with salutary effects on his social development), and seemed to be both intellectually and socially well-adjusted. In the 1922 and 1936 trait ratings, both parents and teachers rated him as very eager to excel.

After college graduation Charles worked briefly in his father's company but was not comfortable there. His father suggested that he start another company in competition. His older brother joined him in the venture, as president, and Charles served as vice-president in charge of sales. Four years later, in 1940, Charles said, surprisingly, that he had "drifted" into this job and possibly would prefer some other, perhaps machine design. He characterized his ultimate goal as "moderate business success, peace and quiet." An early interest in science and mechanics was reflected in his invention of a refrigerated vending machine. In 1950 (at age 38) he commented: "I remain quite tranquil, and don't seem to have any good or bad fortune. I suspect I have some vegetable blood in me."

Charles's father died in 1950, and during the next decade Charles suffered from recurrent depression. In 1953 he sold his company and secured a position as a design engineer. His first year was quite successful but thereafter he lagged in productivity and eventually lost the position. His wife found work that provided meager support for the family (four children) for the next several years. Toward the end of the 1950's, Charles went into a partnership in a ranching venture, but just as the enterprise was beginning to succeed, his partner defected with their capital. His earlier depression became very deep, and he was diagnosed as seriously hypothyroid. His wife had stopped work when his partnership seemed to be successful, but she resumed permanently in 1960 and divorced Charles shortly thereafter, reporting to us independently that he had become "an adolescent," quarreling with their 16-year-old daughter and manifesting other regressive behavior. He found a position as caretaker of a residence club and lived there for a dozen years until he died of cancer in 1976.

Elton was born in 1913 and grew up in a small college town. His early schooling was uneventful, and he completed high school with satisfactory grades. His parents had a poor marriage, however, divorcing when Elton was 14, and this was severely distressing to him. He lived with his mother until he finished high school. He started college with pre-medical intentions, but began failing in his work almost at once and dropped out after a few months to join the Navy.

A brief marriage at age 19 was followed by six others in rapid succession. The last, at age 36, proved permanent and quite satisfactory. Both parents had been in the printing business, his mother as a typesetter and his father as a proofreader. After leaving the Navy, Elton drifted into both these kinds of work, the former for several years until he re-entered the Navy in World War II, where he was assigned to design and manage a weekly ship-board newspaper.

On returning to civilian life, he took a job as proofreader on a large metropolitan daily and soon became departmental supervisor. Shortly thereafter, labor troubles led to his election as the union representative, a job he enjoyed thoroughly for two years. After the strike was settled, he dropped back into the ranks, feeling somewhat rejected in spite of the success of his leadership. He continued in his supervisory position until his retirement at age 63. Twenty years earlier, however, he had secured a real estate broker's license, and for the remaining years he supplemented his income with brokerage and real estate investments. Five years after his retirement from his regular full-time work, he described himself as quite content, fairly cheerful and fairly relaxed, but only "pretty happy," not "very."

The Most Successful

To contrast with these subjects, we present examples of the most successful men in the later-maturity group. After the 1940 follow-up, Terman and Oden (1947) selected 150 "most" and 150 "least successful" men in the Terman sample — the "A" and "C" groups; a "B" rating was assigned to all others. The criteria for selection were: "(a) nature of work, importance of position, and professional output; (b) qualities of leadership, influence, and initiative; (c) recognition and honors (scientific, civic, professional), awards, biographical listings, election to learned societies, etc.; and (d) earned income. For most occupations, except business, income received the least weight" (Oden, 1968, p. 53).

In 1940 perhaps a quarter of the group was too young for their degree of success to be well evaluated. But decades later their ages were fully suitable, and Oden and Dr. Helen Marshall repeated the evaluation. In 1960 they selected only 100 A cases and 100 C cases. (There were not 150 who could be called C's.) There was considerable overlap of the two ratings. The three case vignettes to follow describe men in the later-maturity group who, although in different fields, were rated as "A" in both the 1940 and 1960 ratings of occupational success.

Harold was the son of a merchant and a housewife. He was an exceptionally talented musician in his youth. In fact, during his first two years at a local teachers college his grades suffered owing to a professional job he held as a violinist in a state orchestra. The income he earned during those years enabled him to transfer to a private university for his junior year. His early career aspirations focused on music and show business. But the advent of talking pictures caused him to consider other careers, and he settled on medicine.

He went east for his medical degree, and followed it with an internship, residencies, and a research fellowship. He studied internal medicine. In 1950, at the age of 40, he checked "deep satisfaction and interest" as most descriptive of his feelings toward his present vocation. He married in 1941, when he was 30. His wife was a housewife, and they had three children. He entered military service in 1942, advancing from lieutenant to major in the medical corps before leaving the service in 1946. His military service was uneventful, though it provided him with useful experience. When he left the army, he returned to California to open a private medical practice. He became affiliated with a medical school, eventually becoming a clinical professor of medicine.

He maintained a half-time private practice with half-time involvement in teaching and research throughout most of his career. He published numerous scientific articles in his specialty and was a leader in his field. Music continued to be his chief avocational interest. He gave musical performances from the age of 40, and continued chamber music performances into his seventies. In 1986, most of his time was taken up with paid or unpaid work and music. In his mid-70's he was still active in his profession. He continued university administration, was frequently asked to give lectures, continued to publish, and was appointed to important boards and committees in his later years.

William was always interested in mathematics. His father was a bond salesman and investment analyst, and his mother was a housewife, who had left college in her last year. He was an excellent student. He majored in economics and chose a financial career, which he seems to have enjoyed thoroughly. In 1930 he earned an MBA and entered the business world as an investment analyst. He expressed ambivalence about his choice at times, feeling that he could have made a greater contribution in the academic world. He spoke early of his desire to advance knowledge of sound economic policy in addition to performing well in his business career. This secondary interest in academic matters was fulfilled through the opportunities he found in his job to write economic policy papers and interpretations. Moreover, he wrote a college textbook on investments, coauthored by a professor at his business school. He married in 1934 at the age of 25. His wife was a housewife. They had two adopted children, and a child of their own after almost twenty years of marriage.

William moved up in the ladder easily at his firm as an investment analyst. In

1941, he listed as factors contributing to his happiness, "pleasant work, a happy married life, and a comfortable income. Also, the thought that I have been steadily learning and 'advancing' myself." During World War II, he resigned from the vice-presidency of two investment trusts to take a wartime appointment in Washington and acquired valuable experience in finance during the war, setting the foundation for his subsequent banking career. While stationed in Washington, he attended night school and obtained his Ph.D.

After the war, he moved his family to the midwest, where he became the vice-president of a large bank. He later became president of the bank, and then vice-chairman. He traveled extensively in his banking career, established contacts in many countries, and gained international recognition. When he retired from banking at age 65, he assumed the directorship of the U.S. subsidiary of a large international agribusiness firm, an activity he pursued part-time. His main preoccupation after formal retirement was travel. He and his wife traveled all over the world, including Europe, China, Hong Kong, and South America. His health remained excellent, and in 1977 he mentioned that his only medical condition of note had been a slight muscle problem resulting from a strenuous mountain climb!

Walter was the son of a lawyer and a housewife. Both his undergraduate and graduate majors were biology. He became director and professor of a national biological institute, leading it to great prominence in the field. During his tenure there he undertook several large research programs. He wrote several books and numerous articles. He became nationally and internationally recognized as an expert on the preservation and utilization of natural resources, and highly regarded in the broader scientific community. In the 1960's he was a science advisor to the federal government, and led a panel studying land and water use in a developing country, which resulted in a new direction in his career. Later he became a university dean of research and was instrumental in establishing a branch of his state university system. He subsequently took an opportunity to move east to head an institute on world population problems at a prestigious university.

He was scheduled to retire in 1976, stating in 1972 that he did not expect to enjoy retirement. In 1977, he was still working full-time at the age of 68, having been appointed professor of science and public policy at the university he helped found. In 1986 he was still spending 75 percent of his time in occupational work for pay.

Goals for Work and Family

In this chapter so far we have focused on the men's career development and success in isolation from other areas. An obvious question to ask about a group with such a preponderance of successful men is the role of family goals and satisfactions in their lives. Were these men preoccupied with their work life to the exclusion of family life? Were there variations among the men in the sample? Obviously, not all individuals place the same emphasis on these two important life domains. Upwardly mobile and occupationally high-status men studied at Berkeley favored their work life over their family life more than men who were not as successful, when asked to indicate their hierarchies of preference for activities (Elder, 1969). Bailyn and Schein (1976) reported that the relative importance of work and family involvement varied significantly among three career groupings: scientists and professors; managers; and engineers. The scientists and professors were more involved in work than in family; the two areas were equal for the managers; and the engineers reported higher involvement in family than in work. These authors attributed the differences between the scientists/professors and managers to the greater psychological overload and internalization of job-related role conflict for the former.

As we reported earlier in this chapter, in 1936 the men were asked about their goals for the future in the context of occupational matters. They were in their mid-twenties, on average, at the time. Almost all the men gave an occupational goal, but in response to the same question 40.3 percent of the women mentioned marriage or family, either alone or along with an occupation. The men's 1936 responses suggest that occupations were extremely important for identity development in this cohort of men. Other authors have pointed to the primacy of occupation in men's self-definition. For example, Vaillant reported a significant emphasis on occupation in his sample of Harvard graduates in the Grant Study (1977). Moreover, Levinson and his colleagues (Levinson, et al., 1978) showed the central role of occupational goals for the men in their sample in their discussion of what they called the "Dream" — a man's sense of self in the adult world. Our 1936 results for the men are also consistent with Erikson's (1959) ideas concerning the establishment of identity before intimacy. This pattern seems to fit contemporary college-aged men better than contemporary women of the same age (Schiedel & Marcia, 1985).

Our study also includes a later, retrospective measure of goal orientation that asked about young adulthood goals in a more structured way. Specifically, in 1972, when the subjects averaged 62 years, they were asked to rate the importance of several goals in the plans they had made for themselves in early adulthood, including occupational success and family life (Question B6). The response options were: "(1) Less important to me than to most people; (2) Looked forward to a normal amount of success in this respect; (3) Expected a good deal of myself in this respect; (4) Of prime importance to me; was prepared to sacrifice other things for this." The mean responses of our subjects are tabulated below for men in professional or higher-level business occupations, and men in lower-level occupations; occupational group was determined from their current occupation in 1972/77, or their former occupation if retired.

	Professional			Higher-level business			Lower-level		
	N	Mean	S.D.	N	Mean	S.D.	N	Mean	S.D.
Occupational success	237	3.03	.81	187	2.83	.89	46	2.67	.87
Family life	224	3.05	.89	185	3.08	.84	46	2.87	.89

The men varied in the importance they gave to occupational goals; the professionals rated them the highest and the men in lower-level occupations rated them the lowest. The means for both the professional and higher-level businessmen differed significantly from that of men in lower-level occupations ($p < .01$). Ratings of the importance of family goals differed less. In intragroup comparisons, the professionals gave equal emphasis to work and family goals, while higher-level businessmen rated family goals higher than work. This is perhaps related to the somewhat lower level of intrinsic motivation of men in business, as compared with the professions, which we will report shortly.

These retrospective findings are surprising in the light of the goal responses in 1936. As we shall see in the chapter on women's occupations, there is a better correspondence between goal responses in 1936 and 1972 for women. We do not know how accurate the men's retrospective ratings are. However, some authors have suggested that the fact that men may need occupational definition for achievement of identity, and that they spend vast amounts of time fulfilling their occupational role, does not rule out psychological involvement in the family, or the importance of the family for men's well-being (Pleck, 1985; Veroff, Douvan, & Kulka, 1981). In fact, we will see later (in Chapter 11) that the Terman men's retrospective rating of their satisfaction in marriage and family is quite high. Moreover, we must keep in mind the historical circumstances in which these men reached adulthood. This was a time when gender roles in marriage were sharply differentiated. (This will be verified in Chapter 6, which examines husbands' and wives' performance of various tasks in marriage.) A major component of the husband's role was that of the "good provider" (Bernard, 1981). This definition of men's family role meshed well with their societal and personal task of achieving and developing an occupational identity.

Income in Later Maturity

Own Income

We requested income figures in dollars in 1972 (Question B2) and 1977 (Question 27). In 1972 these figures were for the subject's own earned income, the wife's earned income and the total family income for 1970 and 1971, and an estimate of the annual average of each of these for the decade 1960–69. In 1977, the same figures were requested for 1976 only.

In their later years, most of the men had incomes proportional to the status levels of their occupations. Since income frequently increases with age, especially in institutional settings, we might expect the older men near the ends of their careers to have had higher income than the younger. This expectation that income would increase with age was, however, incorrect. Table 4.4 gives the mean incomes of the three age-groups described in Chapter 2, at the times listed in the left-hand column. As one would expect, the incomes of the youngest increased from 1970 to 1971 — they were still in their fifties and nowhere near

TABLE 4.4
Income of Men in Later-Maturity Group in Three Age-Groups
(in thousands of dollars)

Year	Source of income	Youngest N	Youngest Mean	Youngest S.D.	Middle N	Middle Mean	Middle S.D.	Oldest N	Oldest Mean	Oldest S.D.
1960–69	Self	99	22.7	15.9	183	23.2	17.1	82	21.3	16.2
1970	Self	116	26.8	18.0	199	27.5	19.0	77	23.3	18.4
1971	Self	116	28.6	20.9	194	27.5	19.5	71	23.4	19.1
1971	Family	127	35.7	22.0	227	33.9	21.0	112	29.5	21.9
1976	Self	85	37.9	42.3	139	27.5	27.0	47	20.9	25.3
1976	Family	98	52.4	57.0	201	41.8	34.7	98	36.9	31.1

SOURCE: 1972 and 1977 questionnaires.
NOTE: This table shows subjects' mean earned income and family income in 1970, 1971, and 1976, and retrospective estimate of annual earned income in 1960–69. "Family" income is income of self, wife, and other family members from all sources, including investments, Social Security, etc. The numbers in this table add to smaller totals than in Table 2.1 because some respondents did not report income.

retirement or work reduction. The middle and oldest groups did not increase; a few of them had already started work reduction. By 1976, many more had started, and the earned income of the oldest group actually decreased between 1971 and 1976; the middle group's income remained constant and the youngest group's income increased by $9,300. These latter had not started work reduction, while the older men had. For all three groups, there are consistent positive correlations of .16 to .40 at both ages between earned income and a measure of work persistence (i.e., the opposite of work reduction). This measure will be fully described, and some of its correlates examined, in a later section of this chapter.

Family Income

The difference between earned income and family income was very substantial for all three groups in 1976. A few of the wives were still working and this accounts for at least part of the difference among the age-groups. The following tabulation shows the percentage of wives who had earned income in 1976 and the average amount.

Wives	Youngest	Middle	Oldest
Percent working	16.8%	13.2%	8.3%
Average earned income	$8,116	$10,071	$4,164

Both the middle and youngest men had a larger percentage of wives who were still working, and at a substantially higher salary, than did the oldest group of men. Obviously these differences are not large enough to account for the differences in family income. In the opposite direction, for the men over 65, Social Security payments were added to earned income, which would tend to nullify the effect of wife's income. The major part of the difference between earned and family income was produced by investment income.

TABLE 4.5

Adequacy of Financial Resources of Men in Each Age-Group and Total Later-Maturity Group (1986)

Adequacy	Youngest		Middle		Oldest		Total	
	N	Pct.	N	Pct.	N	Pct.	N	Pct.
More than enough	32	29.6%	79	41.1%	29	36.3%	140	37.2%
Quite adequate	69	63.9	96	50.0	41	51.3	206	54.8
Barely adequate with care	7	6.5	13	6.8	9	11.3	29	7.7
Really insufficient	0	0	1	.5	0	0	1	0.3
Total	108		189		79		376	

SOURCE: 1986 questionnaire.

By 1982 and 1986 there were so many men who had reduced their work that the dollar amounts were no longer of much significance. What was important in these later years was not the dollars but the men's perception of the adequacy of their financial resources. Therefore, in 1986 we asked (Question 24):

Everyone has his/her own level of financial need — how much money it takes to be quite comfortable. How are your financial resources? (Check one.) More than enough, quite adequate, barely adequate with care, really insufficient.

The responses of each age-group are shown in Table 4.5. For each, the left-hand column shows the number of cases for whom data are available. The right shows the percentage of the age-group that that figure represents. Comparable figures for the total group are in the right-hand columns. Only one of the men checked the fourth choice — "finances not really sufficient" — and 29 checked the third — "barely adequate." There are no noteworthy differences among the three age-groups. For each of them and for the later-maturity group as a whole it is evident that financial needs did not bear heavily on these men. Regardless of their lifestyles — what they had accustomed themselves to — the great majority of them considered their income fully adequate or better. This contrasts with the results of a Harris survey conducted for the National Council on Aging in 1981. In that survey 7 percent of men aged 65 or older in the general population said that they could not make ends meet on their incomes, and 38 percent said that they just about managed to get by.

Retirement

The youthful steps mentioned earlier as prelude to full-time employment are matched in later maturity by various steps toward work reduction and retirement. In the general population, the methods of doing this have been found to vary (Quinn, 1981; Quinn & Burkhauser, 1990; Robinson, Coberly, & Paul, 1985). The subjects in our study also showed such variation. Professionals — doctors, lawyers, accountants, and others who were self-employed — could reduce their work in steps if they wished. Men employed by universities and large corporations were more commonly brought to a full halt by retirement rules at 65 or 70 years of age. Some of this latter group sought substitute occupations, usually at a lower level; others became consultants; many others took up volunteer work with community agencies or simply went right on doing what they had been doing, but without pay. This last option was chosen by a number of researchers and writers. For still others, the care of family financial resources became a sufficiently demanding task to be considered "work."

Fortunately for our study, substantial representative data on retirement have recently been collected about the general population, allowing some comparisons with our subjects. The representative data come principally from two major government-sponsored longitudinal studies. The first, the Retirement History Study (RHS), was conducted by the Social Security Administration (Irelan, 1972). In this study over 11,000 men and women between the ages of 58 and 63 were interviewed in 1969 and followed through 1979 (Quinn, 1981). The second study, the National Longitudinal Survey (NLS), conducted between 1966 and 1981, was sponsored by the U.S. Department of Labor, and was based on a sample of over 5,000 men who were between the ages of 45 and 59 in 1966 (Parnes & Less, 1985). Both of these studies include cohorts which overlap considerably in age with our subjects; in 1977 53 percent of our male respondents fell within the age limits of the Retirement History Study and 81 percent fell within the age limits of the National Longitudinal Study.

Regrettably, we did not directly ask the reasons for reducing work load, and they were not always decipherable from the comments that were sometimes added to questions about retirement. For several men, boredom with past occupation had set in during later middle age, and they wanted either a new and totally different kind of job or they just wanted to "play golf and do nuthin'!" However, the largest single cause appeared to be mandatory retirement. Of the professional men in the top occupational category, and among the businessmen of equivalent status, 58 percent were subject to this rule. This figure is higher than the approximately 30 percent of all male workers and 40 percent of all male wage earners in the RHS and NLS who were subject to mandatory retirement. (The figure for all workers includes self-employed men who usually are not subject to mandatory retirement.) Retirement was compulsory for 57 percent of professional and technical wage earners (excluding noncollege teachers) and 43 percent of managers and administrators interviewed in the RHS (Barker & Clark, 1980).

Amount of Work in Later Maturity

The age and rate at which work reduction occurred varied greatly. For the group as a whole, the decrement was steady. It began when the subjects were aged 50. Of the 415 men for whom we had data, 401 were still fully employed at this age, but eleven had reduced their work to 20 to 80 percent, and three had retired completely. The decrement continued without substantial leaps to age 82, when there were still two men who reported working 20 percent of their time.

To obtain measures of "amount of work performed" might seem an easy task but it has its complications. In early and mid-life "work for income" was the norm, and the response to the question, "how much time do you work?" was invariably "100 percent" except in the case of prolonged illness or disability. This 100 percent was work for income. With the coming of formal moves toward retirement, however, men's marginal notes on our questionnaires expressed protest at limiting "work" to activity that produced income. They pointed out that their volunteer work was scheduled, they felt responsible for doing good and regular work, and it was of a kind that might be paid for. Likewise, care of personal finances was mentioned as work — sometimes "hard work." In order to circumvent these difficulties of interpretation, we asked the following question in the 1977 questionnaire (Question 26):

> Below is a time line in years since you were age 50. At what age did you drop down to less than full-time work (100%)? Enter an approximate percent under that year of age to show about how much time you worked. Continue giving percents for each subsequent year to your present age. Work may have been income-producing (i.e., law practice, business), or a continuation of previous work but without pay (e.g., research, writing), or volunteer service (e.g., politics, community organization work). You have to be the judge of what full-time meant to you, and also what work means! If in doubt, add a comment.

The question was repeated in 1982 (Question 12), but with the years 1975 to 1981 given to identify the percentages; these data were then converted to age individually for each subject in order to have continuity with the 1977 data.

While this question avoids the complications involved in the interpretation of "work," it does make a break with all previous queries about "income work." It nevertheless provides a consistent basis for report from mid-life through 1981, when the five youngest of the later-maturity group of men were all 61; three were still working full time, one had reduced to 50 percent the previous year, and one had been at zero for two years. Although the group as a whole had not completely ceased work in 1981, it was sufficiently close to it that further reporting did not seem profitable in the 1986 survey. Instead, we presented a checklist of eight items, asking for percent of time devoted to each (Question 26). These items included (among others) "occupational work with pay," occupational work "without pay," and "community volunteer work." At that time, only two men were working full time for income. One was a 76-year-old lawyer who specified that he worked at his job "eight hours a day, 5 days a week" and did the other things mentioned above in the evening and on the weekend. The other was a 74-year-old engineer who claimed he worked "8 A.M. to midnite every day," and both his productive work and income supported this claim in full. No one else reached more than 90 percent of time by combining (1) "occupation with pay" with (2) "without pay," and (3) "volunteer community work." The 380 men reporting this combination of three types of "work" estimated that they spent an average of 26.8 percent of their time on them.

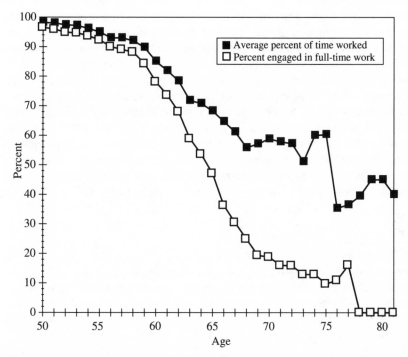

Fig. 4.1. Average percent of time worked and percent of men in later-maturity group in full-time work, by age (N = 436). Data from questionnaires in various years.

Using the annual percentage data obtained in 1977 and 1982, we can get measures of the group's diminishing work level in two ways, one by the average percent of time worked at each age and the other by the percent of men who were still working full time. Both indices are displayed in Figure 4.1. The upper line shows the mean amount of work and the lower line the percent of men still working full time. The number of cases decreases quite rapidly after age 70, due to attrition and the age of the surviving sample, the average being 74 years. The decrease in average amount of time worked is small and steady until 68, after which it varies up and down, the small number of cases making the values less stable. The sharpest decline is between ages 75 and 76, but it is interesting to note that those few hangers-on at the latest ages were still working a third or more of their time.

The second measure, percent of men of each age who were working full time, gives much the same sequential picture of the group's declining activity level, but the values at first seem a little surprising. By age 60 only 78 percent of the men were working full time, and by age 65, just under half were doing so. From the first measure, we saw that the group's average percent of time worked was pretty substantial; at age 60 it was 85 percent, and at 65 they were still spending a little more than two-thirds of their time working. Obviously a large proportion of the men were taking retirement in small steps. By age 70 this principle is very clear — only 19 percent of the men were working full time, but on average the whole group of 279 men aged 70 or more was working 59 percent of their time.

These retirement patterns, showing clear reduction in full-time work before age 65 by some men, are consistent with the national trend toward earlier retirement for men. From 1964 to 1989, the labor force participation rate of men aged 60–64 dropped from 80 to 55 percent (Quinn, Burkhauser, & Myers, 1990). However, our subjects showed substantial continued participation in the labor force in later maturity, much of it part time. To take one year as an example, in 1977 about 30 percent of men aged 65–69 in the general population were employed (Quinn, Burkhauser, & Myers, 1990), while 66 percent of our subjects in the same age-group reported being employed; almost half of these were employed full time and the others part time. (These data were obtained by a question in the 1977 questionnaire [Question 19] asking specifically about income-producing work.)

These findings are of interest to sociologists and economists; they provide some notion of how much this gifted group was providing society with "work" (as defined by the group itself). Psychologists, however, will find the individual records of the retirement process more interesting. Several hundred individual curves, which would vary enormously, would be interesting but hard to assimilate. Something in between the averages of Figure 4.1 and individual curves may be more helpful.

Figure 4.2 shows the percentages of time worked by four cohorts of subjects who began retirement at different ages. The line at the left represents, for a 5-year period, the average percent of time worked by all those men who worked full time through age 64 and began to reduce work at age 65. There were 36 such cases. Note the sharp drop from 100 percent at age 64 to 47 percent at age 65, a very different picture from the slow, steady decrease in the means shown in Figure 4.1. The next curve to the right in Figure 4.2 shows comparable data for the 47 men who began retirement at age 66. The average percent of time they worked also dropped substantially in their first year of retirement (from 100 percent to 41 percent). These two adjacent age-cohorts provide an indication of the reliability of the finding that, on the average, retirement in the mid-sixties in our group led to work reduction by half-time or more. The substantial amount of part-time work in our group contrasts dramatically with exit patterns from career jobs observed in the Retirement History Study. In that study, 73 percent of male wage and salary earners and 49 percent of self-employed men left the labor force entirely upon retirement (Quinn, Burkhauser, & Myers, 1990).

The two curves at the right of Figure 4.2 are similar to the two on the left but show the two small cohorts (Ns of seven and eight respectively) who began their retirements when they were five years older. The decreased number of cases is caused either by death or by the relative youth of the remaining group; some men had not reached 70 in 1977 or 1982, when the data were reported. Comparison of the curves for age 65 and age 70 suggests that the older group reduced their work

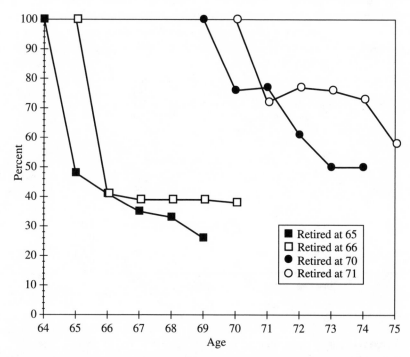

Fig. 4.2. Average percent of time worked by men in later-maturity group who started retirement at age 65, 66, 70, and 71 (N = 36, 47, 7, and 8 respectively). Number of cases in each group decreased by one-third to one-half by the end of the five-year period.

less than the group retiring earlier. These differences in patterns of work reduction between earlier and later retirees are in the same direction as age differences of exit patterns reported for national data by Quinn, Burkhauser, & Myers (1990). These authors suggested that perhaps the same conditions that contributed to later retirement, such as health and opportunities for later work, also contributed to the lesser reduction of work by the older retirees.

Within each of these four groups there were substantial individual differences. By no means all men had a declining monotonic series of work percentages over the five years after the start of work reduction. Individuals' plans for retirement are subject to change by unanticipated events (Anderson, Burkhauser, & Quinn, 1986). Illness, travel opportunities, or family care problems caused some men to stop work for a year or two and then possibly to resume.

Mandatory Retirement

Of all the external — or at least involuntary — causes of retirement, the terms of employment were the most significant. More than half the men were subject to mandatory retirement. Table 4.6 lists the ages at which retirement was required, as reported in 1977 by 415 of the 569 men in the later-maturity sample. In nearly

TABLE 4.6

Retirement Rules for Men in Later-Maturity Group

	N	Percent of total respondents
Mandatory retirement without exceptions	192	46.3
Retirement mandatory but exceptions made	41	9.9
Not officially mandatory but customary	7	1.7
Age of retirement of respondents subject to above rules		
55	1	0.2
60	2	0.5
62	2	0.5
65	166	40.0
66	3	0.7
67	16	3.8
68	4	1.0
69	1	0.2
70	42	10.1
72	3	0.7
No mandatory rule	175	42.2
Total respondents	415	

SOURCE: 1977 questionnaire.

10 percent of cases, exceptions were sometimes made, and in about 2 percent the requirement was only customary, not a part of the employment agreement. In almost all the cases where exceptions were allowed, the rule required retirement at 65, unless exception was granted for some further limited period. These cases have been included in the age listings with those subject to mandatory retirement. Clearly 65 was the predominant age for mandatory retirement, with 70 a distant second.

These data were collected before federal legislation began to influence retirement practices. Since forced retirement below the age of 70 is now prohibited, it is of interest to see how these men felt about retirement, as well as what they did about it.

Retirement Preferences

In 1977 we asked, just after the question on mandatory retirement, which of several arrangements for retirement would be preferable (Question 25). Table 4.7 shows the percentages of the group who would choose each of the four alternatives the question offered, and at what age. The figures for the "regular" or mandated age were obtained from a preceding question about age of mandatory retirement. We have combined the ages into five-year classes, but almost all preferences were stated at the top of each class interval.

Earlier retirement would have been preferred by 19 percent of the men, none above 65. The lowest two retirement ages suggested were 20 and 30, both by younger men — presumably a bit of black humor. The second column shows that 13 percent of the men were satisfied with what they had (regular, mandated age).

Most of these retired at age 65. In the third column are shown the choices of the men (26 percent) who apparently wanted to continue working full time to a given age and then retire completely. Slightly more than a third of these men specified some criterion other than age for retirement; the numbers making each of the four types of comments listed in the table's footnote were almost identical. All the answers representing some form of "I'll never retire" were by members of the middle age-group — no older and no younger men felt this way.

The most common answer to our question was the fourth choice — to start decreasing work at the indicated age and fully retire some years later. This is consistent with the widespread preference in the general population (Jondrow, Bruckling, & Marcus, 1987), which is not often realized in practice. These fourth choices are not shown in the table; they are clustered (43 percent at age 69 or below, mostly at 65, and 57 percent at 70 or above). The highest age chosen, by two middle age-group men, was 90, probably a way of saying "Never!" and still keeping within the format of the questionnaire by giving a figure. A comparison of the third and fourth columns suggests that those men who wanted to quit completely, in one fell swoop, were prepared to wait longer than those who wanted to start decreasing in steps.

The last column on the right of Table 4.7 shows the percentages of men who would prefer the various age brackets. Clearly age 65 is the favorite counting complete retirement and beginning of work reduction together. Age 70 is second, however, and legislation to prevent mandatory retirement before 70 is clearly going to fill the needs of a substantial proportion of these highly motivated and competent workers.

We have not reported these data separately for the three age-groups because

TABLE 4.7

Preferred Age of Retirement of Four Groups of Men in Later-Maturity Group (1977)

Preferred age of retirement	Group preferences (pct.)				N	Pct. of total
	Earlier	Regular	Continue	Decrease		
50 or earlier	9%	—	2%	5%	15	4%
51–55	20	—	1	8	26	7
56–60	39	2	2	23	63	18
61–65	27	79	12	39	124	35
66–70	—	19	33	23	74	21
Over 70	—	—	12	2	14	4
Other[a]	5	—	38	1	40	11
N	66	48	94	148	356	
Pct. of total	19	13	26	42		

SOURCE: 1977 questionnaire.
NOTE: "Earlier" were men who would have preferred to retire earlier than the mandatory age; "Regular" were men who preferred the mandatory age; "Continue" were men who wanted to continue beyond the mandatory age and then retire completely; "Decrease" were men who wanted to start decreasing work at the ages given in the table and fully retire some years later.
[a]Other includes "personal selection," "when health requires," "sufficient income," "never!"

there is little difference among them. The younger men had a general disposition to select an earlier age for retirement than did the other two groups. We have already seen that they had bigger family incomes. Also more of them were in the business rather than the professional sector, and later we will note that the businessmen seem to have gotten less satisfaction from their work than the professional men.

In general, then, we can conclude that in our group there is a lot of idiosyncratic choice involved in selecting both an age and a style for retirement. It appears that the federal legislation setting the lower limit for mandatory retirement at age 70 is in line with the expressed needs of all but a very few of the men in our group.

Effects of mandatory retirement. In the general population, mandatory retirement increases the likelihood of work cessation (Barker & Clark, 1980; Quinn & Burkhauser, 1990). However, the effect of mandatory retirement on amount of work reported by our group is ambiguous. We compared the percent of time worked during the first five years after retirement by men subject to mandatory retirement with the percent worked by men who retired voluntarily. In one cohort, which began work reduction at age 65, the mandatory group worked a little more. In another cohort, which began at age 66, they worked a little less. Neither difference was significant.

Another measure of work activity also leads to the conclusion that the mandatory/voluntary distinction makes little if any difference. We averaged the amount of work reported for ages 51 to 70 and compared the means by t-test. The difference favored the voluntary group by a small margin — they had worked a little more on average ($p < .10$).

Opportunities for continued work. Of clear and much greater significance was a man's perception of future work opportunities. The 1977 questionnaire asked (Question 24): "In general are there opportunities to continue the same occupation after mandatory retirement?" The options for answer by check marks are shown in Table 4.8. The numbers and percentages add to more than 261 and 100 percent respectively because some men checked two or more of the "yes" alternatives. (Thirteen of the men who reported no mandatory retirement in the previous question nevertheless checked an option in this query, maybe finding the question irresistible or wanting to tell what they had actually done.) For the younger men who had not yet retired these judgments were anticipatory; for those who had already retired, they were based on experience.

For more than a quarter of the group, retirement evidently meant the abrupt end of the work which had occupied them all their adult lives, but for the remainder there were other options. This contrasts with the general population, for whom the modal pattern is to cease work entirely after retirement (Quinn & Burkhauser, 1990). The options of our subjects are included in the "percentage of time worked at each age" shown in Figure 4.1, along with whatever different occupational areas the retired men chose to label as "work." One case in point is the carpenter who gave up carpentering and became a mountain guide to raise

TABLE 4.8

*Work Opportunities in Same Occupation Available After Retirement
for Men in Later-Maturity Group (1977)*

Work opportunities	No.	Pct.
No opportunities	73	28.0%
Yes, in other companies or institutions, with pay	41	15.7
Yes, under less advantageous employment circumstances	45	17.2
Yes, as a consultant, free lance, etc.	130	49.8
Yes, same work, without institutional affiliation	20	7.6
Yes, same work on a voluntary basis with same institution	24	9.1
Total respondents	261	

SOURCE: 1977 questionnaire.
NOTE: 188 men gave "Yes" responses, but because some gave two or more, the number of
"Yes" responses exceeds 188 and the total percentage exceeds 100%.

money for environmental agencies. Another man, chief financial officer of a
large corporation, took early retirement and became a professor of linguistics,
thus putting a life-long hobby to satisfying use. Still a third, a mathematics
professor, served as a a free-lance consultant for several years, received a couple
of professional honors, and lived very comfortably on his earnings and his
pension.

Unlike mandatory retirement itself, the perception of opportunities for postretirement work in the same occupation was quite clearly related to the amount
of work done during the first five years after retirement. In Figure 4.3 the men of
the two early cohorts who were subject to mandatory retirement are divided into
two subgroups: those who did not see opportunities for postretirement work in
their usual occupation and those who did. The latter sub-group worked significantly more in both cohorts.

In these figures relating to amount of work at various ages, there is an unavoidable reduction in the size of groups from one period to another, particularly
for the older cohorts. For example, in Figure 4.3, the first curve showed a
constant number of cases (5) from beginning to end of the five-year sequence,
the second curve dropped from 15 to 10 cases after the fourth year, the third
group dropped from 9 to 7 after the second year, and the group farthest to the
right dropped from 29 to 28 after the third year, and further to 22 in the final year.
The reduction is less severe in Figure 4.2, which is based on more cases. These
reductions result from the fact that, at the older ages especially, some of the men
had not yet reached the age they were being asked to report on.

In sum, in contrast to the general population, it does not appear that mandatory retirement rules had much, if any, effect on the work activity of this group of
men. There is no sharp drop in work at either 65 or 70, the two most frequent
ages for compulsory retirement, and there is little difference in the amount of
time worked during the years following 65 and 70 by those who were required to
retire and those who were not. It must be kept in mind that this group of highly
skilled professional and businessmen is far from being a sample of the general

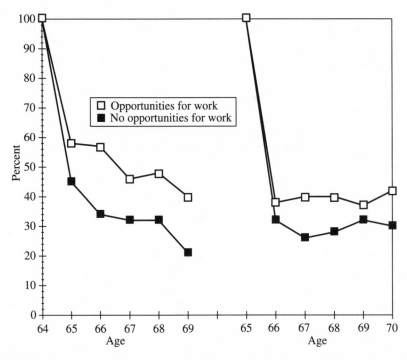

Fig. 4.3. Comparison of average percent of time worked by men in later-maturity group with and without opportunities for their kind of work after retirement. Two cohorts, ages 64–69 and 65–70 (N = 5, 15, 9, and 9 respectively). Data from 1977 questionnaire.

population. We have no comparative data on the perception that an unselected sample of men would have of opportunities for continuing work in the same occupation after retirement, but three-fourths of those in our present group did see opportunities, and obviously many of them took advantage of what options were available.

A Work-Persistence Index

Attitudes toward the continuation of work ranged from an almost violent statement of "I'll never quit!" to a rather indelicate suggestion as to where "work" could go. The men's actual behavior paralleled their feelings. Some quit working as soon as they had enough money to live on, even frugally. Others went along placidly working at one task or another for a few years but dropped off to a professed zero sometime in their late sixties or early seventies. Quite a few, however, worked vigorously and with seeming satisfaction well into their seventies or, in one instance at least, to 80. It is of some interest to search for antecedents, or at least correlates, of these individual differences, because from a societal standpoint the varied amounts of work activity indicate how much contribution the individuals were able to make to the economy. Also to be considered are the benefits resulting from early retirement. Whatever the question, an index is needed to test hypotheses about what may have caused or accompanied those individual variations.

To simplify the index, we have averaged the work-percentages for successive five-year periods beginning with age 51, and then reduced the wide range of resulting percentage values to a five-point scale, with 5 = 0 to 10 percent, 4 = 11 to 39 percent, 3 = 40 to 60 percent, 2 = 61 to 89 percent, and 1 = 90 to 100 percent. Thus, each man could be characterized by a single number describing the percent of time he worked during the successive half-decades of his life beginning at age 51 and continuing until he had reached the age at which the data were collected. An index number was given only if there were at least three years of possible work in a five-year period.

For graphic convenience, the men were divided into three categories of work persistence in each half-decade, those still at full-time work (index value of 1), those in partial retirement (2–4), and those completely retired (5). Figure 4.4 shows the percentages of these three categories at successive half decades. At all ages more men had partially retired than had completely quit work. Even though

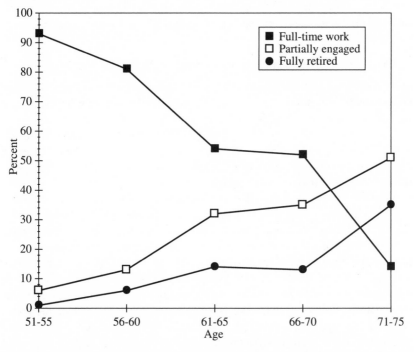

Fig. 4.4. Percent of men in later-maturity group engaged in full-time work (90–100 percent of time), partially engaged (11–89 percent), and fully retired (0–10 percent) in successive half-decades of their lives from 51 to 75 years (N = 528). Data from 1977 and 1982 questionnaires.

about half the group were not subject to mandatory retirement, only 12 percent of them were still fully engaged in the years 71 to 75. The number of cases available at that age is small but a similar graph based solely on the work history of the 72 men who had reached age 75 is indistinguishable from this one. Another indication of the stability of these findings is that, although nearly 100 more cases are available since a similar report was given on the basis of data from the 1972 questionnaires (Sears, 1977), there is no difference in the shapes of the curves then and now.

A final overall index adds the values from the first four half-decades and provides a measure of work persistence to age 70 for 406 of the 569 men in the later-maturity sample. This figure is called "Index70." Its values can range from 4 (rating of 1, which equals full-time work, in all four of the half-decades) to 20 (rating of 5, meaning complete retirement, in all four half-decades). It is to be remembered that the final determination of amount of work at each year of age was obtained in 1982. Hence, we have data available to age 70 — and can use the Index70 — for all the 406 men who were born in 1914 or earlier. We will use this index as a dependent variable to determine what were the antecedents and correlates of a work-persisting career. We have reversed the scale of Index70 in the computations reported below, because our emphasis will be on work persistence, rather than on retirement. Higher values of Index70 will indicate greater work persistence.

Variables Correlated with Work Persistence

A number of variables have been found to be predictive of retirement or cessation of work after retirement (and therefore of work persistence). These include, among others, health, occupational membership, attitudes toward work and retirement, economic means and sources of income, opportunities for work, and job type (Palmore et al., 1985; Parnes et al., 1985; Quinn, Burkhauser, & Myers, 1990). We were able to examine the extent to which a number of these or related variables predicted work persistence.

Health and vitality. A self-report on health status was obtained with a 5-point scale (very poor to very good) in every follow-up from 1936 to 1986. Health during the retirement years has often been found to be associated with earlier retirement (Sammartino, 1987). In our group, the correlations between health ratings and Index70 are zero for the years before 1972. From then on, they are small but consistently positive. The self-report on vitality was obtained with a 4-point scale (1972, Question A3). This measure has been used only in the four later-maturity follow-ups. The correlations between the health and vitality scales and between each and Index70 are given in Table 4.9. Both health and vitality correlated significantly with work persistence, but the coefficients are rather small. Further, they are so highly related to one another that at the level of zero order correlation one can question just how much we are dealing with two variables or only one.

Mental health. Oden's cumulative rating of mental health is available for 379 of the men in the later-maturity group. Its correlation with work persistence

TABLE 4.9
Correlations of Health, Vitality, and Work Persistence
(Index70) of Men in Later-Maturity Group
(1972–86)

| Year | N | With Index70 | | Health with vitality |
		Health	Vitality	
1972	376	.17	.32	.66
1977	378	.16	.18	.58
1982	327	.19	.20	.68
1986	298	.21	.17	.74

SOURCE: Questionnaires in indicated years.

is $-.07$ in the group as a whole, and only in the youngest group is there a separate correlation at all different from zero: $r = .18$. Our conclusion is that this measure of mental health is irrelevant to work persistence.

Two measures — the 1960 and 1986 self-reports on use of alcohol (1986, Question 21) — are equally unrevealing of any connection. Neither for the whole group nor for any one of the three subgroups is there a correlation significantly different from zero in either year.

Marital history. There was a slight tendency for the "always single" men to retire earlier than the others and to work less between ages 51 and 70 (Index70). Otherwise, there was no relation between marital history and work persistence in the group as a whole or in any of the three age-groups.

Education. The achieved level of education offers a quite different picture. All three of the age-groups are within a couple of points of the correlation (.30) between education and Index70 for the whole group (N = 406). The consistency of these correlations indicates that the better-educated men tended to work more during the years from 51 to 70 than the less well-educated.

Occupation. When the work persistence of men in professional, higher-level business, and lower-level business occupations is compared, the difference between the professional and business groups is very clear. The former devoted a higher proportion of time to work during the years 51 to 70 than did the two business groups ($p < .01$). We have seen earlier that these groups were equally subject to mandatory retirement, and hence it seems probable that the difference in work persistence may arise from a combination of perceived opportunities for work and personal feelings about work itself.

Occupational success. Objective occupational success appears to have had less influence on work persistence than did type of occupation, but although its influence was weak it was consistent. The correlations for the group as a whole between Index70 and the A/C occupational success ratings of 1940, 1960, and a combination of the two are .15, .19, and .19 respectively.

Income. It is not surprising that the men who had been working more persistently during their last two decades reported more income in 1972 and 1977 than those who worked less. The correlations between income in the various years and Index70 are as follows:

	Self 1959	Self 1960–69	Self 1970	Self 1971	Family 1970	Self 1976	Family 1976
r	.13	.20	.17	.21	.16	.27	.23
N	374	290	302	291	360	235	357

Except for the self-ratings of health and vitality, variables discussed so far refer to fairly objective events. All of them except use of alcohol and early mental health (1960 and before) provide small positive predictive measures of the amount of time the men would devote to work between ages 51 and 70.

Now we turn to some variables that are less objective. Three from 1940 must be considered; all showed some predictive power, but without statistical significance. Men who reported that they had just "drifted into" rather than "chosen" their occupation tended to work less in the later two decades ($p = .11$). Those who said they would prefer some other work were also less likely to work persistently ($p = .06$). A question on whether they had definitely chosen their life work at that time did not, however, discriminate at all between high and low work persistence.

Two decades later, in 1960, there were stronger predictors. A question on how well the man thought he had lived up to his early promise yielded highly significant answers; on a five-point scale from "my life has been a failure" to "fully," the more persistent workers said they felt they had lived up to their promise more fully than did the men who would later be less persistent ($r = .20$).

A series of 5-point retrospective self-rating scales from 1960 on ambition between ages 30 and 40 were also revealing. They asked for comparison with other men of the same age in ambition for "(1) being excellent at work itself, (2) recognition of accomplishments, (3) vocational advancement, and (4) financial gain." Only the first and third scale showed any relation to work persistence, and those were weak predictors ($r = .14$ and .13, respectively).

In 1960 another question added both confirmation of the importance of interest in work for work persistence and an interesting sidelight: "From what aspects of your life do you derive the greatest satisfaction? (Check once those you regard as important; double check those most important.)" The alternatives were "(1) work itself, (2) recognition for accomplishments, (3) income, (4) avocations, (5) marriage, (6) children, (7) religion, (8) social contacts, (9) community service." Satisfaction with work, children, and marriage showed some relation to work persistence ($r = .24, .20,$ and .12, respectively). None of the other alternatives had any discriminative power whatsoever. We are not prepared to speculate on why high family satisfaction should have been associated with more intensive pursuit of work. Perhaps a happy marriage and home life provided the emotional security and encouragement that allowed the man to work as much as he wished, or perhaps the same vigor and enthusiasm that produced a longer work life also led to a stronger effort to have a happy and successful marriage. The data on marital history did not support this latter suggestion, however; divorce was no more common among the early retirees than among the later.

To provide an overall prediction of work persistence, we entered ten of the

TABLE 4.10

*Results of Multiple Regression Analysis
Predicting Work Persistence (Index70)
of Men in Later-Maturity Group*

Variable	r	β	p
Health and vitality (1972)	.28	.21	.01
Education level	.30	.22	.01
Lived up to promise (1960)	.20	.10	.05
Work satisfaction (1960)	.24	.12	.05
Family satisfaction (1960)	.19	.12	.05
Ever-married	.17	.14	.01
$R = .48; F = 16.89; df = 6,339$			

SOURCE: 1960 and 1972 questionnaires and cumulative education and marriage data.

most promising variables into a multiple regression equation. To avoid possible statistical problems due to multicollinearity of similar variables, we chose a representative variable from each set of variables. Those chosen included: a combined index of health and vitality from 1972; level of education; 1960 cumulative A/C occupational success rating; 1960 self-rating of having lived up to promise; average ambition between ages 30 and 40 with regard to excellence in work and vocational advancement; 1972 family income; business vs. professional occupation; work satisfaction in 1960; family satisfaction in 1960 (the average of satisfaction with marriage and children); and having ever been married. Six produced significant beta weights. The equation was then recomputed with only these six predictors, and the results are presented in Table 4.10, along with their simple correlations with Index70. The multiple R for these six predictors is .48. The most powerful predictors, controlling for the other variables in the equation, were the measures of health and vitality, and highest education level. These were followed by ever-married history, 1960 satisfaction with work, 1960 satisfaction with family, and feeling of having lived up to intellectual promise.

Summary

The Terman men were highly educated for their time. Of the 569 men in the later-maturity group, three-fourths completed college, one-fifth obtained a master's degree or had some graduate work, and one-fourth obtained a doctorate or a major professional degree. The Great Depression and World War II had little effect on the number who obtained undergraduate degrees, but both events approximately halved the proportion of men who obtained doctoral degrees. The Depression had little effect on the pace at which the men obtained their education, but the war clearly retarded both undergraduate and graduate education.

By 1940, over 70 percent of the original group had attained an occupational level equivalent to Classes I (professional) and II (high-level business) of the

U.S. Bureau of the Census classification. This figure rose to almost 90 percent in 1960, and was 95 percent in the later-maturity group. Men in professional occupations expressed a greater desire to continue work and gained more intrinsic satisfaction from their careers than did the businessmen. In 1986, 37 percent of the men said their financial resources were "more than enough" for their needs and another 55 percent rated them "quite adequate." These evaluations of their financial situations were much more favorable than those of older men in the general population.

Examination of the case histories of the 21 men working at occupations in the lower levels of the U.S. Census classification (Classes III–V) in 1972/77 suggested that several characteristics were associated with their more modest achievements. These included relatively poorer and less demanding home backgrounds in childhood, slightly lower IQ, significantly lower intellectual skill in middle age, much less education resulting in part from pressure to earn a living at an earlier age, very much lower level of achievement motivation at all points from early childhood to middle age, and a less directed and integrated effort toward occupational mobility as reflected in job-seeking.

In retrospective ratings in 1972 of the importance of work and family goals in young adulthood, professionals rated occupational success the highest, men in lower-level occupations rated it the lowest, and businessmen's ratings were in between. The three groups of men did not differ significantly in levels of family goals. In intragroup comparisons, the professionals rated goals for work and family equally, while higher-level businessmen rated family goals higher than work goals.

The later-maturity men persisted in work longer than men in the general population. Their retirement from career work did not usually result in a complete cessation of work. Instead, they tended to continue to engage in the same line of work part time or to pursue some other interest. Their continued work and creative endeavors are consistent with other findings showing that precocious individuals tend to be productive longer than others (Simonton, 1990). Contemporaneous factors, such as health and energy, affect work persistence. In addition, the previous high levels of achievement in our sample are clearly operative. It seems that our subjects' continued working is a product of enabling influences that operate at both the individual and societal level to make continued work possible. The previously high educational and achievement levels of many of these men are related to the availability of work opportunities, and to their personal competencies to create such opportunities.

Beyond the contributions of these variables, however, self-assessments of having lived up to promise, and having had positive feelings about work and family at midlife, facilitated longer work. These affective variables suggest that feelings of self-esteem and satisfactions in personal, as well as occupational, life contribute to the enduring interest in meaningful work in the years of later maturity. In stark contrast to the stereotype that gifted children burn out, these men continue to be productive far into their later years.

As we consider the findings concerning the occupational life of the men within the context of successful aging, we conclude that continuing activity in the occupational realm is possible well into later maturity. The continuing work involvement of many of the men is surely a contributing factor to their quality of life in the later years. Moreover, it has been possible for many of these men to experience a gradual reduction in work, rather than an abrupt cessation, the more usual pattern in the general population. A gradual, rather than abrupt, transition to retirement is probably more congruent with the process of aging as experienced by most individuals and requires a less demanding adjustment to the loss of the work role. Thus, with regard to successful aging, the Terman men have been able to enjoy the benefits of productive work well into the later years, while at the same time matching their activity level and involvement in such work with their health and interests in these years.

5

Women's Work History

Nearly all the women in the later-maturity group were born during the first two decades of the twentieth century. They were heirs to a social climate, stemming from the middle of the previous century, that distinguished appropriate employment for men from appropriate employment for women. Although the code was not entirely rigid, women most often found employment as teachers, nurses, clerical workers, stenographers, sales persons, houseworkers, dressmakers, hairdressers, cleaners, and millworkers. The great majority of the mothers of our subjects had held such jobs in their premarital years, but fewer than an eighth of them continued work beyond the birth of a child. Among those who did, two-thirds were in upper professional occupations.

Women of the nineteenth century did not often become professionals or make lifetime careers outside the home. The ones who did were chiefly physicians, college teachers, authors, or performing artists. Women were almost unknown at managerial levels of business.

The tide of immigration late in the nineteenth century brought many young unmarried women to the United States. They sought employment from necessity. The mills of New England, the businesses of the big cities, and the households of the well-to-do all welcomed them — at low wages, but the increasing desire of women to work at a professional level was not so welcome in a male-dominated work force. The difficulties and prejudices they met in their efforts to develop independent careers were well reflected in *The Gilded Age*, a novel written jointly by Mark Twain and Charles Dudley Warner in 1873. Their heroine, a young, obviously capable, politely strong-minded daughter of a successful Philadelphia lawyer, wanted to marry. She also wanted a medical career. Her otherwise estimable family was unsympathetic and persuasively discouraging — about the career.

Her fiancé stood irresolutely between her desires and the proprieties expressed by her father. Her conflict, produced by gentle but smothering tradition and her own yearning for self-actualization, was painfully familiar in the 1920's to girls of her putative granddaughters' generation — our women subjects.

Our women subjects represent the transitional generation between those women who had to struggle for entry into the upper echelons of the work force and those who, at the end of this century, can easily enter any field they choose but may still encounter obstacles to the full acceptance of their achievements at the top levels of the occupational ladder, especially in the business world. During the 70 years since our study started, this change in occupational opportunity has not been smooth nor has it always been in one direction. Indeed, the extraordinary changes in gender roles were not fully apparent, especially at the higher levels of occupations, until the subjects were well into mid-life.

Modest gains were made in women's employment in the professions in the 1920's. Many people saw the combination of marriage with a career as a severe problem, however, especially after the birth of children. Moreover, most professional and semiprofessional women were employed in female-dominated fields, and even there did not receive the same remuneration and advancement as men (Chafe, 1972).

As with many other social movements, initial gains in the expansion of women's occupational opportunities were slowed or lost as new social forces came into play. For example, the proportion of women as members of college faculties reached its height in the early 1930's, declining thereafter, and not increasing until the late 1950's (Bernard, 1964). This was due in part to the Depression, a difficult time for women's entry into careers. The decade of the 1930's heard many arguments against female workers. With unemployment widespread, women who worked were seen as taking jobs away from men supporting families. In some states laws were passed restricting the employment of married women. In fact, and contrary to wide belief, most women who worked during the 1920's and 1930's did so from economic necessity — not for "pin money" (Chafe, 1972). At a more fundamental level, economic instability during the Depression threatened the structure of the family, and resulted in a renewed emphasis on traditional family roles (Banner, 1974).

During World War II, women were recruited to fill jobs vacated by men, particularly clerical and factory jobs. A sizable number of women remained in the labor force after the war, and from 1947 on, the proportion continued to rise. However, women still held the lowest-paying jobs, and their participation in the professions continued to be slight for a number of years. At the same time, the experience of war revived an emphasis on domesticity, and on women's traditional role (Banner, 1974). The late 1940's and the 1950's were accompanied by an increasing birth rate (Bernard, 1964).

Other societal realities, however, led to a steadily increasing participation of women in the work force, especially married women. The expanding economy readily accepted women workers, and in addition, the fact that women lived longer than earlier in the century meant that they faced many child-free years, enabling them to accept employment.

Although disparities still exist between the earnings of American men and women, as well as in their levels of professional status, the occupational world of the 1990's is far different from that faced by our women subjects in the 1930's and 1940's as they reached early adulthood. A majority of women with young children now work, and women have gained admittance to a large number of male-dominated occupations. The issue of the entry of married women to the professions has been largely replaced by a consideration of the problems faced by couples in balancing two professional careers while attempting to maintain a satisfying family life (Holahan & Gilbert, 1979; Rapoport & Rapoport, 1980). Neither women themselves, nor society in general, now question the right of women to challenging careers.

Because these dramatic changes in the role of women in society occurred over the half-century of our group's adult lives, the context is crucial for an understanding of the way in which occupation entered into those lives. In exploring their work histories, we examine their educational preparation and occupational choices, their own characterizations of their work history, the interaction of marital status and parenthood with work history, and the variety of their work patterns. We will also examine how the life goals these women expressed in their youth relate to later career patterns. We also look at other psychological factors which differentiated those women who pursued careers from others in the sample. Finally, we report on the process of retirement and the way in which it related to work history.

Educational Preparation

With a single exception, the women in the later-maturity sample had ended their formal education before they entered later maturity. The last bachelor's degree was in the field of education; it was received in 1961 when the recipient was 49 years old. Another woman obtained a doctoral degree in counseling psychology in 1980 — at the age of 73. Three years later she was still in practice part-time and in 1986 went on a year-long lecture tour around the world.

There was little difference in the amount of education obtained by the men and the women except at the highest level. Two men and one woman did not finish high school, but 70 percent of the women secured a bachelor's degree (or higher), which nearly matches the men's 76 percent. For the women, this figure is in sharp contrast to the 8 percent rate overall for Californian men and women of their generation (Terman and Oden, 1947), and the 8 percent rate Campbell, Converse, and Rogers (1976) found for a representative national sample of women over thirty.

Again at the beginning graduate level the women and men showed similar patterns: 43 percent of the women and 46 percent of the men had some graduate work, with or without advanced degrees. However, only 4 percent of the women

TABLE 5.1

Effect of the Depression and World War II on the Educational Level of Women

Educational level achieved	High school graduates				College graduates					
	1916–29		1930–39		1920–29		1930–39		1940–45	
	N	Pct.	N	Pct.	N	Pct.	N	Pct.	N	Pct.
High school, some college	105	29.1%	41	31.8%	—	—	—	—	—	—
A.B. or B.S. degree	87	24.1	44	34.1	15	21.4%	100	40.5%	10	52.6%
M.A. degree or some graduate work	148	41.0	42	32.6	51	72.9	131	53.0	8	42.1
Doctoral or major professional degree	21	5.8	2	1.6	4	5.7	16	6.5	1	5.3
Total	361		129		70		247		19	
Significance (*p*) by chi square			.05				.05			

SOURCE: Cumulative education data.
NOTE: One woman who did not finish high school is omitted from the table, as are those who completed college after 1945.

obtained doctoral degrees while 27 percent of the men did. The women had relatively more master's degrees and other nondoctoral training than the men. The women's nondoctoral training often consisted of a teaching certificate.

It can be seen from Table 5.1 that the effects of both the Depression and World War II on the higher educational attainment of the women were the same as for the men. Women graduating from high school before the Depression achieved significantly higher levels of education, with 47 percent of pre-Depression high school graduates going beyond the bachelor's degree, while only 34 percent of Depression-period graduates did so. When the groups are separated by date of graduation from college, a similar effect is found, with 79 percent of pre-Depression graduates obtaining some graduate education, in contrast to 60 percent of Depression graduates and 47 percent of those graduating during or after the war.

The effect of the Depression and the war was to curtail the education of both men and women; more of both stopped their education with a bachelor's degree. Among the men, more stopped with an M.A. The difference between men and women even in the pre-Depression period, however, was very substantial in respect to the number obtaining doctoral degrees.

Occupational Levels and Goals for Work and Family

Understanding the men's occupational history was a simple task compared to understanding the women's. The complexities produced by the conflict between marital and family roles and the desire for gainful employment — the latter being increasingly induced by the changing values of the early twentieth century — make it impossible to rely on a single index such as the Index70 used in describing the men's histories. The women's occupations will be listed below, but for deeper analysis, three additional measures have been obtained — in 1972, Question B3 asking subjects for an overall summary of their work patterns, Question 18 in 1977 concerning women's participation in several work-related activities by half-decades of their lives, and the time-line questions of 1977 (Question 26) and 1982 (Question 12) asking about percentage of time worked at each age from 50 on. These provide multiple outcome measures, both of type of occupation and amount of time devoted to it.

Occupational Choices

The occupations of the women in the later-maturity sample who reported occupational data in 1940, 1960, and 1972 or 1977 are listed in Table 5.2. Those women who were retired in 1972 or 1977 were classified by their most recent previous occupation, if they had supplied it on the 1972 questionnaire. The occupations were distributed over three major groups: professional and semi-professional, business occupations, and homemaking. Both the professional and business-related occupations varied considerably in responsibility and prestige. At the top of the professions were medicine, law, and college teaching; lower, in both income and prestige, were nursing and teaching below college level. In the business world, work ranged from executive and managerial to clerical, sales, and service occupations. The professions can be lumped together with the managerial level in business as representative of the top two classes listed by the U.S. Census. The clerical and sales positions belong mainly to Class III. This is similar to the men's classification reported in Chapter 4, though not identical.

The breakdown is dramatically different from the men's. In addition to the fact that women were homemakers, more of the women professionals were concentrated in semiprofessional jobs, rather than in the professions carrying the highest prestige, in contrast to the men. It should also be noted, however, that the women's occupational distribution was very different from that of the general population of women for this cohort. For example, in 1960, 37 percent of the Terman women were in professional, semiprofessional, or managerial jobs, as compared with 17 percent of women in the general population (Hauser, 1964).

Over the twenty years between 1940 and 1960, there was surprisingly little change in the percentages of women employed in each of the three main categories. About 37 percent of them were in professional, semiprofessional, or managerial occupations; 20 percent were in lower-level clerical or sales jobs, farming, or miscellaneous business occupations; and 43 percent were homemakers. From 1962 to 1972/77 there was an increase in the percentage of professional and semiprofessional occupations, caused in part by a rise in the percentage of women in management positions. These positions, however, did not tend to be at the highest levels of management.

Education and Occupation

Whereas higher levels of education are required for professional occupations, in this generation they were not essential for managerial work in business. Sears and Barbee (1977, pp. 50–51) analyzed the kinds of occupation attained, by

TABLE 5.2

*Occupational Categories of Women in Later-Maturity Group
in 1940, 1960, and 1972 or 1977*

Occupational category	1940		1960		1972/77	
	N	Pct.	N	Pct.	N	Pct.
Professional and semiprofessional occupations						
Member of college or university faculty	5	1.2%	17	3.9%	23	6.1%
Member of junior college faculty	1	0.2	2	0.5	—	—
Teaching below college level	56	13.4	53	12.1	30	7.9
Librarian	10	2.4	11	2.5	11	2.9
Social worker or welfare personnel	18	4.3	11	2.5	6	1.6
Vocational or educational counselor	—	—	—	—	5	1.3
Author or journalist	14	3.3	16	3.7	18	4.8
Physician	1	0.2	2	0.5	2	0.5
Economist, political scientist, or related occupation	1	0.2	4	0.9	3	0.8
Physical scientist	2	0.5	—	—	2	0.5
Lawyer	—	—	2	0.5	1	0.3
Psychologist	3	0.7	4	0.9	4	1.1
Nurse or pharmacist	4	1.0	3	0.7	3	0.8
Theater arts	3	0.7	2	0.5	2	0.5
Music teacher	8	1.9	6	1.4	—	—
Fine arts	2	0.5	1	0.2	7	1.9
Applied arts	3	0.7	3	0.7	1	0.3
Other professions	17	4.1	10	2.3	7	1.9
Business occupations						
Executive or managerial positions in business or industry	6	1.4	13	3.0	43	11.4
Secretary, bookkeeper, accountant, or related office work	63	15.0	67	15.3	47	12.4
Sales workers	6	1.4	15	3.4	9	2.4
Miscellaneous	10	2.4	9	2.1	1	0.3
Farmers	3	0.7	—	—	1	0.3
Homemakers	183	43.7	187	42.7	152	40.2
Total in professional, semi-professional, and managerial occupations	154	36.7	160	36.5	168	44.4
Total in lower-level clerical, sales, farming, and miscellaneous business	82	19.5	91	20.8	58	15.3
Total	419		438		378	

SOURCE: Questionnaires from indicated years.
NOTE: In 1972/77, 85 subjects were retired and did not indicate their most recent previous occupation.

1972, by the Terman women in the work force with three different levels of education: college graduation, some college, and high school graduation, and compared these data with those from Campbell, Converse, and Rodgers's (1976) national sample. They found little difference in the proportions of women with college degrees who held professional or managerial positions. There were very large differences, however, among the women with some college but no degree who held such positions, and among the high school graduates. The authors suggested (p. 50) the possibility that "women of high IQ are able to prove

themselves capable on the job, perhaps have higher vocational goals and aspirations because of their family background, and hence succeed in higher-level jobs
and in more employment overall in the labor force than do the women in Campbell's representative sample."

The Women's Own Classification: Career, Income Work, Homemaking

Although a listing of occupational categories provides some clues to understanding the women's work life, such an analysis does not capture the meaning
of activities to the women engaged in them. Neither does it distinguish the many
different work patterns the individuals experience. Because women had more
limited access to formal work roles than did men, it is as important to understand
the psychological meaning of their work to them as it is to understand the content
of it. A woman sometimes engaged in a professional level activity part-time and
this could well have the same meaning for her as a career as a man's full-time
work in the same type of job. And so far as level of occupation is concerned,
talented women such as these could enrich a lower-level occupational position to
an extent not possible for less able individuals.

To understand the women's work lives through their eyes, they were asked in
1972 to describe their work history in terms of four categories (Question B3): "I
have been primarily a homemaker"; "I have pursued a career through most of
my adult life"; "I have pursued a career except when raising a family"; and "I
have done considerable work for needed income, but would not call it a career."
For the purposes of our analysis, this item was used to construct three groups:
homemakers (N = 165), career workers (N = 172), and income workers (N =
77). These figures add to 414 women; 80 members of the later-maturity group
either did not return the 1972 questionnaire or did not respond to this item.

There is considerable correspondence between these categories and the actual
occupations that the women pursued in their later life. In the same 1972 questionnaire, the women were asked to list current occupation or former occupation
if retired; 77 percent of the homemaker group listed homemaking, and 88 percent of career workers listed a professional, technical, or higher-level business
occupation. Almost half of the income workers listed a sales, clerical, or service
occupation. Moreover, almost a fifth of the income workers listed their present or
former occupation as homemaking, suggesting a more limited participation in
work outside the home.

Interaction of Marital Status and Parenthood with Work History

The marital status of these women is helpful in understanding career patterns.
Marital status in a given year can be misleading, however. Seventy-eight of the
414 women in the later-maturity sample who returned the 1972 questionnaire
had divorced, separated, been widowed, or remarried during the twelve years
between 1960 and 1972. In order to get a more stable measure of the relation
between marital status and work history, we have eliminated those 78 cases in
making a comparison. There is a significant relation between the two variables

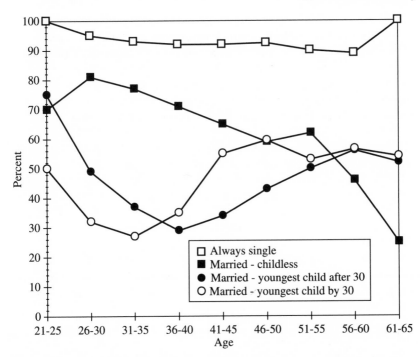

Fig. 5.1. Employment of women in later-maturity group by age, marital status, and age at birth of youngest child (N = 38, 66, 79, and 196 for single, married childless, married with youngest child by age 30, and married with youngest child after 30, respectively). Data from questionnaires in various years.

($p < .01$). Of the single women, 86.5 percent were career workers, while only 31.4 percent of the married women characterized themselves in that way. This finding that a lower proportion of married women had careers is consistent with findings of other studies, including a younger sample studied at Berkeley (Stroud, 1981). Moreover, 50 percent of the separated or divorced women and 74 percent of those who had been widowed considered their lifetime work to be a career. This latter finding suggests that the Terman women met the challenges of widowhood or divorce with considerable resourcefulness, a fact noted in the earlier study by Sears and Barbee (1977).

Having children appears to have inhibited the married women's pursuit of careers. There was a significant relationship between lifetime career pattern and the raising of children ($p < .01$), with 60 percent of childless married women having careers as compared with 33 percent of women with children. The converse holds true as well; women without children were much more likely to have had a career than were women with children.

The age of the mother when she finished childbearing was also very important in determining her lifetime work pattern (P. S. Sears, 1977). Figure 5.1 shows the percentages of women in steady employment in four subgroups in each of the half-decades of their lives between ages 21 and 65. Of the always-single women close to 100 percent were in steady employment until 65 years, paralleling the experience of most men. There were two kinds of differences between the women who bore their last child by age 30 and those whose last child was born after they were 30 years old. The percentage of the first group in employment dropped more and earlier, but also rose again earlier and more sharply. Ultimately the employment percentages in the two groups came together again — and both were substantially more likely to be working by age 61–65 than the childless married women, a much greater percentage of whom had been steadily employed between ages 21 and 45, the childbearing years.

Fulfilling several roles requires a great deal of time and energy and can place constraints on the direction of one's efforts. Those women who could give themselves more or less single-mindedly to the occupational role — single, divorced, widowed, or childless married women — were more likely to develop a career than were those women with conflicting responsibilities — those with children and resident husbands. The principle works in the same way in the opposite direction. Noncareer women had greater responsibilities for children and family than career women. This is verified by the variations in the percent in steady employment during the childbearing years.

Work Patterns

To further unravel the complexity of these work patterns, in 1977 we asked the women to characterize their work life for five-year periods beginning with age 21–25 and ending with age 66–70 (1977, Question 18). This question differed somewhat from the similar 1972 question (A4); it divided work differently — according to fulltime or part-time employment — and added homemaking and volunteer work as explicit categories. This permits us to examine the homemakers, career workers, and income workers separately with respect to the proportion of each group engaged in each of four kinds of activity: homemaking, steady full-time or steady part-time work for income, and volunteer work.

Homemakers. As can be seen in Figure 5.2, most of the 141 homemakers who classified themselves as homemakers in 1972 and who responded in 1977 had engaged in homemaking throughout most of their adult lives. A fair number had worked either full time or part-time for income before 30 — mainly before marriage, or at least before the birth of children. It is interesting to note that as work for income decreased, volunteer work replaced it. By age 45, nearly half the homemakers were engaged in such activity, mostly on a basis of one or two days a week.

Aggregating the work patterns of 141 homemakers in a single graph obscures the great variations among individual women. There was a group of 41 (29 percent) who engaged mainly in homemaking, with slight participation in paid or volunteer work, and 51 women (36 percent) who engaged in full-time or part-time volunteer work during three or more five-year periods. The remaining homemakers, however, pursued a variety of patterns of participation in full-time

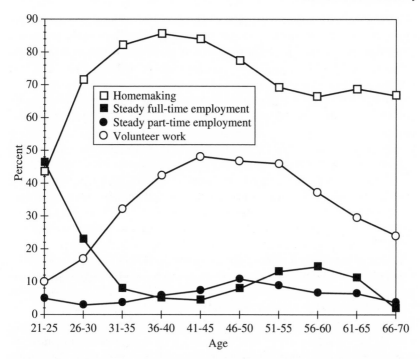

Fig. 5.2. Percent of women homemakers indicating primary activity as homemaking, steady full-time employment, steady part-time employment, and volunteer work during half-decade intervals from age 21 to age 70 (N = 141). Data from 1977 questionnaires. Students and retired women were included in total N, but not graphed. Some percentages add to over 100 because some women were engaged in more than one activity.

or part-time employment, or volunteer work. A few examples will help to portray the variety of life-styles of the homemakers.

Gertrude had been interested in going to college when she was young, but she graduated from high school at the depth of the Depression, and was discouraged from going on to college by teachers because of her financial need. In mid-life she regretted that her teachers had not helped her find a way to further her education. Her father was a retail clerk, as was her mother. She seems not to have been fully aware of her academic potential, saying in young adulthood, "I have been an average girl, and hope to be a better than average wife and mother." She married in her early 20's and had two children. Her husband was a service supervisor for home appliances at a major department store. She had long had homemaking as a goal and pursued it enthusiastically, combining her responsibilities at home with part-time employment and volunteer work. She participated in a number of activities related to her children's lives, such as PTA and scouts. Her employment has consisted principally of sales and office work, but later she became expert at taxes, earning part-time income preparing income tax returns, and teaching other preparers. She has had a busy and satisfying life, and felt that she did not have time for all that she wanted to do. In her older years, she has participated in square dancing, studied geology and natural history, and traveled — all this along with tax work.

Katherine has had an enduring interest in writing, and earned both a bachelor's and a master's degree in English. Her father was a bank officer, and her mother a housewife. She had early plans for a career in journalism, stating at age 25 that she wanted to be "the best editor of the best magazine in the country." She married two years later, and worked as a journalist for a few years. Her husband was a free-lance song writer and taught creative writing, both privately and in a community college. She stayed home with her two children when they were young because she felt this necessary and desirable and later did so at her husband's request. She did not enjoy homemaking, but found deep satisfaction in her writing. She published numerous articles and short stories, including one in a collection of the "best short stories of the year," and in her late 60's a university press published a book she had written. Between her mid-40's and age 60, she completed several walking tours of foreign countries, totaling almost 3,000 miles, with various members of her family. After her husband's death she undertook two solo walking tours of Europe. She used these experiences to develop public speaking programs that she presented for the benefit of her favorite charity. She has been active in her church, and president of its board of trustees. In her late 60's she successfully competed in a swim meet for swimmers over 30 years of age, and in her early 70's she acted in several plays for the first time, including two starring roles, thoroughly enjoying the experience.

Louise has enjoyed being a wife and mother. Her father was a music and drama critic and publicist, and her mother was a music teacher and then a housewife. It had always been taken for granted that Louise would go to college. She majored in English, and graduated with honors, ranking first among the women in her class. After graduating from college she obtained secretarial training in a business school. Shortly thereafter she married, and combined marriage with secretarial work for a number of years. After the birth of her first child, she spent about fifteen years as a full-time homemaker. She had no professional ambitions, and enjoyed her quiet life in a small community with her husband (a botany professor) and her two children. In her late 40's, she worked full time as a secretary for a few years. Then, as a result of the interest she had shown in the libraries of her children's schools, she was asked to be the librarian for several elementary schools in a small New England community. She took courses in librarianship over the years, and enjoyed this work until retirement. She has had an abiding interest in literature and music throughout her life.

Career workers. In Figure 5.3, which summarizes the work patterns of the 136 career workers responding in 1977, we can see the effect of raising children on work participation. As homemaking decreased at midlife as a primary em-

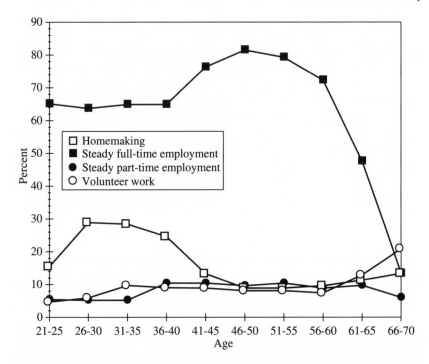

Fig. 5.3. Percent of women career workers indicating primary activity as homemaking, steady full-time employment, steady part-time employment, and volunteer work during half-decade intervals from age 21 to age 70 (N = 136). Data from 1977 questionnaires. Students and retired women were included in total N, but not graphed. Some percentages add to over 100 because some women were engaged in more than one activity.

phasis, full-time work increased. This figure does not separate women who had a last child before or after age 30, as did Figure 5.1, so the period of decreased work is cumulated over a 15-year period. As retirement reduced steady work after age 65, these women increased volunteer work.

When the career workers' patterns were examined individually, there were 68 (50 percent) who showed quite steady full-time employment, with no more than one five-year period without full-time work once it was begun. Thirty-seven (27 percent) pursued homemaking for at least ten years, with most engaging in full-time employment after homemaking. The remaining women in this group followed a variety of patterns, including taking time out from their careers to raise families, as well as participation in part-time and volunteer work. Here are some examples.

Anne graduated from college with highest honors and went on to graduate study of child psychology. Her father was an attorney and her mother a home-maker. Her parents, who had encouraged achievement in their children, supported her pursuit of a higher degree. She was delighted to be hired on the faculty of a small elite women's college in the late 1930's, when jobs were scarce. She became Chair of her department and was eventually appointed Dean of the faculty and Provost of the college. She also served for one year as acting President. A professorship was established in her name at her retirement. Her father went bankrupt in the Depression, and never fully recovered financially. Her mother had a prolonged illness and eventually her father became seriously ill. As the oldest child, Anne assumed major personal and financial responsibility in providing care for them. She also became a substitute mother for a younger sister, a role she enjoyed. Some of her busiest times professionally coincided with these major family stresses, and she felt satisfaction in being able to cope with the many demands on her time and energy. Although she had hoped to marry, she remained single and was fully involved in her professional responsibilities and in caring for her family. She felt fulfilled, and expressed no regrets. In her retirement years she has been active in volunteer work.

Ruth grew up in the country, and became interested in nature studies as a youngster. Her father was an attorney and her mother a housewife who had taught piano. She and her parents decided early that she would be well-suited to teaching, and she went on to a doctorate in zoology. She feels that the Depression and prejudice against women in the professions delayed her professional advancement; but nine years after obtaining her Ph.D., she was hired as an assistant professor at an excellent university, and continued there until her retirement, having become a full professor. She was hired in this position immediately after World War II, when the large enrollments of veterans increased the demand for college teachers. She married in her late 30's, but divorced four years later. The divorce was followed several years later by a marriage to a faculty member in another department at the same university. She did not have children. After retirement she drastically reduced her research activity but then returned to it. She thoroughly enjoyed several recent field trips to faraway places, including Antarctica, to continue her nature studies.

Helen, always interested in children, followed in her mother's footsteps, and became a kindergarten teacher. Her father was a banker. After marrying in her mid-20's, she left teaching for about ten years to raise three children, not intending to return. However, her husband, a businessman (and alcoholic), suffered financial reversals, and she resumed work. Divorced in her 50's, she continued teaching, finding great satisfaction in it. She retired reluctantly at 65, looking back with pride at having helped more than 1,000 kindergarten children in 29 years of teaching. She has filled retirement with varied activities, including travel, time with her family, and public service.

Elizabeth was the daughter of a businessman and a housewife. She earned a bachelor's degree in English, and worked as a journalist in several settings, including a position as assistant story editor and publicist in motion pictures. She took a trip around the world by herself in the late 1930's, and worked briefly as a war correspondent for a major wire service during the outbreak of the Sino-Japanese War. Immediately prior to World War II, she worked for an aircraft public relations firm on publicity concerning the role of aircraft manufacturers in aiding the Allies. After the United States entered World War II she worked as a government analyst of enemy propaganda. She wanted to be transferred to China, but she met her future husband and gave up that possibility. She had had a brief unsuccessful marriage in her early 20's. Now that she was in her mid-30's, she decided that if she was to have a family it was time to marry. Her second husband was an industrial research chemist. She became a stepmother to a four-year-old son, and had a child of her own four years later, at age 40. Since her marriage she has pursued part-time public relations work in a variety of contexts. She has not wanted to work full time, but has found few part-time jobs that offer her the kind of challenge and feeling of accomplishment that she would like.

Income workers. The work sequence for the 60 income workers responding in 1977 is summarized in Figure 5.4. Again the effect of childbearing is very evident; the curve for steady full-time work drops precipitously after age 25 and does not regain its original height until the women were past their mid-40's. In comparison with the career workers, these women had less education and they started work earlier and married earlier. Again we see, too, the replacement of steady paid work with homemaking and volunteer work after age 65.

The individual variations are as great in this group as among homemakers and career workers. Nine (15 percent) of the income workers were steadily employed, working full time for seven or more five-year periods. Over half of the income workers (32) worked full-time during four to six periods, with most of these women (24) resuming or initiating full-time employment after age 40. The remaining income workers worked sporadically or part-time. Below are two examples.

Barbara had prepared to teach English. Her father was a businessman and her mother was a housewife who had been a bookkeeper. She was unable to find a job in the midst of the Depression, and turned to office work, eventually taking courses in accounting. She worked with enjoyment at several firms as a book-keeper and accountant. Her mother was ill for many years, and she cared for both her mother and her aunt until their deaths. She never married. She has been very active in her church, enjoying her church activities. She has spent her spare time helping friends and neighbors who need personal care or assistance.

Susan was raised by an older sister who stressed the need to earn a living rather than obtain advanced education, and stopped Susan's education at high school. Her mother, a housewife who had taught music, had died when Susan was 13. Her father was a businessman. Susan worked as a stenographer until her marriage to a carpenter in her early 20's. She had six children. Her last two (twins) were born when she was 39. After working intermittently on a part-time basis, she took a half-time position at the age of 45 and a full-time supervisory

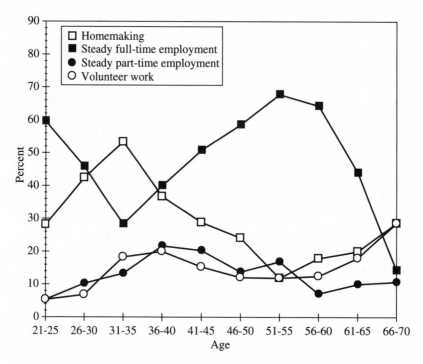

Fig. 5.4. Percent of women income workers indicating primary activity as homemaking, steady full-time employment, steady part-time employment, and volunteer work during half-decade intervals from age 21 to age 70 (N = 50). Data from 1977 questionnaires. Students and retired women were included in total N, but not graphed. Some percentages add to over 100 because some women were engaged in more than one activity.

stenography position several years later. In this latter position she discovered she had leadership capabilities she had not been aware of. She worked at this job until her early retirement in her late 50's.

Career changes. In addition to the variety of patterns of homemaking, paid and volunteer work, entry and reentry, the women's work histories were further complicated by career changes. Career women, in particular, made significant changes after the age of 35. Consider these examples of women who changed fields.

Edith majored in mathematics and minored in German in both her undergraduate and graduate education. Her father was a businessman and her mother a housewife; they had encouraged her to prepare to teach. After receiving a master's degree, she began a career as a high school mathematics teacher. She eventually became disenchanted with the work, and in her late 30's answered an advertisement for a woman college graduate who had majored in mathematics to fill a job with an aircraft manufacturer. She was hired as a mathematician in the aerodynamics group. She studied engineering on the side, and was promoted to work on problems in theoretical aerodynamics. She was the first woman aerodynamicist in the company. In this position she did some technical writing, and translated technical materials from German; she continued these activities part-time after retirement. She remained single. She regularly recorded technical materials for the blind. A leisure activity which she particularly enjoyed was working to stem the deterioration of the English language. She corresponded about correct English usage with several newspaper journalists, as well as columnists and broadcasters who sometimes quoted her.

Marilyn had always wanted to be a teacher. Her father was a patent attorney and her mother a housewife. They sought out the best teachers for their daughter. She decided from the beginning to combine work with marriage and motherhood, and continued teaching elementary school after her marriage and while raising two children. She has been happily married to a banker for over 50 years. In her early 50's she completed work on a doctorate in education, and became an assistant professor of early childhood education at a state university. She was eventually promoted to full professor. She said that the years since she earned her doctorate were the most fulfilling of her life. She had a special interest in gifted children, playing an active role in societies concerning them as well as publishing scholarly articles in that field. She was interested in ecology, and served as a docent for several nature conservancies and parks.

Judith's varied career drew on her interest in the theater and in writing. After graduating from college she spent several years acting in New York. She then worked variously as a literary editor, literary assistant doing research and writing, and in public relations. She did free-lance writing, published a novel, and taught acting and directing. She had her first child after 40, and after her divorce several years later, decided to seek a new career. At the age of 51 she earned a master's degree in public health education, a field to which she had been exposed in an earlier public relations job. She was successful in community health planning, and found her writing and speaking ability helpful. After ten years, she decided to reduce her formal activity in this field and return to her interest in the arts. She worked as the drama and literary director of an educational FM radio station while maintaining a consulting practice in community health planning. She is very proud of her success in raising her daughter, who became a physician. In her late 70's she took a position managing a community theater, finding the skills she had acquired in community health planning to be a major asset for this post.

Volunteer workers. Volunteer work was often pursued as seriously as a career. Each activity provided a welcome outlet for the considerable energies and talents of these women. Their roles as volunteers often included responsibility and influence comparable to those of many paid occupations. As previously noted, many of the homemakers engaged in volunteer work throughout their adult lives. Although most such work was done by the homemakers, it was by no means restricted to them. Career workers and income workers also participated but to a lesser degree; they were most active in volunteer work as a replacement for their paid employment when they retired. Some examples show the significance of this unpaid work.

Dorothy became interested in international relations through a high school teacher. She obtained a bachelor's degree in political science, and did three years of graduate work. She was hoping to enter the foreign service, but found no opportunities there. Several years after leaving school she married a language professor, had two children, and recently she and her husband celebrated their 50th wedding anniversary. Throughout the years she was involved in numerous volunteer activities, holding positions of leadership in many of them. She was particularly active in the League of Women Voters and in state committee work on libraries. Other activities included PTA, Girl Scouts, United Way, Community Chest, and mayoral committees. She received numerous awards for her civic contributions.

Linda earned a bachelor's degree in English and zoology, and a master's degree in zoology. Her father was a forester and her mother a housewife. She married shortly after receiving her master's degree and adopted two children. Her husband was an oceanographer. She was a devoted wife and mother, but participated in many outside activities. She evidently had superb organizational skills and used them in numerous causes related to the preservation of the natural environment; she was honored for the major role she played in establishing several parks in her community. She developed a growing interest in politics over the years, coupled with a concern for human rights, and was active in the League of Women Voters, serving as president of her community chapter. She was not unaware, however, of her abilities, and the choices she had made in not pursuing a paid professional career. In her later years she decreased her volunteer work somewhat, and concentrated on writing. She published four autobiographical books.

Hope taught high school mathematics until her marriage in her late 20's. She had four children, all of whom have professional careers. She returned to teaching when her youngest child was three, and included steady volunteer work in her busy life. She worked in many activities related to her children's lives, including the Boy Scouts, Girl Scouts, and PTA. In addition, she participated in a variety of community activities, such as the Red Cross, Community Chest, and volunteer church work. Most recently she joined a program in which she visited homebound and convalescent elderly persons.

Early Life Goals

These life histories illustrate the influence on occupational outcomes of a host of idiosyncratic variables — marriage, children, financial opportunities, and family responsibilities — as well as the major societal events of economic depression and war. The histories do not tell much about the goals and dreams these women had in their childhood, adolescence, and young adulthood. These were determining variables, too, for they served sometimes to direct the educational and marital plans that influenced life-style. In contemporary terms, we can think of them as "life scripts" (Abelson, 1981; Helson, Mitchell, & Moane, 1984). They dictated methods of coping with responsibilities and other exigencies of life. To the extent that we find congruence between early plans and outcomes in later maturity we can infer the effectiveness of these guiding themes. In searching for such congruence we will examine the women's early and later feelings about three types of occupational outcome which may be labeled as "homemakers," "career workers," and "income workers," based on the women's self-classification in 1972.

Childhood

In 1922, when the girls' age averaged eleven, but ranged from about eight to adolescence, they marked a checklist of 125 occupations they might be interested in. Many of the younger girls chose teaching and musical performance, while the older ones more commonly selected other professions. Age was such a strong correlate of choice that we can get little of value from a detailed analysis in relation to future career. The one question which reveals an early slight indication of differences among the three groups is the one mentioned at the beginning of Chapter 3 — "If you are a girl, do you prefer the duties of a housewife to any other occupation?" Affirmative answers were given by 30 percent of the girls who became homemakers, by 22 percent of those who became career workers, and by 14 percent of the future income workers. The differences suggest a slight congruence between early plans and later outcomes, but do not reach statistical significance.

Young Adulthood

A more telling test of the influence of plans can be made with information obtained in 1936, when the women were in their 20's. After being asked to state their current occupations, the subjects were asked "Have you definitely chosen your life work?" and asked to "Describe your ultimate goals as fully as you can at this time." Nearly all the men answered the goals question with the name of one occupation, but the women's responses were more varied. Most mentioned at least two things, a substantial proportion referring to marriage or motherhood.

The extent to which the women's plans were fulfilled is indicated in Table 5.3. The women are divided into the three classes of homemaker, career worker, and income worker. The categories into which all but a very few of the 1936 answers could be coded are shown in the left-hand columns. The 295 cases in the table were women who returned both the 1936 and 1972 questionnaires, and answered the relevant questions. The column N's add to more than the total N for that column and the column percentages add to more than 100 percent because mentions were counted separately; for example, a woman can be represented in

TABLE 5.3

*Life Plans Reported in 1936 by Women in Later-Maturity Group
Self-Classified in 1972 as Homemakers,
Career Workers, and Income Workers*

| | "As it was" Retrospective self-description (1972) | | | | | |
| | Homemakers | | Career workers | | Income workers | |
Life plans (1936)	N	Pct.	N	Pct.	N	Pct.
Marriage or motherhood	82	67.2%	37	30.0%	28	56.0%
Occupation	62	50.8	103	83.7	37	74.0
Financial success	—	—	1	0.8	—	—
Joy in living	7	5.7	5	4.1	3	6.0
Service to society	2	1.6	4	3.3	—	—
Friendships	1	0.8	—	—	—	—
Cultural satisfaction	5	4.1	3	2.4	—	—
Total respondents	122		123		50	

Significance (p) by chi-square (top two lines only) .01

SOURCE: 1936 and 1972 questionnaires.

NOTE: Column N's add to more than the total N for that column and column percentages add to more than 100 because some respondents reported more than one life plan.

both the "occupation" category (one mention) and the "marriage or mother-hood" category (the other mention).

There is a clear congruence between the plans and the outcomes. It is by no means perfect because, as suggested above, other events also played a role in determining the lifetime outcome. There was, however, a substantial difference between the early plans of the homemakers and of those women who worked outside the home. A chi-square determination applied only to the top two categories, "marriage or motherhood" and "occupation," was significant ($p < .01$), indicating that the distribution of choices was quite different for the three groups of women. The homemakers had more commonly planned for a family life and the others had more frequently planned for an occupation. (There are too few cases of other choices, distributed in such a way as to leave too many empty cells, to permit a useful statistical analysis of them.)

Later Maturity: A Retrospective View

In 1972, when we asked the women to report on their occupational life histories (Question B3), we asked them also to recall the plans they had had in young adulthood ("As I planned it"). These were the data that P. S. Sears and Barbee (1977) had to use for a comparison of plans and outcomes because the 1936 questionnaire had not been coded at the time they made their analysis. We can now compare the original young adulthood report with the women's retrospective reports 36 years later. What is of chief interest, of course, is the accuracy with which they recalled their earlier intentions.

In this comparison, the three classes of homemaking, career, and income working are defined in terms of *recalled plans,* not actual outcomes. The measures obtained in 1936 and 1972 are quite different from one another, and no simple comparison can measure accuracy of recall. Respondents in 1936 were permitted two mentions, and many women actually reported marriage or motherhood and an occupation as parts of their life plan. The 1972 career self-classification included a steady career or one interrupted for childrearing. Also, women could specify in 1972 that they had planned to work, but for needed income only. Nevertheless, as can be seen in Table 5.4, the distribution of early choices displays a clear congruence with later ones. Four out of five of the women who recalled having planned a career actually had mentioned an occupation as part of their life plan, and seven out of ten of those who recalled a plan for homemaking had mentioned marriage or motherhood in 1936. These differences in the distributions were significant, by chi-square, at $p < .01$.

To round out the story we must show the relation of the two 1972 measures of "As it was" and "As I planned it." Table 5.5 shows a very substantial degree of congruence between the two statements, but it is no more perfect than that between the real outcome and the "real" plans just described. The great majority of the homemakers and the career workers reported that they had planned for what actually eventuated. The income workers were another story, however. Few of them acknowledged an early plan for such a life work, and half of them recalled a plan to be a homemaker. In the previous comparison of 1936 and 1972 responses, about half of them had said so at the time. It appears that a life of income working was more likely to have been largely determined by extrinsic events than either homemaking or working at a career.

Predictors of Career Pursuit

The occupational data indicate that many of these active and articulate women were ahead of their time in terms of occupational achievement. Nevertheless, 40

TABLE 5.4

*Life Plans Reported in 1936 by Women in Later-Maturity Group Compared
with Retrospectively Reported Young Adulthood Plans in 1972*

| | "As I planned it" Retrospective young adulthood plans (1972) | | | | | |
| | Homemaking | | Have a career | | Work for income | |
Life plans (1936)	N	Pct.	N	Pct.	N	Pct.
Marriage and/or motherhood	83	70.9%	47	35.6%	5	45.5%
Occupation	61	52.1	109	82.6	8	72.7
Total respondents (N)	117		132		11	
Significance (p) by chi-square .01						

SOURCE: 1936 and 1972 questionnaires.
NOTE: Column N's add to more than total N for that column and column percentages add to more than 100 because some respondents reported more than one life plan.

TABLE 5.5

*Relationship of Young Adult Career Plans of Women in Later-Maturity Group
to Actual Lifetime Career Patterns, as Reported in 1972*

| "As I planned it" (1972) | "As it was" (1972) | | | | | |
| | Homemaker | | Career worker | | Income worker | |
	N	Pct.	N	Pct.	N	Pct.
Homemaking	104	73.2%	31	20.3%	30	50.0%
Have a career	37	26.1	119	77.8	19	31.7
Work for income	1	0.7	3	2.0	11	18.3
Total	142		153		60	
Significance (p) by chi-square .01						

SOURCE: 1972 questionnaire.

percent of them were homemakers with little or no work experience after marriage. Another 19 percent were income workers, and only a small proportion had planned their lives to that end. We cannot help but ask if there were discernible psychological differences between the 41 percent who were career workers — a very high proportion for their time in history — and the others in the sample.

Our first comparison is between all career workers, regardless of interruptions in their careers, and all noncareer women, who include both the homemakers and the income workers. With the thought that the steady and the interrupted career workers represent two different styles of career pursuit, we have also compared the uninterrupted and interrupted career workers with one another. These two comparisons will be considered separately, because there are some differences in the types of experience and personality qualities associated with the two kinds of career women, just as there are between the career and noncareer women.

Career and Noncareer

We have searched for correlates of this difference in life experience among the following variables: family background, intellectual and academic performance, personality qualities related to achievement motivation and self-confidence or self-esteem, and attitudes and activities involving marriage, family, and education. These are areas that others have found to be predictive of women's career choice and development (see Betz & Fitzgerald, 1987). The variables which yielded significant results are listed in Table 5.6. The comparisons are between the two groups of 172 career workers and 242 homemakers and income workers. Whenever possible, we have combined variables into scales to increase reliability and to reduce the number of variables tested. We have used either a *t*-test or chi-square to determine the *p* value, depending on whether a particular independent variable was scalar or non-scalar. Not all of the variables tested in this way showed differences between the groups, and in the paragraphs below we shall comment on these variables, along with some of those that did show differences.

TABLE 5.6

*Variables Characterizing Later-Maturity Group Career Women Contrasted
with Noncareer Women (Homemakers plus Income Workers)*

(N: Career = 172; Noncareer = 272; total = 414)

Year reported	Variable	N	Statistic	p
Intellectual and early academic performance				
1940	Concept Mastery Test: high score	281	t-test	.01
1950	Concept Mastery Test: high score	319	t-test	.01
Family background				
1950	Father encouraged independence in childhood	336	t-test	.05
1950	Mother encouraged independence in childhood	363	t-test	.05
Achievement motivation and behavior				
1922	Liked school (parents' rating)	350	t-test	.01
1922	Liked doing lessons	317	t-test	.05
1922	Liking for arithmetic	312	t-test	.05
1922	Desire to excel (parent rating)	362	t-test	.05
1928	Desire to excel (parent rating)	237	t-test	.10
1928	Achievement motive (field worker's rating)	180	t-test	.01
1940	High grades in college	318	t-test	.10
Cumulative	High level of education	414	chi-square	.01
1960	Ambition, ages 30–40	266	t-test	.05
1960	Ambition since age 40	287	t-test	.05
Self-confidence and purposiveness				
1940	Self-confidence	363	t-test	.05
1950	Self-confidence	364	t-test	.10
1940	Instrumentality	358	t-test	.10
1950	Instrumentality	362	t-test	.05
1922	Perseverance (parents' rating)	414	t-test	.10
1928	Perseverance (parents' rating)	235	t-test	.10
1950	Feel lived up to intellectual abilities	360	t-test	.01
1960	Feel lived up to intellectual abilities	379	t-test	.01
1950	Factors in success: superior mental ability	345	t-test	.01
1950	Factors in success: adequate education	345	t-test	.01
1950	Factors in success: good mental stability	345	t-test	.05
1950	Factors in success: good habits of work	345	t-test	.01
1950	Factors in success: chance	345	t-test	.01
Marriage, family occupation				
Cumulative	Always single status	414	chi-square	.01
Cumulative	Older age at first marriage	369	t-test	.01
Cumulative	Did not rear children	377	chi-square	.01
Cumulative	Marriage disrupted by divorce or widowhood	378	chi-square	.01
1936	Life goals: more toward occupation than family	267	chi-square	.01
1972	"As I planned it" career emphasis	355	chi-square	.01
1972	High importance of occupational goals in young adulthood	328	t-test	.01
1972	Lesser importance of family goals in young adulthood	386	t-test	.01

SOURCE: Questionnaires from indicated years; parents', field-workers', and teachers' ratings; cumulative education data; test scores.

NOTE: All variables are self-reported unless otherwise indicated. The number of cases for most of these variables is fewer than 414 because some of the later-maturity group did not return one or more questionnaires.

Family background. Family background has been shown to be important in women's occupational achievement, although not always to the same degree as for men; parents' education has been a more consistent predictor than father's occupation per se (Betz & Fitzgerald, 1987; Burlin, 1976; Featherman, 1980; Gottfredson, 1981; Greenfield, Greiner, & Wood, 1980; Russo & O'Connell, 1980; Schiffler, 1975; Sewell, Hauser, & Wolf, 1980). Mother's employment also seems to be an important factor (Almquist & Angrist, 1971; Burlin, 1976; Lemkau, 1983; Stephan & Corder, 1985; Tangri, 1972). Moreover, more permissive child-rearing practices on the part of parents appear to facilitate career achievement for women (Kriger, 1972).

In 1950 the participants were asked to assess their family's social and financial positions in childhood. Neither rating differentiated the two groups of women. There was no difference either in the rural/urban character of their early residences. Nor did the groups differ in mother's or father's education, or in level of father's occupation. Because 85 percent of the mothers described themselves as homemakers, the number of mothers who had careers was too small to show whether having a career woman as a mother affected the daughters' careers. We also examined whether the loss of father by death or divorce stimulated daughters to pursue a career, but there was no greater incidence of loss in one group than in the other. A number of retrospective measures of the girls' relationships to their fathers and mothers were recorded in 1950, and two differentiated between the two groups — father's and mother's encouragement of independence.

Intellectual and early academic performance. Variables relating to intellectual ability were examined because of their relation to occupational aspirations and performance (Featherman, 1980; Sewell & Hauser, 1975; Tinsley & Faunce, 1980). There was no difference in childhood IQ or in scores on the Stanford Achievement Test taken during elementary school years. These variables were not promising, in any case, because many of the occupations pursued by the career women were not at the highest level; in all probability these women were capable of higher levels of occupational performance than they actually achieved. However, by 1940 and 1950 a significant difference had developed between the two groups. On the Concept Mastery Test, in both years, the career workers obtained higher scores than the noncareer women. It appears that the intellectual stimulation of career pursuit may have been conducive to maintaining and/or increasing the kind of verbal performance measured by this test.

Achievement motivation. Because of the link between achievement motivation, education, and occupational attainment (Atkinson, Lens, & O'Malley, 1976; Atkinson, 1978; Betz & Fitzgerald, 1987; Farmer, 1985; Fassinger, 1985; Featherman, 1980; Stewart, 1980; Wolfson, 1976), we examined early attitudes to school. Academic self-confidence has been shown to be an important variable in predicting women's career choice (Eccles, Adler, & Meece, 1984; Shavelson, Hubner, & Stanton, 1976). We expected that girls who liked school and for whom achievement in school was important would be more likely to continue their education and therefore have more opportunity for pursuing careers. In

1922, the career women's parents rated them higher on liking for school than did the parents of the noncareer women; the future career women themselves rated liking for lessons higher also. Retrospectively in 1950, they also indicated more often that success in schoolwork had been important to them in adolescence. This latter finding was supported by parent ratings of desire to excel in 1922 and 1928, and by higher average ratings on achievement motivation by the 1928 field-workers. The career women went on to earn better grades in college, and more of them secured master's and doctoral degrees (40 percent) as compared with the noncareer women (20 percent).

An interest in mathematics is gender-typed as masculine in our society, causing many adolescent girls, after having been just as successful at it as boys in elementary school, to dislike and avoid mathematics in both high school and college. Mathematics is necessary for many higher-level occupations, however, especially the scientific and technical ones, and it therefore becomes a powerful screen for career advancement in women (Pedro, Wolleat, Fennema, & Becker, 1981; Fennema & Sherman, 1977; Sherman, 1982). We expected that the career workers would have rejected the traditional role-typing and would have liked mathematics more than did the noncareer women. This proved to be true for the girls in both elementary and high school, if we may judge by how well they said they liked arithmetic in 1922. Six years later, however, different findings emerged for women in high school and those in college. Among girls in high school in 1928, the future career women did not express greater liking for arithmetic and mathematics than their comparison group. The greater preference reappears, however, in those future career women who were in college in 1928; 72 percent of them reported this as a favorite study, while only 48 percent of the noncareer women did.

We also examined the subjects' ambition in adult life, using self-ratings of ambition in four aspects of work from age 30 to 40 and since age 40, all obtained in 1960. Both scales differentiated between the two groups. Of the four kinds of ambition measured — excellence in work, recognition, vocational advancement, and financial gain, only the last appeared to be unimportant in contributing to differences between the two groups.

Self-confidence and purposiveness. We expected that personality traits reflecting self-confidence and purposiveness would be crucial to women's career choice and success (Baruch, 1976; Betz & Hackett, 1981; Helmreich, Spence, Beane, Lucker, & Matthews, 1980; Helson, Mitchell, & Moane, 1984; Marshall & Wijting, 1980; Orlofsky & Stake, 1981; Stake, 1979; Tangri, 1972). In our sample, the career women's parents rated them higher in perseverance in both 1922 and 1928.

As we saw in an earlier section, the career women had early adult plans that were congruent with their future working lives. A few years later, in 1940 and 1950, their self-ratings of relevant personality variables also distinguished them from the noncareer women. To investigate these differences in personality, we constructed two scales of instrumentality — the first for early adulthood. This included self-ratings of perseverance and definite purpose in life, obtained in 1940. The second tapped mid-life instrumentality, and consisted of two ratings in 1950 similar to those on the 1940 scale. Ratings on self-confidence and feelings of inferiority in both 1940 and 1950 were combined into a self-confidence scale for each year (reversing ratings of inferiority feelings). The career women were higher on instrumentality and self-confidence at both times. Moreover, the career women also felt they more fully lived up to their intellectual ability in both 1950 and 1960.

Our results are similar in some respects, but also different from those for two younger cohorts of women studied at Berkeley (see Clausen & Gilens, 1990). The same kinds of instrumental personality characteristics are evident in mid-life for career women in our sample and those with high labor force participation in the sample studied at Berkeley. However, greater directedness of effort earlier in life, especially with respect to school performance, was characteristic of the career workers in our gifted sample.

It is no surprise to go back to 1950 and find a quite relevant precursor to these later recollections. In 1950 the women reported on factors they considered to have been important in contributing to their life accomplishment. The career women checked four items significantly more often than did the noncareer women — all having obvious relevance to occupation: superior mental ability, adequate education, good work habits, and chance. The last may not seem to be immediately relevant to occupational success, but when one considers the greater indeterminacy surrounding women's employment at that time, the implication becomes obvious — and poignant.

Marriage and family. Attitudes and behaviors with respect to marriage and family have been shown to be important factors in women's career development (Card, Steel, & Abeles, 1980; Falk & Cosby, 1978; Featherman, 1980; Matthews & Tiedeman, 1964; Rosenfeld, 1979; Stewart, 1980; Treiman, 1985). In our sample, all but five of the single women belonged to the career group. As will be seen in Chapter 6, they had some exceptional personality qualities and their inclusion in the career group influences markedly certain of the differences we have reported above, especially self-confidence. In contrast, only 37 percent of the married women had careers. However, the married career women also differed sharply from the noncareer women in certain aspects of their experience. The career workers married later; their average age at first marriage was 26.3 years whereas the noncareer women averaged 23.8 years. Fewer married career women had children (73 percent versus 90 percent). Fewer of them had intact marriages, as judged by final marital status in 1986 (33 percent versus 50 percent of noncareer women who married), the difference being accounted for about equally by divorce and widowhood. We examined spouse's occupation, as reported in 1940, but this variable did not differentiate between the two groups.

Attitudes as well as real-life experiences also differentiated the two groups. We have already noted the differences in 1936 planning and 1972 recollection of the plans. There were also differences in the women's recall of the relative importance they placed on family and occupational goals in young adulthood. In 1972 (Question 8), the women were asked to indicate the importance of several life goals in the plans they made for themselves in early adulthood, with four response options: (1) "Less important to me than to most people"; (2) "Looked forward to a normal amount of success in this respect"; (3) "Expected a good deal of myself in this respect"; and (4) "Of prime importance to me; was prepared to sacrifice other things for this." The women's responses to these items by the three career groups are presented below.

	Homemakers			Career workers			Income workers		
	Mean	S.D.	N	Mean	S.D.	N	Mean	S.D.	N
Occupational success	1.86	.93	102	2.68	.74	163	1.94	.87	63
Family life	3.63	.69	158	2.94	.98	161	3.28	.87	67

The career women placed greater emphasis on career and less emphasis on family than the non-career women. It is important to note, however, that among the career women themselves, family was rated as relatively more important than occupation. We will find variation among the career women, however, when we compare the responses of the women who had steady careers with those of women whose careers were interrupted.

Integrative analysis. An integrative descriptive discriminant analysis was run to illustrate the relative importance of each type of variable when combined with the others to predict career group membership. Variables were chosen for the analysis on the basis of their representativeness of each type of variable in combination with the relative completeness of the data. The variables chosen for the analysis were a composite measuring parents' encouragement of independence, parents' rating of the subject's liking for school in 1922, educational level, ambition from age 30 to age 40, self-confidence, having ever married, and 1972 retrospective ratings on the importance of goals for occupational and family life.* The results of the analysis are presented in Table 5.7.

The results of the discriminant analysis show the importance of occupational goals and attitudes and behavior with respect to family life for these women's career pursuit. The variable weighted highest in the analysis was importance of occupational goals in young adulthood. Two other role variables, importance of goals for family life and having ever married, also contributed highly to the prediction. Level of education reached and parents' encouragement of independence were also relatively important variables.

Summary. The women who developed careers did not differ much in childhood from those who followed more traditional patterns. They were no brighter by tested IQ nor did they do better work in school. Their parents did detect some slightly greater ambition to excel and to persevere, however, and field-workers

---

* To provide a large enough sample for a multivariate analysis, mean subgroup substitutions were made on the individual variables making up the composites of family encouraged independence, ambition from age 30 to 40, and on the 1972 retrospective goal items.

TABLE 5.7

*Results of a Discriminant Analysis Predicting Career Work Pattern
versus Noncareer Work Pattern as Reported by Women
in Later-Maturity Group in 1972*

Year reported	Variable	Standardized discriminant function coefficient
1950	Parents encouraged independence in childhood	.20
1922	Liked school (parents' rating)	.05
Cumulative	High level of education	.28
1960	Ambition, ages 30–40	.10
1940	Self-confidence	.15
Cumulative	Always-single marital status	.23
1972	High importance of occupational goals in young adulthood	.65
1972	High importance of family goals in young adulthood	−.27

Wilks's lambda = .71; df = 1,305; $p < .01$

SOURCE: Questionnaires, parents' ratings, and cumulative education data.

clearly detected greater achievement motivation in them. They themselves reported liking school and schoolwork more, and they got better grades in college. By young adulthood their greater interest in occupation and lesser interest in family formation as compared with the other women became evident. More of them remained unmarried; the ones who married did so later than the noncareer women and after they married fewer of them had children. They spent additional years on higher education. By mid-life they had recognized their own competence; they were self-confident and achievement oriented. The plans they had had from young adulthood were being well fulfilled. In sum, it appears that these women had different motives early in life, for reasons we have not detected, and their own personalities interacting with events imposed on their lives resulted in a level of career pursuit uncharacteristic of their generation.

Steady versus Interrupted Career Patterns

This next analysis deals with the career workers only. It divides them into two groups, those who had steady and continuous employment (N = 68), with no more than one five-year period without full-time work once it was begun (as reported in 1977), and those whose work was significantly interrupted, usually while raising families (N = 104). We examined all the variables mentioned in connection with the previous analysis, and those which distinguished these two groups are listed in Table 5.8. All are phrased in such a way as to characterize the steady career workers, in contrast with the interrupted.

None of the differences is surprising if we start with the assumption that the two groups represent women of two levels of commitment to their careers. Seventy-seven percent of the single (never-married) women were in the steady group, while only 31 percent of the married women were. The age at first marriage for the women in the steady group who did marry was higher (28.5 years) than for the interrupted group (25.3 years). Fewer of the steadily employed married career workers had children than did the married interrupted career workers (51 percent compared to 83 percent). More of the steadily employed had their marriages disrupted by divorce or widowhood (71 percent versus 65 percent), but the difference was not statistically significant. All these differences are in the same direction as those between career and noncareer women.

Finally, in 1972, although there was no overall difference between the recollections of the steady-career and the interrupted-career women as to the early adulthood importance of occupation, the steadily employed women did recall a significantly lower importance of family goals in those years, as compared with the other career women. The lesser emphasis on family for the steady-career workers was due to the responses of the single steady-career workers (N = 21), the only group for whom occupational success was more important in young adulthood plans than family life. Moreover, while not evident in the overall comparison of steady-career and interrupted-career workers, occupational success was more important to the single steady-career workers than to the interrupted-career workers. The recollections of the ever-married steady-career workers

TABLE 5.8

Variables Characterizing Steadily Employed Career Women
Contrasted with Women Whose Careers Were Interrupted
by Family Responsibility
(N: Steady = 68; Interrupted = 104; total = 172)

Year reported	Variable	N	Statistic	p
Achievement motivation and behavior				
1940	High grades in college	140	t-test	.05
Cumulative	High level of education	172	chi-square	.01
1960	Ambition, age 30–40	136	t-test	.10
Self-confidence and purposiveness				
1922	Perseverance (teachers' rating)	147	t-test	.05
1922	Conscientiousness (teachers' rating)	145	t-test	.01
1950	Factors in success: good mental stability	149	t-test	.05
1950	Factors in success: persistence in working toward a goal	149	t-test	.10
Marriage and family				
Cumulative	Never married	172	chi-square	.01
Cumulative	Older age at first marriage	136	t-test	.05
Cumulative	Did not rear children	140	chi-square	.01
Cumulative	Marriage disrupted by divorce or widowing	141	chi-square	n.s.
1972	Lesser importance of family goals in young adulthood	161	t-test	.01
1972	"As I planned it" career emphasis	153	chi-square	.01

SOURCE: Questionnaires from indicated years, teachers' ratings, cumulative educational and personal data.
NOTE: The number of cases for most of these variables is fewer than 172 because some of the later maturity group did not return one or more questionnaires.

(N = 42) closely resembled those of the interrupted-career workers, with family life reported as more important in young adulthood plans than occupational success.

Other variables in Table 5.8 are self-explanatory. All the differences parallel those reported in the previous comparison.

Income

As with the men, we must consider age in connection with income, because retirement in later maturity leads to its reduction. With the women, however, it is necessary to take the three categories of work history into account also.

Own Earned Income

In 1972 and 1977 the women were asked to report various income figures. In 1972 these included both the women's own earned income and her total family income for 1970 and 1971, and an estimate of the average annual income in both categories in 1960–69. In 1977, they reported their own earned income and total family income for 1976. Because they had such varied work histories, Table 5.9 contains the income figures for each of the three work history patterns (homemaker, career worker, and income worker) within each of the three age-groups.

The earned income data in Table 5.9 reflect the influences of both age-group and career history. The youngest and middle age-groups generally had approximately the same income in 1970 and 1971, and slight increases from 1971 to 1976. However, the mean income of the oldest group decreased from 1970 to 1971 in all three career groups, reflecting a reduction in paid employment. A higher proportion of career workers reported earned income in comparison with the other two groups. For example, income figures for 1970 were reported by 70 percent of the career workers, 20 percent of the homemakers, and 50 percent of the income workers. As would be expected, the earned income of the career workers was higher than that of the homemakers and income workers. It should be noted that the earned incomes of the women, even the career women, were much less than those of the men.

Family Income

In all the relevant cells of Table 5.9 the average earned income for the women themselves was usually less than half the average family income reported. The average family incomes increased from 1971 to 1976 for all groups. Family income patterns as related to work history group present a different picture from those for the women's own earned income. The homemakers, rather than the career workers, had the highest mean family incomes, in the youngest and middle age-groups. This is due to the fact that a greater proportion of homemakers than either career workers or income workers were married, and their husbands had higher incomes than the women who were single income workers or career workers. In 1972, 82 percent of the homemakers were married compared with

TABLE 5.9

*Incomes of Women in Later-Maturity Group by Age-Group
and Type of Work History for 1960–69 Average,
1970, 1971, and 1976*

(in thousands of dollars)

Year	Source of income	Homemakers			Career workers			Income workers		
		N	Mean	S.D.	N	Mean	S.D.	N	Mean	S.D.
Youngest age-group										
1960–69	Self	4	2.5	3.0	29	8.1	4.8	13	4.5	2.6
1970	Self	11	3.6	2.9	34	11.6	6.0	13	7.2	2.3
1971	Self	12	4.5	3.4	33	12.9	5.8	12	7.5	2.2
1971	Family	40	39.8	25.4	34	28.5	18.2	18	18.9	11.5
1976	Self	5	7.4	6.4	20	15.3	8.0	8	11.6	2.3
1976	Family	32	49.7	47.7	31	29.9	29.7	15	27.9	20.9
Middle age-group										
1960–69	Self	8	4.6	2.4	55	9.3	5.4	18	5.1	1.4
1970	Self	15	4.8	3.2	70	12.5	7.0	22	7.3	2.8
1971	Self	15	5.3	2.5	70	12.3	6.7	22	7.8	3.1
1971	Family	65	26.7	20.7	69	22.1	15.2	29	14.2	8.6
1976	Self	11	12.0	19.9	35	12.6	10.5	12	6.7	5.1
1976	Family	55	27.8	26.5	69	25.2	16.9	24	19.0	15.1
Oldest age-group										
1960–69	Self	5	4.2	1.9	22	10.0	4.3	5	6.6	5.9
1970	Self	6	4.8	4.2	18	16.7	18.9	5	7.8	6.4
1971	Self	4	2.3	1.5	17	12.2	5.7	5	6.2	4.7
1971	Family	30	19.0	12.5	33	20.1	12.7	12	19.9	22.7
1976	Self	2	2.6	2.3	7	8.5	8.7	3	2.8	1.7
1976	Family	28	25.8	17.0	32	22.5	18.8	14	24.8	46.3

SOURCE: Questionnaires for indicated years.

NOTE: Average income for 1960–69 is a retrospective estimate from the 1972 questionnaire. Income in 1970 and 1971 as stated in response to 1972 questionnaire. Income in 1976 as stated in response to 1977 questionnaire. Income from "self" was earned income. Family income includes investment income and husband's earnings.

50 percent of the career workers and 58 percent of the income workers. In 1976, 67 percent of homemakers were married, 35 percent of career workers, and 48 percent of income workers.

Income Adequacy in 1986

In the 1986 survey, questions about the actual dollar amount of income were replaced by a question concerning the subjects' perceptions of the adequacy of their income (Question 24). The checklist permitted four answers: "More than enough," "quite adequate," "barely adequate with care," "really insufficient." There was a relationship between lifetime work history and perceived income adequacy as reported in 1986. This finding is based on the reports of the women who responded to the career history item in 1972 as well as the financial adequacy question in the 1986 questionnaire. Table 5.10 presents the numbers and percentages of responses for each of the career history groups, and for the total later-maturity group. (The total in the right-hand column is larger than the sum of

TABLE 5.10

*Adequacy of Financial Resources of Women in Later-Maturity Group
by Work History and for Total Group (1986)*

Adequacy	Homemakers		Career workers		Income workers		Later-maturity group	
	N	Pct.	N	Pct.	N	Pct.	N	Pct.
More than enough	52	42.6%	41	35.3%	8	15.4%	116	34.2%
Quite adequate	61	50.0	67	57.8	39	75.0	195	57.5
Barely adequate with care	9	7.4	8	6.9	3	5.8	25	7.4
Really insufficient	—	—	—	—	2	3.8	3	0.9
Total	122		116		52		339	
Significance (p) by chi-square .01								

SOURCE: 1986 questionnaire.

NOTE: Numbers for late-maturity group are larger than the sum of the three work history groups because some respondents did not answer the question on career status.

the three work history groups, since some subjects responding to the 1986 questionnaire did not respond to the work history question on the 1972 questionnaire). The two subjects for whom work history was available and who indicated that their income was insufficient were both income workers. Moreover, at the upper end of the scale, income workers, as compared with the homemakers and career workers, were relatively less likely to say that their income was "more than adequate" and more likely to fall into the "quite adequate" category. The homemakers were the most likely to indicate that their financial resources were more than enough.

When the responses of the 339 subjects answering this question were compared across age-groups, no relationship was found between perceived income adequacy and age-group. Three subjects indicated that their income was insufficient, one in each of the three age-groups. Overall, 58 percent of the sample indicated that their income was quite adequate and 34 percent indicated that it was more than enough. These figures are almost identical with the men's (see Table 4.5). These evaluations by our subjects contrast with objective figures for elderly women in the general population (Grambs, 1989), which show that many are in poor financial situations in later-maturity. For example, in the Harris survey conducted for the National Council on Aging in 1981, 11 percent of the women aged 65 and older said that they can't make ends meet with the income they have now, and 42 percent said that they just about manage to get by with their present income.

As far as the subjects' own evaluation of their financial situation is concerned, the women perceived their income in their aging years as either adequate or more than adequate for their needs, and this essentially parallels the men's experience. Among the women, however, the homemakers and career women were better off than the income workers. One final point about gender differences. Most of the men were married at the time of the 1977 report on income. Therefore they are best compared with the women homemakers so far as family income is concerned. Only the youngest group of women reported a family income approximately the same as that of the men; the middle and oldest groups of women reported substantially less (see Table 4.5).

Retirement

Amount of Work in Later Maturity

Research on women's retirement is scarce (Palmore, Burchett, Fillenbaum, George, & Wallman, 1985; Quinn & Burkhauser, 1990); even the two most comprehensive studies of retirement, the Retirement History Study (Irelan, 1972) and the National Longitudinal Surveys (Parnes & Less, 1985) have severe limitations in design for a comprehensive study of women (Gratton & Haug, 1983). However, some recent research has found variations in women's retirement plans and behavior according to factors such as their occupation, work pattern, and marital status (Gratton & Haug, 1983; Shaw, 1984; Szinovacz, 1982). In our sample, the women, unlike the men, most of whom were working full time at age 50, showed a great variety of working patterns, some with steady employment, but many others with much entry, exit, and reentry into the work force. Such discontinuous work histories are common for women in the general population (Gratton & Haug, 1983). Measuring the extent to which the women worked in later maturity, as well as their patterns of work cessation, was therefore not as straightforward as it was for the men. We used data from the same questions as for the men in 1977 (Question 26) and 1982 (Question 12) to determine the percent of time worked at each year of age from 51 to 80, and then averaged these percentages for half-decades over that period. The results of this procedure appear in Figure 5.5, which is comparable to Figure 4.4 for the men. A comparison of the two figures shows a clear similarity in form but some difference in the actual percentages. There was a plateau for both sexes in the frequency of all three classes — full time, partially employed, and fully retired — between the ages of 61 and 70. More of the men remained fully and partially employed throughout the 25 years. These data are consistent with data from the Retirement History Study comparing retirement patterns of men and unmarried working women (Honig, 1985). The number of full retirements among the women increased radically during the last half-decade, with as large a proportion fully retired as were partially retired. As with the men, the number of cases available in the last half-decade is too small to give us confidence in the exact percentages at the oldest age.

These findings come mainly from the career and income workers. Of the 202 women who were reporting for age 51, only 31 had described themselves as homemakers in 1972. As the group grew older, a few more of the original homemakers became employed for a few years. By age 65, there were 44 of them contributing to the figures presented in Figure 5.5. As P. S. Sears and Barbee (1977) reported, some of the homemakers wished in later life that they had had a

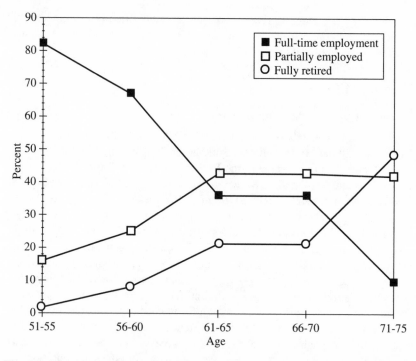

Fig. 5.5. Percent of women in later-maturity group engaged in full-time employment (90–100 percent of time), partially engaged (11–89 percent), and fully retired (0–10 percent) in successive half-decades of their lives from 51 to 75 years (N = 202). Data from 1977 and 1982 questionnaires.

career; at least a few of them were engaged in meaningful and challenging employment in their later years.

Work History Related to Retirement Pattern

Unlike the men, the women varied greatly in the amount of time devoted to work all through their lives. In the present section we will examine the career workers and income workers separately by reference to whether they were fully employed at age 50.

At age 50, 86 percent of the career workers reported working full time, and the remaining individuals reported that they were retired, working between 10 percent and 90 percent time, or had become homemakers. Of the income workers, 68 percent reported working full time at age 50. Most of the women who characterized themselves as homemakers (64 percent) reported that they were engaged in homemaking at age 50. They did not respond to the question on the 1977 questionnaire, since it was to be completed only by those who had had some income-producing work since age 50.

The career and income worker women can be divided into two subgroups:

full-time workers at age 50, and those not fully employed. The average percentage of time worked annually from age 50 onward was computed separately for these two subgroups. Figure 5.6 presents the data for the full-time career and income workers, and Figure 5.7 presents the graphs for those not fully employed.

Figure 5.6 shows that the full-time workers began reducing work well before the age of 65. The two figures show opposite patterns in the rate of work reduction for the career workers and the income workers. The income workers who worked full time at age 50 worked more than the career workers between the ages of 60 and 70. For women not employed full-time at age 50, the opposite was true, with career workers working more than income workers between 60 and 70. These two findings may reflect the intrinsic motivation that usually accompanies career work, in contrast to work pursued solely for income (Price-Bonham & Johnson, 1982). In fact, as compared with career workers in this sample, the income workers were more likely to state in 1972 that financial rewards were among the most satisfying aspects of their work ($p < .07$ by chi square). This is understandable from the income data reported earlier, which showed income workers to be less advantaged financially than career workers. Full-time income workers found it more necessary for financial reasons to persist longer in full-

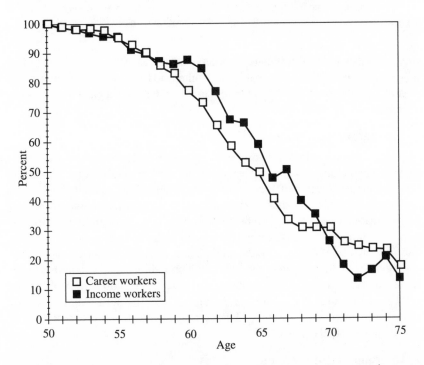

Fig. 5.6. Percent of time worked from age 50 to age 75 by women in later-maturity group who were in full-time employment at age 50 (N = 113 and 39 for career workers and income workers respectively). Data from 1977 and 1982 questionnaires.

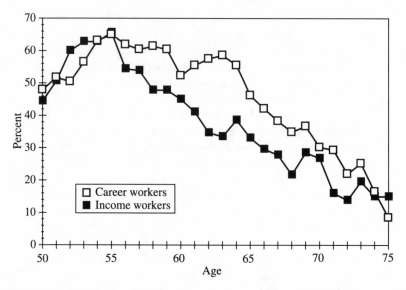

Fig. 5.7. Percent of time worked from age 50 to age 75 by women in later-maturity group who were not employed full-time at age 50 (N = 28 and 19 for career workers and income workers respectively). Data from 1977 and 1982 questionnaires.

time work than did full-time career workers. In contrast, career workers not fully employed at midlife were probably more interested intrinsically in their work than income workers, and were therefore motivated to work a greater percentage of time.

Mandatory Retirement

There was little difference between the career workers and income workers, or between men and women, in the number and ages of people subject to mandatory retirement. Over half the career workers and about half of the income workers were subject to such termination of employment or to one of the two other situations that can be combined with it, retirement required with exceptions, or unofficial but customary retirement. Table 5.11 presents the numbers and percentages of career workers and income workers subject to each retirement condition, together with the ages at which retirement was required. Since these data were collected before changes in federal regulations prohibiting enforcement of retirement before age 70, age 65 was the most common age of mandatory retirement. However, 13 percent of the career workers reported ages for retirement of 70 or above.

Retirement Preferences

Following the question concerning mandatory retirement (1977, Question 23) the women were asked about their preferences for retirement (Question 25).

Table 5.12 shows the numbers of career workers and income workers who would have chosen each of the four alternatives described in the note to the table. The data for the subjects choosing the regular retirement option were obtained from the previous question on age of mandatory retirement (Question 23). The table also includes the ages at which subjects choosing each of the four options would prefer to retire.

There were no important differences between the career workers and income workers nor between women and men. About half would choose 65 or 70 years as optimal, and very few would prefer to retire earlier than their mid-fifties. As with the men, a statute to prevent mandatory retirement before age 70 seems quite suitable for the vast majority of women.

Opportunities for Continued Work

The subjects were asked if there were opportunities for continued work after mandatory retirement, with five opportunities specified (1977, Question 24), as shown in the left-hand column of Table 5.13. Professional women, in particular, tend to have more favorable attitudes toward retirement if they anticipate continuing work activities beyond retirement (Price-Bonham & Johnson, 1982). The table, containing the responses of 89 career workers and 28 income workers subject to mandatory retirement, shows totals of more than the number of subjects and more than 100 percent because many subjects checked more than one of the "yes" categories.

The career workers had more opportunities for continued work than the income workers, 42.9 percent of whom had no opportunities for continued work,

TABLE 5.11
Retirement Rules for Women in Later-Maturity Group

	Career workers		Income workers	
	N	Pct. of total respondents	N	Pct. of total respondents
Mandatory retirement without exceptions	69	54.3%	19	39.6%
Retirement mandatory but exceptions made	12	9.4	4	8.3
Not officially mandatory but customary	3	2.4	1	2.1
Age of retirement of respondents subject to above rules				
55	1	0.8	—	—
60	1	0.8	2	4.2
62	1	0.8	—	—
65	54	42.5	18	37.5
67	10	7.9	2	4.2
68	1	0.8	1	2.1
70	14	11.0	1	2.1
72	1	0.8	—	—
75	1	0.8	—	—
No mandatory rule	43	33.9	24	50.0
Total respondents	127		48	

SOURCE: 1977 questionnaire.

TABLE 5.12

Preferred Age of Retirement of Four Groups of Women in Later-Maturity Group
Who Were Career Workers or Income Workers (1977)

Preferred age of retirement	Group preferences				N	Pct. of total
	Earlier	Regular	Continue	Decrease		
Career workers						
50 or earlier	3	—	—	1	4	3.8%
51–55	3	—	—	2	5	4.8
56–60	7	—	2	11	20	19.2
61–65	7	16	2	5	30	28.8
66–70	1	4	10	8	23	22.1
Over 70	—	—	—	—	—	—
Other	4	4	10	4	22	21.2
Total	25	24	24	31	104	
Pct. of total	24.0	23.1	23.1	29.8		
Income workers						
50 or earlier	2	—	—	—	2	5.3
51–55	—	—	—	—	—	—
56–60	4	—	—	4	8	21.1
61–65	1	4	2	5	12	31.6
66–70	—	3	1	—	4	10.5
Over 70	—	—	1	—	1	2.6
Other	1	5	4	1	11	28.9
Total	8	12	8	10	38	
Pct. of total	21.0	31.6	21.1	26.3		

SOURCE: 1977 questionnaire.

NOTE: "Earlier" were women who would have preferred to retire earlier than the mandatory age; "Regular" were women who preferred the mandatory age; "Continue" were women who wanted to continue beyond the mandatory age and then retire completely; "Decrease" were women who wanted to start decreasing work at the ages given in the table and fully retire some years later.

compared with 22.5 percent of the career workers. There was little difference in the kinds of opportunities that did exist, except that more career workers had opportunities as consultants or free-lancers. In respect to opportunities, then, the career women reported much the same experience as the men (see Table 4.8).

Summary

The Terman women, like the men, were highly educated. Seventy percent of the women in the later-maturity group obtained bachelor's degrees, and over 40 percent secured master's degrees or had some graduate work. However, in contrast to the men, only 4 percent obtained doctoral or major professional degrees. The Depression of the 1930s and World War II decreased the level of the women's education, as it did with the men.

Between 1940 and 1977 there was relatively little change in the proportion of the women who were engaged in the various types of occupations. About 40 percent were primarily homemakers; about 40 percent were in professional, semi-professional, and managerial occupations; and about 19 percent were sales and service workers. Between 1960 and 1977 the proportion of women in managerial occupations increased, with a corresponding decrease in sales/service work. The gifted women with only high school or some college education were employed significantly more often at higher-level occupations than were women of equivalent education in a representative national sample.

By their own retrospective descriptions in 1972, 40 percent of the women had been homemakers, 42 percent had had careers, and 18 percent had been income workers. Career women tested significantly higher than noncareer women on the Concept Mastery Test in both 1940 and 1950. In addition, several measures of achievement motivation favored the career workers. These included parents' and field-workers' ratings at elementary and high school age and self-ratings in adulthood. Career workers' educational attainments were also higher than non-career workers', both in number and quality and in level of degrees obtained. A greater liking for school, and especially for arithmetic, characterized the career workers in both elementary school and college, as did parents' ratings of per-severance in childhood, and self-ratings of self-confidence and purposiveness in young and middle adulthood. Moreover, career workers were more frequently "always single," married at an older age, were less likely to rear children, and were more likely to have had their marriages disrupted by divorce or widow-hood. In young adulthood, career workers also had planned an occupational future rather than a family-oriented one, to a greater extent than had the non-career workers.

The differences between continuously employed career workers and those whose careers were interrupted by family responsibilities paralleled those be-tween career workers and noncareer workers, those with interrupted careers being more similar to the noncareer women. Variables measuring achievement motivation and behavior, self-confidence and persistence, and planning for a career in young adulthood, all favored the steadily employed career women.

TABLE 5.13
Work Opportunities in Same Occupation Available After Retirement
for Women in Later-Maturity Group (1977)

Work opportunities	Career workers		Income workers	
	N	Pct.	N	Pct.
No opportunities	20	22.5%	12	42.9%
Yes, in other companies or institutions, with pay	19	21.3	5	17.9
Yes, under less advantageous employment circumstances	9	10.1	4	14.3
Yes, as a consultant, free-lance, etc.	35	39.3	6	21.4
Yes, same work, without institutional affiliation	3	3.4	—	—
Yes, same work on a voluntary basis with same institution	18	20.2	5	17.9
Other	8	9.0	1	3.6
Total respondents	89		28	

SOURCE: 1977 questionnaire.
NOTE: 69 career workers gave "Yes" responses, but because some gave two or more, the number of "Yes" responses exceeds 69; 16 income workers gave "Yes" responses, but the number of "Yes" responses exceeds 16 for the same reason. Percentages in both groups add to more than 100 for this reason.

Similarly, the steady career workers were more frequently "always single," or married at an older age and were less likely to rear children.

In the decade before 1972 and in 1976 the women's earned income was substantially less than the men's. By 1976 the career workers had the highest earned income, while the homemakers had the highest family income. The career workers and income workers had approximately equal family income. By 1986, 91 percent of the women reported that their financial resources were either "quite adequate" or "more than enough." As with the men, this contrasts with less favorable evaluations of financial adequacy in the general population of older persons. The homemakers and career workers were better off than the income workers, judging by self-evaluations of financial adequacy.

The work patterns of the women were more complicated than those of the men, and the data reveal some retirement patterns for the women. Partial retirement appears to have been an important mode of retirement for the women, as for the men. However, the rate of retirement from work appears to be somewhat faster for the women. The career workers, like the men, reported that they had opportunities for continued work after retirement.

The Terman women, like the men, continued to be quite active in the years of later maturity, aging successfully in this respect. Many of the women who worked, especially the career women, were taking advantage of or creating opportunities to continue occupation-related work well into the years of later maturity. On the whole, however, the kinds of activities in which the women engaged were less oriented toward work for income. They were carrying volunteer work into their later years, some of them substituting volunteer work for work for income as they retired. Many of the homemakers continued volunteer activities begun much earlier. These involvements of the Terman women allowed them, like the men, to pursue meaningful activities while at the same time reducing their level of activity to meet their needs as they aged.

PART III

Social Bonds

6

Marital History

The marital histories of the Terman gifted group seem to display almost all the variety of human relationships that existed in the American population in this period. We know of no homicides, but every other kind of experience appears to have occurred. We have records of single divorces, multiple divorces, intact lifetime marriages, no marriage at all, homosexual partners, and widowing. (The term "widowing" will be applied to the death of a spouse of either sex.) The effects of these relationships (or nonrelationships) on the individual's well-being may range from highly positive to severely negative, the latter including by inference suicide (cf. Shneidman, 1973; Tomlinson-Keasey, Warren, & Elliott, 1986).

Obviously, some of this variation stemmed from life events — who mated with whom, opportunities for forming relationships in a given milieu, favorable or unfavorable occupational experiences, and continuing responsibilities with one's family of origin that seemed to demand other priorities. Not surprisingly, the unique personalities of the individuals themselves also contributed to the variations in their marital histories. We must take these personality differences as given, for we have no means of determining their origins from our present data. Doubtless some differences were genetic, some were the products of early family experiences, and still others were the products of complex adaptations — coping — that the individuals developed to deal with the reality of the external world.

Many of the events and personality qualities that lead to a particular marital history and its final outcome were idiosyncratic. The best we can do is point to a few paths in some brief case vignettes. It is to other, measurable, variables, however, that this chapter will give most attention. We shall search among common demographic variables and several aspects of personality to discover whether there are consistent predictors of marital outcomes. We shall examine, too, how effectively Terman's Marital Aptitude Test, which was constructed and administered to the subjects nearly half a century ago, predicted their marital happiness and success.

Family Formation and Dissolution

The early stages of family formation have been summarized for the Terman group as a whole in previous volumes (Oden, 1968; Terman & Oden, 1947, 1959). With respect to age at first marriage, the later-maturity group does not differ in any respect from the Terman group as a whole. The median in the later-maturity group was 24 years for both sexes, though the mean was 23 for the women and 25 for the men. Four percent of the men and 14 percent of the women married before age 21, and 5 percent of both sexes delayed marriages until after age 36. The latest marriage was that of a man whose first marriage was at 69. Disruption by death and divorce began very soon. In the early years, divorce was the chief source of broken marriages, but in later maturity death played an increasing role.

It is not possible to give a final account of marital matters in this volume, for — as with occupation — people have the potential to change their status as long as they live. For the purposes of the present chapter we will use the marital histories of the later-maturity group as they were when last reported. Only for the 131 men and 70 women who died between 1972 and 1986 are these final. Among those responding in 1986 we can expect a few more remarriages, possibly a divorce or two, and certainly many more widowings. But now that we have a near-final report on marital histories we shall be able to trace antecedents of four of the variety of experiences they had — single status, stable single marriage, single divorce, and multiple divorces. The following chapter will turn to the current marital statuses of the subjects in their later maturity, and finally to the associated matters of living arrangements, children, and family networks.

Patterns of Marriage, Divorce, Remarriage

The parents of nearly all of our subjects were born during the last three decades of the nineteenth century. Most of their parents (the subjects' grandparents) had been born before the middle of that century, when America was largely agrarian except for the Boston-to-Philadelphia east coast. Until well after mid-century, large families were customary; the subjects' parents quite commonly had six or more siblings. These parents, however, belonged to a generation that experienced sharply increased urbanization, still particularly in the northeast but becoming noticeable also in the midwest. Thus while many of our subjects had not-very-distant agrarian roots, they themselves were more likely than their parents to have been born into a middle-class business or professional family. This status, together with the increasing urbanization, was associated with smaller families. In the families the later-maturity sample grew up in, the mean number of children was 3.68 (including the subject).

Both the middle-class status and the recently agrarian background favored a tradition of stability in marriage. Separation and divorce were by no means unknown in the parental generation, but the cultural norm was for a marriage to remain intact until one or the other partner died.

Subjects' Parents

What a society's culture prescribes is not necessarily what all its members do. Among the 962 couples who parented the later-maturity group of 569 men and 494 women, there were 124 divorces or permanent separations (12.9 percent). A few of the latter could properly be called desertions, most often by the husband. Eighty-five percent of these marital disruptions occurred before the subjects had left home. There was no significant difference in this respect between the parents of boys and those of girls.

Divorce was less destructive of marriages than death, however. One hundred and fifty-nine fathers (16.5 percent) and 80 mothers (8.3 percent) died before their children reached age 21. Here again there was no sex difference in the children's experience. Death and/or divorce left more than a third (35.8 percent) of the youngsters to be reared outside the cultural norm of a stable marriage in the family of origin.

The parents who became the children's caretakers were mostly their mothers (80.6 percent). There was no gender difference in this respect. (The children of either sex who stayed with a surviving father tended to be older.) It is also not surprising that the fathers who became caretakers after loss of a wife were much more likely to remarry than were the mothers who remained as caretakers after the loss of a husband. Among the fathers 68.6 percent remarried, whereas only 19.9 percent of the mothers did so.

Though 80.6 percent of the caretakers were the mothers, this figure is misleading as a guide to the customs of the times or to gender differences or similarities in marital choices. If we consider only those cases in which the family of origin was broken by divorce, and the remaining caretaker was either father or mother (disregarding the very few cases of child placement with neither), we find that the mother almost always became the caretaker; in 95.1 percent of the marriages broken by divorce, the child was placed with the mother. In the divorced group there was no difference in the proportions of fathers and mothers who remarried. When the mother was caretaker, 29.6 percent of the fathers and 28.8 percent of the mothers remarried. On the other hand, in the five cases where the divorced fathers were the caretakers four remarried, while none of their ex-wives did.

An additional alleviating circumstance after the breakup of the original families was that a few children were transferred to the care of relatives or family friends who provided two-parent households for their rearing. With these arrangements added to the remarriages and the intact original marriages, 416 boys (73.1 percent) and 394 girls (79.8 percent) were reared in two-parent homes.

It is clear that no matter what the culture prescribed, divorce, in addition to death, made a substantial contribution to departure from the normative ideal of a stable marriage as the foundation for children's rearing in the first two decades of this century. This discrepancy between cultural prescriptions and behavior cannot be cast aside as a perturbation produced by unsocialized deviants; these parents were a part of the stable, productive, and intelligent segment of American society.

The fact that widowed mothers were much more likely than widowed fathers to continue child rearing without a partner calls for explanation. Perhaps, in keeping with tradition and as a result of role training, they were better able to manage the child-rearing function, or at least feared it less. Perhaps they had less choice, because of the imbalance in number of available partners for men and women. Perhaps their children made them less attractive as remarriage partners. Or perhaps they simply chose that life-style; they did not want, or seek to secure, a partner of the opposite sex.

Marriages of the Subjects

The majority of the later maturity subjects had stable marriages. Table 6.1 summarizes the many varieties of their marital experiences in five categories. The sex differences were substantial in some respects, minimal in others. The proportion of women in the later-maturity sample who never married was more than double that of men, the men's rate being slightly lower than that of other men of similar ages, while the later-maturity women's rate was slightly above that of other women of similar ages (see U.S. Bureau of the Census, 1988). Lifelong intact marriages were much commoner for the men than the women. The proportions of intact marriages of men and women are misleading, however, unless taken in conjunction with the proportions of people whose spouses died after a lifetime of living together. The true proportion of intact marriages is obtained by adding the second and fourth lines of the table, and dividing by the total number of later-maturity subjects. This calculation shows that 70.1 percent of the men and 68.2 percent of the women married only once, the marriage, if terminated, being ended only by death of the spouse. The divorce rates of 26 percent for men and 24 percent for women were roughly comparable to those of American marriages during the 1930's and early 1940's when most of the first marriages among our subject occurred (see Preston & McDonald, 1979). However, as noted in Chapter 3 in the discussion of attrition, those with normative marital histories — intact marriages and widowing — are somewhat more highly represented in the later-maturity sample, compared with the full Terman sample.

Marital Roles and Mutual Support

Marriage, like other social roles, carries with it a set of associated responsibilities and tasks. While even today the division of labor in families is somewhat traditional, in our subjects' generation the breakdown of tasks between

TABLE 6.1
Marital History of the Later-Maturity Group at Latest Report

	Men		Women	
	N	Pct.	N	Pct.
Always single	20	3.5%	38	7.7%
Married, no divorce	328	57.6	191	38.7
One or more divorces	129	22.6	90	18.2
Widowed only	71	12.5	146	29.6
Widowed and divorced	21	3.7	29	5.9
Total	569		494	

Significance (p) of sex difference, by chi-square .01

SOURCE: Cumulative marriage data.

genders was especially sharp (Bernard, 1942; Lynd & Lynd, 1937; Pleck, 1985). Women were assigned the major responsibility for homemaking and child care, and men were assigned the major responsibility for breadwinning. For women, the role of helpmate came along with homemaking; many women played a supportive role in their husband's career. Men's sharing in household work tended to be restricted to those tasks less sex-typed as feminine. However, men also had the opportunity to lend support to their wives in their activities outside the home, including community service and paid employment. In this section, we will examine our subjects' reports in later maturity concerning the role division and mutual support in their marriages.

In the 1972 questionnaire (Question 12) the subjects were asked about the division of responsibilities in their marriage, in terms of the husband's relative responsibility for "care and training of children to age 16 and after 16," "day-to-day household work," "care of garden," and "managing family finances and major purchases." Responses were on a five-point scale. The midpoint of the scale (3) represented an equal division of responsibility, with lower numbers indicating that the husband took less responsibility than the wife, and higher numbers indicating that the husband took more responsibility than the wife. Table 6.2 compares the responses of the men and women. In the marriages of both men and women subjects, the division of responsibility for day-to-day household tasks was sharp, with women assuming almost exclusive responsibility. Women also carried predominant responsibility for the care of children, particularly those under age 16. The one large difference between the marriages of the men and women subjects concerned managing family finances and major purchases. The men subjects had more responsibility than their wives for these matters but the women subjects took equal responsibility with their husbands. The only area in which the mean ratings for husband's responsibility were at the mid-point of the scale in the marriages of both men and women subjects was the care of the garden. However, the standard deviation for this item is quite large, indicating substantial variability in couples' assignment of this responsibility. A fair amount of variability also occurred in some of the other areas.

The relation between the women subjects' employment and the domestic

TABLE 6.2

Extent of Husband's Domestic Responsibilities in Marriages of Later-Maturity Group (1972)

	Men subjects' marriages			Women subjects' marriages			
	Mean	S.D.	N	Mean	S.D.	N	p
Care and training of children to age 16	2.31	0.62	414	2.29	0.63	304	n.s.
Care and training of children after age 16	2.64	0.70	402	2.51	0.75	286	.05
Day-to-day household work	1.63	0.67	465	1.65	0.73	376	n.s.
Care of garden	3.13	1.44	460	3.03	1.50	364	n.s.
Managing family finances and major purchases	3.89	1.02	468	3.19	1.17	383	.01

SOURCE: 1972 questionnaire.

NOTE: Responses were coded as follows for men/women, respectively (for present or latest marriage only): 1 = Almost none/almost none; 2 = Less than wife's/less than mine; 3 = About equal to wife's/about like mine; 4 = Greater than my wife's/greater than mine; 5 = Almost entirely mine/almost entirely his. Significance (p) of sex differences was determined by t-test.

responsibilities of their husbands is explored in Table 6.3, which presents the ratings of the husband's responsibility by the three work history groups for women identified on the 1972 questionnaire — homemakers, career workers, and income workers. Although the absolute scale differences were small, husbands' relative responsibilities did vary somewhat according to their wives' work patterns. Most noteworthy is that career workers' and income workers' husbands shared more responsibility for day-to-day household work, compared with the homemakers' husbands. Also, the career workers' husbands took more responsibility than the other husbands for the care and training of young children. Career women and income workers shared responsibility for managing family finances almost equally with their husbands — more equally than the homemakers. However, the homemakers reported a more equal sharing of responsibility in managing family finances than the men reported concerning their marriages.

Interestingly, an analysis of the degree of domestic responsibility of our three male occupational groups — professionals, men in higher-level business occupations, and men in lower-level occupations — showed no significant differences between the groups. However, in 1972 the men were asked to indicate their wife's main occupations since the age of 30. We separated the men into two groups — those who gave "homemaker" as their wife's occupation, and those that gave some other occupation. The domestic responsibilities of the various occupational groups did not differ among the men with homemaker wives, but there were differences among the men with working wives. The professionals and higher-level businessmen took more responsibility than the men in lower-level occupations for the care of young children (means of 2.38, 2.41, and 2.05 respectively; $p < .10$), and the professionals took more responsibility for day-to-day household work when their wives were career workers or income workers (means of 2.00, 1.73, and 1.68 respectively; $p < .05$).

These findings seem to indicate greater sharing of responsibility for household work when wives had jobs, and are consistent with the conclusions of Blood and Wolfe (1960). We do not know to what extent working women's husbands took more domestic responsibility because their wives worked, and to what extent the willingness of the husbands to share in responsibility in household tasks enabled the women to work outside the home. It is also important to keep in mind that a husband's high relative share of responsibility for household work may not indicate a high absolute level of responsibility for the husband, but may result from a lower level of responsibility on the part of the wife who is employed, as Pleck (1985) argues.

In 1972 and 1977, subjects were also asked about the wife's contribution to the husband's career (1972, Question 11 for men, Question 10 for women; 1977, Question 17 for men, Question 16 for women; these questions were identical). Table 6.4 compares the results of the women and men. (The percentages add to more than 100, because many individuals marked more than one option.) As can be seen in the table, the pattern for the women subjects differed from that of the men subjects' wives — more of the Terman women had careers that were independent of their husbands', and, at the same time, they participated more in their husbands' careers. It appears that these capable women brought their abilities, not only to their own activities, but also to those of their husbands.

A further issue is whether the husbands of our subjects extended to their wives the same degree of support in their activities outside the home as the women provided them. The women were asked to indicate the role their husband played in their career or community service in the 1972 questionnaire (Question 11). (A similar question in 1977 proved unusable due to the lack of recording of multiple responses.) Table 6.5 summarizes the women's responses. (The percentages total to more than 100% because many women checked more than one

TABLE 6.3

Extent of Domestic Responsibilities of Husbands as Reported in 1972 by Women Homemakers, Career Workers, and Income Workers in Later-Maturity Group

	Homemakers			Career workers			Income workers			
	Mean	S.D.	N	Mean	S.D.	N	Mean	S.D.	N	p
Care and training of children to age 16	2.24	0.60	147	2.43	0.56	89	2.24	.68	51	.05
Care and training of children after age 16	2.54	0.72	143	2.48	0.70	85	2.44	.87	45	n.s.
Day-to-day household work	1.44	0.59	158	1.92	0.82	127	1.60	.74	66	.01
Care of garden	2.84	1.46	157	3.27	1.50	122	3.02	1.52	61	.06
Managing family finances and major purchases	3.35	1.21	162	3.04	1.04	130	3.07	1.29	67	.06

SOURCE: 1972 questionnaire.
NOTE: Responses were coded as follows: 1 = Almost none; 2 = Less than mine; 3 = About like mine; 4 = Greater than mine; 5 = Almost entirely his. The significance (*p*) of differences among the three groups of women was determined by one-way analysis of variance.

TABLE 6.4

*Wife's Activities in Relation to Husband's Career Reported by Men
and Women Subjects in Later-Maturity Group (1972 and 1977)*

| | 1972 | | | | 1977 | | | |
| | Reported by men | | Reported by women | | Reported by men | | Reported by women | |
Wife's activities	N	Pct.	N	Pct.	N	Pct.	N	Pct.
Wife's career essentially independent of husband's	198	41.9%	185	47.8%^c	148	37.2%	149	46.7%^b
Wife's work contributed directly to husband's^d	89	18.8	107	27.6^a	102	25.6	83	26.0
Wife took substantial responsibility for supporting activities^e	140	29.6	98	25.3	145	36.4	69	21.6^a
Couple discussed husband's work frequently	279	59.0	285	73.6^a	238	59.8	226	70.8^a
Wife knew very little about husband's work	96	20.3	36	9.3^a	78	19.6	25	7.8^a
Total respondents	473		387		398		319	

SOURCE: 1972 and 1977 questionnaires.
^a$p < .01$ by chi-square   ^b$p < .05$ ^c$p < .10$ ^dHelp in planning collaboration, other regular interactions.
^eSocial welfare of associates, activities to build good will for husband's business, etc.

response.) We found that there was appreciable support from their husbands for the women's work or community activities, particularly in regard to discussing their wife's work.

Because a wife's employment ran counter to established gender roles for this cohort, in 1977 subjects were asked to evaluate the effect of the wife's working on their marriage, if the wife had worked for most of the marriage (Question 18). A majority of both the men and the women (61 percent and 56 percent, respectively) felt that the effect of the wife's working was positive, with few perceiving a negative effect. Men's views, however, were relatively more sanguine than women's ($p < .05$ by chi-square for the distribution of responses across sex). In addition to more men perceiving a positive effect, men were more likely to see a neutral effect (29 percent vs. 21 percent), and less likely to see a mixed effect (7 percent vs. 17 percent). The women's report on the effect on the marriage was more positive than that noted in the Berkeley studies (see Clausen, 1990), but the somewhat less favorable view of this issue by the women may indicate role strain or unfavorable attitudes of their husbands toward their working, as was found in the samples studied at Berkeley.

Divorce

As indicated in Table 6.1, 26 percent of the men and 24 percent of the women had a history of divorce at some time in their lives. The total for the group (25.3 percent) was almost twice the percentage among their parents (12.9 percent). A more accurate measure of change from generation to generation can be obtained by focusing on the divorce figures of the married-with-children members of the younger group (because by definition the comparison group includes no childless parents). There were 142 childless married members of the subject group and 58 unmarried, a total of 200. If we eliminate these cases from consideration, 863 couples who had children can be compared with the 962 parental couples. In this selected group the divorce rate was 30.0 percent, a little larger than the divorce rate in the total group. Evidently the presence or absence of children made a small difference in the decision to divorce, the presence of children leading to a slightly higher divorce rate. Although some marriages intact at the time of the subjects' last reports may have subsequently been broken by divorce, there were probably only a few of these. (Only nine of the 1986 respondents had divorced in the ten preceding years.) The 143 percent increase from generation to generation is probably a good estimate of the secular trend of the divorce rate for this kind of group.

Remarriage

In both sexes, divorce was much more commonly followed by remarriage than was widowing, as indicated in Table 6.6. The men were much more likely to remarry under both circumstances.

Much of the difference in remarriage rates after widowing and divorce is attributable to the ages of the subjects when the marriages ended. Divorces came earlier in the life cycle (median age 35 years for both sexes) than did deaths of spouses (median age for women, 62, and for men, 64). The effect of this difference on frequency of remarriage is easily seen when the divorced subjects are divided into two groups — those who divorced prior to and after 1945. Ninety-five percent of the men divorced in 1945 or earlier remarried, but only 70 percent of those divorced between 1946 and 1986 remarried. The outcomes for the two groups of women were far more disparate; 84 percent of those divorced before 1945 remarried compared with only 32 percent of those divorced between 1946 and 1986. There is no way of knowing how much of this gender difference is due to choice and how much to the relative shortage of available men after young

TABLE 6.5
Husband's Role in Career or Community Service of Women
in Later-Maturity Group (1972)

Husband's participation	N	Pct.
Husband knew very little about wife's activities	52	13.5%
Couple discussed wife's work frequently	229	59.5
Husband contributed directly to wife's activities	93	24.2
In many of these activities, husband and wife were full collaborators	75	19.5
Wife did not engage much in such activities during marriage	69	17.9
Total respondents	385	

SOURCE: 1972 questionnaire, women subjects.
NOTE: N's add to more than total respondents and percentages add to more than 100 because many women gave two or more responses.

TABLE 6.6

Frequency of Remarriage by Later-Maturity Group After Divorce or Death of Spouse

| | Men | | | | Women | | | |
| | Divorce | | Death | | Divorce | | Death | |
Remarriage	N	Pct.	N	Pct.	N	Pct.	N	Pct.
No	28	18.5%	32	45.7%	46	38.7%	132	90.4%
Yes	123	81.5	38	54.3	73	61.3	14	9.6
Total	151		70		119		146	
Significance (*p*) by chi-square			.01				.01	

SOURCE: Cumulative marriage data.
NOTE: This table gives outcomes after the first marriage only.

adulthood, or to the possible unattractiveness of taking on stepchildren with a new spouse.

The categories in Tables 6.1 and 6.6 are arbitrary, of course; they combine all the subjects who have had a divorce into a single percentage, no matter how many divorces they had or whether they remarried or not. The same is true for those who lost a spouse by death. This hides many individual differences in marital experience, a few of them spectacular. In Table 6.7 all those in the later-maturity group who experienced divorce or widowing are divided into more revealing subgroups. The table shows what percentage of the later maturity group had each marital record. The most notable figure is that slightly more than a quarter of the women who were widowed remained unmarried. This proportion is about five times the rate for men in the same circumstance.

It should be kept in mind, when assessing the stability of marriage, that most of those men and women who divorced or lost a spouse by death early in their lives and then remarried had almost as stable a marital history as those who were more fortunate in their first marriage. The same can be said for those whose lifelong stable marriage was terminated only by death of one of the spouses.

Prediction of Marital Outcomes

During the late 1920's and the 1930's, a number of social scientists turned to the study of marital happiness. The burgeoning child guidance clinics, the developing profession of marriage counseling, and the broadening of psychiatric practice to include people with disturbances not requiring hospitalization led to a realization that the broken home, especially a home broken by divorce, could be detrimental to the mental health both of the marriage partners and of the children concerned.

Divorce was viewed as an index of marital unhappiness, a sign of the failure of the institution of marriage. Single marital status — which we will call "nonmarriage" — was viewed as either a misfortune or a sign of possible maladjustment, mitigated in some instances by the specialized demands of a religious calling. These two kinds of marital (or non-marital) experience were deviations from the cultural norm, and therefore could carry a threat to the welfare of people who experienced them. To a psychometrician of that time, the construction of a predictive test to measure marital aptitude was a natural step.

The Marriage Study

During the late 1930's, Terman turned his attention to psychological factors conducive to marital happiness (Terman, 1938). For his study of nearly 800 married couples, unselected for intellectual level, he constructed two tests that later became important to the present research. The first was a measure of marital happiness. No precise theory guided this effort, but it drew from previous research by G. V. Hamilton (1929), Dickinson and Beam (1931), and Burgess and Cottrell (1938). It was composed of 65 items relating to the subject's congeniality with and complaints about his or her partner, and five items on sexual compatibility. The split-half reliability was .89 for both spouses. The scores of husband and wife correlated .52 with each other.

Terman's purpose in constructing this test was to provide a criterion score, i.e., a dependent or outcome variable, that he could use as an index of happiness in marriage. He looked forward to constructing a test of marital aptitude, a test that he hoped would predict an individual's marital happiness before a marriage was undertaken. A preliminary form of the Marital Aptitude Test was used in the original marriage study, but Terman constructed a more extensive one for use with the gifted group. Like the marital happiness scale, it did not rest on a detailed theory of the correlates of happy marriage, but it did draw on previous studies of the qualities of personality associated with marital happiness and on Terman's own matchless intuition. The test as used with the gifted group was labeled "Personality and Temperament" (Terman and Oden, 1947, chapters 18–19, and pp. 418–24). It was administered to 637 married gifted subjects and their spouses in 1940. Of these, 567 couples, including four in which both

TABLE 6.7
Divorce, Widowing, and Remarriage in Later-Maturity Group

Divorce, widowing, remarriage at latest report	Men N	Men Pct.	Women N	Women Pct.
Married once; separated or divorced	28	4.9%	46	9.3%
Married once; widowed	32	5.6	132	26.7
Married, divorced, remarried	72	12.7	20	4.0
Married, widowed, remarried	37	6.5	11	2.2
Two marriages, both broken by death or divorce	18	3.2	36	7.3
Three, four, or five marriages, ending married	27	4.7	11	2.2
Three, four, or five marriages, ending broken	7	1.2	9	1.8
Total widowed or divorced	221	38.8	265	53.6
Total later-maturity group	569		494	

SOURCE: Cumulative marriage data.
NOTE: Percentages relate to total later-maturity group.

spouses were gifted, took both the test of marital aptitude and test of marital happiness.

The Marital Aptitude Test had 104 items: 38 from the Bernreuter Personality Test, 10 from the Strong Vocational Interest Inventory, 27 questions designed to sample retrospective feelings (and a few facts) about family background and childhood and adolescent experiences, 15 about current views of the ideal marriage, and 14 self-ratings on personality dimensions. The items were individually weighted according to their correlation with the Marital Happiness Test. The validating correlation of Marital Aptitude scores with Marital Happiness scores was .53 for the men and .48 for the women with split-half reliabilities near .85. For both male and female married subjects, the correlations between husbands' and wives' scores were close to .30.

In 1940 Terman secured Marital Aptitude scores from nearly all of the subjects still available, whether married or not, but only subjects already married were asked to take the Marital Happiness Test. In our smaller later-maturity group the husband-wife correlations for marital aptitude were .30 and .33 for the men and women respectively. The same correlations for marital happiness were .54 and .52, almost identical with the larger sample. Terman concluded that these values accounted for so small a part of the variance as to suggest that both happiness and aptitude were dependent more on qualities of individual personalities — what he labeled loosely as "happiness of temperament" — than on the specific character of the dyadic relationships between the husbands and wives.

Terman's Validation of the Marital Aptitude Test

The 1940 correlations of the Aptitude Test with the Happiness Test were quite modest, .53 for the men and .48 for the women. Terman recognized the need for a more robust test of validity, and in 1946 was able to compare the mean scores of 45 couples who had divorced since the tests were given six years earlier with those of subjects who had not divorced. The divorced group had significantly lower mean scores on the aptitude test than the non-divorced, the difference being greater for the women than the men. When the husband and wife scores were averaged, the difference between the divorced and non-divorced was still larger. Terman and Oden (1947, p. 263) concluded that the Marital Aptitude Test showed promise as a predictor of the success of marriages, but added: "Follow-up of the marriages for another 10 or 20 years will establish more accurately the predictive value of the tests."

Evidence from the Later-Maturity Group

Forty years is better than the "10 or 20" they asked for, and we can now give a reasonably final report on the validity of the Marital Aptitude Test, using divorce as the criterion. With divorce scored as a binary measure (presence or absence), the point-biserial correlations between the marital aptitude score and absence of divorce were low — for women and their spouses .22 and .25, respectively, and for men and their spouses, .12 and .20. The point-biserial correlations of the combined subject/spouse aptitude measure and non-occurrence of divorce were .24 for female subjects and .25 for male subjects. A separation of single divorces from multiple divorces does not improve prediction by the test, though as will be seen later this distinction has some value in identifying antecedents of stable versus unstable marriages. In Terman's earlier analysis of the data (1947), he found that the combined scores of husband and wife correlated better with marital stability than the score of either partner alone. A similar pattern of relationships was found for the later-maturity group, with only negligible differences.

Another test of validity is the comparison of marital aptitude scores of the subjects who never married with scores of those who did and had stable marriages. The point-biserial coefficient is .14 for the men and .04 for the women. None of the correlation coefficients exceeds .29. While any value above .10 is significant at the .05 level, the value of the test as a predictive instrument is low; at best the aptitude score can account for no more than 8 percent of the variance.

So, after waiting nearly half a century to complete the validation process, we reach two conclusions: (1) the Marital Aptitude Test was obviously measuring some personality qualities that differentiated men and women who differed in their marital success, but (2) its psychometric efficiency was not sufficient to make it a useful clinical instrument.

Antecedents of Divorce

In the search for correlates of divorce we continue to distinguish between subjects who divorced only once and those who had two or more divorces. The appropriate comparisons are between each of these separately and the much larger group who married but did not divorce. The independent variables which we have examined include intellectual performance, early parent-child relationships, adolescent sex behavior, age at first marriage, personality traits, emotional adjustment, and occupational experience.

Other investigators have found differences between divorced men and women and persons with intact marriages, especially satisfied married persons, on several of these dimensions. For example, in the Berkeley study (Skolnick, 1981), the strongest difference between divorced men and women and those in intact marriages was a tendency to be more erotically inclined, but divorced men and women were also lower in cognitive investment (ease and skill in intellectual matters, reflectiveness, and interest in achievement) than satisfied married individuals, perhaps as a result of socioeconomic differences. Earlier age of marriage has been found to be associated with divorce (Glick, 1975), as has extraversion, invulnerability, poor ego controls, psychopathy in males, and low congeniality in females (Bentler & Newcomb, 1978; Dworkin & Widom, 1977; Johnson & Harris, 1980). Multiple divorce has been associated with greater impulsivity and nonconformity (McCranie & Kahan, 1986). Also, studies showing those with better marital adjustment to be more emotionally mature, considerate, sensitive to other's feelings, nurturing, companionable, yielding, self-confident, and dependent are also suggestive (Burgess & Wallin, 1953; Cole, Cole, & Dean, 1980; Murstein & Glaudin, 1968; Skolnick, 1981; Terman, Buttenwieser, Ferguson, Johnson, & Wilson, 1938). Our anticipation was that the multi-divorced subjects would differ from the never-divorced subjects more than would the single-divorced group.

The 1940 Personality and Temperament questionnaire (as the Marital Aptitude Test was labeled) is a convenient place to start, for we know in advance that we will find some significant differences. Likewise, the Marriage Study questionnaire of the same year provides useful information. By 1940 the subjects in the gifted group had reached an average age of 30 years; some of the questions called for answers that were retrospective to earlier childhood and adolescent feelings and experiences, while others were more relevant to the subjects' then-current young adulthood. The same can be said for the 1950 Supplementary Biographical Data and Rate of Reproduction questionnaires. Still other information, mainly parents' ratings of subjects' personality traits, is available from the actual period of childhood; these are found in the Home Information questionnaires of 1922 and 1928.

Intellectual Performance

In the later-maturity group, subjects who never divorced, those who divorced once, and those who had two or more divorces did not differ in intellectual or educational performance in childhood, adolescence, or young adulthood. These measures include the 1922 IQ, the 1922 Stanford Achievement Test, the 1940 and 1950 Concept Mastery Tests, number of high school "college recommended units," and average college grade. Intellectual potential and achievement contributed little or no variance to this area of emotional and social behavior.

Family Background

Several measures of the social and economic background of the family were obtained, both from the field-workers in 1922 and retrospectively from the subjects themselves in 1940. None of these differentiated the divorced from the nondivorced men; neighborhoods, homes, the children's perception of social status, and family income were all similar in the two subgroups. The homes of the multi-divorced women were rated slightly lower on the Whittier Home Index ($p < .10$), however, and they recalled more limited family financial and social circumstances ($p < .05$ and $p < .10$ respectively).

Although we have no measures of emotional relationships between the subjects and their parents from the earlier years, some of the differences between divorced and never-divorced subgroups on the adulthood retrospective measures are large enough to warrant attention. Table 6.8 reports on remembered affection, conflict with parents, and happiness of parents' marriage as the subjects reached young adulthood (1940) and middle age (1950). The key stimulus words were a little different in the two questionnaires (e.g., "attachment to father" in 1940, and "deep affection and understanding between you and your father" in 1950), but the basic affective implications were quite similar, and both sets of self-ratings

TABLE 6.8

Early Parent-Child Relationships and Family Background of Never-Divorced and Divorced Persons in Later-Maturity Group

	Never-divorced		Once-divorced		Multi-divorced	
	Mean	S.D.	Mean	S.D.	Mean	S.D.
	MEN					
	(N = 323–356)		(N = 87–100)		(N = 22–26)	
1940						
Conflict with father	2.1	1.1	2.2	1.1	2.3	1.2
Attachment to father	3.3	1.0	3.4	0.9	3.1	1.0
Conflict with mother	2.0	1.0	2.2	1.1	2.8[a]	0.9
Attachment to mother	3.8	0.8	3.7	0.8	3.4[b]	1.0
Happiness of parents' marriage	4.8	1.8	5.0	1.7	3.9[b]	1.8
Happiness in childhood	3.5	0.9	3.5	1.0	3.1[b]	0.9
1950						
Rebellion against father	2.3	1.0	2.6[b]	1.2	2.6	1.3
Rebellion against mother	2.2	1.1	2.7[a]	1.1	2.5	1.2
Affection for father	3.1	1.0	2.9	1.1	2.6	1.0
Affection for mother	3.6	1.0	3.3	1.0	3.2	1.1
	WOMEN					
	(N = 260–289)		(N = 64–76)		(N = 23–28)	
1940						
Conflict with father	2.0	1.1	2.2	1.3	3.0[a]	1.4
Attachment to father	3.6	1.0	3.6	1.0	3.3	1.2
Conflict with mother	2.2	1.1	2.4	1.2	2.9[a]	1.2
Attachment to mother	4.0	0.8	3.9	0.9	3.4[a]	1.0
Happiness of parents' marriage	5.5	1.4	4.9[a]	1.4	4.3[a]	1.9
Happiness in childhood	3.7	0.9	3.5	1.0	3.1[a]	1.1
1950						
Rebellion against father	2.3	1.2	2.4	1.3	2.6	1.3
Rebellion against mother	2.6	1.2	2.7	1.1	3.2[b]	1.3
Affection for father	3.4	1.2	3.4	1.1	2.9[b]	1.2
Affection for mother	3.6	1.1	3.5	1.1	3.0[b]	1.2

SOURCE: 1940 and 1950 questionnaire.
NOTE: All measures are subjects' retrospective reports. N's varied between limits indicated. All significant differences are between the "never-divorced" and the indicated divorced group.
[a]$p < .01$ by *t*-test.   [b]$p < .05$ by *t*-test.

were on a 5-point scale — with one exception of the estimate of "happiness of parents' marriage" on a 7-point scale.

Subjects who had only one divorce did not differ materially on these measures from those who had none. In the once-divorced group, there is evidence of difficulty between sons and mothers and fathers in the 1950 ratings, and a clue lies in another 1950 variable (not in the table) — mother's resistance to son's independence. The mean for this scale was significantly higher in the once-divorced group than in the never-divorced. Beyond this there is little to be noted, except that once-divorced women rated their parents' marital happiness lower than did the never-divorced women.

The multi-divorced women had a stormy time in childhood and adolescence. They had less affection for their parents and more conflict with them, and rebelled against their mother more. On another 1950 scale, not listed in the table, the multi-divorced women reported significantly more rejection by the mother than did the never-divorced. The multi-divorced men reported more conflict with their mother and less attachment to her than did the never-divorced. On a more global estimate, both the multi-divorced men and women characterized their childhood as less happy.

Doubtless a key contributor to this conflict and lack of affection was the marital unhappiness of the parents themselves. Both the men and the women of the multi-divorced group judged their parents' marriage significantly less happy than did either the once-divorced or the never-divorced groups. There was no difference, for either sex, among the three groups in the number of actual divorces that occurred in the parental generation.

Adolescent Sexuality and Marriage

Measures of adolescent sexuality and age at first marriage showed differences between the once-divorced and the multi-divorced subgroups. As can be seen in Table 6.9, on almost all the variables we have examined relating to adolescent sexual behavior, courtship, and first marriage, the multi-divorced subjects of both sexes differed significantly from the never-divorced. They married earlier and hence the interval between puberty and first marriage was briefer; they tended to be therefore both sexually and socially less mature.

The U.S. Census for 1940 reported the average age at first marriage to be 24.3 years for men and 21.4 years for women in the U.S. population as a whole. The averages for our total group, combining the three subgroups in Table 6.9, are 26.7 years for men and 24.8 years for women, substantially higher than the U.S. Census figures.

Three measures of sexual attitudes and behavior in high school, reported retrospectively in 1940, showed significantly greater interest and activity in the multi-divorced group. They had greater pleasurable anticipation of sex, did more petting, and had more opposite-sex friends. They appear to have had stronger or perhaps more impulsive sexual motivation. If this were so, one might expect a greater frequency of certain external events that are sometimes found clinically to be associated with greater sexuality — early introduction to sexual stimulation or over-emphasis of sexual instruction. The 1940 inquiry uncovered no differences among the three subgroups in the occurrence of sex shocks, or in the age, adequacy, or sources of sexual education, nor were there any differences in the sibling gender constellations of their families. While these findings came from rating scales on a questionnaire rather than from deep therapeutic searching, there was no indication of the influence of extrinsic events on early sexual attitudes or behavior.

In the light of the evidence about greater conflict with parents, it is possible that social-sexual peer group activity and an early marriage were forms of flight from a conflictual home and a search for affectional stability in dyadic relationships of the children's own making. This interpretation is reinforced by the fact

TABLE 6.9

Adolescent Sexuality and Age at First Marriage of Divorced and Never-Divorced Persons in Later-Maturity Group

	Never-divorced			Once-divorced			Multi-divorced		
	N	Mean	S.D.	N	Mean	S.D.	N	Mean	S.D.
					MEN				
Age at puberty	239	14.3	1.1	64	14.2	1.1	17	14.4	1.4
Age at first marriage	398	27.2	6.1	115	26.2	4.5	30	24.4[a]	3.6
Years between puberty and first marriage	237	13.4	5.8	61	12.1	4.7	16	10.1[a]	3.8
Favorable attitude toward sex in high school	356	2.6	0.6	99	2.8[a]	0.7	26	2.9[a]	0.5
Amount of petting in high school	356	2.2	1.1	100	2.4	1.2	25	2.4	1.0
Number of premarriage opposite sex friends	218	2.6	0.9	52	2.8	0.9	14	3.1[b]	0.9
N/percent wish to be opposite sex		354/6.5%			98/10.2%			26/11.5%	
					WOMEN				
Age at puberty	284	12.6	1.2	77	12.6	1.2	29	12.9	1.5
Age at first marriage	326	25.1	5.5	85	24.7	4.7	31	22.4[a]	3.9
Years between puberty and first marriage	279	12.3	5.4	76	12.2	5.1	28	9.5[a]	4.0
Favorable attitude toward sex in high school	288	2.3	0.6	77	2.4	0.6	30	2.7[a]	0.7
Amount of petting in high school	289	1.9	1.1	76	2.3[b]	1.2	30	2.4[b]	1.1
Number of premarriage opposite sex friends	194	3.0	0.9	40	3.4[a]	0.7	14	3.3	1.0
N/percent wish to be opposite sex		287/46.7%			76/43.4%			21/70.0%[c]	

SOURCE: 1940 questionnaire and cumulative data on age of subjects and first marriage.

NOTE: Adolescent sexuality measures are subjects' retrospective reports. All significant differences are between the "never-divorced" and the indicated divorced group.

[a]$p < .01$ by t-test.   [b]$p < .05$ by t-test.   [c]$p < .05$ by chi-square.

that the multi-divorced women much more frequently recalled having wished they could have been boys than did the other two subgroups of women. Seven times as many of the never-divorced girls recalled this wish to be of the opposite sex as did never-divorced boys. Such a gender difference has commonly been attributed to girls' adolescent fantasies of greater social status and greater power. The greater frequency of this wish among the multi-divorced women may be one of the products of their conflictual childhood and adolescent home life and a coping method, in fantasy, parallel to early marriage in reality.

Personality Traits

How did these people see themselves, and how did others see them? We can start with their self-perceptions in 1940, when they were between 20 and 40

TABLE 6.10

Personality Trait Self-Ratings in 1940 by Divorced and Never-Divorced Persons in Later-Maturity Group

	Never-divorced		Once-divorced		Multi-divorced	
	Mean	S.D.	Mean	S.D.	Mean	S.D.
		MEN				
	(N = 354–357)		(N = 98–100)		(N = 26)	
Emotionality	18.0	4.1	18.5	3.9	19.3	5.0
Self-confidence	12.8	3.3	13.3	3.3	14.2[c]	3.4
Purposiveness	14.0	2.8	14.6[c]	3.1	14.2	3.3
Easygoing	14.4	2.8	14.3	2.9	13.8	3.2
Conformity to authority	5.7	1.8	5.3[c]	1.8	4.3[a]	1.5
Impulsiveness	5.2	1.8	5.4	1.8	6.7[a]	1.5
		WOMEN				
	(N = 286–288)		(N = 76–77)		(N = 28–30)	
Emotionality	19.4	3.8	20.5	3.7[b]	21.3[b]	4.0
Self-confidence	11.6	3.2	12.2	3.2	10.9	3.4
Purposiveness	13.2	2.7	13.4	3.4	14.4[c]	3.0
Easygoing	14.6	2.8	14.2	2.8	14.4	3.3
Conformity to authority	5.9	1.7	5.6	1.8	4.9[a]	1.9
Impulsiveness	6.0	1.8	6.0	1.9	6.7[b]	1.8

SOURCE: 1940 questionnaire. 1922 score on masculinity of interests in childhood games.

NOTE: All significant differences are between the "never-divorced" and the indicated divorced group.

[a]$p < .01$ by t-test.　　[b]$p < .05$ by t-test.　　[c]$p < .10$ by t-test.

years of age and averaged 30. In the Personality and Temperament questionnaire the subjects rated themselves on several 11-point scales. On the basis of factor and item analyses we constructed several scales from 11 of these items for the purposes of analysis. The "emotionality" scale consisted of ratings on emotionality, moodiness, and sensitive feelings. The "self-confidence" scale consisted of a self-confidence item and an item on feelings of inferiority, which was reverse scored. "Purposiveness" was composed of an item measuring persistence and one measuring having a definite purpose for one's life. The "easygoing" scale consisted of items measuring happiness of temperament and being easy to get along with. Two other items were of interest — "impulsiveness" and "conforming to authority" — and they were analyzed separately. In Table 6.10 we list the results of comparisons between the never-divorced and divorced groups. Again there is little difference between the never-divorced and the once-divorced groups, but what there is may well be genuine. Among men, those with one divorce rated themselves somewhat higher on "purposiveness," as a result of differences in scores on the persistence item; they also rated themselves as less "conforming to authority." The women rated themselves higher on the "emotionality" scale, as a result of differences in scores on the emotionality item.

More important, and more robust, are the differences between the never-divorced and the multi-divorced. Both the male and female multi-divorced groups reported greater "impulsiveness," and less conformity to authority. The men showed somewhat greater "self-confidence." The multi-divorced women also showed greater "emotionality," especially on the moodiness and sensitivity of feelings items, and also greater "purposiveness" as shown particularly on the persistence item. Some 1922 ratings by parents and teachers (not shown in the table) showed some significant differences. Parents' 1922 ratings on "moodiness" and "persistence" showed the future multi-divorced males and females to be more moody and less persistent, as did teachers' 1922 ratings of the females. There are no early ratings of refusal to conform to authority, but it is worth noting that the teachers rated both sexes of the multi-divorced group as less "tractable to punishment" than the never-divorced group.

Although more than half of the subjects had spouses who participated in the 1940 follow-up, the spouse ratings are not useful for this present comparison. Only 11 women and 13 men in the multi-divorced groups had participating spouses. Both the husbands and wives of these few cases, however, reported the same tendency not to conform to authority ($p = .05$).

Most of the youngsters conformed to personal and cultural authority in at least one respect — they never divorced from their spouses. The smaller group who divorced more than once obviously had different styles of coping and went down different paths to adulthood. These paths cannot be traced easily with the types of data we have available. We can conclude, with little doubt and some profit, that at the beginning of a long lifetime which would eventuate in multiple divorces these people already perceived themselves differently from the way the more conventional majority perceived themselves. They were more moody, impulsive, willful and persistent, emotional, and resistant to authority.

One other personality quality for which we have measures is masculinity/femininity of interests. In 1922 about 500 of those children in the gifted group who were in elementary school were given a test of their knowledge and interest in childhood games (Terman et al., 1925). One score on the test evaluated the masculinity of these interests. In 1940, most of the men and about a third of the women filled out the Strong Vocational Interest Blank, which also was scored for masculinity of interests. On both measures the men of the divorced groups were a little less masculine in their interests than were the men of the never-divorced group. The divorced women showed a similar tendency in 1940 but not in the 1922 data. None of these differences, however, is even marginally significant.

Emotional Adjustment and Mental Health

We have three reasonably direct measures of emotional adjustment and mental health. The first is the Woodworth-Cady test, an empirically validated instrument that provides an index of emotional stability as contrasted with neurotic tendencies (Terman et al., 1925). This test was given to some of the subjects in 1922. The second measure is alcohol use as reported by the subjects themselves on a 5-point scale ranging from "I have never used liquor" through "alcohol is a problem; I drink periodically or steadily, am drunk fairly often, and attempts to stop have been unsuccessful." This scale was included in the 1940 and 1960

TABLE 6.11

Mental Health of Divorced and Never-Divorced Persons in Later-Maturity Group
by Percentage of Subjects Rated in Each Category
After 1940, 1950, and 1960 Follow-ups

Mental health rating	Never-divorced			Once-divorced			Multi-divorced		
	1940	1950	1960	1940	1950	1960	1940	1950	1960
				MEN					
Satisfactory	87%	81%	78%	78%	70%	64%	55%	52%	41%
Some difficulty	11	15	19	21	26	31	36	34	33
Considerable difficulty	2	4	4	2	4	6	10	14	26
N	386	387	361	107	105	104	31	29	27
Significance (*p*) by chi-square				.05	.05	.05	.01	.01	.01
				WOMEN					
Satisfactory	87	74	70	73	57	50	70	48	43
Some difficulty	12	23	26	21	28	28	13	33	36
Considerable difficulty	2	3	4	6	15	22	17	18	21
N	329	312	303	84	81	78	30	27	28
Significance (*p*) by chi-square				.01	.01	.01	.01	.01	.01

SOURCE: Cumulative ratings by staff, based on 1940, 1950, and 1960 questionnaires.
NOTE: All significant differences are between the "never-divorced" and the indicated divorce group.

follow-ups; a 4-point scale (omitting the middle point) was used in 1950. The third measure was the summary rating on "mental difficulties" made by the research staff after the 1940, 1950, and 1960 follow-ups. Subjects who had no apparent difficulty were rated 0, those with some problem perhaps requiring counseling or psychotherapy were rated 1, and those with considerable difficulty, including hospitalization, were rated 2. The rating was cumulative from follow-up to follow-up; a person once rated as having some degree of difficulty would continue to be so rated even if his or her adjustment improved.

There was some tendency for both the multi-divorced men and women to have had a score on the Woodworth-Cady more predictive of neuroticism than the never-divorced ($ps < .10$). The Woodworth-Cady test does reflect emotional disturbance in children, and if the multi-divorced subjects were accurate in their recall of conflict and unhappiness in their childhood family life, it is not surprising that such feelings might have been reflected in their responses to this test in childhood.

When the three measures of alcohol use (in 1940, 1950, and 1960) were combined into one scale, both the men with one divorce and the multi-divorced men had higher overall alcohol use ($p < .01$ and $p < .10$ respectively). Among women, only the multi-divorced group differed from the never-divorced ($p < .05$), showing higher alcohol use.

The final mental health variable is displayed in Table 6.11. Both divorce groups were consistently rated by the staff as having poorer adjustment than the never-divorced. The multi-divorced, especially the men, were generally more extreme in this respect. By 1960, the percentage of multi-divorced men and women rated as having had "considerable difficulty" was over five times greater than among the never-divorced. Because the data for this measure were ratings by a staff who perforce were familiar with the divorce record of each subject as well as other facets of his or her life, the question of bias in rating arises. Did one or more divorces in a case history lead the raters to give a more serious "difficulty" score? Probably not to a great extent, if we may judge from the fact that the 1940 ratings — made before more than a handful of divorces had occurred — already showed substantial differences between the never-divorced and those who would later be multi-divorced. The differences in the "2" category, which included hospitalization and loss of employment, were as great as in the "1" category. We conclude that a good many of the divorced subjects, especially the multi-divorced, showed symptoms of mental disturbance from their earliest adult years.

In some cases we can infer from the uncoded records of events and reports that an unfortunate marital mismatch and the ensuing divorce were themselves responsible for the emotional stress. In other instances, and especially in the multi-divorced group, the emotional maladjustment appears to have been primary, and the later divorce history more a consequence than a cause.

Education and Occupation

Both multi-divorced men and women had somewhat less education than the never-divorced, but as we saw earlier, they married earlier also. The early marriage was possibly a primary cause of stopping education short of a bachelor's degree and was doubtless partly a product of early home conflicts.

Occupational measures did not differentiate among the three marital groups. Differences in marital history were not related to the professional vs. business distinction in men, to the distinction between women career workers and income workers, to different scores on the index of work persistence of men, or to differences in men's rated occupational success (the A/C rating by Terman and Oden in 1940 or by Oden and Marshall in 1960).

Integrative Analysis

To help understand the ways in which the various kinds of variables we have reviewed work together in predicting multi-divorced status, we computed descriptive discriminant functions for the men and women separately. The variables chosen reflect the findings we have just reviewed, and are displayed in Table 6.12. The 1940 retrospective relationship variables with each parent sum the scores for conflict and lack of attachment. The childhood happiness composite is the sum of standardized scores on childhood happiness and happiness of

TABLE 6.12

Results of a Discriminant Analysis Predicting Multiply-Divorced
versus Never-Divorced in Later-Maturity Group

Year reported	Variable	Standardized discriminant function coefficient	
		Men	Women
1950	Parents' favorable financial and social position	—	−.28
1940	Retrospective negative relationship with father	.19	—
1940	Retrospective negative relationship with mother	.00	.39
1940	Childhood happiness composite	−.45	−.25
	Age at first marriage	−.27	−.25
1940	Sexual attitudes in high school[a]	.07	.45
1940	Emotionality	—	.38
1940	Self-confidence	.49	—
1940	Purposiveness	—	.32
1940	Conformity to authority	−.35	−.09
1940	Impulsiveness	.48	.07
1940	Cumulative mental health difficulties	.37	.27
	Wilks's lambda	.82	.69
	Degrees of freedom	1,345	1,208
	p	.01	.01

SOURCE: Questionnaires for indicated years; cumulative marriage data; staff ratings of mental health.
[a]Higher score indicates more interest and anticipation and more petting.

parents' marriage. The sexual attitudes measure is the sum of attitude toward sex and amount of petting in high school. Variables where no entry appears were not included in the equation for the men or women.*

The results of the discriminant analysis show somewhat different patterns of weighting for men and women. For men, childhood unhappiness, cumulative mental health difficulties, and the personality characteristics of self-confidence, impulsiveness, and lack of conformity to authority were the strongest predictors. For women, the strongest predictors were sexual attitudes in high school, a negative relationship with mother, and the personality characteristics of emotionality and purposiveness.

Case Studies

The realms in which we have sought antecedents are necessarily limited and the idiosyncratic events of the subjects' lives contain many other causative factors. Some case vignettes will help to place the simple fact of divorce, or non-divorce, in the context of other experiences.

Alice graduated from college at the bottom of the Depression. She was independently well-to-do and spent the two years after college graduation in European travel. Her father was a widely known and much respected public figure, her mother a suitable consort. Alice married a former classmate when she re-

* To make the multivariate analysis possible, subgroup means were substituted for missing data for the multidivorced groups.

turned to California. He had begun work in a large firm, learning the business "from the bottom" (a current expression half a century ago), and progressed rapidly in the company. They had three children in rapid succession, and then settled into an active program of income work for the husband and volunteer work for Alice. Their children were all successful, made happy marriages, and produced several grandchildren. In 1986, Alice wrote in answer to the question (Question 34) about what changes she would have made, in retrospect: "None. Of course, there have been ups and downs, but we've had a wonderful life and my husband is still the best there is. Now we just enjoy the grandchildren!"

Beth illustrates the essential similarity between the never-divorced and the once-divorced groups. She was the third child in a troubled family. Her parents, both high-school graduates, divorced when she was eight years old, and she had no further contact with her father. Her mother worked hard to maintain the household but suffered from much ill health. Beth was a good student in high school, working part-time to add to family income. She graduated at Christmas time in 1929 and immediately married a classmate. They had a baby girl the following November. Neither youngster was prepared for earning a living, and within a year Beth secured a divorce on grounds of non-support.

Her life thereafter was continuously difficult but up-grade all the way. She got a job as a waitress at a Woolworth lunch counter, was promoted to manager after nine months, there met and fell in love with a high-school graduate who was also just 20, and married him in 1933. A year later he formally adopted her child. He found a better position as an appliance salesman, and she was soon able to transfer to his store as a bookkeeper. She found the sales aspect of the store appealing and was transferred to that section. Her mother had become a chronic invalid and lived with them until her death from a stroke in 1939.

Both Beth and her husband were hard workers, frugal, and successful in their retail positions. She became a buyer in a department store and he became manager of the appliance section. By 1950 they had saved enough money to buy a partnership in a good appliance store in a small but prosperous community. Beth worked without salary at first, but after a couple of years began taking a salary and using it to pay off the purchase loans for the store. A few years later, when their income had become very substantial, she stopped work altogether and began volunteer community work at a less demanding pace. The daughter was married in 1958, after graduating from college, and Beth and her husband built a charming rustic home in some nearby hills. Their business partner died and they bought his share from his widow. The daughter's marriage failed in 1970, but Beth's continued strong. In 1986 she wrote: "As I must have said many times before [she had], the best thing in my life has been my marriage. It's been just perfect."

Carla, a brilliant and vigorous young woman, had professional training to the master's degree level. At age 23 she married an equally brilliant man in the same field who was five years older, then found herself refused admission for doctoral work in their university because her husband was on the faculty. She found a remunerative but unsatisfying job as a buyer in a department store. After ten years of marriage and two children, the couple divorced and both remarried, she taking the children. She had one child by her second husband, but this youngster was killed in an accident, and shortly thereafter the father died. Our subject married a third time but divorced this husband very soon after the marriage.

In the meantime her first husband had married a young faculty woman (who already had her Ph.D.), and they had two children. This second wife died after 25 years. Within a few weeks he had searched for and found his now-widowed first wife — Carla — and they remarried, living together congenially and affection-ately until he died five years later at age 82.

Elton was an energetic self-reliant man who supported himself almost en-tirely while getting an A.B. in economics at a large state university. He won varsity letters in three sports. He obtained a position as an accountant on gradua-tion, in 1933, and the next year married a high-school graduate who had a minor managerial position in a large store. He was reasonably successful in his work, but not very happy with his marriage. His primary pleasure came from sports. He entered the Army as a 1st Lieutenant in 1942 and retired as Lieutenant Colonel at the end of the war. He started his own accounting firm and experienced rapid success, but his marriage dissolved in divorce in 1948. Athletic activity took much of his non-working time during the next few years, and in 1954 he won the national championship in his favorite sport. He married for the second time that same year, again to a high school graduate; this wife quit work at marriage and they had two children in their first two years. When after 20 years this second wife died, Elton soon married again, this time to a woman 15 years younger than he. She quit her very good position as a secretary to a top manager of a large business. The marriage was intact as of 1986. In the 1977 questionnaire (Ques-tion 41), Elton listed five events that had been of critical importance to him; three related to sports, one to occupation, one to education, none to marriage or other relationships.

Gina's parents first separated when she was eight years old, quarrelled con-stantly (according to her recollection), and finally divorced as she entered adoles-cence. She had an older sister with whom she was not friendly; the mother appears to have incited jealousy between them as a means of maintaining her own insecure status. Gina left home after high school and went to a neighboring state for teacher training. She married impulsively at 18 but separated from her husband after six weeks and was divorced. Not caring for teaching, she went to business college for a year. In 1935 she married a second time; this union produced a son three years later just as the husband went into military service as an enlisted man. During his year and a half of service, Gina lived unhappily with his mother. The marriage did not survive her husband's return, and Gina secured a divorce on grounds of "extreme cruelty." She shifted from clerical and secre-tarial work to a position as a counselor with the juvenile court. She worked effectively at this until she married again in 1952. This third husband was, like the others, a high-school graduate, and successful as an entrepreneurial real estate investor. Gina quit work, had a second child (14 years junior to her first), and lived comfortably for the next 25 years until her death in 1977.

Irwin was the son of a happily married and occupationally successful urban business couple. He graduated from college in 1935 and had several short-term jobs in stores and factories, each seemingly for the purpose of "learning the business." None was satisfying and promotion was slow, so at age 25 he started his own manufacturing company, which was an immediate success. In 1952 he took a commission in the Navy, where he progressed to Lt. Commander during three years of service. In early 1943 he married a woman whose health did not at that time permit her to have a child. They adopted one immediately. After his wife died two years later, Irwin kept his son at home, rearing him with outside help until marrying again in 1955. In the meantime Irwin had become active in a number of community organizations; the financial success of his business allowed him to drop down to about half-time work. Irwin became quite active as a philanthropist.

Shortly after his second marriage, the couple had a child, but the marriage ended in divorce after less than three years. Two years later, Irwin married for a third time, but his wife became alcoholic, and they were divorced after a dozen years; she died two years later. Since then Irwin has lived alone with a full-time housekeeper, has limited his occupational activity to investment, and has continued his social and philanthropic work.

Antecedents of Never-Married Status

To explore the antecedents of never-married status in the later-maturity group, we compared the never-married with those who married but never divorced, in terms of the same variables used to compare the divorced and the never-divorced. This similarity in data analysis is not matched by any similarity in findings, however; whereas the divorced men and women appeared to have much the same personality qualities, the men and women who never married differed from one another in a few quite important respects. Other studies have also found differences between single women and single men. For example, single women have been shown to be happier than single men, more active in dealing with their problems, and stronger in meeting challenges in their lives (Gurin, Veroff, & Feld, 1960). Unmarried men in the general population tend to have lower educational levels, occupational status, and income than married men, but single women compare favorably in these respects with both married women and unmarried men (Austrom, 1984; Spreitzer & Riley, 1974).

Intellectual Performance

In both sexes, there were no differences between the never-married and the never-divorced in early intellectual performance (initial IQ, Stanford Achieve-

TABLE 6.13

Intellectual Performance of Never-Divorced and Never-Married Persons in the Later-Maturity Group (1940, 1950)

	Men				Women			
	Never-divorced (N = 272–299)		Never-married (N = 11–13)		Never-divorced (N = 234–265)		Never-married (N = 26)	
	Mean	S.D.	Mean	S.D.	Mean	S.D.	Mean	S.D.
1940								
Concept Mastery Test	98.2	29.5	105.7	29.4	92.1	27.2	106.8[b]	27.3
1950								
Concept Mastery Test	139.7	26.4	156.2[b]	16.6	132.1	26.7	146.1[a]	20.3

SOURCE: Concept Mastery Test scores, 1940 and 1950.

NOTE: Form A of the Concept Mastery Test was given in 1940, and Form B was given in 1950. The means presented here are calculated from the raw scores. The significant differences are between never-married and never-divorced.

[a] $p < .01$ by *t*-test   [b] $p < .05$ by *t*-test

ment Test). Academic performance as represented by the number of "recommended units" for college and school failure records did not differ, but the never-married women had higher college grades.

The Concept Mastery Test scores of the never-married subjects in 1940 and 1950 were, however, clearly superior to those of never-divorced (see Table 6.13). We have data from only about two-thirds of the subjects in the later maturity group, but the differences are so large that there seems little doubt that the never-married had not only improved their positions vis-a-vis the others by 1940 but that this progress continued during the following decade. As will be seen later, many of these people were in occupations, and had had the education, that would be conducive to continuing intellectual development.

Family Background

The never-married subjects did not differ significantly from the never-divorced subjects in family background variables, including feelings and experience. They recalled no more conflict or rebellion in their relations to their parents than did the comparison group, and they expressed equal affection and attachment. The only variable that differentiated the two groups — and only among the women — was the subjects' estimate of the happiness of their parents' marriage. But this had not led to any feeling of rejection, so far as the women recalled. These findings differ sharply from those reported in the previous section for the multi-divorced subjects; the subjects who never married show no indication of having chosen this path as a result of earlier unhappiness in the family setting.

Adolescent Sexuality

If we may judge by the age of puberty, the never-married subjects did not differ in physiological maturity from those who married but never divorced. There is a suggestion of social immaturity, however. In Table 6.14 it can be seen that the boys of the never-married group had less interest in sex at high-school age, as they judged retrospectively in 1940, and both boys and girls reported significantly less petting in high school. In 1928 there had been no differences in the mothers' ratings of their children's amount of interest in the opposite sex. The picture is confused by one other 1940 self-report. The boys in the never-married group reported an earlier knowledge about the origin of babies than did the never-divorced boys, but the girls in the never-married group reported the opposite, namely a later discovery of these facts of life than the never-divorced girls. As is usually found, very few of the boys of either group had ever wished to be of the opposite sex, while almost half of the girls in both groups recalled such wishes.

Personality Traits

As young adults, the never-married men expressed a rather poor opinion of themselves, as evidenced by ratings on both the self-confidence and feelings of inferiority items making up the "self-confidence" scale (see Table 6.15). In contrast with the never-divorced, they were also relatively less "easygoing," particularly reflected by their responses to the unhappiness of temperament item. The never-married women showed no signs of such self-derogation, and on the positive side, rated themselves higher on "purposiveness," particularly on the persistence item, than did the never-divorced women.

TABLE 6.14
Adolescent Sexuality of Never-Divorced and Never-Married Persons in Later-Maturity Group

	Never-divorced		Never-married	
	Mean	S.D.	Mean	S.D.
	MEN			
	(N = 239–357)		(N = 11–20)	
Age at puberty (years)	14.3	1.1	14.0	1.3
Age learned about babies[a]	2.2	0.7	1.8[c]	0.4
Favorable attitude toward sex in high school[b]	2.6	0.6	2.3[d]	0.7
Amount of petting in high school	2.2	1.1	1.4[c]	0.8
Interest in opposite sex[b]	2.6	0.6	2.7	0.5
Percent wishing to be opposite sex	—	6.5%	—	10.5%
	WOMEN			
	(N = 219–290)		(N = 26–35)	
Age at puberty (years)	12.5	1.2	12.3	1.1
Age learned about babies[a]	2.1	0.7	2.5[d]	0.7
Favorable attitude toward sex in high school[b]	2.3	0.6	2.3[d]	0.5
Amount of petting in high school	1.9	1.1	1.3	0.7
Interest in opposite sex[b]	2.9	0.5	2.6	0.6
Percent wishing to be opposite sex	—	46.7%	—	45.7%

SOURCE: 1940 questionnaire and cumulative data on age at puberty, and 1928 mothers' ratings.
[a]High score indicates late discovery: 1 = before age 6; 2 = 6 to 11; 3 = high school age.
[b]Mother's ratings on a four-point scale: 1 = aversion; 4 = great interest.
[c]$p < .01$ by t-test.   [d]$p < .05$ by t-test.

TABLE 6.15

*Personality Trait Self-Ratings in 1940 by Never-Divorced
and Never-Married Persons in Later-Maturity Group*

Personality trait	Never-divorced		Never-married	
	Mean	S.D.	Mean	S.D.
	MEN			
	(N = 355–356)		(N = 20)	
Emotionality	18.0	4.1	18.0	5.2
Self-confidence	12.8	3.3	10.9[b]	2.4
Purposiveness	14.0	2.8	12.9	2.9
Easygoing	14.4	2.8	12.2[b]	2.6
Conformity to authority	5.7	1.8	5.8	1.8
Impulsiveness	5.2	1.8	5.0	2.2
Masculinity — play (1922)[a]	3.6	0.8	3.0	1.2
Masculinity — SVIB (1940)[a]	6.0	2.1	4.6[c]	2.5
	WOMEN			
	(N = 291)		(N = 35)	
Emotionality	19.4	3.8	19.4	4.0
Self-confidence	11.6	3.2	11.4	3.0
Purposiveness	13.2	2.7	14.3[d]	3.0
Easygoing	14.6	2.8	14.4	2.3
Conformity to authority	5.9	1.7	6.4	1.8
Impulsiveness	6.0	1.8	5.9	1.4
Masculinity — play (1922)[a]	3.0	0.9	3.3	1.0
Masculinity — SVIB (1940)[a]	6.7	2.0	6.0	2.5

SOURCE: 1940 questionnaire; 1922 score on masculinity of interests in childhood games; 1940 Strong Vocational Interest Blank scored for masculinity.

NOTE: The Strong Vocational Interest Blank was given in 1940 to only those women who expressed an interest in taking it (*N* = 200). For our comparison of the M/F scale, *N* = 102 for never-divorced women and *N* = 18 for never-married women.

[a]A high score means high masculinity.   [b]$p < .01$ by *t*-test.
[c]$p < .05$ by *t*-test.   [d]$p < .10$ by *t*-test.

Except for the happy temperament rating, the mothers' ratings of the never-married men were similar to the men's self-ratings. The mothers' ratings of the men's "self-confidence" and "inferiority feelings" and of women's "persistence" showed the same direction of differences from the mothers' ratings of the never-divorced subjects as the subjects' self-ratings ($p < .10$).

One other finding is of interest. As can be seen in Table 6.15 the measures of masculinity, based in 1922 on masculinity of interests in play and games and in 1940 on the whole array of interests tapped by the Strong Vocational Interest Blank, showed the never-married men to have more feminine interests. The "never-married" women did not differ significantly from the married women on these measures.

Emotional Adjustment and Mental Health

Neither the Woodworth-Cady test of 1922 nor the self-reported use of alcohol in 1940, 1950, and 1960 indicated any difference between the never-married subjects and the never-divorced. The staff rating of mental health, however, gave a somewhat different picture (Table 6.16). Both men and women of the never-married group were rated more poorly in 1940 than the never-divorced. This difference became quite robust for the men in the following two decades — but disappeared almost entirely for the women. Neither the men nor the women had shown any such differences in the two-point rating of 1928.

Education and Occupation

There was no difference in the proportions of never-married and never-divorced men who obtained various levels of education; about half of both groups had some graduate work or received graduate degrees. Their occupational outcomes, however, were very different. Forty percent of the never-married men ended up in lower-level occupations, compared with only 11 percent of the never-divorced. The 60 percent of the never-married men who were in the upper two occupational levels were mainly professional, by a proportion of 47 percent to 13 percent, but as a group they were not very successful.

After the 1940 follow-up, Terman and Oden (1947) selected 150 "most successful" and "least successful" men — the "A" and "C" groups. A "B" rating was assigned to all others. (No such rating was made for women.) The criteria for selection were: "(a) nature of work, importance of position, and professional output; (b) qualities of leadership, influence, and initiative; (c) recognition and honors (scientific, civic, professional), awards, biographical listings, election to

TABLE 6.16

Mental Health of Never-Divorced and Never-Married Persons in Later-Maturity Group by Percentage of Subjects Rated in Each Category After Follow-ups in 1940, 1950, and 1960

Mental health rating	Never-divorced			Never-married		
	1940	1950	1960	1940	1950	1960
	MEN					
Satisfactory	87%	81%	78%	65%	47%	56%
Some difficulty	11	15	19	30	32	22
Considerable difficulty	2	4	4	5	21	22
Total respondents	386	387	361	20	19	18
Significance (p) by chi-square				.05	.01	.01
	WOMEN					
Satisfactory	87	74	70	78	81	75
Some difficulty	12	23	26	14	14	18
Considerable difficulty	1	3	4	8	6	8
Total respondents	329	312	303	37	36	36
Significance (p) by chi-square				.05	n.s.	n.s.

SOURCE: Cumulative ratings by staff, based on 1940, 1950, and 1960 questionnaires.

learned societies, etc.; and (d) earned income. For most occupations, except business, income received the least weight" (Oden, 1968, p. 53).

In 1940 perhaps a quarter of the group was too young to be well evaluated. But decades later their ages were fully suitable, and the evaluation was repeated in 1960. In 1960 only 100 A cases and 100 C cases were selected. (There were not 150 who could be called C's.) There was considerable overlap of the two ratings (Oden, 1968), but there was enough shuffling of position to make it useful to examine both sets of ratings with respect to attrition. Half the never-married men were rated as "C" in the 1960 evaluation of occupational success, none as "A." The emotional problems that plagued some of the unmarried men were apparently of sufficient importance to interfere with their occupational lives.

Although the never-married and never-divorced men had similar levels of education, the never-married women had much more education than the never-divorced women. Eighty-one percent of them had some graduate work or a graduate degree, compared with only 41 percent of the never-divorced. At the other end of the distribution, 29 percent of the never-divorced lacked a bachelor's degree, in contrast with only 8 percent of the never-married women. As for occupations, the single women were predominantly professional (67 percent); the never-divorced were less so (45 percent). Far more radical were the differences in amount of work and kind of occupation. Eighty-nine percent of never-married women had full lifetime work histories; this contrasts with only 34 percent of the never-divorced women. The kinds of work they did also contrasted sharply. Almost half the never-divorced women were homemakers — a status held by only one of the never-married women, one who had an inherited income. There was not much difference between the two groups, however, in the proportion who worked solely for income. Both occupational level and level of success were definitely higher among the never-married women than among the never-married men.

Integrative Analysis

To understand better the relative strength of each kind of variable in the prediction of never-married status, representative variables were entered into a descriptive discriminant analysis for the men and the women. The results of the analysis are presented in Table 6.17. Sexual attitudes in high school is the sum of favorable attitude to sex and amount of petting in high school. The lifetime A/C designation for men combines the 1940 and 1960 ratings into a numerical scale, with those rated "C" at both times rated lowest, and those rated "A" at both times highest.*

The results capture differences in the kinds and importance of variables that predict never-married status for men and women. Sexual attitudes in high school receives a higher weight in the men's equation than the women's. The predictors

---

* To make the multivariate analysis possible, subgroup means were substituted for missing data in the never-married groups.

TABLE 6.17
Results of a Discriminant Analysis Predicting Never-Divorced
versus Never-Married Status in Later-Maturity Group

Year reported	Variable	Standardized discriminant function coefficients	
		Men	Women
1940	Sexual attitudes in high school	−.52	−.21
1940	Self-confidence	−.01	
1940	Easygoing	−.47	
1940	Purposiveness		.02
1960	Lifetime A/C designation for men[a]	−.60	
1972	Noncareer versus career work history		.70
Cumulative	Education level		.49
1950	Cumulative mental health difficulties	.32	.16
Wilks's lambda		.87	.84
Degrees of freedom		1,350	1,273
p		.01	.01

SOURCE: Questionnaires for indicated years; cumulative education data; staff ratings of mental health.

[a]This rating combines the 1940 and 1960 ratings of occupational success into a numerical scale, with those rated "C" at both times rated lowest, and those rated "A" at both times highest.

of never-married status for men emphasize a lesser degree of sexual interest in high school and of occupational achievement than the never-divorced men, and personality characteristics that would not be conducive to marital adjustment. Among women, the importance for this generation of women of the relation between never-married status and the choice of a career is evident.

Case Studies

As is always the case, there were individual characteristics of the life histories that seem to have been salient aspects of a particular person's development but were not reflected in statistical comparisons. Four brief case descriptions exemplify this observation.

Paul was born in San Francisco in 1910. His father had been a grocery clerk for a number of years but became an accountant in a small business about the time Paul was born. Paul's mother had taken a business course after graduating from the eighth grade and then worked as a stenographer until she married. The father became a chronic invalid (with Parkinson's disease) when Paul was nine years old. This led Paul to take much part-time employment to help provide family income; even so, he was a "straight-A" student through elementary and high school.

Until he graduated from high school, Paul had been attracted to law and to writing as possible careers, but then his interest turned firmly to religion and the ministry. He completed his work in a pretheological college in the Bay Area with high honors, after which, leaving home for the first time, he went east to a church college. For several years he served as a minister to small congregations, inter-spersing work for the national administrative arm of his church with his parish duties. His father died when Paul was 30, and his mother came to live with Paul permanently as his homemaker. By 1945 he had become widely known in his profession, and in that year was appointed president of a small church college. In both 1940 and 1950, Paul's questionnaire reports indicated a warm and affection-ate relationship with his mother, and a complete lack of interest in marriage. His recollection of high school feelings about sex were of "disgust and aversion" and an entire lack of sexual activity. He never developed close friendships with either sex, though as an adult, at least, he was socially able and worked effec-tively in various middle-level administrative positions. In 1977, two years after his mother's death, "with whom I lived all my life, in all places of my resi-dence," he referred to the event as the most crucial turning point of his life. Now 67 years old, he said "[I] must now face remainder of life living alone." He had already published seven religious books, now published another, served for three more years in an important missionary role, and died of cancer at age 70.

Cedric was born in a small town near San Francisco, the oldest of four brothers. His parents were upper middle-class business people, originally from the Carolinas. Cedric was an excellent student and quite popular in high school. His primary interest was in dramatics. From age seven his favorite reading was plays and his other chief leisure-time activity was drawing. His family, teachers, and friends expected him to become a cartoonist. In high school he acted in many plays, painted scenery, and wrote one-act plays for the drama club. After high school he went to a famous playhouse training school for two years. Immediately thereafter, in spite of the Depression, he was able to get steady work as a radio dramatist and actor. At age 21 he met another man engaged in the same work, and they became successful collaborators and life-long house-mates. After their initial success in Hollywood, they moved to New York, where they became a well-known team as radio theater writers. They bought a farm in Connecticut, lived relatively quietly, but, by the nature of their occupation, under continuous high tension. Cedric reported in his thirties that alcohol and smoking were big problems for him. In 1940, at age 27, his interests were scored as "A" level for physician, actor, musician, and writer.

By 1960, the pressure of constant creativity and deadlines had exhausted both his partner and him, and they began a partial retirement, starting with a six-month tour of Europe. Thereafter Cedric worked only part-time, since he no longer needed much income, and used his leisure to work on plays, teach part-time in a theatrical college, and prepare special TV extravaganzas on assign-ment. In 1972 he reported that his drinking was under good control but he was still unable to stop smoking. He died of lung cancer three years later.

Elizabeth was born and reared in a small mid-western town where her father was the successful president of a college. He was 48 and her mother 40 when Elizabeth was born. Her mother was quite active in community work, especially with their church. Elizabeth, with three much older brothers and a younger sister, had an apparently comfortable childhood until she was 12. Then her father retired and the family, without the older boys, moved to a small city to live with ailing grandparents.

The transition from small town to city was difficult, and during the next few years Elizabeth became somewhat reserved, isolating herself from social life. Her father died about the time she started college. She had trouble adjusting to the first school she entered and eventually went to four different colleges before graduating in 1930. Her main interest was in writing, and she thought of herself as a future writer. For financial reasons she planned to begin a career in library work, and entered library school. Again for financial reasons she dropped out after a year and found a position in a small library. Her mother reported in the mid-1930's that Elizabeth was still trying to write in her spare time but was not very successful. Elizabeth was "too tired after long days in the library." The two of them lived together until World War II, when Elizabeth turned to clerical work in an airplane factory. In 1944 she resigned and entered the Women's Army Corps as a private. Her assignments during the next three years, to Paris and London, were a mixed blessing; her work and travel were stimulating but she missed her Californian home life. After her discharge she was able to return to library school and finish her training.

By this time (1948) writing was more a wistful hobby than an occupation, and Elizabeth settled into a new position in a large and sophisticated state library. Over the next 25 years she progressed well professionally, finally becoming a top level administrator. Her mother had died when Elizabeth was 40, leaving her alone without a housemate. Eventually she found a congenial woman friend with whom she lived the rest of her life. In 1977 she answered the financial questions on her questionnaire with, first, her own income (which was substantial), and then added "T. earns about the same and so our family income is —."

In the early part of her career, Elizabeth referred frequently to writing stories and articles as her real vocation and rated her library work as a poor source of satisfaction. In successive reports over 30 years, however, writing was put on the back burner, the library work was put in first place, and in her final questionnaire she rated "my work itself" as her most important source of life satisfaction.

Jean was the oldest of four children in a financially comfortable family, the father a commercial publisher, the mother a homemaker whose college degree was in electrical engineering. Jean's mother and teachers, both elementary and high school, suggested teaching as her probable vocation, and all agreed that her ability in mathematics was exceptional. She majored in it at the University of California, where she received the A.B. and M.A., but her interests also included psychology and education. The combination led her to a position in the psychological test construction program at a major university. In the mid-thirties she moved to a large eastern city with a large black population and began teaching mathematics in high school. Her interest in testing and counseling continued, and she published a substantial number of articles in technical journals.

One of her major values from her high school years had been the improvement of interracial relations; in college she was active in interracial clubs, and in her new city school system she immediately became active in the desegregation movement. She was active also in several professional organizations. Her technical work continued, however, in spite of her organizational activity, and at age 60 she retired from teaching to become managing editor of an important technical journal, a position she held until her final retirement in her late 60's.

Jean rejected homemaking with a firm "no" on her first questionnaire about interests, in 1922, and she evidently continued this feeling for the rest of her life; she lived first in a small apartment for a few years, then bought a house (where her main interest was gardening), and finally returned to an apartment. In all these dwellings she lived alone. Social issues were exceedingly important to her. Boys and men were not. She had many women friends but no housemates.

Summary

The majority of the later-maturity subjects had stable marriages. About 70 percent of both sexes married only once, with the marriage, if terminated, ending by the death of the spouse. About a quarter of both the men and the women divorced at least once. These divorce rates were roughly comparable to those for American marriages during the 1930's and 1940's when most of the first marriages among our subjects occurred. The proportion of women in the later-maturity sample who never married was more than double that of men; the men's rate was slightly lower than that of other men of similar age, and the women's rate was slightly higher than that of women of similar age. Terman's Marital Aptitude Test discriminated significantly between never-divorced subjects and those who never married, divorced once, or divorced more than once.

As compared with the Terman men's wives, more of the Terman women had careers independent of their husbands' careers. Also, the Terman women participated more in their husbands' careers than did spouses of Terman men. After marriage, both the men and women had adopted a traditional division of responsibility for household tasks and childrearing. However, the Terman women's work outside the home was accompanied by slightly greater participation by husbands in day-to-day household work; husbands of the career workers also participated more in the care and training of the children. Women income workers and career workers shared more financial management responsibilities with their spouses than did homemakers. In marriages in which the wife had worked for most of the marriage, a majority of the men and women saw the effect of the wife's work on the marriage as positive, but this was relatively more true for the men than for the women. The husbands of the Terman women provided appreciable support for their wives' community service or paid work, particularly with regard to discussing the wife's work.

A distinction between marital histories showing a single divorce and those showing multiple divorces was especially informative. The once-divorced group differed relatively little from the never-divorced group in respect of family background, adolescent sexuality, age at first marriage, and several personality traits self-rated by the subjects in young adulthood. The multi-divorced groups of both sexes, however, differed more sharply from the never-divorced group. The multi-divorced subjects perceived their childhood as unhappy and their relationships to their parents as unaffectionate and conflictual. Both the boys and girls tended to marry early, and were less mature as measured by the interval since they had entered puberty. This, in turn, led to an abbreviation of education. The salient personality traits — emotionality, impulsiveness, and refusal to conform to authority — that the multi-divorced people perceived in themselves (and which their mothers judged similarly) can be viewed both as products of early parent-child maladjustment and as seedbeds of difficulty for later marital adjustment.

The once-divorced groups, however, were not entirely free of difficulty. The mental health measures, based on an evaluation of all the information available from 1940 to 1960, suggested that they, too, had more emotional difficulties, neuroticism, and serious affective interference in their adult lives than did the subjects who never divorced. In young adulthood, however, once-divorced subjects did not remember their childhood as more unhappy nor did they recall more conflict, rebellion, and lack of affection in their relations to their parents. We have no way of knowing whether this difference in recollections is a real difference in the childhood situation or whether the once-divorced people simply coped more effectively with earlier family problems, and by young adulthood no longer viewed their earlier lives as unhappy and conflictual.

In contrast to their respective same-sex comparison groups, we see that there are important similarities as well as differences between the never-married men and women. Never-married subjects of both sexes had no intellectual advantage in their early years over children in the study who later married. However, by young adulthood — their thirties and forties — both never-married men and women had developed superior competence as measured by the 1940 and 1950 Concept Mastery Tests. In childhood, never-married subjects of both sexes were slightly sex-typed toward the opposite gender, and in adolescence, both were little interested in sex behavior and had relatively little experience with it. By young adulthood the single subjects' interests still leaned toward those typed as opposite to their own gender, the men more so than the women, and the men had begun to diverge toward unhappiness, low self-confidence, and feelings of inferiority. The women, on the other hand, had become more persistent in their seeking of life goals. In middle age this difference was reflected by more serious adjustment difficulties for the never-married men, which appears to have interfered significantly with their occupational activity; a disproportionately large segment of the never-married men settled for a low level of occupation, and by and large they were not very successful. The never-married women, in contrast, had a significantly higher level of education than the never-divorced, were predominantly professional, and were quite successful in their continuing full-time occupational careers. Single subjects of both sexes were predominantly professional in their occupational choices, and tended to be full-time career workers throughout their lives.

7

Family and Social Networks

Marriage is commonly viewed as a social institution providing a convenient and efficient setting for sexual gratification and procreation. Of course it is, but there are other assets — companionship, sharing of housework, mutual caretaking, emotional support, and freedom for intimacy and the expression of feelings. When these rewards have been experienced for a near lifetime, they add up to a learned reliance on a partner, an interdependence which is the essence of a dyadic relationship.

But marriage is not the only social form that can provide the necessary conditions for the satisfaction of interpersonal needs. Single persons of the same sex can pair up to form households, with or without sexual intimacy. Parent and child may also create a dyad. A variety of alternatives to marriage are possible, and indeed the only limit to these relationships is set by their function — to provide reciprocal support and satisfaction of mutual needs for help and companionship.

Living arrangements usually reflect the presence of a supportive relationship. However, many older people who live alone have meaningful interpersonal relationships. Some have relatives and friends living elsewhere with whom they maintain contact by visits, telephone, or mail. While the actual interactive behavior of such partners will necessarily differ from that of housemates, the affective quality may be much the same (Chappell & Badger, 1989).

Such relationships usually go beyond a simple pairing connection such as marriage and involve a number of persons who constitute a network of partners. Couples as well as individuals are usually embedded in small groups of people who rely on one another for the kinds of rewards — satisfactions — we have mentioned above. Few individuals are without network membership (Antonucci, 1990), and these networks tend to be fairly stable (Costa, Zonderman, & Mc-

Crae, 1985; Field & Minkler, 1988; Wellman & Hall, 1986). Social networks and associated social support have been extensively studied in aging, because of their associations with both physical and psychological well-being (Antonucci & Jackson, 1987; Cutrona, Russell, & Rose, 1986; Holahan & Holahan, 1987; House, Landis, & Umberson, 1988; Krause, 1986a; Krause, Liang, & Yatomi, 1989; Lowenthal & Robinson, 1976; Norris & Murrell, 1990).

This chapter describes such supporting relationships in the Terman group's later maturity, beginning with current marital status. We will then consider living arrangements and support by children, siblings, and friends. All these matters will illustrate the increasingly tenuous structure of dyads, especially marriage, that stems from the ever-more-likely loss of partners through death.

Current Marital Status

The subjects reported their current marital status on each of the four follow-up questionnaires between 1972 and 1986, together with a description of any changes since their previous report. Table 7.1 shows how many reported each status in the latest report. Comparisons of the marital statuses of the members of the later-maturity group who were aged 65–74 in 1986 with the general population show that there were proportionately more married men in the group and fewer of the other statuses than in the general population (U.S. Bureau of the Census, 1988). More of the women were single or divorced, and fewer were married or widowed, than in the general population of women. The most dramatic difference is in the divorced category for women, where 14.6 percent of the later-maturity group were divorced in 1986, compared with 5.5 percent in the general population. The higher proportion of single women in our sample is consistent with the greater tendency for educated women to remain single (Ward, 1979). The lower rates of widowhood among both the men and the women are consistent with data from other samples showing lower rates of widowhood with individuals of higher socioeconomic status (Palmore, 1981).

The gender differences in marital status are enormous. Nearly twice as many men as women were still married — not necessarily to the same partner — and four times as many women as men were widowed and now unmarried. Nearly three times as many women remained unmarried after divorces. These gender differences in marital status are consistent with patterns in the general population, which are thought to be due to differences in the death rates of men and women, the tendency for women to marry men older than themselves, and the greater likelihood of remarriage among men (Bengtson, Rosenthal, & Burton, 1990; Palmore, 1981).

Since the subjects varied in age at the time of responding and not all of them returned all four questionnaires, the data we report on current marital status are based on responses made at quite a range of ages, though 90 percent of the subjects were between 65 and 85 years old at the time we secured the latest information. A table of the numbers and percentages of the subjects who re-

TABLE 7.1
*Current Marital Status of Later-Maturity Group
at Latest Report*

Marital status (at latest report)	Men		Women	
	N	Pct.	N	Pct.
Single	20	3.5%	38	7.7%
Married	474	83.3	224	45.3
Separated	3	0.5	2	0.4
Divorced	28	4.9	61	12.3
Widowed	44	7.7	169	34.2
Total respondents	569		494	
Significance (*p*) by chi-square		.01		

SOURCE: Questionnaires in 1972, 1977, 1982, and 1986.

ported each marital status by half-decade age-groups showed no noteworthy departures from the pattern in Table 7.1.

In another decade there will be more deaths of spouses and possibly an occasional divorce or separation. As the Terman group have reached later maturity they have more and more returned to the single status from which they started as adolescents and young adults. This was twice as frequent among the women as among the men.

Living Arrangements

Household Composition

In later maturity there was a substantial reduction in number of household living-partners or housemates. Table 7.2 shows the numbers and proportions of our later-maturity group who were living alone, or with various combinations of household members at latest report. These data were obtained in the last three follow-ups only (1977–86); hence the number of cases is reduced by post-1972 attrition. The gender differences were very great. Only 12 percent of the men were living alone, while 46 percent of the women were. The main alternative was two-person households, for which the respective values were 80 and 48 percent. (These percentages are not shown separately in the table.) Most of these two-person households consisted of subject and spouse, but not all, and by no means equally for the two sexes. In 1977, for example, five women and one man were living with a "friend of the opposite sex." Very few had a parent or person of an older generation living with them. Somewhat more had children and/or grandchildren in the house, but not nearly as many as had had them in their younger years. Only three women and one man had as yet employed a nurse, caretaker, or companion. It is clear that, in later maturity, the two-person household was the predominant pattern for men, but it applied to only about half the women.

Presenting the data cumulatively at latest report obscures an important fact.

Over the decade from 1977 to 1986 there was a steady decrease in two-person households. The following tabulation illustrates change in household composition:

	1977		1982		1986	
	Men Pct.	Women Pct.	Men Pct.	Women Pct.	Men Pct.	Women Pct.
Living alone	8	32	11	39	12	47
With spouse	81	56	79	51	79	42

There was only a small reduction in the percentage of men living with spouses, but the percentage of women doing so fell dramatically. A trend in the opposite direction occurred in the percentages living alone.

The percentage of Terman men living with their spouses in 1986 is comparable with that in the general male population aged 65 and older (U.S. Bureau of the Census, 1988). However, the percentage of Terman women living with spouses or with other family members was smaller than among older women in the general population in 1986, because they were less likely to marry or have children than were others in their cohort, and because there were more divorced women in the later-maturity sample than in the general population of similar ages. The Terman women were more likely than the men to be living with nonfamily members. Like the general population of this age, rather than living with their families, they preferred to preserve their independence. This was particularly true of the women, who were more likely to be faced with this issue by the death of a spouse.

Housing

At latest report, the great majority of the subjects were living in single-family housing (93 percent of the men and 88 percent of the women). This included single houses, duplexes, apartments, and condominiums. Another 3 percent of

TABLE 7.2
*Composition of Households of Later-Maturity Group
at Latest Report*

Composition of household (at latest report)	Men		Women	
	N	Pct.	N	Pct.
Living alone	61	12.2%	210	45.7%
With spouse only	389	77.6	196	42.6
Spouse and child(ren)	24	4.8	9	2.0
With child(ren)	14	2.8	12	2.6
Other relatives	3	0.6	9	2.0
Non-family persons	10	2.0	22	4.8
Institution	0	0.0	2	0.4
Total respondents	501		460	
Significance (*p*) of sex difference, by chi-square		.01		

SOURCE: 1977, 1982, and 1986 questionnaires.

each sex were living in mobile homes and about the same percentage in retirement homes. Only one man and five women had yet gone into nursing homes.

Satisfaction

Not all of the subjects had found a fully satisfying living arrangement. In 1977 and 1982 we asked questions about satisfaction, expected changes, recent changes, and reasons for change (1977, Questions 6–8; 1982, Questions 6–8). More than 80 percent of the group reported themselves, in 1977, to be in the top two categories of a 5-point scale of satisfaction, but most of the remainder were unhappy or dissatisfied. This satisfaction measure cumulates feelings about number of housemates, relationships with them, and housing style, but it permits us to examine the reasons for dissatisfaction and what people planned to do about it. As there were no significant gender differences in these matters we will not report the findings separately by sex.

In general, those who were well satisfied with their arrangements had no plans for change in the near future, 83 percent saying they did not expect any changes in the next five years. The point-biserial correlation between the 5-point scale of satisfaction and the intention to change was .44 for the men and .35 for the women. Of those who did plan a change, 82 percent intended to move into a smaller or more convenient residence or a more congenial neighborhood. The other 18 percent were divided equally in their planning for (1) a change of housemates, (2) a move to be nearer their children, and (3) a move into a retirement home. None spoke of the need to employ a caretaker or to enter a nursing home.

By 1982, only about half of those who had planned a change had actually made one. Those who changed were about equally divided among the three categories of change mentioned above. The coding of responses to these questions was based partly on motivation and partly on objective characteristics, however, and we cannot be too sure of the accuracy of every interpretation. The fact of change was coded accurately enough, but the not-always-certain reasons force us to report the proportions only as approximations.

Expectancy

It is not surprising that some people who did not plan to change their living arrangements actually did so, and that about half those who intended to change did not do so. According to one interpretation of expectancy theory (Sears, 1981), the subjects who did not expect to change should have had less satisfaction after their change than those who expected a change. The reasoning is simply that expectation of change offers an opportunity for the preparatory rehearsal of new activities and responses to new arrangements while an unexpected change produces frustration of accustomed responses without opportunity for replacing them with new and adaptive behavior.

A test of this hypothesis is presented in Table 7.3. The critical comparison is between the mean 1982 satisfaction ratings for (1) those subjects who had not

TABLE 7.3

Satisfaction with Living Arrangements in 1982 of Members of Later-Maturity Group by Comparison Groups of Planned Change in 1977 and Actual Change by 1986

| | Satisfaction (1982) | | | | | |
| | Men | | | Women | | |
Comparison groups	N	Mean	S.D.	N	Mean	S.D.
1977–no plans for change; 1982–no change reported	237	8.15	.99	212	7.90	1.28
1977–no plans for change; 1982–some change reported	50	6.84	1.95	65	7.44	1.71
1977–planned a change; 1982–no change reported	37	7.43	1.34	29	7.41	1.05
1977–planned a change; 1982–some change reported	29	7.52	1.35	26	7.38	1.94

SOURCE: 1977 and 1982 questionnaires.

planned a change in living arrangements at the time of the 1977 follow-up but nevertheless did make one before 1982, and (2) those who did so plan and did make the change. These 1982 means are given in the second and fourth rows of the table. Among the men, the former experience was associated with slightly lower satisfaction ratings than the latter, though the difference was not statistically significant. Among the women, the two ratings were almost identical.

Since 1977 and 1982 ratings of satisfaction were correlated (rs of .44 for men and .35 for women), a more stringent test would control for initial level of satisfaction. An analysis of covariance was conducted for each sex separately, controlling for satisfaction in 1977, and comparing the same groups (those who had had no plans for change but experienced change, and those who had planned for change, and experienced it). This analysis was significant for men ($p < .05$), but not for women. It appears that expectation of change was important for the satisfaction of men five years later, but it was not important for women. Perhaps men are accustomed to controlling their lives and are not satisfied when things do not turn out as they plan. Women may be more accustomed to making accommodations to changing life circumstances throughout their lives, and may be better able to adapt to unexpected occurrences.

Networks

People reach later maturity with a variety of resources for securing the kinds of dyadic satisfactions mentioned earlier (Adams & Blieszner, 1989; Antonucci, 1990; Bengtson, Rosenthal, & Burton, 1990; Cicirelli, 1989; Depner & Ingersoll-Dayton, 1988; Larson, Mannell, & Zuzanek, 1986). One such resource is living arrangements. As we have seen, many of our women subjects and a few of the men were living alone. Parents or other supportive members of the older generation were no longer available. There remained children, grandchildren, siblings, and friends of the older person's own generation. The ways and the extent to which these partners are affiliated with our subjects were indicated by the answers to a number of questions asked in 1977 (Questions 9–13, 41), 1982 (Questions 9a–10b, 16–17), and 1986 (Questions 7–10, 34).

Resources

Since all of our information about networks comes from these last three follow-ups, we will exclude those subjects in the later-maturity group who left the study after 1972. This leaves 504 men and 460 women who answered at least one of the questionnaires from 1977 through 1986.

Siblings. In 1977 the average number of living siblings was 1.30 for men and 1.24 for women. One hundred twenty-five of the men (29 percent) and 120 of the women (31 percent) were only children, or had no living sibling; if the only children are excluded, these averages are 1.84 and 1.81 respectively. Siblings were far from being a universal source of comradeship and support, and the amount available to the later-maturity group is less than that available in the general population of similar age. The 1980 U.S. Census reported an average of 2.52 siblings for the comparable cohort.

Children. In 1977 the men in the later-maturity group reported that they had raised an average of 2.2 children (including their own children, their stepchildren, and their adopted children). The women averaged 1.8 children. This difference is significant ($p < .05$ by t-test) and is partly a result of the greater nonresponse by single men, and the more frequent remarriage of men, with the ensuing increase in the number of stepchildren. In 1977, 15 percent of the men reported having raised no children and 23 percent of the women reported having raised none. Slightly less than half of both the men and the women had raised one or two children, but 37 percent of the men had raised from three to eight, while only 28 percent of the women had raised that many.

If we exclude the subjects who had raised no children the men still had significantly more on average than the women. The average numbers were 2.6 for men and 2.4 for women ($p < .01$).

Communication

There were five measures of the amount of communication between the subjects and various people important to them. The first four were obtained in 1977 (Questions 9–13), and refer to the frequency of telephoning and correspondence with their children and siblings. The fifth was from a 1982 query (Questions 9a–9b) about the number of hours of close personal interaction, with friends or others.

There was no difference in the frequency with which men and women saw or had had telephone conversations with their children, but the women significantly more often talked with siblings ($p < .05$). Men, however, corresponded with their children more frequently than did women, while women were in more frequent written communication with siblings than the men ($p < .05$). As a minor generalization, it can be said that the women were more communicative

TABLE 7.4
Amount of Interaction of Later-Maturity Group with Others
and Degree of Satisfaction with That Amount
by Current Marital Status (1982)

| | Men | | | Women | | |
Marital Status	N	Interaction mean	Satisfaction mean	N	Interaction mean	Satisfaction mean
Always single	13	4.77	5.23	32	6.78	5.69
Married	353	6.12	5.35	208	6.85	5.46
Divorced/separated	16	6.00	5.88	38	5.76	5.79
Widowed	27	6.56	5.78	117	6.47	5.56
Total respondents	409			395		
Significance of difference (p) among marital groups by analysis of variance		.10	.05		.01	n.s.

SOURCE: Marital status from latest report in 1972, 1977, 1982, or 1986 questionnaires. Interaction and satisfaction from 1986 questionnaires.

NOTE: Both interaction and satisfaction were measured on 9-point scale. On the satisfaction scale, "5" represents "fully satisfied with present amount," lower scores indicating a preference for less interaction and higher scores a preference for more interaction.

with siblings than men, by either method, while men wrote more to their children than women did; women talked more to their children than men did.

The scales used for securing these estimates were not suitable for exact measurement of just how often communication occurred, but the median frequency for phoning children was at a substantially shorter time interval (once a week) than for written correspondence (less than once a month). Communication with siblings by either method was less frequent than with children.

In 1982 the subjects were asked to indicate the extent to which they interact with others (Question 9). The question was asked on a 5-point linear scale, which was converted to a 9-point scale. This interaction measure of communication did, however, show very substantial gender differences in both behavior and degree of satisfaction. Such gender differences in social networks have been well documented (see Antonucci & Akiyama, 1987; Huyck, 1990; Rossi, 1985; Wright, 1989). The women in the later-maturity group reported a mean amount of interaction of 6.63 on the 9-point scale, but the men's mean was 6.03 ($p < .01$ by t-test). The subjects' satisfaction with the amount of interaction they had was measured on a 5-point linear rating scale converted to a 9-point scale, with the midpoint — 5 — representing full satisfaction with present amount; lower scores indicated a preference for less interaction and higher scores a preference for more. Both the men and women were quite satisfied, the women being slightly more desirous of more interaction (means of 5.39 and 5.54, respectively; $p < .10$ by t-test).

The mean differences among the marital status subgroups are shown in Table 7.4. The "always single" men had by far the lowest interaction but the "always single" women had the second highest amount, almost tying with the married women. This difference corresponds well with many other differences between the never-married men and women which were reported in Chapter 6. It is worth noting, however, that the never-married men were the most satisfied with the amount of interaction they had. In the years of later maturity, they appear to have found an appropriate level of interaction with others and to be in less need of a network than the divorced and widowed men, who also lack a marital companion. Similar differences in interaction patterns and associated satisfaction have been found with other samples (see Babchuck, 1978–79; Braito & Anderson, 1983; Depner & Ingersoll-Dayton, 1988; Keith, 1989; Kohen, 1983; Longino & Lipman, 1981; Reisman, 1988; Ward, 1979).

Intimacy and Companionship

The communication and interaction variables provide a measure of a network's existence, but not of its quality. Qualitative dimensions of social support have been shown to be important for well-being in the elderly (Carstensen, 1987; Cutrona, Russell, & Rose, 1986; Fredrickson & Carstensen, 1990; Holahan & Holahan, 1987; Liang, Dvorkin, Kahana, & Mazian, 1980; Lowenthal & Haven, 1968; Strain & Chappell, 1982; Ward, Sherman, & LaGory, 1984). In 1986, two questions concerned this matter. We asked, separately for family and friends, how many provided opportunities for intimate exchange of feelings, how many just companionship, and how many were casual relationships (Questions 7–10); for family, there was also a fourth category of "indifference or hostility, with active avoidance." Separate rating scales asked how satisfying these amounts of intimacy and companionship were.

The question about friends specified "your 10 best friends." The subjects answered in terms of the reality of their lives rather than the demands of our question. Some did not have 10 "best friends" and others had more. We placed no limit on the number of family members to be considered, but the subjects varied considerably in the number they gave. The following tabulation shows separately the baseline numbers the men and the women used for answering the questions.

	Men		Women	
	Mean	S.D.	Mean	S.D.
Number of friends	8.20	4.63	8.72	7.05
Number of family	8.42	7.45	8.23	9.04

The means of the sexes did not differ significantly, but the variation as measured by the standard deviations, both between men and women and among individuals of both sexes, make it difficult to use the reported figures in their raw form. Instead, for other comparisons, we have used a coarser and simpler measure, namely, whether none or one (or more) friends or family were mentioned in connection with each degree of intimacy. This permits us to report the percentages of subjects who did or did not have persons with whom they had each type of relationship. Thus various groups can be characterized by percentages of

TABLE 7.5
*Intimacy of Relationships of Later-Maturity Group
with Friends and Family Members (1986)*

Relationship	Percent of men	Percent of women	p
Friends			
Intimate	46.6%	71.0%	.01
Companion	78.7	86.2	.05
Casual	64.3	50.3	.01
Family members			
Intimate	80.7	83.6	n.s.
Companion	70.7	70.0	n.s.
Casual	57.6	47.0	.01
Indifferent/hostile	13.9	8.8	.05
Total respondents	367	334	

SOURCE: 1986 questionnaire.
NOTE: *p* by chi-square.

positive responses rather than by average of figures stemming from differing baselines.

It is clear from the values in Table 7.5 that the men were considerably less likely to have intimate relationships with friends. Even companionship was a little less common for them. Their friendships in later maturity were significantly more likely to be casual. This reserve, or withholding of responsiveness, did not apply to family relationships, however; they were as likely as the women to have at least one family member with whom they could feel intimate, and another (or more) with whom they could be companionable. The men were clearly more likely than the women to have relationships limited to casual interaction. Finally, perhaps a kind of end-point to the men's more isolated affective lives, they were a little more likely than the women to feel indifferent, avoidant, and even hostile toward some of their family members.

These gender differences are displayed even more sharply in the combination of friend and family relationships. Almost twice as many men as women had no person with whom they had an intimate relationship (13.8 percent to 7.3 percent, $p < .01$). At the other end of the dimension, significantly more men have casual relationships with someone, either a friend or family member (79.9 percent and 67.9 percent respectively, $p < .01$).

Intimacy and marital status. While these gender differences are impressive, and seem to suggest that men are deprived — or deprive themselves — of intimacy with others, the fact is that much depends on their marital status. Not all men differ as much from women as the gross figures seem to show. Without presenting a maddening maze of comparisons in tabular form, the salient points can be summarized below:

1. Most of the gender difference in intimacy was produced by men and women not currently married; this includes the never-married, the divorced, and the widowed. All these three groups of men had many fewer intimates among

either friends or family members than did the women of those statuses. The differences were highly significant in all but one instance — frequency of family intimates among the divorced men and women.

It is to be remembered that those men and women who had divorced and widowed status in later maturity had quite different marital histories, on the average. The men had mostly been divorced or widowed recently, while the women had been divorced or widowed for a much longer time, and had an opportunity to develop a new life-style more similar to the "always single" women. These differences were discussed in Chapter 5 in connection with occupational histories.

2. There was a small but not statistically significant gender difference in the number of married men and women who had an intimate friend (44.7 percent and 56.3 percent respectively); there was almost no difference in the number who had an intimate family member (84.2 percent and 90.8 percent respectively). Presumably the spouse serves in this role for both sexes.

3. Nonetheless all four kinds of men were approximately twice as likely as women to report indifferent or hostile family relationships. The divorced men (of whom there are only 16) were three times as likely as divorced women (N=40) to have someone they avoid. Again we must remember the longer time the women had to adapt to a new life situation.

Satisfaction with degree of intimacy. Satisfaction with amount of intimacy and companionship was assessed by two 9-point rating scales (1986, Questions 8, 10). A mid-point rating of "5" indicated full satisfaction with present amount of interaction; a lower rating meant the person would like less interaction and a higher rating meant a desire for more. The following tabulation shows the averages and standard deviations for both men and women in respect to their feelings concerning both friends and family members.

	Men			Women		
	N	Mean	S.D.	N	Mean	S.D.
Friends	370	5.80	1.00	321	5.92	1.15
Family members	367	5.63	0.87	313	5.85	1.11

Both sexes were reasonably close to full satisfaction with the amount and kinds of interaction they had with both friends and family members. The women, however, wanted a little more than did the men, significantly so in the case of family members ($p < .01$). The small size of the standard deviations shows that there was little variation in these feelings among the subjects of either sex. This relative unanimity of desire for just a little more interaction was reflected in the average ratings by the four marital statuses of each sex; they ranged from 5.50 to 6.13 and none of the differences between statuses approached significance.

Disappointments, Bereavements, and Happiness

A network plays a role in both good and bad experiences. The role is likely to be a little different, however. The good things that happen often involve other

TABLE 7.6

*Aspects of Life Causing Disappointment and Bereavement
for Later-Maturity Group Reported in 1940 and 1986*

	Men		Women	
Aspects of life	1940 Pct.	1986 Pct.	1940 Pct.	1986 Pct.
Marital difficulties	8.3%	4.5%	12.2%	6.2%
Occupational situation	6.8	2.4	7.4	1.8
Educational problems	3.8	0.0	2.6	1.2
Financial difficulties	1.7	2.6	2.2	0.9
Own health problems	0.5	10.5	1.5	1.8
Others' health	1.0	0.0	2.0	0.0
Children's problems	0.0	0.5	0.4	1.2
Deaths	7.7	27.4	14.4	48.4
Spouse or lover	0.7	7.4	1.6	15.9
Child	0.5	0.8	0.7	2.1
Parents	5.2	0.8	9.6	2.9
Siblings	1.2	3.7	1.3	8.0
Other relatives	0.2	1.8	1.3	3.5
Friends	0.0	12.9	0.0	15.9
None reported	66.7	58.9	48.8	42.5
Total respondents	601	380	457	339

SOURCE: 1940 and 1986 questionnaires.
NOTE: Data for 1940 from whole Terman group at that time. Data for 1986 from later-maturity group. Percentages may add to over 100 because up to two aspects mentioned by a respondent were counted in 1940 and up to three aspects mentioned in 1986. The percentages in column 3 add to less than 100 because not all aspects mentioned were included in the table.

people, the members of the network, and the happy event may be either a product of continuing interaction (e.g., a happy marriage) or a terminal situation (e.g., a satisfactory arrangement for retirement). The network may be similarly involved in the bad happenings (e.g., death of a loved one). It has another function that is more frequently noted in sad circumstances than happy ones; it serves as an alleviating and therapeutic agent after the event has occurred. It is this latter function — rarely relevant to happy events — that is so important in later maturity because the problem of bereavement is so pervasive.

The reason for emphasis upon the supportive role of the network can be easily seen in Table 7.6, which shows the percentage of men and women who reported various sources of disappointment or bereavement in their 1940 and 1986 questionnaires. We have used data from the full Terman sample in 1940 in order to maximize the amount of data. The difference between 1940 and 1986 in frequency of death as a cause is enormous. Approximately four times as many of the people experienced such loss in later maturity as did in their young adulthood. The difference in probable severity of loss is even more telling when we examine the persons who died. In young adulthood, parents were much more frequently lost, while in later maturity, spouses and friends were the chief ones who died. The loss of parents in young adulthood is likely to be less traumatic than the loss of spouses at older ages.

TABLE 7.7
*Aspects of Life Causing Disappointment or Happiness
for Later-Maturity Group Reported in 1982*

	Men		Women	
Aspect of life	Disappointment Pct.	Happiness Pct.	Disappointment Pct.	Happiness Pct.
Marriage	5.8%	50.2%	8.2%	35.2%
Occupation	3.6	25.2	2.3	14.6
Education	0.0	0.7	0.0	1.5
Finances	2.6	20.9	1.3	17.8
Health (own)	7.2	23.1	8.5	23.4
Death	21.2	0.0	43.2	0.0
Children	0.0	27.9	1.0	42.5
Recreation	0.0	9.1	0.5	8.0
Travel	0.5	6.2	0.5	11.3
Character (own)	4.1	27.9	5.5	26.6
Living arrangements	1.2	4.1	0.8	9.0
Friends; social activities	2.9	13.7	6.3	30.4
Political situation	1.0	0.0	0.5	0.0
Religion	0.0	3.1	0.0	8.0
None mentioned	63.9	7.5	48.2	5.8
Total respondents	416		398	

SOURCE: 1982 questionnaire.
NOTE: Percentages add to over 100 because some respondents gave more than one response.

The percentage of men who did not report any disappointments was higher in both periods than the percentage of women. For both sexes, there were more reports in the later years than the earlier. The figures in Table 7.6 add to over 100 percent because up to two aspects mentioned by a respondent were recorded in 1940 and up to three in 1986. (Several minor causes of disappointment have been omitted to save space; none involved more than two or three persons.)

The sex difference is of little consequence, being largely caused by the greater frequency of deaths of women subjects' spouses. Other deaths — children, siblings, friends — were also more frequently reported by women, but it was death of spouse that provided the biggest difference. We can only speculate as to why women report more disappointments, a fact replicated in the 1982 questionnaire, results of which will be summarized below. We suggest, on the basis of the other communication and interaction evidence cited earlier, that women's networks were broader than men's. They had more friends, were noticing of and interactive with more siblings, and retained more intimate contact with children. Therefore they had more people in their lives who could cause them both happiness and disappointment, and more people who can die and leave them bereft. Other authors have noted that women's more extensive networks carry costs in addition to their benefits (Antonucci & Akiyama, 1988; Brody, Kleban, Johnsen, Hoffman, & Schoonover, 1987; Kessler, McLeod, & Wethington, 1985).

In 1982, we asked about both disappointments (Question 16) and happiness (Question 17). Table 7.7 shows a list of causes of both similar to the list in Table

7.6, but without the details of who died. (Deaths of friends, spouses, children are included only in the category "death," not in "marriage," "friends," or "children.") Less than 10 percent of either sex failed to mention some source of happiness, and the proportions for disappointments were about the same as they had been 42 years earlier and still would be four years later—about half the women and two-thirds of the men.

The table summarizes the causes of joy and sorrow in gifted older people. By 1982, with their ages mostly in the sixties and seventies, marriage, occupation (sometimes its continuation, a few times its relinquishment), finances, health, children, the person's own character and accomplishments, and friendships were prominent causes of happiness and rarely mentioned as disappointments. Recreation, travel, and religion were much less frequently mentioned, and education hardly at all. Only death and the political situation were no sources of happiness for anyone.

A higher percentage of men than of women mentioned marriage and occupation as sources of happiness, but there were no other important gender differences in sources of happiness. The greater mortality of husbands than of wives was responsible for the former difference, and the less frequent occupational involvement of women for the latter. The role of religion was small but not negligible, as always with this group. We shall consider this matter, and its earlier manifestations, in Chapter 9, which is devoted to goals and ideals.

Summary

The Terman men and women differed markedly in current marital status in later maturity. Nearly twice as many men as women were still married (83 percent as compared with 45 percent); less than 10 percent of men were unmarried widowers, as compared with one-third of women who were widows. Nearly three times as many women as men remained unmarried after divorce; and more than four times as many women as men remained unmarried after being widowed. Similarly, almost four times as many women as men were living alone. The great majority of the subjects were living in single family housing at the latest report, and more than 80 percent reported that they were satisfied with their living arrangements in 1977.

The men and women differed in later maturity in amount of interaction with other people, the women reporting more interaction. Both men and women were quite satisfied with the amount of interaction, but on average, women were slightly more desirous than men of more interaction. The men and women also differed in the types of relationships they had with friends and family. The women were more likely to have intimate or companionship relationships with friends, and less likely to have casual friendships. The men were as likely as women to have intimate or companionship relationships with family, but more likely than women to have casual or indifferent or hostile family relationships. Most of the gender difference in intimacy was produced by men and women not currently married, including the never-married, the divorced, and the widowed. All three of these groups of men had many fewer intimate relationships with either friends or family members than did the women of the same statuses.

There was no difference in the frequency with which the men and women had telephone conversations with their children, but the women talked with siblings more frequently. Men, on the other hand, corresponded with their children more frequently than did women, while women were in more frequent written communication with siblings. There was a small gender difference in the number of married men and women who had an intimate friend (women being higher), but almost no difference in the number who had an intimate family member. More important, in 1986, both sexes were reasonably close to full satisfaction with the amount and kinds of interaction they had with both friends and family members.

In both 1940 and later maturity, fewer of the men than the women reported disappointments. The gender difference in disappointments in later maturity is largely due to spousal deaths. A higher percentage of men than women mentioned marriage and occupation as sources of happiness, but there were no other important sex differences in sources of happiness. The greater mortality of husbands than of wives is responsible for the former, and the less frequent occupational involvement of women for the latter.

In light of the literature suggesting that social network membership makes an important contribution to both physical and psychological well-being in aging (see Antonnuci, 1990), the prospects of the later-maturity group for successful aging seem auspicious. Although the women desired slightly more social interaction they were quite close to full satisfaction with the amount they had. Despite the differences in patterns of interaction by sex and by marital status, a generally high level of satisfaction held for all marital status subgroups. Many members of the sample had extensive social networks, but more importantly, almost all had attained at least a threshold level of social functioning necessary for positive adaptation in aging.

PART IV

Personal Involvements

8

Interests and Activities

Leisure and avocational activities become increasingly important in the later years. They can provide a source of meaning in their own right; and, to the extent that they involve shared interests and the demonstration of competencies, they can create a sense of belonging and self-worth. In addition, activities that challenge the older person can help maintain established knowledge and competencies. Also, activities in aging compensate for some of the loss, with retirement, of positive aspects of interactions with others in the work setting (DeCarlo, 1974; Kelly, Steinkamp, & Kelly, 1987; Lawton, 1985; Lawton, Moss, & Fulcomer, 1986–87; Palmore, 1981).

Individuals commonly look forward to their aging years as a time to pursue new interests. In reality, there is remarkable stability in the kinds of activities pursued across the life cycle, especially from middle age onward (Atchley, 1988; Bosse & Ekerdt, 1981; Lawton, 1985). Individuals are thus confronted with the challenge of developing, at least by middle age, a set of interests and competencies that they can continue into their later years. This is particularly the case for those whose lifelong occupations do not lend themselves to part-time or voluntary participation after formal retirement.

Laying the foundation for meaningful nonvocational activity in aging is complicated by the ambivalence in our culture concerning leisure. In ancient cultures, leisure — frequently involving cultural pursuits — was valued as a source of fulfillment in life. In our contemporary work-oriented culture, leisure is often disparaged as simply nonwork. This attitude is reinforced by the fact that many popular leisure activities require little intellectual or physical effort. This ambivalence toward leisure has the potential for leaving older persons unprepared to meet the need for creating structure and meaning in their lives after they leave work (Gordon, Gaitz, & Scott, 1976; Troll, 1982).

Both the aging process itself, and the social conditions surrounding aging, can influence the kinds of activities that people pursue. Declining health and energy, decreasing financial resources, and de facto age-segregation in our culture, all limit the activities pursued by some of the elderly. Activities that make strong physical demands are dropped in favor of those that do not. Activities that require leaving the home are replaced by inside activities, and those with a social orientation are replaced by more solitary ones. However, these declines are far from inevitable, and depend to a great extent on the individual characteristics and life situation of the aging person (Atchley, 1988; Burrus-Bammel & Bammel, 1985; Gordon, Gaitz, & Scott, 1976; Tinsley et al., 1987).

Earlier volumes reporting on the Terman longitudinal study have described the avocational interests and activities of the Terman subjects from childhood to middle age. Far from the stereotype of the gifted as one-sided in abilities and interests (current when Terman began this study in the early 1920's), the subjects have demonstrated a breadth of interests and avocational activities. We are interested now in how these subjects have spent their time in their later years, especially when their involvement in formal work roles is reduced. This chapter looks at the activities of the subjects during later maturity, using reports from 1977, 1982, and 1986. In addition, we will use data from earlier reports to investigate continuity in activity participation over the life cycle.

Activities in 1977

In an item in the 1977 questionnaire, subjects were asked about their participation in income-producing work, and were offered five response options ranging from "none" to "essentially full time." About a third of the 1977 male respondents were working full time and about a third had no paid work at all in 1977; only 15 percent of women were working full time and two-thirds had no paid employment. (Women who had no income-producing work after age 50 [150 women] are included in the "none" category.) The totals would not be greatly altered by counting time spent in continued unpaid vocational activity; only 47 (14 percent) of the men and 21 (7 percent) of the women reported such activity half-time or more.

In 1977, the average age of the group was 67, and the retirement process was well under way. With the reduction in work for pay, the subjects had more time for other activities. Lifetime homemakers whose children had long left home were free for other activities.

To explore the subjects' activity level in later maturity, we asked them in 1977 (Question 37) about their participation in 33 activities. Response alternatives were: (1) "Never," (2) "Seldom," (3) "Occasionally," and (4) "Frequently." In 1977, the count of activities the individual engaged in occasionally or frequently ranged from 1 to 29. The men reported an average of 17 activities at the occasional or frequent level, and the women reported participation at these levels in an average of 17.7 activities. These data are consistent with earlier descriptions of the Terman men and women as an active group, with diverse interests. The subjects' activity level compared quite favorably with that of the general population. For example, Peppers (1976) reported an average number of 12 activities by a heterogeneous sample of men after retirement.

The individuals in the later-maturity group varied widely in the types of activities they reported. To facilitate our discussion of the kinds of activities they engaged in, we have formed five scales, after conducting factor and item analysis, and considering item content. The scales and their items are presented in Table 8.1. The first scale, Intellectual Activities, includes serious reading, self-improvement in knowledge or skills, and unpaid professional or technical work. The Cultural Activities scale covers both receptive and productive cultural and artistic pursuits. The Social Activities scale covers informal socializing and entertaining, as well as several kinds of community service. The Active Recreational Activities scale includes nine diverse activities that require leaving the home, physical exertion, skill, or psychological investment. The last scale, Passive Recreational Activities, consists of light reading, watching TV, and solitary games and puzzles.

Table 8.1 also presents item and scale means for the men and women. In addition, the nominal significance of the sex difference is indicated. The scale score is the average of the scores on the items in the scale. Scale scores are computed only for those subjects who responded to all the items in the scale. Thus, the scale scores are sometimes based on markedly reduced Ns in comparison with the total N responding to this section of the questionnaire.

The intellectual activities most favored in the group in later maturity were serious reading and increasing knowledge or skill by independent study. These ratings averaged near 3, "Occasionally," on our four-point scale. Men read professional publications and did unpaid professional or technical work more than women. Women were more likely than men to read nonfiction and to attend continuing education classes. It should be noted that there was no difference between the men and women on the scale score, because their scores were balanced by an emphasis on different kinds of intellectual activities.

The group tended toward the two receptive cultural activities in later maturity. At least occasionally, most subjects listened to recorded music and attended cultural events. Women participated in all four of the cultural activities more frequently than the men. Social interaction most often consisted of informal contact with friends, neighbors, and relatives, and entertaining. Our subjects also engaged in community service, particularly in helping friends or neighbors. The women were more active socially than the men.

The Active Recreation items are more diverse than items in the other scales. Among them, the most popular activities were travel, physical self-improvement, such as exercise or dieting, noncompetitive physical activity, hobbies, and home repairs (for men). More than half the subjects participated in all of these activities

TABLE 8.1
Participation by Later-Maturity Group in 32 Activities in 1977

Activity	Men (N = 323–421)		Women (N = 247–380)	
	Mean	S.D.	Mean	S.D.
Intellectual activities				
Scale score	2.62	0.58	2.53	0.65
Reading: books (nonfiction)	3.25	0.75	3.42[b]	0.76
Reading: avocational publications	2.83	1.02	2.73	1.03
Reading: professional publications	3.07[b]	1.06	2.35	1.13
Increasing knowledge or skill (independent study)	2.74	1.02	2.77	1.00
Continuing education (classes)	1.86	1.03	2.23[b]	1.17
Unpaid professional or technical work	2.04[b]	1.08	1.73	1.07
Cultural activities				
Scale score	1.97	0.44	2.21	0.60
Listening to recorded music	2.88	0.96	3.12[b]	0.95
Going to concerts, plays, lectures, museums, etc.	2.80	0.90	3.05[b]	0.87
Playing a musical instrument	1.40	0.86	1.70[b]	1.09
Playing or singing with a musical group	1.24	0.69	1.41[b]	0.91
Creative writing, painting, sculpture, dramatics	1.67	1.05	1.89[b]	1.18
Social activities				
Scale score	2.50	0.57	2.79[b]	0.57
Informal visiting with friends and neighbors	3.13	0.75	3.41[b]	0.69
Visiting and communicating with relatives	3.00	0.77	3.38[b]	0.78
Entertaining	2.84	0.78	2.99[b]	0.77
Community service: helping friends and neighbors	2.41	0.87	2.82[b]	0.90
Community service: with a group	2.16	1.12	2.36[a]	1.15
Community service: work done at home	1.62	0.77	1.88[b]	0.99
Active Recreation				
Scale score	2.54[b]	0.46	2.42	0.46
Traveling	3.18	0.84	3.19	0.85
Attending movies	1.90	0.73	1.89	0.67
Attending sporting events	1.96[b]	0.87	1.64	0.77
Self improvement — physical (exercise, diet)	3.00	1.01	3.11	0.98
Noncompetitive physical activity	3.06[b]	1.03	2.80	1.11
Participating in competitive sports	1.74[b]	1.16	1.34	0.81
Competitive card or board games	2.26	1.12	2.42[a]	1.15
Working on hobbies (collections, gardening, handicrafts)	2.93	1.10	3.13[b]	1.01
Home repairs and maintenance	3.00[b]	0.99	2.47	1.10
Passive Recreation				
Scale score	3.03	0.46	3.14	0.47
Reading: newspapers, magazines	3.95[a]	0.29	3.89	0.37
Reading: books (fiction)	3.06	0.87	3.42[b]	0.78
Watching TV: educational, cultural	3.13	0.79	3.42[b]	0.75
Watching TV: entertainment	3.03	0.90	3.14	0.85
Watching TV: sporting events	3.08[b]	0.97	2.51	1.05
Solitary games or puzzles	2.02	1.06	2.53[b]	1.18

SOURCE: 1977 questionnaire.

NOTE: Raw scores varied from 1 to 4, as follows: 1 = Never; 2 = Seldom; 3 = Occasionally; 4 = Frequently. Significant differences indicated are between men and women.

[a] $p < .01$ by t-test.   [b] $p < .05$ by t-test.

at least occasionally. Men engaged in more sports-related activities and did more home repairs than women. Women, more than men, chose hobbies and competitive card or board games.

The responses to the first item on the Passive Recreation scale, reading newspapers and magazines, suggest that the members of the sample kept well-informed in their later years. Both averages were near 4 and this item had the lowest variability of all the activity items. Most subjects also read fictional books and watched various kinds of TV. Men watched sports on TV more than women, while women averaged higher on watching educational TV, reading fiction, and playing solitary games.

Many of the sex differences in activity patterns follow traditional gender roles. Other authors have found similar patterns with less advantaged samples (see Cutler & Hendricks, 1990; Gordon, Gaitz, & Scott, 1976; Lawton, Moss, & Fulcomer, 1986–87). The largest gender differences were in the social and cultural realms, where women's activity level was noticeably higher. In addition, men generally participated more in active recreational activities, while women's recreational activities were more passive. Men consistently favored both active and passive sports-related activities more than women — participation in sports and physical activities, attending sporting events, and watching sports on TV. Their interest in sports has been greater than women's throughout the years of the study (see Terman & Oden, 1959). As previously noted, men also engaged more in work-related activities — both unpaid professional or technical work and professional reading.

Comparison with Other Samples

How do the activity patterns of the Terman subjects compare with those of other samples? Traditional indicators of socioeconomic status, such as income, education, and occupational history, have been associated with more varied and intellectually or socially demanding leisure activities (Harris, 1975; Lawton, 1985; Lawton, Moss, & Fulcomer, 1986–87; Palmore, 1981; Schmitz-Scherzer, 1976). As an advantaged group, especially with regard to education, the Terman subjects might be expected to have varied and complex activity patterns.

Table 8.2 presents comparison data from the later-maturity group with six other studies. For this table, the later-maturity group has been restricted to those 65 years of age or older, to allow better comparisons with the other samples. The first column gives the percentage of the later-maturity group 65 years or older who participated in each activity occasionally or frequently, and the second column gives percentages of those participating frequently. Some items and associated percentages for the later-maturity group were computed by combining the subject's endorsement of several related items. For example, the entry for reading frequently represents frequent reading of at least one of the five types presented on the questionnaire — newspapers and magazines, fiction, nonfiction, avocational, and professional. Similar aggregates were created for watching TV, physical activity, and visiting with family and friends. The seven studies pre-

TABLE 8.2

Activity Participation in 1977 by Later-Maturity Group Aged 65 and Over Compared with Other Samples of Same Age

Activity	Later-Maturity Group		Other Samples					
	Occasional or frequent Pct.	Frequent Pct.	A Pct.	B Pct.	C Pct.	D Pct.	E Pct.	F Pct.
Reading	99%	98%	51%	87%	36%	37%	67%	66%
TV	93	78	78	96	36	28	69	76
Participation in sports/physical activity	68	46	—	—	3	10	—	—
Attending sporting events	20	3	—	—	—	2	—	—
Listening to music	70	37	16	—	—	2	—	—
Competitive card or board games	43	20	16	—	—	23	29	—
Travel	81	42	29	—	—	10	—	—
Travel: alone	—	—	—	—	—	—	—	47
Travel: group	—	—	—	—	—	—	—	66
Working on hobbies	71	47	—	—	—	—	—	—
Participating in recreational activities and hobbies	—	—	—	—	26	—	—	—
Arts, crafts, etc.	—	—	37	53	—	26	46	—
Gardening	—	—	27	—	39	9	49	57
Visiting and communicating with relatives	83	41	—	—	—	—	—	—
Visiting with immediate family	—	—	60	—	—	—	—	—
Informal visiting with friends and neighbors	86	43	—	—	47	—	—	78
Visiting with neighbors	—	—	32	—	—	—	—	—
Visiting relatives or acquaintances	—	—	32	—	—	—	—	—
Visiting family/friends	93	67	—	89	—	19	75	—
Community service: helping friends	56	18	—	—	—	—	—	—
Community service: group	42	20	—	—	—	—	—	—
Community service: at home	21	5	—	—	—	—	—	—
Participation in fraternal or community organizations	—	—	8	—	17	2	20	—
Volunteer work	—	—	—	19	8	3	—	—

SOURCE: 1977 questionnaire and the following studies: (A) German subjects age 65 and older, participated often or very often, 1971, reported by Schmitz-Scherzer, 1979; (B) National Longitudinal Survey, representative sample of retired men age 60–74 (N = 1599), participated in the last year, 1981 (Morgan, Parnes, & Less, 1985); (C) representative sample of men and women age 65 and older (N = 2797), spending "a lot of time" (Harris, 1975); (D) Men and women age 50 to 94, average age 71 (N = 245), activities mentioned as leisure (Roadburg, 1981); (E) Men and women age 65 and older (N = 540), top five recreational activities (McAvoy, 1979); (F) Retired men (N = 206), participating in activities (Peppers, 1976).

sented used different methods for their data collection, so that we would not expect identical results. Some, such as the Harris (1975) study for the National Council on Aging, asked the subjects to list activities on which they spend "a lot of time," and the Roadberg (1981) study asked subjects to list those activities they considered "leisure." We would expect that the frequencies would be smaller when the subjects were asked to provide the categories, rather than respond to a checklist. Other methodologies, such as that used by Morgan, Parnes, & Less (1985), who asked respondents to indicate if they had participated in a short list of activities in the past year, would tend to inflate frequencies.

Nonetheless, the differences between the activity patterns of the later-maturity group and the other samples are striking. Most noticeably, as expected, the subjects spent more time reading than the other samples. Almost all the subjects reported reading newspapers and magazines occasionally or frequently, while 60 to 78 percent reported the other four types of reading occasionally or frequently. More interesting, however, is the fact that the Terman group also had higher participation in other, nonintellectual areas, such as physical activity, visiting family and friends, and travel. Their contributions in terms of community service are also noteworthy. It is interesting to note, however, that most of them watch TV (more of them than in five of the other samples). Their TV watching was fairly evenly distributed across educational, entertainment, and sports, with 84 percent of the sample reporting frequently or occasionally watching educational TV, 76 percent entertainment, and 63 percent sports. The wide variety of activities pursued by the Terman group, as well as their high levels of participation in nonintellectual activities, again belie the early stereotypes of gifted individuals as one-sided in interests and abilities.

Changes in Activity Patterns

In addition to their present participation, we asked the subjects if they had recently taken up any of the activities, or if they had dropped activities they used to engage in during their middle years. Several authors have noted relationships between age and type of activity and degree of pursuit. For example, Gordon, Gaitz, & Scott (1976), in a cross-sectional study across the life span, found a correlation of $-.49$ between the level of general leisure activity and age. However, while participation in some activities was lower in older persons, participation in others was greater or showed no difference when compared with that of persons in earlier life stages. The activities most likely to show reductions were more intense, required more physical exertion, and tended to take place outside the home. Harris (1975) also found some differences between older and younger respondents in participation in activities, but these were not dramatic. Schmitz-Scherzer (1976) found small changes in general activity, with slight increases in watching TV and reading newspapers as subjects in the Bonn Longitudinal Study grew older. Finally, Palmore (1981), in a discussion of social activities, reports slow but discernible reductions with aging in the Duke Longitudinal Studies.

Table 8.3 presents the percentage of men and women in the sample who had dropped or added each activity previously listed from the 1977 questionnaire. Our subjects were more inclined to discontinue activities than to take on new ones. Sixteen activities were dropped by five percent or more of the men or women. Activities that require intense concentration, interaction in a social group, leaving the home, or physical activity were more likely to be dropped after midlife. The intellectual activities most often reduced were professional reading and formal continuing education. Cultural activities that showed the greatest declines were playing a musical instrument and playing or singing with a group. The social activities declining most were community service with a group and

TABLE 8.3

*Percentage of Men and Women in Later-Maturity Group
Dropping and Adding Activities in Later Maturity*

Activity	Men (N = 424)		Women (N = 381)	
	Dropped since middle years	Taken up recently	Dropped since middle years	Taken up recently
Intellectual activities				
Reading: books (nonfiction)	2%	2%	3%	1%
Reading: avocational publications	2	2	1	2
Reading: professional publications	12	<1	10	1
Increasing knowledge or skill (independent study)	3	1	5	2
Continuing education (classes)	9	2	12	4
Unpaid professional or technical work	3	2	4	1
Cultural activities				
Listening to recorded music	5	1	2	1
Going to concerts, plays, lectures, museums, etc.	5	1	6	0
Playing a musical instrument	7	1	9	2
Playing or singing with a musical group	7	1	8	1
Creative writing, painting, sculpture, dramatics	3	2	7	4
Social activities				
Informal visiting with friends and neighbors	1	1	2	0
Visiting and communicating with relatives	1	1	2	<1
Entertaining	4	0	7	<1
Community service: helping friends and neighbors	1	1	5	1
Community service: with a group	5	2	10	4
Community service: work done at home	1	1	5	1
Active recreation				
Traveling	4	3	6	3
Attending movies	12	1	12	1
Attending sporting events	10	1	11	0
Self improvement — physical (exercise, diet)	1	1	2	3
Noncompetitive physical activity	4	4	5	3
Participating in competitive sports	15	2	7	2
Competitive card or board games	6	1	6	2
Working on hobbies (collections, gardening, handicrafts)	3	2	5	3
Home repairs and maintenance	4	2	4	1
Passive recreation				
Reading: newspapers, magazines	1	<1	1	1
Reading: books (fiction)	4	3	4	1
Watching TV: educational, cultural	<1	3	1	4
Watching TV: entertainment	<1	2	1	4
Watching TV: sporting events	1	2	2	3
Solitary games or puzzles	2	1	2	2

SOURCE: 1977 questionnaire.

entertaining. The greatest declines in active recreational activities were in attending movies and sporting events and participating in competitive sports. None of the passive recreational activities showed much decline.

It should be emphasized, however, that at the individual level, these changes do not indicate large alterations in activity pattern. Overall, approximately 40 percent of the sample did not drop any activity, while 20 percent dropped only one. Furthermore, although there was a range of 24 years in the ages of the subjects in 1977, the correlations between individual activity participation and age were quite small. The highest correlations occurred for four activities that require leaving the home: $-.19$ for attending movies, and $-.10$ for attending sporting events, playing or singing with a musical group, and attending continuing education classes.

Although less common than dropping activities, some subjects took up new activities in later maturity. The most frequent increases in women's activities were in continuing education, creative activities, community service with a group, physical self-improvement, and watching entertainment TV, all increasing for three to four percent of the women. For both sexes, noncompetitive physical activities and watching educational TV also increased by three to four percent. About a third of the subjects added a new activity since middle age.

We also asked retired subjects to indicate whether any of the activities listed had replaced their occupation as a principal focus for their efforts and energy. Response rates were low and the responses varied widely. The most frequent choices among the men were hobbies, or "other" activities, community service with a group, creative writing, painting, sculpture, or dramatics, and unpaid professional or technical work (frequencies ranged from 13 to 7 subjects). For women, hobbies were the most frequent substitute for their occupation, followed by creative activities and unpaid work (frequencies ranged from 12 to 7 subjects).

Summary of 1977 Findings

The respondents remained quite active in the early years of later maturity. Although there was variability among subjects in the level of activity participation, the average level was impressively high. As a group, the subjects showed considerable diversity in the wide range of activities pursued. Changes in their activities in their later years were largely consistent with trends in the larger society toward activities that are less demanding. However, these declines in activities were not substantial, and some subjects added activities that involved considerable energy and engagement.

Activities in 1982 and 1986

By 1982 the subjects' average age was 70, and most had retired from the work force. In 1982 and 1986 we asked again about their activities, but listed only fifteen specific activities to allow more attention to other topics. Respondents were asked to check those activities occupying them "occasionally" or "frequently" (scored "1" and "2" respectively); activities not checked were scored "0." These items were included in the 1977 activity scales. Table 8.4 presents the items in the 1982 and 1986 version of the scales. The Active Recreation scale is the most conceptually diverse, and contains one item not included on the earlier questionnaire — managing personal property and finance.

Because we had identical measures in 1982 and 1986, we were able to em-

TABLE 8.4

Scales Used to Measure Participation by Later-Maturity
Group in Various Types of Activity (1982 and 1986)

Intellectual Activities
  Reading: nonfiction or professional or avocational publications
  Continuing education, increasing knowledge or skills
Cultural Activities
  Serious practice on arts (music, art, writing, dramatics, etc.)
  Going to concerts, plays, lectures, museums, etc.
Social Activities
  Informal visiting with friends, neighbors, children
  Helping others (friends, neighbors, children)
  Meeting of social groups, clubs
  Community service with organizations
Active Recreation
  Physical self improvement (exercise, diet)
  Competitive activities (bridge, golf, etc.)
  Working on hobbies (collections, gardening, handicrafts, etc.)
  Managing personal property and finance
Passive Recreation
  Reading books: fiction
  Watching TV: educational, cultural
  Watching TV: entertainment

SOURCE: Constructed from 1982 and 1986 questionnaires.

pirically analyze differences in activity participation as the group aged. Table 8.5 breaks down the data by sex and date of data collection. The results of an analysis of variance by repeated measures are also presented. Over the four-year period, the subjects showed an increase in passive recreation, and a decrease in the other four areas. The increase in passive activities was principally accounted for by more frequent watching of TV. On those scales where declines were noted, decreases occurred on almost all items. These findings reinforce the 1977 findings indicating a movement by our group toward less demanding activities in aging.

Men and women differed on four of the activity dimensions. Women engaged in more cultural and social activities, and scored higher than men on almost all of the activities on these scales. Women were also higher in passive recreation; more frequent watching of educational TV and reading fiction accounted for this finding. These sex differences were consistent with the 1977 results. Men were higher on the active recreation scale, due to a greater participation than women in managing personal property and finances. There were no statistically significant data by sex interactions for the activity scale analyses.

To investigate the stability of our subjects' activities in later maturity, we computed the intercorrelations of parallel activity scales for 1977, 1982, and 1986 responses. These analyses show the extent to which subjects ranked similarly in their participation across years. There was moderate stability in interest patterns over the years of later maturity. The correlations ranged from .33 to .69; the average correlation was .53.

Constraints on Activity

Personal resources and environmental constraints can influence activity participation. Health, in particular, has been considered as an important prerequisite for many activities (Lawton, Moss, & Fulcomer, 1986–87; Schmitz-Scherzer, 1976). Financial constraints have also been seen as important, but the findings concerning their relationship to activity participation in aging are inconsistent (Cutler & Hendricks, 1990). We asked the subjects in 1982 if their pattern of activities was their own choice. The responses were scored on a 9-point scale ranging from (1) hardly at all to (9) entirely, with the midpoint (5) labeled moderately. Men and women scored almost identically. Although responses covered the entire range of the scale, the median score for the two groups combined was 8, indicating that most members of the group felt that their activity patterns were of their own free choice.

The subjects were also asked if any of six factors interfered with their preferred activity pattern. Table 8.6 presents the number and percentage of subjects who felt that each of the listed factors made their activity pattern different from what they would prefer. About two-fifths of the men and a third of the women indicated that none of these factors kept them from a preferred activity. However, three-fifths of the men and two-thirds of the women checked at least one of the listed factors. The most frequently noted factors were limited health and energy, the wishes and needs of spouse or children, and limited financial resources. The lack of opportunities for older persons was not seen as an important restricting factor.

Because health was the factor most commonly listed as interfering with activity participation, we correlated self-reported health in 1977, 1982, and 1986 with the activity scales. A health score summed the standardized scores on two items included in all three questionnaires: self-reported health, and energy and vitality. The relationships were positive between self-reported health and participation in those activities in later maturity that make demands on the older

TABLE 8.5
Participation in Activities by Men and Women in Later-Maturity Group (1982 and 1986)

Activity	Men (N = 345)				Women (N = 310)				Significance level	
	1982		1986		1982		1986		Years	Sex
	Mean	S.D.	Mean	S.D.	Mean	S.D.	Mean	S.D.	*p*	*p*
Intellectual activities	1.99	1.04	1.85	1.05	1.97	1.11	1.75	1.11	.01	n.s.
Cultural activities	1.04	1.01	.92	0.97	1.35	1.06	1.24	1.09	.01	.01
Social activities	2.61	1.70	2.39	1.78	3.45	1.82	3.18	1.91	.01	.01
Active recreation	3.47	1.65	3.06	1.72	3.24	1.57	2.85	1.67	.01	.05
Passive recreation	2.88	1.33	3.07	1.40	3.46	1.36	3.66	1.42	.01	.01

SOURCE: 1982 and 1986 questionnaires.
NOTE: Significance of differences between 1982 and 1986 and between men and women determined by repeated measures analysis of variance.

TABLE 8.6
*Factors Interfering with Preferred Activity Patterns
of Later-Maturity Group*

	Men		Women	
	N	Pct.	N	Pct.
None	181	43.0%	135	33.9%
Limited health and energy	113	27.1	137	34.4
Wishes and needs of spouse or children	86	20.6	86	21.6
Limited financial resources	74	17.7	55	13.8
Sense of responsibility for an activity or organization	28	6.7	31	7.8
Lack of opportunities for older persons	12	2.9	15	3.8
Other	40	9.6	68	17.1
Total respondents	417		398	

SOURCE: 1982 questionnaire.
NOTE: Numbers add to more than the total number of respondents, and percentages add to over 100, because some respondents gave more than one response.

person. The highest correlations were between active recreation and health, which averaged .29 for men and .27 for women. Passive recreational activities showed rather little relationship to health, but the correlations tended to be negative.

Relation of Occupational History to Activity Participation

Occupations can shape entire life-styles, as well as work behavior, and are seen as an important determinant of activity participation in aging (Burrus-Bammel & Bammel, 1985; Lawton, 1985). We wondered whether the occupational histories of our subjects would predict their activity patterns in later maturity. We examined the scores on the activity scales for the men and women according to the occupational breakdowns used previously. For the analysis, we included the five activity scales from each of the three years — 1977, 1982, and 1986. For men, we used the three categories of occupation based on present or previous occupation as reported in 1972 or 1977 — professional, higher business, and lower-level occupations. For women, we used the 1972 self-classification of homemaker, career worker, or income worker.

Among men, the most pronounced activity differences between the occupational groups were reported in 1977 and applied to intellectual and cultural activities. Professionals were highest in intellectual activities ($p < .01$) and professionals and higher level businessmen were higher on cultural activities ($p < .05$) than men in lower-level occupations. The finding for the intellectual scale reflected differences in professional reading, avocational reading, unpaid work, and increasing knowledge and skill by independent study. In 1982, professionals were highest, and men in lower-level occupations were lowest, in cultural activities; this difference arose mainly from differences in the frequency of attending cultural events.

Differences in activity participation were also found for the three occupational groups of women (see Holahan, 1981, for an earlier report). Again, participation in intellectual and cultural activities differed between groups. Career workers tended to be highest on these scales, in contrast to both the homemakers and income workers. An exception was the 1982 Intellectual Activities scale on which income workers matched career workers. A 1977 finding that career workers participated more in intellectual activities reflected higher levels of unpaid work and professional reading among career workers. In 1982 and 1986, homemakers participated less than the other groups in continuing education and reading of nonfiction. Differences in cultural participation in 1982 and 1986 were most strongly influenced by attendance at cultural events.

The women's occupational groups also differed in social activities. The career workers tended to be highest on these scales, although in 1977 their participation was matched by the homemakers. This 1977 finding mostly arose from differences in informal visiting with friends. In 1982 the career workers were highest in participation in social groups, in visiting with friends and relatives, and service with organizations; the last of these contributed most to 1986 differences.

Stability of Activity Participation Over the Life Cycle

Are the individuals who were most active earlier in life also those who are most active in aging? How much continuity is there in activity participation across the life cycle? There is considerable evidence for continuity in types of activities in adulthood and aging (Atchley, 1988; Bosse & Ekerdt, 1981; Cutler & Hendricks, 1990; Morgan, Parnes, & Less, 1985; Simpson, Back, & McKinney, 1966), and also evidence that childhood activity is related to adult participation (Kelly, 1974, 1977; Yoesting & Christensen, 1978). The Terman study, with its duration of over sixty years, presents an ideal opportunity to examine these questions. At a number of earlier points in the study, the subjects were asked about their interests or activities. We selected data from the years 1922, 1936, 1940, and 1960 to relate to the later-maturity data.

In 1922, the study was just beginning, and the subjects were an average age of 11. They were asked about their liking for 12 activities, such as studying, reading, artistic activities, various games, social activities, and domestic activities. These interests were scored on a five-point scale ranging from (1) "dislike very much" to (5) "like very much," and the scores were summed to provide the total interest level for each subject. From the 1936 questionnaire, we coded the number of activities participated in while in high school. In 1940, when the subjects were an average age of thirty, they reported their level of interest in twelve activities, including travel, outdoor sports, social life, and cultural activities. These were scored from (1) "none" to (5) "very much," and the scores were summed to provide a measure of overall interest level. From 1940, we also have

TABLE 8.7

Cultural Activities Included in Each Score for Participation in Cultural Activities by Terman Group (1922–86)

Date	Items	Score
1922	Interest in practicing music, drawing, dancing, etc.	Cultural interest
1936	Music (singing, glee clubs, playing instruments, dancing, choir) Dramatics Art Writing Study of art Music appreciation Attending plays	Number of cultural activities and hobbies during high school
1940	Same as 1936	Number of cultural activities during high school
1940	Same as 1936	Number of cultural avocational activities since leaving school
1940	Interest in music Interest in art	Cultural interest
1960	Music Art Creative writing Dramatic and theater arts	Number of cultural avocational interests
1977	Listening to recorded music Playing a musical instrument Playing or singing with a group Creative writing, painting, sculpture, dramatics Going to concerts, plays, lectures, museums, etc.	Level of cultural participation
1982	Serious practice on arts Going to concerts, plays, lectures, museums	Level of cultural participation
1986	Same as 1982	Level of cultural participation

SOURCE: Questionnaires in indicated years.

the number of activities participated in during college and a five-point rating which considers both extent and success in extracurricular activities in college. From 1940 and 1960, we have the number of avocational interests since leaving school and in mid-life, respectively; and finally, we have counts of activities from 1977, 1982, and 1986 reports. Thus, most of these measures reflect breadth of interests; the 1922 and 1940 interest measures reflect both breadth and level of interest.

The earlier measures of activity interest and participation correlated modestly with the number of activities pursued in later maturity. The largest correlations, between 1940 interest level and breadth of activity at the three points in later maturity, averaged .24 for men. The relations between earlier and later variables were stronger for men than for women.

We also explored the degree of continuity in type of activity. We selected cultural activities as an area to examine over the years because they seemed especially relevant to a gifted group, and, among the diverse measures of interests, they were relatively easy to operationalize. We used the scores for interest in cultural activities from 1923 to 1940, summing items that belonged to appropriate categories for each year. In 1940 and 1960, we summed subjects' reported avocational interests in the appropriate categories. From 1977, 1982, and 1986, we used the previously defined cultural scales. Table 8.7 lists the items from each survey that make up the cultural scores.

Table 8.8 presents the correlations of earlier cultural interest and participation with participation in later maturity. There is evidence of moderate continuity of cultural interests across the life cycle, with the correlations stronger for men than for women. The predictive relations are strongest from the young adulthood and mid-life surveys. However, the correlations among the men of activities in childhood with those in later maturity are also noteworthy. The evidence for continuity in cultural activity pursuit is all the more impressive in view of the fact that different items were used in the measures at the various measurement times.

Summary

Overall, the Terman subjects were leading involved and active lives in their years of later maturity. They participated in a wide range of activities, and exceeded the general population in their participation in both intellectual and nonintellectual pursuits. There were moderate correlations among parallel activity scales over the years of later maturity. Modest correlations also were found across the life span for the breadth of activity participation, and the subjects showed moderate stability across the life span in their interest and participation in cultural activities, an area examined from childhood onward.

Some of the choice of activity is consistent with traditional gender roles.

TABLE 8.8

Correlations of Measures of Cultural Activities of Later-Maturity Group from 1922 to 1960 with Parallel Activities in 1977, 1982, and 1986

| | Cultural activities | | | | | |
| | Men (N = 270–380) | | | Women (N = 236–365) | | |
	1977	1982	1986	1977	1982	1986
1922 — Interest level	.19	.20	.22	.09	.02	.01
1936 — Avocational activities in high school	.22	.27	.25	.20	.09	.07
1940 — Avocational activities in college	.29	.27	.30	.27	.14	.14
1940 — Avocational activities since leaving school	.29	.29	.29	.31	.21	.15
1940 — Interest level in music and art	.43	.34	.36	.29	.21	.17
1960 — Avocational activities	.36	.33	.29	.39	.22	.19

SOURCE: Questionnaires in 1977, 1982, and 1986.
NOTE: For N = 300, a correlation of .11 or above is significant at .05 level; a correlation of .15 or above is significant at .01 level.

Women consistently participated more in social and cultural activities, and tended to engage in passive recreational activities more than men. Overall, men participated more in active recreational activities, including all sports-related activities. Men also pursued work-related activities more than did women. Moreover, occupational groups differed in their activities. Among men, professionals were highest in both intellectual and cultural activities, while those in lower-level occupations were the lowest. Among women, career workers tended to be highest in intellectual, cultural, and social participation.

The subjects gradually dropped activities in their later years. The greatest declines were in activities that require intense concentration, group interaction, leaving the home, or physical activity. Yet, overall, the subjects felt that even in aging their choice of activities was little constrained by disabilities or external factors. The most frequently noted factors interfering with preferred activity pattern were limited health and energy, the wishes and needs of spouse and children, and limited financial resources. The lack of opportunities for older persons was not seen as a limiting factor. There were modest relations between measures of self-reported health in later maturity and participation in demanding activities.

In terms of successful aging, some authors have stressed that it is not activity participation per se, but participation in meaningful activities, that is important for satisfaction in the later years (Howe, 1988; Lawton, 1985). The fact that the activity patterns of the group were primarily of their own choosing suggests that their activity participation contributed to the quality of their lives in later maturity. They succeeded in maintaining and creating structure in their lives, even after their involvement in formal work roles ended. The group appeared to have the opportunity, as well as the inclination, to pursue a large number of activities, some of which required considerable commitment. They were not, however, immune to a change in activity with aging. As with other samples, as the subjects grew older the trend, although modest, was toward less demanding activities.

9

Values and Goals

Values and goals are essential to a sense of meaningfulness in life (Reker & Wong, 1988), and are important in life satisfaction and mental health. The congruence between desired and achieved goals has been used as an indicator of life satisfaction in aging (Neugarten, Havighurst, & Tobin, 1961). Similarly, poor mental health has been associated with a sense of hopelessness in reaching desired goals (Erickson, Post, & Paige, 1975). Among the Terman subjects (Holahan, 1988), individuals who still reported commitment to goals at an advanced age also reported greater psychological well-being. This was particularly true of goals reflecting an involvement with people or activities, or relating to achievement. The relationship between goals and well-being seemed to operate directly, as well as indirectly, through activity participation. Having goals was related to greater participation in activities, which contributed to well-being. Over and above that effect, having goals was in itself associated with greater well-being.

The later-maturity group brought a superior set of personal resources to aging. They were advantaged compared to others of their generation in their intellectual ability, lifetime achievement, and income. The study of their values and goals in later maturity may provide some insight into the potentials, as well as limitations, for a meaningful life in the later years. This chapter examines the values and life goals of the later-maturity group as expressed in their responses to the four questionnaires from 1972 to 1986.

Goals can be thought of as the values that an individual is committed to strive for (Klinger, 1977). Values may include abstract, guiding principles by which persons live as well as more concrete wants and desires. Values may thus reflect both desired outcomes and the means by which outcomes are achieved (Rokeach,

1973). Persons have both short-term and long-term goals, and goals vary in their importance to the individual as well as in their likelihood of being achieved. Values and goals are inextricably bound up with each person's background and experience, and are influenced by beliefs about life in general and about the individual's own life. In addition to reflecting the concerns and desires of each individual, values and goals are also influenced by opportunities and incentives for the fulfillment of those desires.

Only a comparatively small number of major values and goals appear in discussions of development across the adult life cycle. For example, Erikson's (1959) theory of the life cycle includes changes in commitments at each developmental stage. Thus, in young adulthood, the individual is faced with the challenge of attaining intimacy, while generativity — a concern with the next generation — is the challenge of mid-life. In later maturity, the older person must achieve integrity despite despair, in the face of physical decline and changing life circumstances. Four clusters of major adulthood commitments have been described by Fiske (1980): interpersonal, altruistic or moral, competence or mastery, and self-protective. It has been suggested that the salience of each of these areas will vary according to an individual's life stage and life circumstances (Fiske, 1980). Additional sources of meaning include creativity, hedonism, religion, and legacy (Fiske & Chiriboga, 1990; Thurnher, 1975; Yalom, 1980).

The values and goals of the older person surely emerge from his or her unique life history. In aging, individuals may deal with declining physical and mental capacities by emphasizing areas of strength in order to compensate for deficits (Baltes, Dittmann-Kohli, & Dixon, 1984). An important skill in adulthood, and particularly in aging, may be the ability to move to the periphery those goals and commitments that are unattainable, while replacing them with ones more easily fulfilled (Lazarus & DeLongis, 1983). This adjustment process may include a reintegration of values and life goals, as well as alterations in them (Clark & Anderson, 1967; Fiske & Chiriboga, 1990). Erikson, Erikson, & Kivnick (1986) have described a process by which earlier intrapsychic conflicts are revisited and reinterpreted within the life context of the later years.

This chapter begins with a discussion of goals and ambitions in later maturity, and proceeds to an examination of underlying values as expressed in religious interest and practice, political interest and participation, and contributions to others. Stability and change in values and goals is examined whenever earlier comparable data are available. Using related measures from the data archives, we also examine antecedents of the values our subjects bring to later maturity.

Goals and Ambitions

Goals in 1982 and 1986

Maintaining a sense of purpose may become more challenging as older persons experience the cumulative losses of aging (Dittmann-Kohli, 1990; Reker, Peacock, & Wong, 1987; Ryff, 1991). However, we have seen in the previous

TABLE 9.1
Goals of Men and Women in Later-Maturity Group (1982 and 1986)

	Men		Women	
Goal	1982 Pct.	1986 Pct.	1982 Pct.	1986 Pct.
Autonomy				
Remain independent	88%	92%	89%	94%
Financially secure	85	90	81	85
Remain healthy	95	90	91	93
Involvement				
Many pleasant relationships	64	62	79	75
Intimacy with others	32	28	47	43
Hobbies and other activities	67	61	69	61
Achievement motivation				
Contribution to society	45	47	59	54
Continue to work	47	35	31	21
Growth personally, be creative and productive	55	54	66	63
Produce social change	13	13	16	19
Opportunities for achievement and competition	17	22	17	13
Acceptance				
Take each day as it comes	54	61	64	73
Die peacefully	42	55	51	67
Family goals				
Contribute to children	57	62	54	55
Contribute to spouse	72	71	48	37
Total respondents	416	377	397	335

SOURCE: 1982 and 1986 questionnaires.
NOTE: Percentages add to over 100 because many respondents mentioned two or more goals.

chapter that the Terman group maintained significant meaningful activities into their later years. In this chapter, we examine some of the motives and values that may account for their remarkable activity patterns.

We asked our subjects about their goals and purposes for their lives in 1982 and 1986 (Question 26 and Question 29, respectively). The same goals were presented in both years. The subjects were asked to check all goals that were important to them. (They were also asked to indicate three goals as most important, but in fact a number of subjects checked more or fewer than three.) We scored ratings of "most important" and "important" as 2 and 1, respectively; not checking was scored as zero.

We grouped fifteen of the goals on the basis of content and a factor analysis. Table 9.1 lists the goals within each group and the percentages of men and women in 1982 and 1986 who indicated that each goal was important or very important (single or double check). "Autonomy" refers to maintenance of independence, including health and financial security. These self-protective goals are basic to the attainment of other goals, and they may become increasingly important as health declines. "Involvement" refers to investment in relationships and activities. "Achievement motivation" refers to desire for personal achievements and achievements in society. "Acceptance" combines the goals of "take each day as it comes" and "die peacefully." The last two, "Family goals," concern contributions to children and spouse.

The most striking feature of Table 9.1 is the high degree of endorsement of many of these goals. The goals related to autonomy were mentioned particularly often. The degree of attainment of these goals will affect the realization of many of the other goals being considered. The data on involvement goals show that the subjects had considerable interest in pursuing interpersonal relationships and hobbies and other activities. We have already seen in Chapter 8 on activities that they were indeed attaining these goals.

Endorsement of achievement goals was mixed. On average, these subjects were highly productive and have made significant impact on society in their earlier lives. As they reached their later years, their achievement motives were expressed in personal rather than competitive ways; personal growth was the most frequently endorsed of the achievement goals. Moreover, while they maintained considerable interest in making a contribution to society they did not have an interest in changing it. At the same time, they appeared to be accepting some of the limitations of aging and to be seeking a peaceful resolution at the end of their lives.

The data on family goals show the maintenance of interest in contributing to their children and spouses. The gender differences in contribution to family reflect the realities of differential mortalities of husbands and wives, and the different number of children of the men and the women (see Chapter 7 on social networks).

We shall now examine differences in goals at the two dates, for those subjects answering at both times. In 1982 and 1986 the subjects averaged 70 and 74 years of age, respectively. We have constructed scales for the first four groups of items by summing the scores on the individual items on each scale. (We will not pursue the family goals further, because of difficulties in meaningful interpretation without breaking the sample down by marital and child history. Initial such analyses produced nothing worthy of note.) The remaining four scales are presented in Table 9.2 by sex and year. The results of an analysis of variance by repeated measures are also presented. Follow-up t-tests on scales and sometimes individual items were used to clarify these findings.

Both the men and the women reduced their commitment to involvement and achievement goals, and increased their emphasis on acceptance goals. These changes in goals are understandable in terms of the diminished physical capacities of some of the individuals in the sample and the shortened time horizon of the later years. They are consistent with other studies showing an awareness of future uncertainty in aging, and a decrease in positive expectations and goals for the future (Dittmann-Kohli, 1990; Reker, Peacock, & Wong, 1987; Ryff, 1991). However, although statistically significant, these differences are not large in magnitude. As is also suggested by the data in Table 9.1 for all individuals

TABLE 9.2
Comparison of Goals of Men and Women in Later-Maturity Group (1982, 1986)

	Men (N = 345)				Women (N = 310)				Level of significance		
	1982		1986		1982		1986		Years	Sex	Sex × year
Type of goal	Mean	S.D.	Mean	S.D.	Mean	S.D.	Mean	S.D.	*p*	*p*	*p*
Autonomy	4.18	1.29	4.02	1.34	4.12	1.46	4.30	1.41	n.s.	n.s.	.01
Involvement	1.86	1.21	1.66	1.17	2.30	1.22	2.07	1.35	.01	.01	n.s.
Achievement motivation	2.30	1.85	2.09	1.88	2.39	1.84	1.97	1.60	.01	n.s.	n.s.
Acceptance	1.05	.95	1.38	1.07	1.35	1.00	1.68	1.06	.01	.01	n.s.

SOURCE: 1982 and 1986 questionnaires.
NOTE: Goals not checked by respondents were assigned a score of "0," goals checked once were scored "1," and a score of "2" was given to goals that respondents indicated were among the "three most important" goals for them. The scale score on each type of goal is the sum of the scores on all the goals included in the type (listed in Table 9.1). Only subjects responding to this question in both years are included in this table. The column on the extreme right reflects relative differences across years for men and women.

responding in 1982 or 1986, the proportion of subjects who continued to maintain goals indicating an active, optimistic approach to their lives remained impressively high.

Some differences in the changes and/or levels of goals held by men and women suggest that the sexes had somewhat different orientations to aging. As we saw in Chapter 7, the women had more close relationships than the men, despite the loss of spouses through widowhood or divorce. Our analyses of goals confirmed these earlier results. The women scored higher on involvement goals in both 1982 and 1986, with the differences due to a greater emphasis on personal relationships, both in terms of intimacy and numbers ($ps < .01$) (see also Table 9.1).

In addition, many more of the women were living alone (see Chapter 7), and issues of autonomy appear to be more salient to them than to the men. The women were higher than the men in autonomy goals in 1986 ($p < .05$), particularly with regard to maintaining independence and health. Men's emphasis on autonomy goals decreased between 1982 and 1986 ($p < .05$). This was caused by their lower emphasis on the goal of maintaining health ($p < .01$). This decline was paralleled by a drop in their self-rated health at the two dates ($p < .01$). We do not know the extent to which this decline in health goals for the men was a cause or an effect of age-related changes in health. (Chapter 10 considers health in greater detail.) Another sex difference was that women appeared to have come to a greater acceptance of the realities of aging, indicated by their greater endorsement of acceptance goals in both years.

The lack of a gender difference in achievement motivation may seem surprising at first, given the differences in occupational histories for the men and women. However, as can be seen in Table 9.1, the men's relatively higher interest in continuance of work and achievement and competition is balanced by the women's greater interest in personal growth and productivity and in contributing to society. These findings show both differences from and similarities to those of a study of lower-middle class and blue collar workers reported by Fiske and Chiriboga (1990). They found that the oldest men in their study decreased in achievement goals over time, as we found here; however, the oldest women in their sample outranked the men in achievement orientation at all times of measurement.

Since the subjects differed in achievement style and history, we examined the later-life goals of the subjects in relation to these earlier occupational orientations. For the men, the three groups discussed in Chapter 4 were used for analysis: professional, higher-level business, and lower-level occupations. For the women, we used the self-classification in 1972 (see Chapter 5) of homemaker, career worker, and income worker.

Differences among the three occupational groups of men were concentrated in achievement and autonomy goals. In particular, the professional men ranked first in achievement motivation in 1986 ($p < .05$). Their higher scores on goals concerning the continuation of work, growing personally, and making contributions to society accounted for this finding. As noted in Chapter 4 on the men's work history, the professionals had more opportunity to continue work after formal retirement, and also tended to pursue intrinsic more than extrinsic motives.

On autonomy goals, the higher-level businessmen had the highest average scores in both 1982 and 1986; the professional men had the lowest ($p < .05$). In both years, differences in health goals contributed the most to the significant difference on the total scale. However, an analysis of the self-assessments of general health of these three groups in 1982 and 1986 failed to yield any differences. Perhaps the professional men's personal investment in achievement transcended their interest in health preservation.

The goals of the three career groups of women also differed. The career women had more active goal orientations than the other women (greater concern with autonomy in 1982, greater involvement in 1986 [$p < .05$]). They also reported more concern for achievement in both years ($p < .01$), particularly in comparison with the homemakers. The career workers' ratings of the importance of achievement goals surpassed those of the entire sample of men, and were most comparable to those of the professional men. Although a greater emphasis on achievement was expected for the career workers, it is noteworthy that they were also higher in involvement goals. This came principally from their emphasis on intimacy in relationships and enjoyment of avocational activities.

It appears that the active mastery the career women exhibited in their careers continued into aging. These results probably reflect lifelong patterns of coping, in combination with the opportunities that careers provide for the continuation of achievement-related pursuits later in life. They may also reflect the demands for self-support and the active creation and maintenance of social networks for those who never married, or who were widowed or divorced.

Finally, we were interested in the stability in these goals over the four years from 1982 to 1986, when most of our subjects moved from their early 70's to their mid-70's. Were the individuals who were most goal-oriented in 1982 also higher in 1986? We found that those who stated strong goals in 1982 also tended to score higher in 1986. The correlations ranged from .35 to .67; the average correlation was .51.

These analyses of the goal orientations of the later-maturity group in 1982 and 1986, when on average they were in their early 70's to mid-70's, suggest that on the whole they were maintaining commitments to meaningful goals, while at the same time accepting some of the realities of aging. They tended to emphasize personal bases for maintaining a sense of mastery and productivity, rather than formal work roles or achievement via competition. Moreover, they continued to be interested in personal relationships, both within and outside their families. There were, however, on average, modest reductions in the importance they attached to more active goals over the four years from 1982 to 1986, while acceptance goals increased in importance.

Ambitions in Later Maturity and Earlier Life

The gifted Terman sample always had considerable achievement orientation. Achievement-related measures from the earlier follow-ups make it possible to assess changes in ambition from adulthood to aging, as well as the relation between earlier and later ambition. In 1960, reports were obtained on ambition since age 40 in four areas: excellence in work, recognition of accomplishments, vocational advancement, and financial gain. In 1977, the latter two items were replaced by ambition in avocational pursuits and maintaining an excellent standard of living. The 1986 question asked about their ambition for excellence in whatever projects they were presently engaged in. The 1960 and 1977 responses were scored on a five-point scale comparing themselves with others of their age and sex, the mid-point of the scale indicating "average" ambition. The original 9-point scaling of the 1986 question was converted to a 5-point scale. Table 9.3 presents the means for each sex along with the results of significance tests on mean differences between 1960 and 1977.

Overall, the group rated themselves as "average" to "somewhat above average" in ambition, the means ranging from near "3" to "4." The greatest ambition for both men and women was in the area of excellence in work (reported in both 1960 and 1977), followed by the 1986 rating of excellence in whatever the subjects engaged in. The ambition for financial gain was the lowest for both men and women in 1960. Where 1960 items concerning excellence in work and recognition of accomplishment were repeated in 1977, there was a small shift upward in the means, which may indicate a slight tendency for the group to see themselves as more ambitious than others of their cohort as they age.

The sex differences in ambition in later maturity were consistent with gender roles for this cohort and suggested a greater channeling of men's ambition into employment-related pursuits and of women's into avocational pursuits. Men were higher in 1977 in ambition for recognition of accomplishment ($p < .05$) and maintaining an excellent standard of living ($p < .06$), while women were

TABLE 9.3

*Self-Ratings of Later-Maturity Group on Ambition Since Age 40
(Reported in 1960) and on Present Ambition
in 1977 and 1986*

Ambition	1960 (Since age 40)		1977 (Current)		1986 (Current)	
	Mean	S.D.	Mean	S.D.	Mean	S.D.
	MEN					
	(N = 477–497)		(N = 397–406)		(N = 368)	
Excellence in work	3.98	0.73	4.05	0.78		
Recognition of accomplishments	3.22[a]	0.86	3.40	0.86		
Vocational advancement	3.20	0.95				
Financial gain	3.10	0.93				
Avocational pursuits			3.38	0.97		
Maintaining excellent standard of living			3.40	0.95		
Excellence in whatever engaged in					3.67	0.87
	WOMEN					
	(N = 355–388)		(N = 344–361)		(N = 330)	
Excellence in work	3.85[b]	0.80	3.98	0.81		
Recognition of accomplishments	3.14[a]	0.80	3.24	0.91		
Vocational advancement	3.08	0.99				
Financial gain	2.77	0.99				
Avocational pursuits			3.53	0.92		
Maintaining excellent standard of living			3.27	0.91		
Excellence in whatever engaged in					3.49	0.88

SOURCE: Questionnaires for indicated years.
NOTE: Significance levels are for the comparison of 1960 items with identical 1977 items. Items were phrased to measure ambition in comparison to others of the same age and sex. The midpoint, "3," indicated average ambition, with lower scores indicating less ambition than others, and higher scores indicating more than others. The original 9-point scale on 1986 ambition was converted to a 5-point scale for this analysis.
[a]$p < .01$ by t-test.   [b]$p < .05$ by t-test.

higher in ambition for hobbies and avocational pursuits ($p < .05$). Men were also higher than women in overall ambition in 1986 ($p < .01$).

In 1977 the subjects were asked to assess directly the change in their ambition in the last 10–15 years. Responses were on a 5-point scale, with the midpoint of the scale, "3," indicating no change, lower scores indicating a decrease in ambition, and higher scores indicating an increase. Consistent with the results on their comparative level of ambition, women reported a larger increase in ambition for avocational pursuits (means of 3.13 and 3.25 for men and women, $p < .06$), and men reported greater increase in maintaining an excellent standard of living (means of 3.23 and 3.08 for men and women, $p < .01$).

We expected to find differences in ambition among our subjects in later maturity that were related to their lifetime occupational patterns. When we examined the ambition items for the men by occupational group, one comparison was significant. Professional men were highest in ambition for excellence in work in 1977, with the men in lower-level occupations the lowest ($p < .05$).

When we looked at the 1977 and 1986 items by occupational group for women, we also found differences. The career women rated themselves as relatively more ambitious in excellence in work compared to others in 1977, as well as in overall ambition in 1986. It is noteworthy that the career workers' ratings on these items matched those of the men.

The only significant difference in change in ambition for the three occupational groups of women occurred in excellence in work in the last 10–15 years ($p < .05$). Income workers showed the greatest increase (mean = 3.35), and homemakers reported no change, the career workers' mean being in between. The income workers' greater increase in ambition in work may be due to their lower income levels (see Chapter 5), leading to later retirement; it could also be a consequence of increased investment in their jobs for income workers whose responsibilities increased later in life.

In Chapters 4 and 5, in our discussions of the prediction of career achievement of the men and women, we examined the relationship of earlier achievement orientations to later achievement. Our more recent data collections in later maturity provide the opportunity to explore the stability of ambition from childhood to later maturity. A summary of the relations among earlier measures of ambition and ambition in later maturity appears in Table 9.4. For 1977, we summed the four ambition ratings, and the 1986 entry refers to the single 1986 item concerning current ambition in any project undertaken.

For the remaining computations in this table, we summed the four items for each of the two time periods reported in 1960 — age 30–40, and since age 40. In addition, we have included measures from the 1950 supplementary blank. In this questionnaire subjects were asked to rate their ambition in five areas at three time periods — before age 12, from age 12–20, and after age 20. These areas included sports, leadership, money, social, and school. We summed the ratings for the 1950 items for each time period.

Assessments of ambition as early as childhood were related to ambition in

TABLE 9.4
Correlations of Earlier Ambition Total Scores with Ambition in Later Maturity

	Correlation between earlier ambition and ambition in later maturity			
	Men		Women	
	Date of report		Date of report	
Earlier ambition	1977 (N = 313–354)	1986 (N = 287–319)	1977 (N = 232–292)	1986 (N = 209–284)
Before age 12 (1950)	.15	.19	.22	.09
Age 12–20 (1950)	.19	.14	.19	.07
After age 20 (1950)	.26	.20	.27	.16
Age 30–40 (1960)	.24	.15	.39	.19
Since age 40 (1960)	.30	.24	.42	.28

SOURCE: Questionnaires in years indicated in parentheses.
NOTE: For N = 200, a correlation of .14 or above is significant at the .05 level, and a correlation of .18 or above is significant at the .01 level. For N = 300, a correlation of .11 is significant at the .05 level, and a correlation of .15 is significant at the .01 level.

later maturity in both men and women. The trend of the size of the correlations from top to bottom of each column shows that we also find for men and women, as we would expect, a tendency for the prediction of later ambition to become progressively stronger as the assessments are closer in time.

These analyses of the group's ambition over the life cycle supplement the consideration of achievement goals in the earlier part of the chapter. Here we observe evidence for continuity in ambition over the life cycle in this highly achieving group. Moreover, in later maturity, the subjects see themselves as slightly higher in ambition than others of their same age, and this is increasingly the case as the subjects grow older. As was true for goals, the men and women, on average, emphasized different areas — the men were more work-oriented. However, among the women, the career workers matched the men on some of the ambition ratings.

Religion

Religion is intrinsic to some individuals' value systems, and is of particular interest in later maturity. It can become increasingly salient in the later years as a means by which older persons resolve philosophical issues concerning the meaning of existence. At a day-to-day level, religion may provide a means of coping with deaths of loved ones, as well as other vicissitudes of aging (Moberg, 1990). We shall see, here, however, that the study of religion in aging is complex and multifaceted, as we explore our group's interest and participation in religion in later maturity.

Past Religious Participation

There is generally strong cross-generational continuity in religious orientation (Troll & Bengtson, 1979), and our subjects were no exception. About 80 percent of our subjects who reported religious affiliation in adulthood were Protestants (see Table 9.5). Their religious choices were highly consistent with the national origins of their parents and grandparents (see Chapter 2).

As a group, our subjects in adulthood were about as religious as the general population, at least as far as their report of affiliation or interest in organized religion is concerned (Terman & Oden, 1959). The later-maturity group showed much the same pattern of affiliations as the full sample. In 1940, at age 30, about 55 percent of the men and 57 percent of the women reported at least an informal religious affiliation (see Table 9.5). Our subjects increased their affiliation somewhat by 1950. By that time, about 70 percent of men and two-thirds of women expressed at least an informal interest in an organized religion. The subjects were then an average age of 40.

Data From Later Maturity

Although the elderly are commonly thought to turn to religion as a source of comfort, not all research concurs. Evidence for stability, increases, and decreases

TABLE 9.5
Religious Affiliations of Later-Maturity Group (1940 and 1950)

	Men				Women			
	1940		1950		1940		1950	
Religion	N	Pct.	N	Pct.	N	Pct.	N	Pct.
Protestant	210	42.1%	253	54.2%	196	45.6%	215	53.6%
Catholic	23	4.6	31	6.6	22	5.1	24	6.0
Jewish	31	6.2	33	7.1	25	5.8	23	5.7
Other	11	2.2	6	1.3	4	0.9	3	0.7
None	224	44.9	144	30.8	183	42.6	136	33.9
Total (N)	499		467		430		401	

SOURCE: 1940 and 1950 questionnaires.

in religiosity can be found. Partly, the conflicting findings reflect investigators' attention to different aspects of religion. For example, data from the Duke Longitudinal Studies showed that religious attitudes remained stable, whereas formal religious activity such as church attendance declined (Blazer & Palmore, 1976). When changes in religious orientation are found in aging, increases tend to be in interest and in private devotional practices; formal participation is what most often declines (Moberg, 1970). Part of the retreat from religious activities outside the home can be attributed to difficulties of health and transportation. Another influence may be congregations' lack of responsiveness to the needs of their elderly members (Atchley, 1988; Hendricks & Hendricks, 1986).

In 1977, when the subjects were in their late 60's, they were asked in two separate questions to indicate whether their interest in religion or their formal association with it had decreased, remained the same, or increased since their middle years. About 70 percent reported no change in either interest or association. However, one-fifth of the sample reported a decrease in formal association—twice as many as an increase. As in other samples (e.g., Moberg, 1970), more women than men indicated increased interest in religion since mid-life (24 percent of the women in comparison to 16 percent of the men).

In 1986 we supplemented our initial inquiry into religious orientation in later maturity with more detailed questions about the importance of eight aspects of religion. Most of the subjects were then near their mid-70's. Three questions related to spiritual aspects of religion, three to religion as a social activity, and two to social-welfare activities. The subjects were asked to indicate how important each aspect was to them on a three-point scale: (1) "not at all," (2) "moderately important," (3) "very important." Table 9.6 summarizes the responses.

The most noteworthy finding was that religion was not highly important to either the men or women, on average, in the later-maturity group. Most means were noticeably below (2) "moderately important" on the three-point scale. This result differs from that of a Harris poll indicating in 1975 that more than 70 percent of persons in the general population over 65 rated religion as "very important." According to a Gallup survey also (Princeton Religion Research

TABLE 9.6

Importance of Eight Aspects of Religion to Later-Maturity Group (1986)

Aspects of religion	Men (N = 316–351)		Women (N = 258–306)	
	Mean	S.D.	Mean	S.D.
Spiritual				
Worship and prayer	1.57[a]	0.74	1.90	0.84
Spiritual reading, radio/TV	1.24[a]	0.53	1.50	0.72
Trying to understand religious truths more deeply	1.57[a]	0.70	1.88	0.79
Social				
Going to church as a social activity	1.25[a]	0.49	1.46	0.69
Participating in church pageants, socials and the like	1.12[a]	0.36	1.24	0.53
Participating in church government, committees	1.18[b]	0.48	1.29	0.60
Social welfare				
Supporting social betterment causes	1.70[b]	0.66	1.83	0.71
Welfare activities	1.60[a]	0.60	1.74	0.66

SOURCE: 1986 questionnaire.
NOTE: Levels of statistical significance refer to mean differences between men and women.
[a]$p < .01$ by t-test.   [b]$p < .05$ by t-test.

Center, 1982), 67 percent of the elderly in the general population in 1981 reported that religion was "very important" in their lives. In the later-maturity group, the highest percentages of "very important" ratings were found for worship and prayer (15 percent of men and 30 percent of women) and trying to understand religious truths more deeply (12 percent of men and 26 percent of women). Thus, on average, our respondents rated the importance of no aspect of religion much above "moderate." While several aspects of religion were rated as "moderately important" by the women (worship and prayer, trying to understand religious truths, and supporting social betterment causes), none were so rated by the men. Among both men and women, the spiritual and social-welfare aspects of religion were the most important. On average, the subjects expressed little enthusiasm for church-related social activities, particularly participating in church pageants and socials and in church governance.

In 1986, we asked about recent increase or decrease in the importance of each of these eight aspects of religion. An analysis of the proportion of men and women showing increases or decreases in each category showed changes consistent with the changes in interest and formal association recorded in 1977. The greatest increases in importance were in the spiritual aspects of religion, while the greatest decreases were in its social aspects.

As evident throughout our discussion of religion, the women in the later-maturity group were more religious than the men. All eight aspects of religion were more important to them. Moreover, the personal aspects of religion assumed relatively more importance for women as they aged. Women, more than men, reported increases in the importance of the spiritual aspects of religion and of going to church as a social activity (although to a smaller extent). However, the more public aspects became relatively less important for women; they

showed greater decreases than men in participating in church socials and pageants, and in the two social welfare aspects of religion.

The increases in religious orientation in aging are intriguing. Do people tend
to discover religion in later life, or do those already religiously inclined increase
their interest? An examination of the relations of earlier religious orientation
with changes in aging suggests that it is the latter that was more likely to occur in
this sample. For example, looking at the relation of change in interest in religion
reported in 1977 and extent religiously inclined in 1950 at an average age of
forty, a very clear pattern emerges. The percent of individuals who reported
increased interest in religion as they aged gradually increased across levels of
inclination at mid-life. Interest in religion increased from 10 percent of men and
14 percent of women with no religious inclination at mid-life to 32 percent of
men and 34 percent of women who were strongly religiously inclined by later
maturity. In contrast, over 80 percent of both the men and the women who had no
interest in religion at mid-life reported no change in their interest when they grew
older. Lower proportions of subjects (one half of the men and about two-thirds of
the women) with strong religious inclinations at mid-life reported no change in
their interest in their later years.

Predictors of Religious Orientation in Later Maturity

Does the importance of religion in later maturity relate to childhood training
and to religious practices in earlier adulthood? As a preliminary step to investigating this issue, we created three composite scores from the 1986 responses on
the importance of spiritual, social, and social welfare aspects of religion. The
correlations of these scores with information from the data archives concerning
religious training, behavior, and interest in earlier years are presented in Table
9.7. The 1940 variables regarding church membership, Sunday School attendance, and number of church activities appeared in the Personality and Temperament questionnaire. The subjects were asked to report their participation at the
time of their marriage.

The importance of religion in later maturity was moderately related to interest
and participation at least 30 to 40 years earlier in young adulthood and mid-life,
whereas the correlation with recollected childhood religious training was somewhat lower. The importance of spiritual aspects of religion in 1986 was best
predicted by interest in religion in young adulthood and religious inclination as
an adult, whereas religious participation in young adulthood matched these variables in predicting the importance of social and social welfare activities. The
importance of religious social welfare activities in aging was less well predicted
from earlier variables, as compared with the spiritual and social aspects of
religion, especially for women.

Integrative Multiple Regression Analyses

These religion variables are correlated, and the simple correlations with religious attitudes in later maturity may obscure the unique predictive power of

TABLE 9.7

*Correlations of Aspects of Earlier Religious Experience with Importance
of Spiritual, Social, and Social Welfare Aspects
of Religion to Later-Maturity Group in 1986*

	Men (N = 207–285)			Women (N = 142–242)		
Aspect of earlier religious experience	Spiritual aspects	Social aspects	Social welfare aspects	Spiritual aspects	Social aspects	Social welfare aspects
Strictness of religious training (1940)	.23	.18	.17	.28	.10	.02
Strictness of religious training (1950)	.19	.17	.17	.22	.16	.02
Church membership	.31	.42	.25	.37	.34	.15
Sunday School attendance (1940)	.38	.34	.23	.30	.27	.06
Number of church activities (1940)	.30	.24	.27	.34	.36	.19
Amount of interest in religion	.50	.37	.24	.44	.35	.13
Extent religiously inclined, as an adult (1950)	.50	.42	.28	.57	.40	.14

SOURCE: Questionnaires in indicated years.

NOTE: For N = 200, a correlation of .14 or more is significant at the .05 level, and a correlation of .18 or more is significant at the .01 level. For N = 300, a correlation of .11 is significant at the .05 level, and a correlation of .15 is significant at the .01 level.

each of the earlier variables. Accordingly, we computed multiple regression equations for men and women separately for the importance of each of the three aspects of religion in later maturity. Table 9.8 presents the beta weights for the six multiple regression equations. We have used only the 1940 variable for strictness of religious training because of its high association with the same variable measured in 1950. As can be seen from the table, the extent of religious inclination as an adult, as reported in 1950 when the subjects were an average age of 40, was by far the strongest predictor, when the other religion variables were controlled. Sunday School attendance and amount of interest in religion in young adulthood are relatively more important for men as a predictor of interest in religion in later maturity, while church membership and activities are stronger predictors for women. Strictness of religious training emerged as a significant negative predictor of the importance of social aspects of religion for women within the context of the other variables, suggesting that it was correcting for irrelevant components in other predictors (see Cohen & Cohen, 1975, for a discussion of suppression in multiple regression).

Religion and Well-Being

Is religion related to a sense of well-being in later maturity? Some investigators have found an association between religious orientation and well-being in aging (Hunsberger, 1985; Koenig, Kvale, & Ferrel, 1988). For the women in our sample, three measures of well-being in 1986 — self-rated calmness, cheerfulness, and happiness — were modestly correlated ($r = .10$ to $.21$) with the reported importance of spiritual activities. Happiness was also related to an increase in spiritual activities for women ($r = .11$). For men, the importance of social aspects of religion was correlated with cheerfulness and happiness ($r = .11$ and $.19$). We wondered whether marital status, especially widowhood or divorce, would be related to any of the 1986 indexes of religious orientation. We found that the total increase in spiritual activities for married women was lower than for the single, divorced, or widowed women ($p < .05$).

Political Participation and Beliefs

We turn now to the political views and activities of our subjects. While the stands that people take on political issues are indicators of their values, political participation is complex and reflects the interplay of many factors. For example, people's participation in the political process reflects not only their interest in current issues, but also their belief that society can be influenced through political means. As we will see, the members of the later-maturity group had been politically active to a greater than average degree.

Voting Regularity

Voter participation in the group has been extraordinarily high. In 1977 the subjects were asked about their voting frequency. They were an average age of 67. More than 90 percent said that they always voted in national elections. The

TABLE 9.8
*Results of Multiple Regression Analyses Predicting Importance
of Three Aspects of Religion to Later-Maturity Group in 1986*

| | Standardized multiple regression coefficients | | | | | |
| | Spiritual | | Social | | Social welfare | |
Religious variables	Men (N = 108)	Women (N = 112)	Men (N = 109)	Women (N = 107)	Men (N = 108)	Women (N = 105)
Strictness of religious training (1940)	.01	.05	−.05	−.35^a	.09	−.06
Church membership (1940)	.03	.18^b	.13	.21^b	.18^a	.22^a
Sunday school attendance (1940)	.20^c	.04	.34^a	.13	.01	−.05
Number of church activities (1940)	.08	.00	.02	.25^b	.12	.15
Amount of interest in religion (1940)	.20^b	.12	.15	.05	.06	.00
Extent religiously inclined as an adult (1950)	.30^a	.48^a	.21^a	.25^b	.18	.07
R	.61	.67	.63	.60	.45	.30
R^2 (Adjusted R^2)	.37(.34)	.45(.42)	.40(.36)	.36(.33)	.20(.14)	.09(.04)

SOURCE: Questionnaires in indicated years.
NOTE: Levels of statistical significance refer to the unique predictive contribution (β) of the variable for the indicated group.
$^a p < .01$. $^b p < .05$. $^c p < .10$.

TABLE 9.9

Political Party Preferences of Terman Group (1940, 1950, 1960, and 1977)

| | 1940 | | | | 1950 | | | |
| | Men | | Women | | Men | | Women | |
Political party	N	Pct.	N	Pct.	N	Pct.	N	Pct.
Republican	161	36.3	138	35.9	299	55.7	227	50.3
Conservative	29	6.5	15	3.9	—	—	—	—
Democratic	107	24.1	102	26.6	174	32.4	181	40.1
Liberal	56	12.6	50	13.0	—	—	—	—
New Deal	17	3.8	6	1.6	—	—	—	—
Progressive	3	0.7	3	0.8	—	—	—	—
Socialist	17	3.8	17	4.4	13	2.4	13	2.9
Radical	7	1.6	5	1.3	—	—	—	—
Communist	0	0.0	1	0.3	—	—	—	—
Other	—	—	—	—	10	1.9	5	1.1
None or independent	47	10.6	47	12.2	41	7.6	25	5.5
Total (N)	444		384		537		451	

SOURCE: Questionnaires for indicated years.

percentages who always voted in state and, particularly, local elections, were somewhat smaller, but when those who "usually" voted were also considered, these percentages were also over 90 percent. These levels of participation clearly exceeded those for other older persons and for the population as a whole. For example, of American voters 65 years and older, 62 percent reported voting in the presidential election in 1976, and 51 percent reported voting in the congressional elections in 1974; comparable figures for the population as a whole were 59 percent and 45 percent, respectively (Hendricks & Hendricks, 1986). One likely contributing factor to the group's voting frequency is their relatively high socioeconomic level, a variable which has been found to be associated with greater political participation (Erikson, Luttbeg, & Tedin, 1988).

As might be expected, the group's voting participation in later maturity has its roots in earlier life. Their high levels of participation were continuous throughout adulthood. We compared their 1977 responses to questions about voting regularity to their responses in 1950 and 1960. Ninety-four percent of men and 97 percent of women who answered the 1950 and 1977 questions said at both times that they always or usually voted in national elections; similar levels of stability were found in the 1960 and 1977 responses.

Political Party Preferences

The Terman group formed their political affiliations in a time of political diversity and upheaval. The elections in which some 70 percent of the later-maturity sample were first eligible to vote were those of 1932 and 1936, when Franklin Roosevelt's sweep made the Democratic Party the majority party. Voters who entered the electorate in this time have been liberal on average, and most registered as Democrats throughout their lives (Abramson, 1983; Erikson, Lutt-

TABLE 9.9
(*Continued*)

| | 1960 | | | | 1977 | | | |
| | Men | | Women | | Men | | Women | |
Political party	N	Pct.	N	Pct.	N	Pct.	N	Pct.
Republican	304	62.7	245	57.9	227	57.5	164	46.6
Conservative	—	—	—	—	—	—	—	—
Democratic	162	33.4	162	38.3	123	31.1	146	41.5
Liberal	—	—	—	—	—	—	—	—
New Deal	—	—	—	—	—	—	—	—
Progressive	—	—	—	—	—	—	—	—
Socialist	8	1.7	7	1.7	—	—	—	—
Radical	—	—	—	—	—	—	—	—
Communist	—	—	—	—	—	—	—	—
Other	—	—	—	—	4	1.0	2	0.6
None or independent	11	2.3	9	2.1	41	10.4	40	11.4
Total (N)	485		423		395		352	

beg, & Tedin, 1988). The Terman group, on average, was somewhat more conservative, although the members' political views varied considerably.

Table 9.9 summarizes responses of the later-maturity group from 1940 through 1977 to questions on political leanings. Eleven codes were used in 1940 and only four thereafter. If we group Conservatives with Republicans, and Liberals, New Dealers, and Progressives with Democrats, we see that in 1940 the men's political preferences were almost equally divided between the two major parties, and the women leaned toward the Democrats. In addition to these affiliations, 5 percent of both men and women identified themselves as Socialists or as having radical views, and one woman had Communist leanings. By 1950, and increasingly so in 1960, a majority of our sample was Republican, somewhat more so among the men than the women. The political leanings of the later-maturity group in these earlier years were roughly similar to those of the Terman group as a whole.

In 1977, a majority of the men identified with the Republican Party; the women were more equally balanced between the two parties, although more women reporting affiliation were Republicans than Democrats. Thus, the group, in contrast to others in their cohort, has maintained a greater identification with the Republican than the Democratic Party from mid-life into later maturity. The proportion of Independents was larger in 1977 than in the years since 1940. This is consistent with a trend in the larger society toward declining party identification since the mid-1960's (Abramson, 1983; Erikson, Luttbeg, & Tedin, 1988).

We were curious about the extent to which party preferences throughout the group's lives were continuous or shifting affiliations for the individuals in the group, and examined the joint distributions of Democratic and Republican party leanings in the same years as in Table 9.9. For the 1940 data, we grouped

Conservatives with Republicans, and those identifying with Liberals, the New Deal, and Progressives with Democrats.

We found that while there was considerable stability in affiliation, there also were shifts in membership along the way for some members of the group. The stability in party identification was somewhat greater from mid-life onward (1950 to 1977) than earlier. From young adulthood to mid-life (1940 to 1950), over 60 percent of both men and women reported that their party identification had not changed. However, in the two later comparisons (1950 to 1960 and 1960 to 1977), 75 to 80 percent reported no change. For men who moved between parties, the strongest shift was from the Democratic to the Republican Party between 1940 and 1950 (10 percent), and shifts in 1960 and 1977 from the previous reports were approximately equal in direction (about 5 percent). Among women who changed party membership between reports, there was a noticeable shift from Democratic to Republican membership from 1940 to 1950 (11 percent), and in 1960 (9 percent). However, in later maturity the direction of change reversed for women, with 8 percent of women moving from the Republican to the Democratic Party between 1960 and 1977.

Self-ratings on Radicalism/Conservatism

In 1977 the group was asked about their political and economic viewpoints. This question was modeled on similar questions in the 1940, 1950, and 1960 questionnaires. The 1977 responses are summarized in Table 9.10. The group's views covered the entire range from radical to strongly conservative. Twenty-three percent called themselves middle-of-the-road. The median for men was slightly on the conservative side and for women was slightly on the liberal side. Almost 27 percent of men stated that they tended to be liberal or very liberal, as compared with 40 percent of the women. In contrast, 46 percent of the men described themselves as tending to be conservative or very conservative, while only one-third of the women did so.

In 1940, 1950, and 1960 the subjects were asked a similar question about their political philosophy. The question was phrased slightly differently in those years, with the term "political and social viewpoint" used instead of "political and economic viewpoint." The question was coded on a 9-point scale, with five points labeled: (1) "Extremely radical," (3) "tend to be radical," (5) "average," (7) "tend to be conservative," and (9) "very conservative." Responses midway between the labeled points were assigned the appropriate values.

Intercorrelations across the four reports of political and social/economic viewpoint were computed. As with political party membership, there is considerable stability in the rankings of the members of the group over the 37 years these variables were measured. The correlations ranged from .44 to .68, the average being .61.

Comparing 1977 reports of radicalism-conservatism with earlier reports is problematic because of the differences in the scale labels. The scaling of the item used in the earlier years differed markedly from the scaling of the 1977 item on

TABLE 9.10
Self-Rated Political and Social/Economic Viewpoints
of Later-Maturity Group (1977)

Political and economic viewpoint	Men N	Men Pct.	Women N	Women Pct.
Radical	5	1.2	2	0.5
Very liberal	19	4.6	34	9.0
Tend to be liberal	91	21.9	115	30.6
Middle of the road	91	21.9	93	24.7
Tend to be conservative	127	30.5	86	22.9
Quite conservative	65	15.6	36	9.6
Strongly conservative	18	4.3	10	2.7
Total (N)	416		376	
Significance (p) by Wilcoxon test		.01		

SOURCE: 1977 questionnaire.
NOTE: Statistical significance level is for difference between men and women.

the liberal side of the scale. In 1940 through 1960, the terms "extremely radical" and "tend to be radical" were used, rather than "liberal," while in the later scale "radical" was used only at the scale endpoint. Oden commented in 1968 on the asymmetry of the earlier scale, and noted that "liberal" was probably a more appropriate term to use with "conservative"; the original scale had been retained to make comparisons with previous years possible. In 1977 the scale was modified to fit the contemporary political spectrum.

To deal with the change of scale, we pooled responses above the middle category for each year, and also those below it, providing general categories for percentages of liberals and conservatives. Table 9.11 displays the progression of subjects' ratings from 1940 to 1977. Again, we see the shift toward conservatism in midlife, but the women moved perceptibly in the liberal direction as they reached later maturity.

Correlates of Political Beliefs

As we have seen, the group's political and social views covered the entire spectrum. It is natural to ask whether the variability in their views was linked in any systematic way to other factors. In fact, some social and demographic factors were found to correlate with these views in earlier surveys and have been noted in previous volumes. We compared political views across our three occupational groups of men and across our three career groups of women. For these analyses we compared the mean ratings on the radicalism-conservatism scale for each year. There was a consistent tendency for the professional men to be more liberal than the other two male groups. Among the women, the homemakers' views were consistently more conservative than those of the career women and income workers.

We also wondered whether personality was related to social and economic viewpoint. In 1940 the Terman group were asked to describe themselves on a list

TABLE 9.11
Self-Rated Political and Social/Economic Viewpoints of Terman Group
(1940, 1950, 1960, and 1977)

	1940		1950		1960		1977	
	N	Pct.	N	Pct.	N	Pct.	N	Pct.
				MEN				
Liberal-radical	205	41.3	128	24.2	126	25.2	115	27.6
Middle of the road/average	102	20.6	145	27.5	109	21.8	91	21.9
Conservative	189	38.1	255	48.3	265	53.0	210	50.5
Total (N)	496		528		500		416	
				WOMEN				
Liberal-radical	153	34.6	112	24.8	111	25.3	151	40.2
Middle of the road/average	130	29.4	157	34.7	127	29.0	93	24.7
Conservative	159	36.0	183	40.5	200	45.7	132	35.1
Total (N)	442		452		438		376	

SOURCE: Questionnaires in indicated years.

of twenty personality traits. The only trait that showed consistent relationships to political and social or economic viewpoint was "conforming to authority," which was related positively with more conservative views. The correlations ranged from .37 to .13 for the men for the four ratings from 1940 to 1977, and from .39 to .27 for the women. The average correlation was .21 for the men and .31 for the women. (For a discussion of similar findings with the samples studied at Berkeley, see Mussen & Haan, 1981.)

Contributions to Others

Contributions to others can be made in a variety of arenas, including religious and political organizations and their activities. They may also be undertaken privately on an individual basis. Although contributions to others may be an indicator of an important altruistic personal value, they also can be an indicator of positive functioning. Persons unable to take care of themselves are probably less able to contribute to others. Moreover, both middle-aged and older persons believe that having positive relations with others and caring about others are significant components of healthy adjustment (Ryff, 1989b).

Organizational Membership

The later-maturity group were asked about their organizational memberships in 1977. Almost three-fifths of the men and two-thirds of the women belonged to at least one organization. These figures are slightly lower than the 69 percent of persons aged 64 to 70 reporting attending organizations one or more times per month in the Duke adaptation study (Cutler, 1985). The later-maturity men belonged to more professional and business organizations than the women, while the women's participation was higher than the men's in community health, religious, political, and educational or cultural organizations. This probably resulted partly from sex differences in employment patterns earlier in life.

We investigated continuity in organizational participation to see whether individuals tended to join organizations later in life, or whether those who had participated earlier were more likely to do so later. We examined the correlations between several indices of organizational involvement in later maturity and the number of service activities and organizational memberships reported in 1950 and 1960. These included: presence or absence of volunteer activities in 1972, number of organizations in 1977, and how often engaged in community service activities in 1982 and 1986. The results are presented in Table 9.12. The correlations in this table suggest, as in Chapter 8 on interests and activities, that activities in aging often have their foundation in earlier involvements. These findings are important, because organizational participation has the potential for providing

TABLE 9.12

Relationship of Community Service Activities and Organizational Memberships in 1950 and 1960 to Community Service and Organizational Memberships in Later Maturity

Community service activities and organizational memberships	Participation in voluntary community service activities (1972) r	Number of organizational memberships (1977) r	Frequency of community service (1982) r	Frequency of community service (1986) r
	MEN (N = 266–436)			
Service activities (1950)	.25	.24	.24	.29
Organizational memberships (1950)	.17	.28	.18	.10
Service activities (1960)	.26	.34	.29	.35
Organizational memberships (1960)	.25	.23	.15	.11
	WOMEN (N = 251–377)			
Service activities (1950)	.25	.08	.10	.19
Organizational memberships (1950)	.23	.30	.19	.17
Service activities (1960)	.28	.24	.11	.12
Organizational memberships (1960)	.13	.32	.21	.20

SOURCE: Questionnaires in indicated years.

NOTE: For N = 300, a correlation of .11 or above is significant at the .05 level, and a correlation of .15 or above is significant at the .01 level. For N = 400, a correlation of .10 or above is significant at the .05 level, and a correlation of .13 or above is significant at the .01 level. 1972 data are presence versus absence of volunteer activities taking up a substantial amount of time in the period 1970–72; 1977 data are the number of organizations to which subjects have committed a substantial amount of time or interest; 1982 and 1986 data are how often subjects engaged in community service activities coded as 0 = "none," 1 = "occasionally," and 2 = "frequently."

meaning and integration in the later years, and it is easier for the older person to continue or increase participation in an organization than to find and join a new one.

Personal Contributions to Others

A 1982 question asked whether subjects were providing care for a friend or relative. About a quarter of the men and a third of the women reported that they were caring for someone. Both the men and women helped relatives as well as friends. However, almost twice as many women as men were helping friends. These results reinforce our earlier findings that the women had broader networks than the men, and also reflect the fact that more of the women were widowed.

Summary

On the whole, the group were maintaining meaningful goal commitments in later maturity, although they were, at the same time, accepting some of the realities of aging. Their goal emphasis tended toward maintaining a sense of mastery and productivity in a personal way, rather than through formal work roles or competitive achievement. Both men's and women's goals showed moderate stability from 1982 to 1986. However, from 1982 to 1986, both men and women showed modest reductions in their commitment to involvement and achievement goals, but increased their commitment to acceptance goals.

The men and women also showed some differences in their goal orientations in later maturity. The women were higher on involvement goals, with a greater emphasis on personal relationships. Autonomy was also more salient to the women, particularly in regard to maintaining independence and health. The women also stressed acceptance goals more than the men.

Goal orientations of both men and women also varied according to their occupational histories. Professional men were more achievement-oriented than both higher-level business men and men in lower-level occupations. Professional men put least emphasis, however, on autonomy goals, and higher-level business men the most. The strongest contributor to this latter difference was the goal to maintain health. The later-maturity goals of the career women were more active in nature than the goals of the women income workers and homemakers. The career women put more emphasis on autonomy, involvement, and achievement goals, and less on acceptance goals.

There was a slight tendency for the later-maturity group to see themselves as more ambitious than others of their cohort as they aged. The men had higher employment-related ambitions than the women in 1977; the women channeled their ambition into avocational pursuits. Professional men had the highest ambition for excellence in work in 1977 and the men in the lower-level occupations had the lowest. Among women, the career workers saw themselves as relatively more ambitious compared to others in regard to excellence in work in 1977 and in overall ambition in 1986. Assessments of ambition as early as childhood were related to ambition in later maturity of both men and women.

Religion was not highly important to either the men or women in later maturity, and did not appear to be as important to them as to other elderly persons. Overall, the women were more religious than the men. The most important aspects of religion for both men and women were spiritual and social welfare activities; the social aspects of religion were relatively less important. Increases in religious orientation as the group grew older most often concerned interest in religion and greater emphasis on the importance of the spiritual aspects of religion. Decreases in religious orientation most often involved formal religious participation and declining concern with the social aspects of religion. The importance of religion to different individuals in later maturity was related to earlier religious training and participation. The strongest predictors of later religious orientation were religious participation and interest in young adulthood and religious inclination reported in mid-life. Several measures of well-being showed small positive correlations with religious orientation in aging, including the importance of spiritual aspects of religion to women and emphasis on the social aspects of religion in men.

The Terman group demonstrated an extraordinarily high level of voter participation in later maturity, as well as earlier in their lives. On the whole, they were more conservative in their political affiliation than others of their generation, the men being more conservative than the women. In 1940, the men were almost equally divided between the two major parties and the women leaned toward the Democrats; by mid-life the majority of both sexes favored the Republican Party. In 1977, a majority of the men identified with the Republican Party, while the women's support for the two parties was more equally balanced. Party allegiance and political and social/economic viewpoint showed considerable stability from mid-life onward, but the women moved perceptibly in the liberal direction in later maturity. The professional men were consistently more liberal than the higher-level businessmen and the men in lower-level occupations. Among women, the homemakers were consistently more conservative than the career workers and income workers.

In later maturity, both the men and women made contributions to others through organizational participation or by providing personal assistance on an individual basis. Over half the men belonged to at least one organization, as did two-thirds of the women. Participation in organizations in mid-life was related to such participation in later maturity. About a quarter of the men and about a third of the women reported in 1982 that they were providing care for someone.

The findings in this chapter concerning the values and goals of the later-maturity group have important implications for successful aging. In this chapter, we see the motivational bases of the broad range of activities these subjects engaged in (as described in Chapter 8). Many of the individuals in the sample were highly committed to making personal contributions to society and to their own personal growth. They continued to be involved with people in both personal and organizational ways. Their high level of political participation is a sign that they remained interested in the world around them, and that they felt that their voice could make a difference.

At the same time, there were also signs of a realistic assessment and awareness of the aging years. The modest declines in involvement and achievement goals, and the corresponding increase in acceptance goals reflect this phenomenon. This is in accord with other research and theory related to goals in aging (Dittmann-Kohli, 1990; Erikson, 1959; Ryff, 1991). Even individuals as advantaged as these subjects must come to terms with the existential realities of aging. However, they were doing so within the overall context of highly positive functioning, and of an optimistic and proactive orientation to life.

PART V

Overall Adjustment

10

Health and Well-Being

Physical health is a key component of well-being, particularly in aging, when people are increasingly subject to chronic ailments, and are more susceptible to serious life-threatening diseases. However, individuals vary considerably in their functioning in later life, including their physical health (Rowe & Kahn, 1987). Some individuals reach their later years without apparent physical or mental illness, while others must deal with chronic or episodic health problems and clearly evident disease processes. Baltes and Baltes (1990) have distinguished between these two paths to aging, calling them "normal" and "pathological," respectively. In addition, they discuss a third category, "optimal" aging, which refers to the ideal of aging under optimal physical and environmental conditions.

Physical health has consistently been found to correlate with self-assessments of well-being in aging (George & Landerman, 1984; Larson, 1978; Okun et al., 1984). Physical illness and psychological dysfunction often interact, and each may cause, mask, or exacerbate dysfunction in the other realm (Brody & Kleban, 1983; LaRue, Dessonville, & Jarvik, 1985). For example, psychological stress can contribute to physical illness, and physical illness can lead to negative emotional reactions and to a curtailment of social interaction. Moreover, older individuals place greater emphasis on health as a criterion for well-being than do younger persons. For example, in a recent study comparing views of well-being of middle-aged and older adults, older subjects were more likely to mention health as the most important factor in their lives, and as the thing they were most unhappy about (Ryff, 1989b).

Some older individuals with severe medical problems do function well. In a developmental sense, dealing with diminished physical health presents one of

217

the most demanding challenges of the later years. Poor health in the later years is likely to require more accommodative strategies for effective coping than typical demands earlier in the life cycle (Brandtstadter & Renner, 1990; Folkman et al., 1987).

In addition to physical factors, gerontologists, in particular, have been interested in the study of psychological well-being, as they search for ways to optimize the experience of the later years (George, 1981; Larson, 1978; Lawton, Kleban, & diCarlo, 1984; Stock, Okun, & Benin, 1986). However, psychological or "subjective" well-being is complex (see Bryant & Veroff, 1982; Diener, 1984). Subjective well-being has several aspects, including life satisfaction, happiness, morale, and psychiatric symptoms (George, 1981). Measures of subjective well-being commonly include assessments of positive and negative affect, as well as comparisons of ideal conditions and attainments with reality. In addition to traditional approaches to the definition of well-being, Ryff (1989a) has proposed other aspects, such as autonomy, positive relations with other persons, and purpose in life, that have their roots in theories of positive psychological functioning.

A number of objective factors have been found to be important in predicting psychological well-being in aging. Among these are health, socioeconomic status, activity, social interaction, and aspects of the individual's living situation. It is important to realize, however, that the direction of causality is not always clear. Moreover, persons of higher socioeconomic status are in a better position to mitigate many of the negative effects of aging, and, thus, socioeconomic status may moderate the influence of some of the usual causal factors (Larson, 1978; Longino, Warheit, & Green, 1989; Shanas & Maddox, 1985).

We begin this chapter by summarizing the mortality and causes of death of the sample to 1986. We then take the assessments of health and well-being in the 1986 questionnaire as our principal focus, and describe the later-maturity group's status on these dimensions, at 74 years of age, on average. We also investigate antecedents and correlates of health and well-being. Finally, through selected case studies, we allow the subjects to speak for themselves, as they face the issues of physical and emotional well-being in their aging years.

Mortality and Objective Health Status

Mortality

Table 10.1 shows, within birth cohorts, the percentage distribution of deaths at various ages, to September 1986. At that date, 40 percent of the original sample of men were known to be deceased, and 28 percent of the women, but Table 10.1 excludes voluntary withdrawals who can no longer be located and other lost subjects, showing adjusted figures of 43 percent and 31 percent, respectively. Particularly after age 50, men's mortality was greater than women's.

There is some evidence for a relationship between precocity, productivity, and length of life (Simonton, 1990). The mortality data for the Terman subjects are

TABLE IO.I

Percentage of Deaths in Terman Group at Various Ages, by Birth Cohort, to 1986

Birth cohort	N	Percent deaths in age-groups							Age of death unknown	Total deaths	
		<30	30–39	40–49	50–59	60–69	70–79	80–89		N	Pct.
					MEN						
1900–1904	68	3%	1%	3%	7%	18%	19%	6%[a]	3%	41	60%
1905–9	261	3	3	2	9	13	14[a]	1[a]	<1	119	46
1910–14	391	4	3	4	8	14	7[a]	—	3	163	42
1915–19	82	4	2	1	10	6[a]	—	—	1	20	24
1920–25	8	12.5	0	0	0	12.5[a]	—	—	—	2	25
Total	810	4	3	3	8	13	9	1	2	345	43
					WOMEN						
1900–1904	23	4%	9%	0%	4%	13%	17%	0%[a]	4%	12	52%
1905–9	196	2	3	2	4	7	12[a]	1[a]	3	65	33
1910–14	320	4	1	3	4	9	6[a]	—	3	95	30
1915–19	73	3	4	4	4	8[a]	1	—	—	18	25
1920–25	11	9	0	0	9	0	—	—	9	3	27
Total	623	3	2	2	4	8	8	<1	3	193	31

SOURCE: Cumulative data on deaths.

NOTE: N's exclude lost cases.

[a]Not all members of this group had reached the upper limit of this interval in 1986. The final death rate in the cell may be higher than shown here.

far from complete, but what there are suggest that the group, on average, is comparatively long-lived. We use two bases for comparison. First, presented below, are the percentage surviving to age 70 in 1987 in two United States cohorts: 1900–1902, and 1909–11 (National Center for Health Statistics, 1989), compared with the survival rates for two cohorts of the Terman group derived from Table 10.1.

Terman Group			
Men		Women	
1900–1904	1905–9	1900–1904	1905–9
68%	70%	70%	82%
United States			
Men		Women	
1900–1902	1909–11	1900–1902	1909–11
30%	31%	37%	35%

It should first be noted that the United States statistics include all races, and would be somewhat higher than those shown if restricted to whites. Second, the median age of death of white males in the 1900–1902 cohort was 57.2, and of white females was 60.6. As can be seen from Table 10.1, the median age of death for both the men and women in the group in the 1900–1904 cohort was over 70. We must qualify these comparisons by noting that infant and childhood mortality was much higher in these earlier cohorts than is presently the case, and that the

TABLE 10.2

Causes of Death in Terman Group by Age-Group (to 1986)

Cause of death	Number of deaths in age-groups							Age of death unknown	Total deaths	
	<30	30–39	40–49	50–59	60–69	70–79	80–89		N	Pct.
MEN										
Cardiovascular	1	4	9	24	29	22	2	—	91	26%
Stroke	—	1	2	3	2	2	—	—	10	3
Cancer	1	4	5	14	24	18	—	—	66	19
Infections	6	—	1	1	4	1	—	—	13	4
Renal	2	—	—	1	3	—	—	—	6	2
Respiratory	—	—	—	—	2	—	—	—	2	1
Neurological	1	—	1	1	—	4	1	1	9	3
Gastrointestinal	2	—	—	1	1	1	—	—	5	1
Accidents	13	4	3	2	1	1	—	—	24	7
Suicide	4	4	6	7	4	—	—	—	25	7
War	—	4	—	—	—	—	—	—	4	1
Other	1	—	—	12	36	26	4	13	92	27
Total deaths	31	21	26	66	106	75	6	14	345	
(with pct.)	(9%)	(6%)	(8%)	(19%)	(31%)	(22%)	(2%)	(4%)		
WOMEN										
Cardiovascular	1	1	1	5	9	5	—	—	22	11
Stroke	—	—	1	1	2	3	—	—	7	4
Cancer	2	3	27	10	13	16	1	—	42	37
Infections	10	4	—	1	1	2	—	—	18	9
Renal	1	1	—	—	1	—	—	—	3	2
Respiratory	1	—	—	—	—	5	—	1	7	4
Neurological	—	—	—	—	1	2	1	—	4	2
Gastrointestinal	1	—	—	—	1	—	—	—	2	1
Accidents	3	1	2	2	3	—	—	—	11	6
Suicide	1	3	3	1	—	—	—	—	8	4
War	—	—	—	—	—	—	—	—	—	—
Other	1	—	1	6	20	15	—	16	59	31
Total deaths	21	13	15	26	51	48	2	17	193	
(with pct.)	(11%)	(7%)	(8%)	(13%)	(26%)	(25%)	(1%)	(9%)		

SOURCE: Cumulative data on deaths.

Terman subjects are a part of the population that had survived these early years. The percentage of individuals surviving to age 10 in the United States cohorts above was approximately 80 percent, indicating a 20 percent loss due to infant and early childhood mortality. Even with this qualification, however, the Terman subjects appear to have survived longer than their peers.

The causes of death in each age-group are presented in Table 10.2. It should be noted that these data may not be completely accurate; they are based primarily on death certificates, which often list a secondary illness, rather than the underlying cause of death. While accidents and infections account for a greater proportion of earlier deaths, there is a trend toward a higher incidence of cardiovascular disease, stroke, and cancer as causes of death from mid-life onward. This is consistent with national statistics which show that heart disease, cancer, and stroke account for over three-quarters of deaths among the elderly (U.S. Senate Special Committee on Aging, 1987–88). In the Terman group, cardiovascular disease and cancer were the most frequent causes of death in both sexes, cardiovascular disease accounting for the highest percentage of men's deaths and cancer the highest percentage of deaths among women. Our data on cardiovascular disease are consistent with national data showing that men were more than twice as likely as women to die of heart disease (U.S. Senate Special Committee on Aging, 1987–88). However, national data show that, on average, men are also more likely than women to die of cancer (Verbrugge, 1989). The generalization that both sexes tend to die of the same causes, however, applies to the Terman group as well to national samples.

Specific Health Problems

We now consider the specific health problems reported by the later-maturity group. In 1986 they were asked to indicate any changes in their physical and mental well-being since 1981, and to indicate areas that cause them to worry about their well-being over the next few years. About a third of the sample listed no changes and about 40 percent listed no concerns.

The health conditions most often reported were cardiovascular problems and muscular-skeletal problems. Cardiovascular problems were slightly more prevalent among men than women, being mentioned as a change or concern by 18 percent and 15 percent of men, and by 14 percent and 11 percent of women, respectively. Cardiovascular problems ranged from high blood pressure or irregular heart beats to having had a heart attack or bypass surgery. Muscular-skeletal problems were more prevalent among women, mentioned by 13 percent and 9 percent of men as a change or concern, compared with 23 percent and 12 percent of women. General problems of aging, visual difficulties, psychological changes, and cancer were the next most frequently mentioned. Problems of aging included miscellaneous aches and pains, becoming forgetful, and general slowing down.

Some of the changes and concerns corresponded with causes of death for the sample, particularly cardiovascular disease and cancer. Others, such as muscular-skeletal problems, and general concerns about growing older, represent chronic disabilities of aging. The sex differences in the group were consistent with data for the general population showing that elderly men are more likely to experience life-threatening acute illness, and elderly women more likely to experience chronic, nonfatal, illnesses, such as arthritis, that cause physical limitations (U.S. Senate Special Committee on Aging, 1987–88; Verbrugge, 1989).

Personal Assistance

Because serious medical problems can lead to a need for personal assistance, we also explored the degree to which our subjects needed help from others. An item in the 1986 questionnaire, scored on a nine-point scale, asked the subjects to indicate to what extent they needed personal care or assistance. The two endpoints of the scale were: (1) "must have considerable help" and (9) "need little or no help," the midpoint of the scale being (5) "have some recurrent needs." The distribution of responses was highly skewed, with the great majority of the 1986 respondents needing little assistance. Almost 60 percent indicated that they need little or no help; 7 percent of men and 8 percent of women indicated that they had recurrent need for help or for considerable help. There was no difference in the distribution of responses on this variable for men and women. (These figures did not include one man and four women whose questionnaires were filled out by a relative or caretaker because the subjects were unable to fill them out.)

The men and women did differ, however, in their satisfaction with the availability and quality of their health care. The question was posed on a nine-point scale labeled (9) "highly satisfied," (7) "generally satisfied," (5) "somewhat satisfied," (3) "not very satisfied," and (1) "not at all satisfied." The means of 7.29 (S.D.=1.41) for men and 6.73 (S.D.=1.40) for women indicate that the group were, on average, generally satisfied with their health care. However, the sex difference was significant ($p < .01$). The difference was produced principally by responses at the high end of the scale; 18 percent of men were highly satisfied, while none of the women were. The group reported spending an average of only about 4 percent of their time meeting their health care needs.

Appraisal of Health and Well-being

We shall now examine the group's self-ratings of their health and psychological well-being. We shall also examine the extent to which these self-assessments of current health status correspond with the physical health disorders they listed in the open-ended questions about recent health changes and concerns.

Health Ratings

General health. The first rating we examine is a five-point self-rating of health since 1981, made in 1986. The distribution of responses appears in Table 10.3. More than 80 percent of the men and 75 percent of the women reported that they were in good or very good health. These percentages exceed the level of favorable self-ratings in national surveys. We present below comparisons with national data for 1986 (Verbrugge, 1989), where health was also measured on a five-point scale, but where the points on the scale were labeled "excellent," "very good," "good," "fair," and "poor." The figures for the later-maturity group are the percentage rating their health as very good or good, and for the national sample, the percentage rating their health as excellent, very good, or good.

	Terman		United States	
Age	Men	Women	Men	Women
65–74	89.5%	76.0%	72.9%	72.2%
75–84	73.6	73.8	65.9	66.6

TABLE IO.3

Self-Ratings by Later-Maturity Group of Recent Health, and
Energy and Vitality (1986)

	Men		Women	
	N	Pct.	N	Pct.
Health				
Very good	111	30.4	109	33.1
Good	187	51.2	139	42.3
Fair	49	13.4	64	19.5
Poor	14	3.8	15	4.6
Very poor	4	1.1	2	0.6
Total respondents	365		329	
Energy and vitality				
Vigorous, have considerable endurance	78	20.7	69	20.8
Adequate for a full program of activities	192	51.1	147	44.3
Have to limit myself	78	20.7	87	26.2
Lack of energy very much limits my activities	28	7.5	29	8.7
Total respondents	376		332	

SOURCE: 1986 questionnaire.

Also, a 1981 Harris survey conducted for the National Council on Aging re-ported that 21 percent of individuals aged 65 and older reported poor health to be a very serious problem. Both these comparisons show more favorable self-ratings of health by the Terman group.

The group's ratings are high, considering the numerous health problems they listed. To explore whether there was a correspondence between their self-ratings of general health and their specific health problems, we examined the distribu-tions of ratings of overall health for the most frequently mentioned changes and concerns. Table 10.4 reports the percentage of individuals who rated their overall health since 1981 as "very good" or "good," broken down by those who men-tioned no changes and concerns, and those who mentioned some of the most frequent problems. The first row of the table shows a strong correspondence between a high self-rating of health and listing no health changes or concerns.

The health ratings of those who list negative changes in aging, muscular-skeletal problems, or problems with vision, were quite positive, particularly among men. Most strikingly, even for life-threatening disease, such as cancer, a majority of the subjects rated their overall health as good or very good. Several of the group had cancer that was considered to be cured, but there were others who had had recent cancer surgery and were maintaining an optimistic outlook despite uncertainty about the future. For example, one woman who had had breast cancer recently rated her health as very good; she said she was aware of her own mortality, but did not worry.

The fact that the subjects rated their health favorably in the face of numerous health changes and concerns is consistent with other samples (see, for example,

TABLE 10.4

Number and Percent of Later-Maturity Group Reporting Each
of Several Health Changes or Concerns and Reporting
Good or Very Good Health

Health change or concern	Reporting change in health				Reporting concern about health			
	Health good or very good		Psychological well-being very good		Health good or very good		Psychological well-being very good	
	N	Pct.	N	Pct.	N	Pct.	N	Pct.
				MEN (N = 363)				
None	118	97%	61	50%	143	93%	64	42%
Aging	29	85	9	26	30	79	11	29
Muscular-skeletal	37	79	9	19	28	88	8	25
Vision	27	79	10	29	18	86	6	29
Cardiovascular	42	67	7	11	39	72	9	17
Cancer	12	54	1	5	8	53	3	20
				WOMEN (N = 329)				
None	88	95	53	57	128	91	72	51
Aging	38	85	7	16	22	61	7	19
Muscular-skeletal	47	62	9	14	28	68	9	22
Vision	21	68	5	16	18	56	6	19
Cardiovascular	23	50	8	17	28	76	8	22
Cancer	15	68	3	14	12	80	3	20

SOURCE: 1986 questionnaire.

Bayer, Whissell-Buechy, & Honzik, 1981). In a recent study of subjective health ratings of individuals aged 51 to 91 (Walker & Volkan, 1989, cited in Walker, 1990), results showed that these ratings stress in descending order, functional, eudaimonistic (exuberant well-being, realization of intrinsic potential), and adaptive factors, clinical definitions (the absence of disease) being given the least weight. Our findings, as well as those of others, suggest that when individuals rate their health they take their functioning into account, and also compare their health status to others of their own age, rather than focusing on a clinical diagnosis of freedom from pathology. These more positive, lived definitions make it possible for older people to feel well, even in the presence of chronic or life-threatening disease (Walker, 1990), and probably account for the finding that discrepancies between self-ratings and ratings by physicians tend to be in the direction of more optimistic ratings by individuals (LaRue et al., 1979; Maddox & Douglass, 1973).

It is, however, important to note the essential validity of self-ratings of health. They tend to be positively correlated with physicians' ratings (LaRue et al., 1979; Maddox & Douglass, 1973). Moreover, they predict mortality above and beyond prediction on the basis of objective indicators, such as physicians' assessment based on physical examinations (Idler & Kasl, 1991; Kaplan, Barell, & Lusky, 1988).

Self-ratings of energy and vitality, also summarized in Table 10.3, were somewhat less favorable than the general health ratings, but still quite good, considering the age of the group. The mean ratings of health and energy and vitality of men and women did not differ. They did differ by age, as would be expected. The oldest subjects had the lowest self-ratings, and the youngest had the highest on both variables ($p < .01$). Moreover, mean differences in the two ratings in 1982 and 1986 for those subjects responding at both times were lower in 1986 for both men and women ($p < .01$). The correlation with age was $-.17$ for both ratings by men. Among women, the correlation was $-.10$ for health and $-.21$ for energy and vitality.

Health hassles. Table 10.5 reports the self-ratings on a number of health problems. These items measure some chronic problems of the elderly, such as sensory and motor deficits, as well as general health and personal energy. A growing literature suggests that chronic daily stressors are associated with poorer mental health, especially in the elderly (Chiriboga & Cutler, 1980; Holahan, Holahan, & Belk, 1984; Lazarus & DeLongis, 1983). The health problems appeared within a larger list of items, with the following instructions: "Here is list of experiences that many elderly people find troubling. Some of them can be real hassles. Check once those that have troubled you recently, but that in one way or another you are able to handle without too much stress. Check twice those that you cannot handle very well and that are causing you fairly severe stress." These ratings thus explicitly took into consideration not only the presence of a problem, but the difficulty it was causing. We shall speak of those that the subjects could handle fairly easily as "minor hassles," and the more difficult ones as "major hassles." The respondent's score on an item was the number of checks (0, 1, or 2). The item scores were summed to create a total health has-

TABLE 10.5
Number and Percent of Later-Maturity Group Reporting Each of Several Minor and Major Health Hassles (1986)

	Men (N = 359)				Women (N = 324)			
	Minor		Major		Minor		Major	
Health hassle	N	Pct.	N	Pct.	N	Pct.	N	Pct.
Hearing	151	42.1%[a]	15	4.2%	87	26.9%	9	2.8%
Vision	139	38.7	10	2.8	108	33.3	12	3.7
Health	106	29.5	17	4.7	84	25.9	24	7.4
Muscular strength and control	127	35.4	16	4.5	114	35.2	21	6.5
Not enough personal energy	111	30.9[a]	13	3.6	130	40.1	21	6.5

SOURCE: 1986 questionnaire.
NOTE: Measure of statistical significance refers to difference in the distribution for men and women.
[a]$p < .01$ by chi-square.

sles score, ranging in value from 0 to 10. The mean hassles score was 2.17 (S.D.=1.67) for men and 2.16 (S.D.=1.75) for women.

As the table shows, although these health problems were prevalent in the group, only a small percentage of the subjects found them very difficult to handle. More women than men found lack of personal energy a problem; more men than women reported hearing problems.

Psychological Well-Being

Psychological well-being was assessed directly by three variables: two measures of mood (depression and anxiety) and a measure of happiness. The first question asked the respondents to indicate the range within which their mood had fluctuated during the last month or two on a nine-point scale ranging from (1) "Very depressed; gloomy" to (9) "Very cheerful; elated." The second question asked them to do the same on a nine-point scale ranging from "Very tense, worried; anxious" to "Very relaxed; calm." Thus, respondents were asked to give an upper and a lower score on each scale.

The high upper scores ranged from 3 to 9 for depression and 2 to 9 for anxiety in both men and women; the median upper score on each variable was 7. The lower scores ranged from 1 to 8 on both variables, the median being 5. Thus the subjects' mood tended to be positive, with upper scores tending toward the high end of the scale and lower scores toward the middle of the scale. On average, both men's upper and lower scores on anxiety were slightly more favorable than those of the women.

Some subjects did not indicate a fluctuation of mood, giving only one rating. The differences between the low and the high scores on each variable thus ranged from 0 to 7 for depression and 0 to 8 for anxiety; the median spread was 2 for both variables. Thus, most subjects indicated that their mood was fairly stable.

We will use the average of the high and low scores for depression and anxiety in the following discussions of psychological well-being. The happiness variable was scored from 1 to 3, the scale points being labeled "Not too happy," "Pretty happy," and "Very happy." Table 10.6 presents the means on these three variables by sex. On average, the scores on the two mood variables were above the midpoint of the scale. The group's average happiness score was near 2 ("pretty happy"). The distribution of the responses for happiness — 33 percent of men and 30 percent of women "very happy," and only 8 percent of men and 12 percent of women "not too happy" — compares favorably with national data from 1986 for both sexes combined showing 32 percent of the general population "very happy" and 11 percent "not too happy" (Niemi, Mueller, & Smith, 1989).

To combine the three variables into a single measure of overall psychological well-being, we standardized the scores on each item and summed them. As can be seen in the table, the men scored higher on overall well-being, due to the difference in the anxiety rating. We did not find the gender differences in depressed mood in aging reported of some other samples (Grambs, 1989). Finan-

TABLE 10.6

Psychological Well-Being Reported by Later-Maturity Group (1986)

Dimensions of psychological well-being	Men			Women		
	N	Mean	S.D.	N	Mean	S.D.
Depression/cheerfulness	375	6.08	1.10	332	6.00	1.32
Anxiety/calmness	372	6.23[a]	1.33	331	5.92	1.55
Happiness	372	2.24	0.59	333	2.17	0.62
Psychological well-being (overall)	368	.19[b]	2.32	327	−.20	2.75

SOURCE: 1986 questionnaire.

NOTE: Levels of statistical significance refer to differences between means of men and women. For explanation of scores see text.

[a]$p < .01$ by t-test. [b]$p < .05$ by t-test.

cial difficulties are thought to play a significant role in greater incidence of depression in older women as compared to men (Krause, 1986b). The fact that the majority of the Terman women reported that their finances were adequate may mitigate the experience of depression in this sample.

The relations between age and the overall psychological well-being measure, as well as each of its components, tended to be negative, but extremely small (see Aldwin et al., 1989 for a discussion of mental health and age). However, there were small but statistically significant differences between mean levels in 1982 and 1986 of those subjects responding in both years, the ratings in 1986 in all cases being slightly lower ($p < .01$ for both men and women on all three variables, with the exception of anxiety for men ($p < .05$).

In addition to the ratings of mood and happiness, we saw earlier that a number of subjects mentioned changes and concerns that were primarily psychological in nature. About 7 percent of men and 8 percent of women mentioned at least one of these changes. They included changes such as anxiety, depression, loneliness, insomnia, and various other frustrations and adjustments.

To determine whether we could consider the health and psychological self-ratings as two different dimensions, we performed a factor analysis on the six items. For health these were the rating of health, the rating of energy and vitality, and health hassles. The psychological items included the two average mood ratings and the happiness rating. An oblique rotation indicated two distinct, but related, factors. When the physical health scores were standardized and summed (with the total health hassles score reversed) to form a total physical health score, this score correlated moderately ($r = .48$) with the total psychological well-being score for both men and women. Therefore, as we consider the antecedents and correlates of health and psychological well-being below, we shall present the results for each variable separately in each table. We expected that although some variables would relate more strongly to health or psychological well-being, the relational patterns of the variables would often show some similarities.

It should also be noted here that the correlation between health and well-being in this group is somewhat larger than that usually found (see Okun et al., 1984, for a meta-analysis). In the light of our discussion above concerning self-ratings of health, it is interesting that the highest correlation between individual health measures and the psychological well-being composite occurred for the overall health rating (.49 for men and .48 for women). The correlations with energy and vitality were .41 and .39, and with health hassles .38 and .41 for men and women respectively in each case.

Correlates of Health and Psychological Well-Being in Later Maturity

In this section we shall consider contemporaneous factors and their relation to physical health and psychological well-being. In approaching the prediction of health and well-being, we shall rely on many of the constructs from previous chapters that have been found to be important in the lives of older persons. These include both personal and situational factors. It should be noted that causality may go in either or both directions for many of these variables.

Demographic and Situational Factors

Although, as we have seen, men and women tend to report different types of medical problems, their general self-ratings of their physical health are comparable. Levels of happiness and depression also are equivalent for men and women. However, their ratings of psychological well-being differ because the men give more positive self-ratings of anxiety.

As people age, the probability of health problems increases, on average, and age was negatively correlated with health for both the men and the women in the later-maturity group. (See Table 10.7 for the simple correlations of age and other variables with health and well-being. The results of the multiple regression analysis will be discussed below.)

We examined several health related variables because of the importance of health to well-being in the later years (Palmore, 1981). The need for assistance and satisfaction with health care were some of the strongest single correlates of both health and well-being, as can be seen in the simple correlations in Table 10.7, the time spent in meeting health care needs was also an important indicator. The use of alcohol (not included in the table), however, tended to relate more to psychological well-being than to physical (r of $-.10$ and $-.11$ with psychological well-being of men and women).

Another important variable that can relate to many of the conditions of aging is income (Shanas & Maddox, 1985), one of the common components of measures of socioeconomic status. In our group, most of whom were fairly well satisfied with their financial situation, the respondents' assessment of the adequacy of their finances in 1986 was positively related to their physical and psychological well-being (see Table 10.7). Satisfaction with present living arrangements, reported in 1977 (see Chapter 7 for details) was related to psychological well-being in 1986 ($r=.24$) for both men and women; the correlations with health were .13 for men and .08 for women. However, reports of objective

TABLE 10.7

Contemporaneous Correlates of Health and Psychological Well-Being of Later-Maturity Group (1986)

	Men				Women			
	Health (N = 263)		Psychological well-being (N = 266)		Health (N = 164)		Psychological well-being (N = 165)	
	r	β	r	β	r	β	r	β
Age	−.22	—	−.02	—	−.16	—	−.03	—
Adequacy of finances	.19	—	.25	—	.16	—	.14	—
Not being alone	.07	—	.14	.12[b]	.08	.12[c]	.04	—
Would like more interaction with friends	−.11	—	−.19	−.11[c]	−.21	—	−.24	—
Would like more interaction with family	−.09	—	−.12	—	−.25	−.14[c]	−.21	—
Need assistance	−.50	−.39[a]	−.31	—	−.46	−.29[a]	−.23	—
Percent time meeting health needs	−.31	—	−.20	−.10[c]	−.31	−.23[a]	−.16	—
Satisfaction with health care	.26	—	.27	.11[b]	.22	.14[b]	.32	.18[a]
Ambition in whatever engaged in	.33	.14[a]	.36	.23[a]	.30	—	.26	—
Proactive goals	.26	—	.19	−.11[c]	.28	—	.19	.19[b]
Importance of spiritual aspects of religion	−.02	—	.03	—	.02	—	.18	.18[b]
Importance of social aspects of religion	.03	—	.13	.16[b]	.00	−.17[b]	.10	—
Proactive activities	.29	.14[b]	.22	.18[a]	.26	.16[b]	.25	.16[b]
Non-health hassles	−.21	−.14[b]	—	—	−.25	−.20[a]	—	—
Total hassles	—	—	−.40	−.30[a]	—	—	−.42	−.45[a]
R	.60		.60		.65		.67	
R^2 (Adjusted R^2)	.36 (.33)		.36 (.33)		.42 (.37)		.45 (.40)	

SOURCE: 1986 questionnaire.
[a]$p < .01$.   [b]$p < .05$.   [c]$p < .10$.

living arrangements (house, apartment, etc.) in 1986 showed no relation to these variables.

Goals, Ambitions, and Activities

Being psychologically invested in life and being behaviorally active might be expected to contribute to the physical and emotional well-being of the later-maturity group. Such relationships have been found in other samples, such as the Duke longitudinal studies (George, 1978; Palmore, 1979, 1981). They are related to constructs such as personal optimism, which represent hopeful, rather than hopeless, stances toward life (Reker & Wong, 1985). We began by examining the relations of the group's 1986 goals and ambitions (see Chapter 9; also Holahan, 1988; Vaillant & Vaillant, 1990) to health and psychological well-being. The results are presented in Table 10.8. As can be seen in the table, ambition in whatever the subjects engage in as compared to others of their age and sex, had the highest relation with physical health and psychological well-being. Involvement in relationships and activities, and achievement motivation were positively

TABLE 10.8
Correlations of Ambitions, Goals, and Importance of Religion
with Health and Psychological Well-Being
of Later-Maturity Group (1986)

	Men (N = 342–368)		Women (N = 317–327)	
	Health	Psychological well-being	Health	Psychological well-being
	r	r	r	r
Ambition and goals				
Ambition in whatever engage in	.33	.36	.30	.26
Autonomy	−.01	.00	.18	.06
Involvement	.15	.19	.17	.21
Achievement motivation	.24	.13	.19	.14
Family	.18	.10	.05	.01
Acceptance	−.13	−.08	−.04	.04
Proactive goals[a]	.22	.17	.29	.21
Importance of religion				
Spiritual aspects	−.02	.03	.02	.18
Social aspects	.03	.13	.00	.10
Social welfare aspects	.02	.04	−.03	.01
Activities				
Intellectual	.13	.04	.11	.10
Cultural	.21	.14	.20	.11
Social	.21	.18	.16	.21
Active recreation	.24	.21	.27	.23
Passive recreation	.04	.00	−.04	.00
Proactive activities[b]	.29	.22	.26	.25

SOURCE: 1986 questionnaire.
NOTE: For N = 300, a correlation of .11 is significant at the .05 level, and a correlation of .15 is significant at the .01 level. For N = 400, a correlation of .10 or above is significant at the .05 level, and a correlation of .13 or above is significant at the .01 level.
[a]Proactive goals is the sum of Autonomy, Involvement, Achievement Motivation, and Family Goals.
[b]Proactive activities is the sum of Intellectual, Cultural, and Social Activities, and Active Recreation.

related to both dependent variables for both men and women, and autonomy was related to health for women. Family goals were more strongly associated with both variables in men than in women. The total proactive goals measure is the sum of Autonomy, Involvement, Achievement Motivation, and Family Goals; it shows positive relations with both physical health and psychological well-being.

Chapter 9 on values and goals discussed the importance to the group of various aspects of religion. Religious orientation in aging has been found to be related to well-being in other samples, such as the Duke Longitudinal Study (Palmore, 1981). Although our sample, on average, was not strongly oriented to religion, Table 10.8 shows some positive, but weak, relations of spiritual and social aspects of religion to psychological well-being.

Table 10.8 also presents the correlations of health and psychological well-being with participation in activities in 1986. Activity participation was related to both physical health and psychological well-being, the association being the strongest for active recreation, social, and cultural activities. The proactive activities score sums the first four activities (omitting passive recreation); it related positively to health and psychological well-being.

Hassles

Returning to our discussion of hassles, or chronic stressors (see Chiriboga & Cutler, 1980; Holahan, Holahan, & Belk, 1984; Lazarus & DeLongis, 1983), we list in Table 10.9 the remaining items from this section of the questionnaire. These represent several areas of chronic stress that we thought relevant to the lives of older people. Several of them, notably rising prices, family difficulties, managing finances, and misplacing or losing things, were checked as difficulties by at least a fifth of the respondents. In Table 10.7, we saw that both nonhealth hassles and total hassles have a definite negative relation to reports on psychological well-being, and nonhealth hassles are negatively related to self-reported health. Since health hassles were used in the computation of the measure of health, correlations are not computed between these two variables. However, the correlation of health hassles with psychological well-being, not noted in the table, was identical to that of total hassles, among both men and women.

Social Support and Marital Status

A substantial literature documents the association of social support with health and psychological well-being. Moreover, it is well accepted that the availability of meaningful personal relationships plays an important role in the well-being of persons in their aging years (Antonucci, 1990; Cutrona, Russell, & Rose, 1986; Holahan & Holahan, 1987; Ryff, 1989a,b). A recent study (Russell & Cutrona, 1991) found that part of the contribution of social support was its preventive role in the experience of minor stressful events, such as hassles. The recent emphasis in the research on social support has been on the quality of support, rather than its quantity.

TABLE 10.9

Number and Percent of Later-Maturity Group Reporting Each of Several Minor and Major Nonhealth Hassles (1986)

	Men				Women			
	Minor		Major		Minor		Major	
Nonhealth hassle	N	Pct.	N	Pct.	N	Pct.	N	Pct.
Care of a family member	56	15.6	9	2.5	30	9.3	12	3.7
Not seeing enough people	43	12.0	2	0.6	53	16.4	11	3.4
Rising prices of goods and services	94	26.2	10	2.8	83	25.6	11	3.4
Local transportation	15	4.2	7	2.0	26	8.0	5	1.5
Children's/grandchildren's difficulties	91	25.4	12	3.3	80	24.7	10	3.1
Too many things to do	66	18.4	9	2.5	66	20.4	9	2.8
Managing property and accounts	74	20.6	5	1.4	68	21.0	13	4.0
Misplaced or lost things; poor memory	104	29.0	16	4.5	89	27.5	15	4.6

SOURCE: 1986 questionnaires. Percentages add to over 100 because some respondents checked more than one hassle.

In 1986 respondents were asked to indicate their degree of satisfaction with the amount of intimacy and companionship they had with both friends and family. The variables were scored from (1) "would like much less" to (9) "would like much more," with the mid-point (5) labeled "fully satisfied." The means of these scores were slightly above the midpoint for both men and women, indicating that most were close to being fully satisfied with their social relationships (see Chapter 7 on Networks for a detailed description of findings). We rescored these variables to reflect sufficiency of support by collapsing the first 5 points on the scale; this yielded two five-point satisfaction variables, with higher levels indicating that more interaction was desired. The correlational patterns of the variables, presented in Table 10.7, show stronger relations to both health and psychological well-being of women than of men.

Other investigators have found that marital status is related to psychological well-being in aging, married subjects reporting higher levels of well-being (Larson, 1978). In the later-maturity group, divorced and separated men were lowest in psychological well-being ($p < .05$). There was no difference in health by marital status among men, or on either measure among women. To broaden the analysis in terms of social support, we created a related binary variable indicating whether or not an individual lived alone. Consistent with the results for marital status, there was a positive correlation ($r = .14$) between not living alone and psychological well-being in 1986 for men.

Integrative Multiple Regression Analyses

Along with the simple correlation coefficients in Table 10.7, we have presented the standardized beta weights for more integrative multiple regression analyses of the correlates of both health and well-being. We examined variables relating to physical health status, social support, ambitions, goals, importance of religion, activities, and chronic hassles. These analyses show the association of our dependent variable measures with each of the independent variables, when the operation of the other independent variable is controlled for. (The use of alcohol was not significant in any of the equations, and was excluded from the final analyses.) We included both age and adequacy of finances as control variables, even though they did not have significant beta weights, because of their demonstrated association with health and well-being in aging. The table also shows the multiple R and the variance accounted for in each equation. The multiple Rs are impressive, ranging from .60 to .67 and accounting for from 33 to 40 percent of the variance.

Need for assistance was significantly associated with the health of both men and women. The women's health was also associated with two other variables — percent of time spent meeting health needs and satisfaction with health care. Proactive activities were associated with the health of both men and women, as was the level of chronic stress, reflected in nonhealth hassles. Level of ambition was also associated with men's health. Social support was associated with women's health; women who did not live alone and did not desire more interaction with family had better health. The importance of social aspects of religion emerged as a significant negative predictor of health for women within the context of the other variables, suggesting that it was correlating for irrelevant components in other predictors (see Cohen & Cohen, 1975, for a discussion of suppression in multiple regression).

The psychological well-being of both men and women was associated with satisfaction with health care. Men's well-being was associated with percent of time spent meeting health needs. Social support variables, especially not living alone, were significantly associated with men's well-being. Having ambition (for men) and proactive goals (for women) were also significantly associated with psychological well-being. However, proactive goals had a negative weight for men, within the context of the other variables. Consistent with the correlational patterns, spiritual aspects of religion was associated with the well-being of women, and the importance of social aspects of religion with that of men. In both sexes, but especially in women, chronic stress as measured by total hassles was negatively associated with psychological well-being.

Antecedents of Health and Psychological Well-Being

The foundations for our subjects' experiences in aging were set earlier in their lives, and it is necessary to explore how the major variables examined in earlier chapters were related to their health and psychological well-being at the time of the latest follow-up in 1986, when they were in their mid-70's. In this section, we present the results of these analyses, which include variables such as family and occupational history, attitude toward achievement, previous activity level, and previous health and psychological well-being.

Previous Health and Well-Being

We begin by examining the relation of earlier measures of health and psychological well-being to the 1986 measures. We expected to find evidence of considerable continuity, with persons who had the best health and the most favorable psychological outlook earlier ranking higher on our 1986 scales.

The correlations of 1986 health and psychological well-being with several such antecedent measures are presented in Table 10.10. The 1982 measure of psychological well-being was identical to the 1986 measure, but the 1982 health variable lacked the 1986 measure of health hassles. The 1977 and 1972 health measures were single items, as was the 1977 measure of happiness. The 1960 mental health measure was a cumulative staff rating of mental health to that date, taking into account all psychological symptoms to 1960. The results showed moderate continuity between earlier and later health and psychological well-being. Overall, as would be expected, both health and psychological well-being in 1986 correlated higher with like antecedent measures than with measures in the other domain.

One attitudinal variable that seemed likely to be related to our subjects'

TABLE IO.IO

*Correlations of Previous Health and Psychological Well-Being
of Later-Maturity Group with Their Health and Psychological Well-Being
in 1986*

Measure of previous health or psychological well-being	Men (N = 292–329)		Women (N = 255–299)	
	Health *r*	Psychological well-being *r*	Health *r*	Psychological well-being *r*
Health (1982)	.62	.44	.70	.36
Health (1977)	.46	.52	.40	.43
Health (1972)	.46	.33	.48	.28
Health (1960)	.23	.21	.38	.34
Psychological well-being (1982)	.38	.66	.32	.57
Happiness (1977)	.31	.50	.13	.40
Cumulative mental health (1960)	.12	.17	.14	.23
Alcohol use (1960)	−.02	−.10	−.03	−.14
Expectations about aging (1972)	.04	.27	.07	.22

SOURCE: Questionnaires in indicated years and staff ratings of mental health.

NOTE: For N = 200, a correlation of .14 or more is significant at the .05 level, and a correlation of .18 or more is significant at the .01 level. For N = 300, a correlation of .11 is significant at the .05 level, and a correlation of .15 is significant at the .01 level.

enjoyment of their later years was their earlier expectations about these years. One reason is that expectancy, by providing the basis for constructive planning, may reduce maladaptive responses to changing life circumstances (Sears, 1981). A question about expectations about the years from 70 to 75 appeared in the 1972 questionnaire, with the responses scaled to indicate negative expectations at the low end of the scale and expectations of enjoyment of those years at the high end. (Responses of those with no idea about the future were excluded from the analysis.) The correlations with the 1986 health and psychological well-being variables appear in Table 10.10. For these correlations, the sample was restricted to subjects who were at least 70 years old in 1986. As can be seen in the table, 1972 expectations about these later years were related to psychological well-being 14 years later, but not to physical health.

Career History and Ambition

Since career patterns are related to life-styles as well as to economic factors, we examined the relation of career history to physical health and psychological well-being in 1986. The men were divided into the three occupational groups we used earlier, based on their 1972 to 1977 occupational level: professional, higher-level business, and lower-level occupations. For the women, the 1972 self-classification of homemaker, career worker, and income worker was used. There were no differences in either health or psychological well-being among the three occupational groups of men. The women's health did not differ between the occupational groups, but the career women exhibited more positive psychological well-being ($p < .10$), owing to their more favorable scores on depression

($p < .05$). Two important variables for occupational success, IQ and educational level, failed to show relationships with health and well-being. This replicates findings from the Duke Longitudinal Studies, which included a measure of life satisfaction (Palmore, 1979), but conflicts with another study of the Duke sample which focused on physical health (Nowlin, 1977). It is not surprising that IQ and educational level failed to predict for the later-maturity group, because most of them are above the threshold for the influence of these variables in most studies.

We also looked at other behavioral and attitudinal indices of earlier ambition or involvement in work, particularly those in the early years of later maturity. These correlations are presented in Table 10.11. The 1977 ambition variable summed ambition scores in four areas: excellence in work, recognition by others of accomplishments, proficiency in avocational pursuits and hobbies, and maintaining an excellent standard of living. The 1960 ambition variables included the first two of the above, along with vocational advancement and financial gain. Subjects were also asked in 1960 if they felt they had lived up to their intellectual ability. Finally, as described in Chapter 4, in 1940 the 150 most and least successful men were assigned the ratings "A" and "C." A "B" rating was assigned to all others. In 1960 the 100 most and least successful cases were selected. The lifetime A/C designation combined the two ratings into a numerical scale, with those rated "C" at both times rated lowest, and those rated "A" at both times highest.

Overall, there were modest relations between these variables and health and

TABLE 10.11

Correlations of Career Variables with Health and Psychological Well-Being of Later-Maturity Group (1986)

	Men (N = 183–347)		Women (N = 84–299)	
	Health	Psychological well-being	Health	Psychological well-being
Career variable	r	r	r	r
Percent time worked (1981)	.10	.07	.19	.09
Percent time worked (1977)	.21	.06	.11	−.03
Feelings about work (1977)	.15	.24	.09	.22
Feelings about work (1972)	.07	.16	−.02	.25
Ambition (1977)	.15	.20	.12	−.05
Change in ambition (1977)	.21	.23	.16	.03
Lifetime A/C designation for men (1960)	.22	.11	—	—
Noncareer/career self-rating for women (1972)			.06	.15
Lived up to intellectual abilities (1960)	.09	.11	.10	.20
Ambition age 30 to 40 (1960)	−.04	−.13	.05	.15
Ambition since age 40 (1960)	.03	−.01	.19	.13

SOURCE: Questionnaires in indicated years, staff ratings of mental health, and staff classification of men as "most successful" occupationally (A), and "least successful" (C).

NOTE: For N = 200, a correlation of .14 or more is significant at the .05 level, and a correlation of .18 or more is significant at the .01 level. For N = 300, a correlation of .11 is significant at the .05 level, and a correlation of .15 is significant at the .01 level.

psychological well-being. Enjoyment of work in later life tended to relate more strongly to subsequent psychological well-being than to physical health. In men the level of 1977 ambition, and change of ambition reported in 1977, related to both 1986 variables. In women there were modest correlations with physical health. The correlations of the 1960 ambition ratings also differed between the sexes, women's earlier ambition tending to correlate positively with health and psychological well-being, whereas a small negative correlation was observed between ambition between ages 30 and 40 and psychological well-being in men. However, the lifetime A/C rating in 1960 was positively related to both men's physical health and psychological well-being in 1986.

Previous Activity Level

We expected that higher activity levels in earlier life would predict positive outcomes in later maturity. The group was highly active throughout their lives (see Chapter 8 for a detailed discussion). We expected that these earlier activity patterns might be related to later physical health and psychological well-being by providing opportunities for meaningful lives, the maintenance of adaptive skills, and continued social interaction. Previous activities might also serve as an index of prior mental and physical health. We therefore computed the correlations between the 1977 and 1982 activity scales and health and well-being in 1986. Social activities and active recreation showed the strongest relation between previous activities and our 1986 measures. A summary proactive activities score for each year (summing intellectual, cultural, and social activities, and active recreation) was positively related to both health and well-being, with correlations ranging from .16 to .35. However, a 1960 activities measure of number of avocational pursuits failed to show any relation with later health and well-being.

Family History

Does a person's family history relate to his or her well-being in later maturity? We first examined the relation of lifetime marital pattern to 1986 physical health and psychological well-being by breaking the subjects into five groups: always single; intact marriage to 1986; history of divorce or separation only; widowhood without divorce or separation; and widowhood with divorce or separation. We compared the 1986 physical health and psychological well-being of these groups and found no relation to our variables. However, when we collapsed marital history into a binary variable for correlational analysis, contrasting those with normative marital histories — intact marriages or widowhood — with those who were single or divorced, we found a positive correlation in men ($r = .11$), but not in women.

We also looked at whether subjects had, or had not, raised children. We found positive relations to our 1986 variables in men (r of .15 and .14 for health and well-being, respectively), but no relations for women. Comparisons of the means

TABLE 10.12

Antecedents of Health and Psychological Well-Being of Later-Maturity Group in 1986

	Men				Women			
	Health (N = 262)		Psychological well-being (N = 276)		Health (N = 150)		Psychological well-being (N = 154)	
Personality variable	r	β	r	β	r	β	r	β
Easygoing (1940)	.25	.27[a]	.34	.33[a]	.12	—	.29	.22[a]
Self-confident (1940)	−.03	—	.10	—	.10	.16[c]	.17	—
Purpose (1940)	.11	—	.18	.13[b]	.00	—	.10	—
Health (1960)	.23	.10[c]	.21	—	.38	.33[a]	.34	.30[a]
Alcohol (1960)	−.02	—	−.10	—	.03	—	−.14	−.14[c]
Ambition age 30–40 (1960)	−.04	−.12[c]	−.13	−.21[a]	.05	*	.15	*
Ambition since age 40 (1960)	−.03	*	−.01	*	.19	.17[b]	.13	—
Men's cumulative A/C rating (1960)	.22	.23[a]	.11	.10[c]				
Women's career groups (1972)					.06	—	.15	—
R	.42		.45		.44		.49	
R^2 (Adjusted R^2)	.18 (.15)		.20 (.17)		.20 (.15)		.24 (.20)	

SOURCE: Questionnaires for indicated years and staff ratings of occupational success.
*Not included
[a]$p < .01$.   [b]$p < .05$.   [c]$p < .10$.

on health and psychological well-being showed that men who had raised children had higher scores on both variables ($p < .01$), but again there were no differences for women. We wondered if these results might be influenced by the differences in the life-styles and outcomes of single men and women (see Chapter 6 for details). However, when only married subjects were considered, the above pattern of results continued to hold.

Personality

It seemed possible that personality dimensions might relate to well-being in later life. We had no measures of personality in later maturity, but decided to explore the relation of the 1940 personality variables we discussed earlier with regard to occupations and marital experience. These included dimensions we have labeled "easygoing" (happiness of temperament and easy to get along with), "self-confidence," "sense of purpose," "emotionality," "impulsive," and "nonconforming." Correlational patterns suggested that the first four might prove important in predicting later health and well-being, the strongest correlations being between easygoing and psychological well-being for men and women. The correlations for easygoing, self-confidence, and sense of purpose are presented in Table 10.12 with results of a multiple regression analysis to be discussed below. Men's emotionality correlated .18 with their psychological well-being; women's emotionality correlated $-.18$ with health and $-.25$ with their psychological well-being. The variables are similar to some of those found to be predictive of either health or well-being in the Berkeley studies (Bayer, Whissell-Buechy, & Honzik, 1981; Mussen, Honzik, & Eichorn, 1982), the Duke Longitudinal Studies (George, 1978), the Baltimore Longitudinal Study (Costa, McCrae, & Norris, 1981), and the Grant Study (Vaillant, 1990).

Integrative Multiple Regression Analyses

We decided to explore the role of antecedent variables from early adulthood and midlife, along with marital and family history, as predictors of well-being in later maturity in integrative multiple regression analyses. (The family variables failed to contribute to the prediction, and were eliminated from the equation.) The final variables selected focus on four areas: personality, mental and physical health, earlier ambition, and attained career status.

With respect to personality, emotionality failed to contribute beyond the other variables, and was eliminated from the analyses. Cumulative mental health (as measured in 1960) was also nonsignificant, but the 1960 use of alcohol measure was significant and was retained. The two ambition measures in 1960 (ambition between ages 30 and 40 and ambition since age 40) were correlated (.67 for men and .56 for women), and one was chosen for each sex for inclusion in the regression equation on the basis of the simple correlations with the dependent variables. Thus, ambition from age 30 to age 40 was entered for men, and ambition since age 40 was entered for women. Men's lifetime A/C status was also included. Finally, we also included women's career status, scored in the direction of 1972 classification of career versus noncareer status, for reasons of symmetry between the equations for men and women.

The resulting equations are very interesting, and at first surprising. Having an easygoing disposition at age 30 was predictive of both health and psychological well-being at age 74 for both men and women. Men's achieved occupational status (their A/C rating) was a predictor of health and, to a lesser extent, of psychological well-being. Men's psychological well-being in later maturity was predicted by an early sense of purpose, which is positively correlated with career attainment. However, ambition between age 30 and 40, which also is correlated positively with eventual occupational achievement, was a negative predictor. Men with the highest earlier ambitions may have had difficulty in adjusting to some of the curtailments of achievement in their later years.

Previous health was very important in predicting women's health and psychological well-being in later life. Ambition since age 40 entered as a positive predictor of women's health in aging, as did earlier self-confidence.

Case Studies

While our objective variables can provide clues to approaches to life and conditions that can influence physical health and psychological well-being in the later years, they cannot capture the uniqueness of individual lives. We offer the following as examples of the orientations and experiences of some individuals in the later years.

Alan had been interested in history from childhood, and even before high school he spent much of his leisure time reading stories and novels about historical events. He went on to a distinguished career as a professor of history. He was the author of numerous articles and books in his field, one a noted reference volume. During his career, he was twice department chairman, and was also a vice chancellor for academic affairs. In his late 50's he became the director of a prestigious historical archive at his university. While pursuing his scholarly interests, he served on various boards, and was the president of the Board of Trustees at a nearby college. He received numerous honors in his work. His wife was a homemaker who participated actively in community service. They had two children, and he was very happy in his family life.

In his late 60's he completed what he believed was one of his two most important books, while continuing to produce scholarly articles at the same rate as earlier. His wife died then, and he subsequently remarried. His three most important goals at the age of seventy were to remain independent, healthy, and to have opportunities for achievement or competition, with secondary goals to be financially secure, make a contribution to society, continue to work, and continue to grow personally. His most frequent activities in his seventies were reading, professional writing, and community service, followed by hobbies, attending cultural events, and socializing with friends and relatives. In his mid-70's he was still employed half-time as director of the archive, and continuing to publish as well. His health was very good through his mid-70's, as was his reported mood and happiness.

Mark was a TV comedy writer and producer. He began in radio with considerable early success, having a natural talent for this line of work. He stated that he thought his early poor social adjustment contributed to his accomplishments in comedy writing by providing him with material. He had a special interest and ability in music and took both singing and piano lessons. His Strong Vocational Interest scores were high for artist, musician, author-journalist, and lawyer. His wife was a housewife; they had two children. He listed his marriage as a turning point in his life between an unhappy childhood and an extremely happy and rewarding adult life. He held several patents for equipment used in television production, one for an optometric device for visual training, and several for athletic instruction devices. He received his greatest satisfaction in his work from his creative activities, including both his professional activities and his inventions.

He had a heart attack at 61, but by age 64 considered his general health good; in his early 70's he experienced chest pains on exertion. He had cut back to about three-quarters time in his sixties, still finding his work as a writer/producer of occasional TV shows rewarding; by his late 60's he was working 20 percent time. He stated that the factors contributing most to his happiness then were health, financial independence, and having his family close by. He expected then to enjoy the years from 70 to 75, and his reports in those later years were quite positive. In his early 70's his most frequent activities were reading, informal visiting, and golf (which consumed half his time). His three most important goals were to be healthy, to make a contribution to society, and to continue to grow personally, be creative and productive.

Josephine received her doctorate at the Sorbonne in Paris. She had always been career-oriented, and enjoyed her career thoroughly, traveling widely to attend professional conferences. She was a research microbiologist, and was listed in "American Men of Science." (There was no equivalent volume for women.) She worked at several major research institutes in Europe and the United States. She retired early because of funding problems, but in her early 60's was appointed to a noted research institute, where she collaborated on important work in her field, and where she did some of her most exciting research. She says of that period, "So one advantage of 'old age' is the accumulated 'know-how' which only comes with experience or trial and error."

She worked full-time at her research into her late 60's, and then began gradual retirement. She worked regularly in a summer camp for children, teaching them to make flutes. Her initial reaction in her late 60's to her arthritis was to say that "she couldn't complain too much," since it "hadn't affected my tennis serve or trick shots — merely my ability to run or cover the court." However, as the years passed, arthritis became an increasing burden. In her mid-70's, she listed her three most important goals as to remain independent, to be as healthy as possible, and to continue to work. Her activities included reading, TV, hobbies, attending cultural events, and informal visiting. Despite her arthritis, she made scientific sojourns to Europe and Asia in her early 70's, giving conference talks. By her mid-70's, she described herself as more or less finally retired, and was working on a part-time volunteer basis at a research institute. In her late seventies she says, "So I am gradually winding down and trying to accept the debilities of old age and arthritis 'gracefully.' "

Nancy had originally trained as a teacher, but found her first experience unsatisfactory, so she trained to be a secretary. Her bachelor's degree was in chemistry. Her husband was a rancher who raised and warehoused fruit. She left secretarial work to raise their four children, and considered rearing them to be her most successful project. She eventually became a part-time newspaper correspondent for local newspapers. She then reentered teaching in her 40's, first as a substitute teacher, then as a regular elementary teacher, and finally as a high-school teacher.

Upon her retirement from teaching, she engaged in hobbies, gardening, arts and crafts, and travel, and spent much time with her husband, children, and grandchildren. Her husband of 40 years died of cancer when she was in her late 60's, and she found this loss to be difficult to cope with. After feeling devastated for a year, she began to put her life together. By her mid-70's, she considered her health good, although she had developed a heart problem and some arthritis; her mood was upbeat and she described herself as very happy. Travel had been her most interesting activity, and she took several major trips, including a 30-day trip around the Pacific, and trips to South America and China.

Summary

On the whole, the subjects' appraisals of their health in later maturity were quite positive. Over four-fifths of the men and almost three-fourths of the women reported that they were in good or very good health from 1981 to 1986. A majority of the subjects also reported that their level of energy and vitality was adequate for a full program of activities. Moreover, the favorability of their health ratings exceeded that of national samples.

The most frequent health problems reported were cardiovascular problems, muscular-skeletal problems, vision, cancer, and problems of aging. Although chronic health problems were fairly prevalent in the group, only a small percentage found them to be extremely difficult to handle, and most did not need personal assistance. Although the men and women tended to report different types of medical problems, their general self-ratings of their physical health were comparable. The men, however, were more satisfied with their health care than were the women.

Cardiovascular disease and cancer are the most frequent causes of death, with cardiovascular disease accounting for the highest proportion of men's deaths and cancer the highest proportion of women's deaths. By September 1986, 40 percent of the original sample of men were known to be deceased, as were 28 percent of the women. Excluding lost subjects, the adjusted percentages were 43 and 31, respectively. The subjects appeared to be living longer than others of their cohort.

Both the men's and women's subjective well-being was high. The levels of happiness and depression of the men and women were equivalent. However, their ratings of psychological well-being differed because the men gave more positive self-ratings of anxiety. Self-rated health and well-being in both sexes were moderately correlated. Age was negatively correlated with health; the relations between age and well-being tended to be in the negative direction, but were very small. However, repeated measures analysis of health and well-being items measured in both 1982 and 1986 showed small declines on all measures.

There were multiple contributors to the health and psychological well-being of our subjects in their 70's. The most important were health-related variables, such as the need for assistance, time spent on health care, and satisfaction with health care. Beyond health, however, social relationships and positive approaches to life, as represented by goals and ambitions and behavioral involvement in activities, both made positive contributions to health and well-being at this life stage. Married men had a higher level of psychological well-being than other men, but women's marital status was not related to their psychological well-being. Adequacy of finances (as assessed by respondents) contributed modestly to their well-being. The level of chronic stress in respondents' lives was one of the strongest predictors of lower well-being.

Moderate stability was observed between earlier measures of both health and psychological well-being and the corresponding 1986 measures. Some behavioral and attitudinal indices of earlier ambition or involvement in work, and of activity in earlier years were associated modestly with good health and well-being in later maturity. Several personality variables, measured when the subjects were an average age of 30, were positively related to 1986 health and/or well-being in later maturity, including easygoingness, self-confidence, sense of purpose, and high emotionality. In the integrative multiple regression analyses, easygoingness was one of the most important predictors of health and psychological well-being in the later years.

In examining life history variables that predict health and well-being in aging, we found, surprisingly, that family variables were stronger predictors for men than for women, in terms of both marital and parenting history. For this gifted group, previous occupational attainments were positive predictors of health and psychological well-being of both men and women. However, there was an intriguing difference in the positive role of earlier ambition (between the ages of 30 and 40). Women's ambition at this stage was positively related to later well-being, but men's was negatively related. The relation for women was probably related to the finding showing better psychological well-being for women with careers. For men, however, although early ambition and ultimate success were positively related to each other, their predictors were opposite so far as health and well-being in aging were concerned.

As we viewed our subjects' overall health and psychological well-being in their later years, we considered them to be aging successfully. On the most basic issue of survival, the data indicate that they were outliving others of their cohort. Moreover, their quality of life during their aging years was also comparatively good. They outranked national samples in their self-appraisals of good health, and their levels of subjective well-being were quite high. Although there were signs of modest declines in both health and well-being as the subjects grew older, overall they appeared to be handling the difficulties they encountered quite well.

11

Life Satisfactions

As an individual nears the end of a long life, it is natural to pause to reflect on the past and to evaluate experiences and satisfactions. In fact, contemporary theorists view this process as both a necessary and productive part of successful aging. For example, Butler (1963) sees the "life review" as providing the opportunity for the achievement of wisdom in the later years. And Erikson (1959) has placed in those years the last developmental crisis in his theory of the life cycle. In successfully resolving the conflict of integrity versus despair, the aging individual makes peace with his or her life, and comes to terms with the role of historical circumstances in shaping the life course.

In this chapter, we focus on the group's retrospective evaluations of their lives. The evaluations of such a talented group of individuals, living during a period of immense social change, can provide insights into the kinds of experiences and approaches to life that lead to satisfying lives. How contented were our subjects as they looked back on their lives? Which aspects of their life experience did they rate as most satisfying? What life events and personal characteristics were precursors of greater-than-average satisfaction? These and related issues will be addressed in this chapter.*

We shall use a set of responses from 1977; the subjects, in their late 60's on average, were asked to evaluate their lifetime satisfaction in several areas. We

* This chapter was written by Lee J. Cronbach, with the exception of the sections on turning points and life choices, which were written by Carole K. Holahan. The chapter is based on an incomplete plan made by Robert Sears. It revisits the questions treated in his award address (R. Sears, 1977) on the men and in the paper on women by Pauline S. Sears and Ann Barbee (1977), using more recent data. The analysis is different; for good reasons, R. Sears proposed not to make another multivariate ("path") analysis here and not to weight subjects' satisfaction scores by their ratings of importance.

shall explore both correlates and antecedents of these responses. We shall conclude the chapter with respondents' comments about the turning points in their lives, and about the choices they might make differently if they had the opportunity to live their lives again, using the insights gained over a lifetime.

The Profile of Life Satisfactions

The 1977 questionnaire asked for a report, on a five-point scale, of "the overall level of satisfaction you have experienced" in ten aspects of life. These included the core areas of work and family life, as well as several other areas with potential for providing meaning in life (see Table 11.2).* "Does not apply to my life" was a sixth option. Percentages, averages, and other statistics here ignore nonresponders and persons who checked this sixth option. Five of the areas had appeared in the 1972 questionnaire with somewhat different wording and a different response scale. Analyses of the 1972 data appear in R. Sears (1977) and P. Sears and Barbee (1977).

Work Satisfaction as an Example

By way of introduction to our discussion, Table 11.1 presents a full cross-tabulation of ratings on "the overall level of satisfaction you have experienced [in] income-producing work." The salient fact in this table is the concentration of responses at the two highest scale-points. The subgroup distributions differed, but even in the least contented subgroups five-sixths were at least "generally" satisfied with their work. All the 1977 scales exhibited the skewness seen here, though it was not always so extreme. Because skewness makes the mean a poor summary statistic, we concentrate on percentages in this section.

The table subdivides the sexes, using categories introduced in Chapter 4 for men and Chapter 5 for women. Clearly, the overall summary for either sex tells only part of the story. The percentages calling their work histories "Highly satisfying" were appreciably higher among career women and professional men than among other subgroups. (Thirty-six housewives said "Does not apply" and 30 more did not respond to the question.)

Satisfaction in Nine Areas

The ratings assigned to nine areas of satisfaction are summarized in Table 11.2. This table does not report subgroup percentages, but we shall mention noteworthy differences in the discussion. (The number of "Lower-level" men and "Income worker" women was too small to warrant specific reports on them.)

The first conclusion from Table 11.2 is that both sexes expressed much gratification in the four areas at the top in the table. Approximately half the sample

---

* One variable refers to satisfaction with a former marriage. This was coded only for persons who indicated (by a second, uncircled check) that their satisfaction with a former marriage did not match that of the latest marriage. We might infer that if a person had remarried and checked the marriage item only once the rating applies to all marriages. But we chose not to analyze the "former marriage" variable.

TABLE II.I

*Retrospective Ratings of Work Satisfaction of Later-Maturity Group
by Career Group (1977)*

Occupational group	N	Percentage of career group giving each response				
		Not at all satisfying	Not very satisfying	Somewhat satisfying	Generally satisfying	Highly satisfying
		MEN				
Professional	208	<1	2	4	35	58
Higher-business	168	2	3	7	44	44
Lower-level	40	0	8	10	58	25
Total	416	1	3	6	41	49
		WOMEN				
Career	135	0	1	3	32	64
Income worker	56	0	7	11	46	36
Homemaker	83	1	4	12	45	39
Total	295	<1	3	11	39	50

SOURCE: 1977 questionnaire.

NOTE: Two men and 40 women who checked "Does not apply to my life" are ignored; so are 8 men and 51 women who gave no satisfaction ratings. Twenty-one women who could not be assigned to one of the three categories but who gave a rating are counted in the total, so total percent adds to more than 100.

checked "Highly" and another 40 percent checked the slightly less positive "Generally" in evaluating family, work, and avocation. (On "avocation," see below.) Women's satisfaction over children was especially positive. Indeed, women expressed more satisfaction than men in all areas save work and most recent marriage.

Sears, interpreting the 1972 satisfaction data for all men together, ended his paper with the generalization that even the most gifted man gets more satisfaction from his family than his work. Our overall finding supports this, but the conclusion is reshaped when men are subdivided. In the higher-business group, the "Highly satisfied" percentages were 44, 65, and 55 for work, marriage, and children respectively — very much in line with Sears' statement (which also fits the men in lower-level occupations). His statement applies also to the home-maker women, whose percentages were 39 (work), 63 (marriage), and 71 (children). Among professional men, however, the percentages were almost equal: 58 (work), 61 (marriage), and 55 (children). Career women had a distinctive profile: 64 (work), 51 (marriage), and 77 (children). (The notably high figure of 77 comes from only 78 women who responded to the item on children.)

With regard to friendship and recreation there is just one unsurprising detail to add to the facts in the table. The percentage of homemakers who were highly satisfied with recreation was 7–9 percent above career women. (This was also true of the Leisure variable described below.)

The men's ratings on the three aspects lowest in the table suggest lack of enthusiasm. Lukewarm response to religion and cultural activities fits the sex

TABLE 11.2

Satisfaction of Later-Maturity Group with Various Aspects of Life Experience (1977)

Aspects of life experience	N		"Highly satisfying"		"Highly or generally satisfying"	
	Men	Women	Men Pct.	Women Pct.	Men Pct.	Women Pct.
Children	357	283	56%	71%	89%	93%
Present or most recent marriage	402	336	63	57	90	87
Income-producing work	416	295	49	50	90	89
Avocational activities, hobbies	393	325	43	56	88	95
Friendships, social contacts	410	365	30	47	82	92
Recreation	400	333	30	41	85	88
Cultural activities	311	310	17	37	65	85
Religion	253	253	18	33	44	65
Community service	316	285	15	27	52	78

SOURCE: 1977 questionnaire.

NOTE: The percentages in the two columns on the right are the sum of respondents answering "Highly satisfying" and those who answered "Generally satisfying."

stereotype. Since persons who avoided voluntary service would have checked "Does not apply," one must conclude that community service was less central than other areas to the men. Religion and community service ranked lower for women also. Subgroup differences within the sexes were small.

Results from the equivocal avocation-recreation-culture triad cannot be taken at face value. Terman had introduced "Avocational interests or hobbies" in a question about satisfaction in the 1950 supplementary blank (and we know from a question in the principal 1950 blank that he had in mind "sports, music, art, writing, collections, gardening, woodwork, etc."). In the 1972 questionnaire, a question about use of time employed the categories "Participation in cultural activities" and "Recreation." These terms and the "Avocational" phrase from 1950 and 1960 were made parallel entries in the 1977 query on satisfaction, with no further defining text. It was left to the respondent to decide which rubric to use in reporting on bridgeplaying, say, or nudism, or writing poetry. With no way to resolve the ambiguity, we have integrated the three into a new satisfaction variable named "leisure occupation." Our rule is to count only the highest of the responses to the three items. The percentages saying "Highly satisfactory" regarding at least one of the three elements were 52 for men and 69 for women. This count — obviously biased upward — puts leisure activities on a footing with the most satisfying elements in Table 11.2. It is of some interest that the men in lower-level occupations fell 22 percentage points below the professional and higher-business groups. One might have hypothesized that they would have found compensatory satisfaction outside the job. They did not.

Reliability from survey to survey. The 1977 report on satisfaction with income work correlated in the .4–.5 range with the 1972 counterpart. The 1977 report on satisfaction with present or recent marriage correlated in the .5–.7 range with the 1972 report on "family." For community service and culture the correlations were in the neighborhood of .3–.4. Recalling that the wording of questions changed and that most 1977 responses fell at the two highest satisfaction scale points, major differences among subjects in feelings of satisfaction appear to have been reasonably stable. However, unreliability severely limits the size of the correlations between satisfaction and other variables to which much of this chapter is devoted.

The profile in midlife. How did the ordering of satisfactions in Table 11.2 compare with reports on satisfaction at earlier dates? In 1950 and 1960, seven of the nine areas (all save recreation and cultural activities) were presented with essentially the same wording as in 1977. The respondent was to check or double check those aspects from which he/she was at that time deriving greatest satisfaction. This choice response is not logically equivalent to the 1977 ratings on scales separately. The differences between 1950 and 1960 are too small to be worthy of report; an adequate summary of the data appears to be a percentage of endorsements, averaged over the two years, with no extra weight given to double checks. (Persons making a checkmark on at least one element are counted in the base for all percentages, as the "Does not apply" option was not offered. Such an option would have raised the percentages, and the relative position of satisfaction with children, marriage, and women's work.)

Responses of the respondents included in Table 11.2 give the following percentages for sources of greatest satisfaction in 1950–1960.

	Children	Marriage	Work	Avocation	Friends	Religion	Service
Men	73%	77%	80%	53%	31%	17%	19%
Women	71	70	48	54	51	28	34

Although change of technique precludes exact comparisons, we see that the ordering of the areas was the same retrospectively as it was in real time. As the group grew older on average they did not cast a rosy light on some memories while forgetting their joy in other areas.

Was Retrospective Satisfaction Colored by Current Life Conditions?

Posssibly, an older person's expressed satisfaction with life in retrospect is strongly conditioned by present well-being. To check on this we related other 1977 characteristics to a "general satisfaction" measure, the proportion of the person's responses that fell at "Highly satisfactory." Persons rating fewer than 5 aspects were ignored. We did not carry the composite variable into later analyses, first because about 40 percent of each sex marked too few aspects to provide a score. Second, the components cohered so poorly as to make dubious a construct of individual differences in "general lifetime satisfaction." Rather typical was the within-sex correlation of about .16 between work satisfaction and avocational satisfaction. Several correlations were below .10.

We correlated this summary variable with reports on the person's current life situation. Almost all correlations for men were appreciably larger than those for women; after several attempts to check possible reasons we have no plausible explanation. In the following list of specific correlations, those above .15 are nominally significant at the .01 level.

	1977 General Satisfaction	
	Men	Women
Happiness	.33	.30
Energy, vitality	.32	.09
Satisfaction with living arrangements	.28	.17
Health	.25	.11
Current activity level	.16	.05
Education level	.13	.04
Current income	.07	.17
Age	.10	−.03

Activity level combines responses to questions about time devoted to paid and unpaid work; we gave somewhat greater weight in the composite to paid work because many subjects left the second question unanswered.

We have made no serious search for antecedents of overall satisfaction, but we did check whether more successful men reported more ultimate satisfaction. When the 1940 and 1960 staff ratings of occupational success were combined into a single scale, the composite correlated .20 with overall satisfaction. Objective conditions such as age were little related to reported satisfaction. In the list above, the four sizable correlations for men and the one for women were produced by variables that are partly subjective; a person with some health problems, for example, is expressing feeling as well as fact in choosing "Good" rather than "Fair." Evidently, men who in their 60's and 70's felt good about their current lives also tended to think well of their pasts. No doubt the correlations reported here were raised a bit by the fact that, among persons with the same feelings, some tend to speak well (and others less well) of both present and past. If a mood-driven response tendency were operating strongly, however, areas of satisfaction would intercorrelate more than they do.

Occupational Satisfaction

We intend to carry the sexes along in parallel, to the extent possible, so that men's and women's data on a given question can be reviewed on the same page. We shall, however, shift back and forth between the sexes where parallel treatment is not feasible or appropriate.

Before considering the 1977 data further, it seems well to recapitulate a striking finding of P. S. Sears and Barbee (1977), based on the 1972 data regarding satisfaction. It will be recalled that a 1972 question asked the women which one of four sentences best summed up her work history. We pooled women who had careers except in the years when they reared children with women who

TABLE 11.3

Actual and Preferred Career Patterns of Three Career Groups
of Women in Later-Maturity Group (1972)

| | | | "As I would now choose" | | |
"As it was"	N	Pct.	Career Pct.	Income worker Pct.	Homemaker Pct.
Career	157	41%	**94%**	1%	5%
Income worker	64	17	62	**25**	12
Homemaker	159	42	40	1	**59**
Total	380		66	5	29

SOURCE: 1972 questionnaire.
NOTE: These numbers differ slightly from the similar table of Sears and Barbee, as we found it possible to assign to categories 15 women previously coded as "other." The second column shows the percentage of respondents who actually were in each career group. The other percentages are the percentage of each career group who would choose each alternative in 1972. The figures in bold type are the percentages of each career group whose 1972 preferences corresponded to their actual work histories.

checked the simple "career worker" description. A companion question with the same response options asked which track "you would prefer to have been in, as you look back now"; again we pool the two "career" categories. This leaves three categories: self-designated career workers, income workers, and homemakers.

As these subjects reflected on their lives, careers were popular, desired by 66 percent of the women. Table 11.3 shows that the income workers' and homemakers' retrospective preference for careers differed markedly from their actual work patterns. Only 41 percent of the women were career workers in fact, but 66 percent would have preferred to be. Forty-two percent were homemakers, in contrast to 29 percent overall who preferred this pattern. The income worker pattern was the least practiced and least desired, but the 17 percent who were income workers was much larger than the 5 percent who would have chosen to be income workers. Almost none of the career women would have wished otherwise. Three-fifths of those who worked primarily for needed income longed for the career they had missed, and few longed for the traditional homemaking role. Although a majority of homemakers did favor that lifework in retrospect in 1972, nearly 40 percent of them would have preferred the career option. P. S. Sears and Barbee (1977, p. 34) offer this interpretation: "The proportion of women in the United States who are in the 'work' (according to this definition, 'work' does not include homemaking) force has been steadily rising, and possibly some of the homemaker women felt that they had missed an interesting and challenging part of life."

Sources of Satisfaction in Work

We can gain some psychological understanding of work satisfaction from reports on its sources. Table 11.4 summarizes two kinds of reports. An open-ended question in the 1972 questionnaire asked "What aspects of your work have given you the greatest satisfaction in recent years?" and the categories in

TABLE 11.4

Importance of Sources of Work Satisfaction of Later-Maturity Group (1972 and 1977)

	1972 free responses		1977 checklist	
Aspect of work	Men (N = 329) Mean	Women (N = 217) Mean	Men (N = 422) Mean	Women (N = 331) Mean
Creativity, learning, stimulation, personal growth (e)	.33	.31	.40	.47
Administrative, organizational, pride in getting things done (d)	.17	.20	.41	.35
Friendly relationship with people in work (b)	.06	.18	.39	.42
A helping or teaching relationship with people in work (a)	.19	.51	.31	.34
Financial gain (c)	.03	.10	.29	.24
Recognition, competition (f)	.22	.09	.23	.14

SOURCE: 1972 and 1977 questionnaires.

NOTE: Men not placed in an occupational group were included if they responded to the question. Means were computed as the ratio of total checkmarks to the possible total. Means therefore ranged from 0 to 1. When the 1977 responses were scored by counting double checks only, among men "Helping" tied with "Friendly" and "Financial" dropped to a tie with "Recognition." Among women, the double checks yielded the same profile as the count of all checks, save that "Administrative" dropped to a tie with "Friendly." Letters in parentheses indicate the order of response choices in the 1977 blank.

the table were developed as a coding adequate to cover nearly all responses. The same phrases constituted a checklist in the 1977 blank. The wording of the question became "Which of the following aspects . . . ?" Beyond checking those regarded as important, the respondent was to double-check "those most important." Retired persons were asked to respond in terms of preretirement satisfaction. (We do not summarize the diverse responses written on a final "Other:" line.)

A startling contrast between the 1972 and 1977 data no doubt carries a methodological lesson for survey researchers. Although the 1972 question spoke of aspects in the plural, only two men gave responses coded into as many as two categories. It is surprising that so few offered plural responses; the word "greatest" seemingly took on more weight than was intended. Among women the story was dramatically different. Of those giving one reason, 40 percent went on to give a second and 8 percent gave a third. (More precisely, their multiple responses were coded differently.) In 1977 men and women both averaged close to four checkmarks. The 1977 responses seemingly reflected the prompting or inhibiting effect of various words. A person who responds to one of the elements within the *d* or *e* string might not have come up with such a term spontaneously.

The ratio of total checkmarks to the possible total was computed for 1972 and 1977, so the means range from 0–1. These ratios are displayed in Table 11.4. For 1972 the base of the ratio was the number of persons giving any response to the question, not necessarily a response coded into a category of the table. The 1977 figures are means that gave double weight to a double check; thus the base of the ratio was twice the number of persons who checked at least one option. The responses to the different questions in the two surveys cannot be made fully comparable by any conversion. A count of 1977 double checks only might be more comparable to the 1972 data for men, and a footnote in the table adds some detail on double checks.

We concentrate on findings from the better standardized 1977 question. The four options that head the list were rated almost equally high, and the sex groups differed little. The overall picture was one of satisfaction from self-expression or development and achievement on the one hand, and from interpersonal relations on the other. In the 1972 free responses, the strongest tendency was for women to mention helping or teaching; apart from that, self-development values were high in both groups.

Men's occupational subgroups had distinctive patterns, exhibited in Table 11.5; this also considers subdivisions with respect to success, as rated by the staff in 1940 and 1960. As noted in Chapter 4, in 1940 the 150 most and least occupationally successful men were assigned the ratings "A" and "C." A "B" rating was assigned to all others. In 1960 the 100 most successful and the 100 least successful cases were selected. In Table 11.5 the "most success" groups consist of men with a success rating of A in either year; the "less success" groups are all others. The overall mean was calculated by averaging the means on the six aspects for each subgroup. The comparative dissatisfaction of the men in lower-level occupations was observable in their lower overall mean.

Professional men emphasized "Creativity" and "Helping" more than others. "Recognition" was comparatively salient for the more successful professionals

TABLE 11.5

Importance of Sources of Work Satisfaction in Occupational Groups of Men in Later-Maturity Group (1977)

| | Occupational group | | | | |
| | Professional | | Higher-level business | | Lower level |
Aspect of work giving satisfaction[a]	Most success (N = 62) Mean	Less success (N = 143) Mean	Most success (N = 42) Mean	Less success (N = 125) Mean	Less success (N = 36) Mean
Creativity	.61	.47	.36	.31	.17
Administrative	.31	.36	.56	.49	.29
Friendly relations	.34	.41	.39	.39	.43
Helping relations	.44	.37	.29	.22	.19
Financial gain	.26	.24	.31	.34	.28
Recognition, competition	.31	.19	.29	.26	.12
Mean overall satisfaction	.38	.34	.37	.34	.24

SOURCE: 1940 and 1960 staff ratings of occupational success and 1977 questionnaire.
NOTE: Means were computed as the ratio of total checkmarks to the possible total. Means therefore ranged from 0 to 1. Success ratings classified men in three groups: "Most successful" (A), "Least successful" (C), and all others (B). For the table, men rated A in either year were counted as "Most success," and all others were counted as "Less success." Only two men in lower-level occupations were rated A; they are not included in the table. "Mean overall satisfaction" is the average of the means for the six aspects in each subgroup.
[a]See Table 11.4 for full wording of the aspect.

(but still not especially high). "Friendly" was somewhat less salient for them than for others. It is striking that, even among the more successful professionals, inner-directed satisfactions from "Creativity" count for much more than the outer-directed joys of "Recognition." This agrees with a common conclusion in industrial psychology, that among high-status workers "intrinsic" aspects of work are a more significant source of satisfaction than "extrinsic" aspects (Locke, 1976).

In the higher-business group a similar finding was the predominance of the "doer": "Administrative" satisfaction over "Financial" and "Recognition." The two success subgroups differed little. To the men in lower-level occupations, the most satisfactory aspect of work was "Friendly relations"; it is not surprising that affiliation is a principal reward for those with less power or status. These men, as a group, seemed to have lost out on most of the satisfactions that come from making a personal contribution and from personal development through one's work.

The mean work satisfaction of the self-designated career women, income workers, and homemakers was .37, .35, and .27, respectively. Among career women "Creativity" held first place, with "Helping" and "Friendly" tied for second. Only their mean for "Helping" (.43) appreciably exceeded the mean for all women. The income workers, like lower-level men, were far above average on "Friendly" (.53) and "Financial" (.41); "Creativity" tied with "Financial" for second rank. The homemakers' two highest means, "Creativity" and "Administration," were near the mean for all women. Homemakers fell below other women on "Helping" (.24) and "Financial" (.10).

All in all, the career women were much like the BC-level professional men in their sources of work satisfaction. The income workers' main satisfaction was "Financial" (along with the social aspects of work, which are ranked highly in nearly every subgroup). The homemakers who worked found their satisfaction in the work itself, plus friendly relations; more emphatically than any other group, they "weren't in it for the money."

Antecedents of Satisfaction

Sears's 1977 paper examined a great number of hypotheses about predictors of men's retrospective work satisfaction. We made a similar study of 1977 ratings, using a similar list of variables, and also investigated women on these insofar as the data permitted. We brought in additional variables from the 1977 report on women by P. S. Sears and Barbee. They related background factors to satisfaction defined as correspondence between occupational preference and work history (indicated by the boldface cells of Table 11.3), not by the rating variable. (From the variables that were candidates for predictors of 1977 satisfaction we omitted indicators of work satisfaction from 1940–60. These correlated with 1972 satisfaction and no doubt would predict 1977 responses also.)

To reduce the list of candidate predictors we formed composites of intercorrelated variables, or selected a single report (for example, on health) rather than

TABLE 11.6

Percentage of Men in Later-Maturity Group Giving 1977 Retrospective Report
of Satisfying Work Experience, Classified by Occupational Group and Success

| | | Occupational group | | | | |
| | | Professional (N = 204) | | Higher business (N = 165) | | Lower level (N = 36) |
Level of occupational success	N	"Highly satisfying" Pct.	"Highly or generally satisfying" Pct.	"Highly satisfying" Pct.	"Highly or generally satisfying" Pct.	"Highly or generally satisfying" Pct.
Most success	108	71%	100%	56%	91%	—[b]
Moderate success	223	56	92	41	86	33[a]
Least success	74	22[a]	78[a]	35[a]	88[a]	23[a]

SOURCE: 1940 and 1960 staff ratings of occupational success and 1977 questionnaire.
NOTE: In 1940 and 1960 men were classified, on the basis of ratings by research staff, into three groups: "Most successful" (A), "Least successful" (C), and all others (B). For the table men who were rated A in either year were counted as "Most success," those who were rated B in both years were counted as "Moderate success," and the rest as "Least success."
[a]Percentages based on fewer than 40 cases.
[b]N < 20; too small for useful report.

using a string of reports. Even so, in a study with many variables chance has considerable influence on which ones rise above the "noise" level. In general, we attended to correlations at and above .15, even though the number of cases made many of the lower *r*'s nominally significant. We considered number of cases and logical relevance in deciding what to report. The unreliability of one-item variables limited all the correlations.

Men's occupational success. As described above, men (and not women) were rated on success and accomplishment in 1940 and 1960. Here we averaged the two ratings, giving greater nominal weight to the 1960 figure. (It was based on more information and has a smaller standard deviation than the 1940 rating.) Men rated A in either year were counted as "Most success"; those rated B in both years were counted as "Moderate success," and the rest as "Least success." For the few men in the 1977 sample who lacked one of the ratings, we construct an estimate. Our compositing formula differed slightly from that used by R. Sears in 1977. The success ratings ran low in the lower-level occupational group; the percentages above BB in the three groups were 30 (professional), 25 (higher-business), and 5 (lower-level).

Satisfaction clearly went with success; the correlation for all men was .27. As Table 11.6 shows, the relation was strongest among professionals. On this point R. Sears reported a correlation of .36; that higher figure makes sense because, as was noted at the start of this chapter, his dependent variable explicitly brought in success and commitment as well as satisfaction.

Life history correlates. The relation of the men's occupational satisfaction to type of career, first seen in Table 11.1, is echoed in Table 11.6. It will be recalled that type of career was a strong correlate for women's occupational satisfaction also.

Among background factors, only earned income correlated with retrospective work satisfaction (.22 for men and .26 for women). Earnings in 1970 and 1971 make up the predictor variable. This cannot tell the whole story, as some persons were wholly or partially out of the work force in those years. If we had had an accurate, inflation-adjusted measure of peak earnings (and the peak earning rate of part-time workers) the correlation would surely have been higher.

Age at first degree is of interest because it reflects the acceleration some subjects experienced, as well as some other advantages; the correlations were in the expected direction but low ($-.09$ for men and $-.03$ for women). Older members of the sample expressed more occupational satisfaction than younger members (correlations of .18 and .07, respectively) and health showed a weak correlation among women only (correlations of .00 and .13, respectively).

A life event or circumstance that, for example, curtails or postpones one's education no doubt can have a substantial effect on one's career and satisfaction. The effects, however, are idiosyncratic; a variety of life courses can follow from particular kinds of adversity or opportunity. We doubt that correlation analysis of many further life-event variables, even in a sample much larger than ours, would shed light on work satisfaction. The dynamics of circumstances, coping, and gratification are proper subjects for a case-history approach.

Motivational variables. Following the lead of the 1977 papers, we made a correlational study of twelve indicators of motivation collected during early and middle adulthood. Variables were scored to indicate positive motivation and self-esteem. Although every one of the 24 within-sex correlations with work satisfaction was positive, only 5 variables correlated in the neighborhood of .15 or better in one or both sexes. We give the correlations beside the coded name of the variable before we describe the variables.

	Correlation with work satisfaction	
	Men	Women
Ambition (age 30–40)	.26	.16
Ambition (since age 40)	.28	.13
Importance of schoolwork	.21	.13
Self-confidence	.24	.09
Drive	.19	.11

Correlations in the 1977 report on men were quite similar; the report on women did not include correlations of this kind.

Ambition (age 30–40) was formed by summing 1960 retrospective self-ratings on ambition at age 30–40 with regard to excellence in work, recognition, advancement, and financial return. Ambition (since age 40) was identical save that the ratings referred to "since age 40" and thus were concurrent, not retrospective. The correlations indicate that men ambitious in their work tended, on average, to end their careers with greater than average satisfaction; the same relationship was present, but much weaker, among women.

Taking one's schoolwork seriously shows much the same correlations. Impor-

tance of schoolwork was the sum of three 1950 self-ratings on interest in succeeding at schoolwork at ages before 12, 12–20, and since age 20.

Self-confidence combined 1940 and 1950 self-ratings on confidence and,
with the scale reversed, feelings of inferiority. Drive combines four items from
1940 and 1950 on persistence or perseverance and having "a program with
definite purposes" with a 1950 self-rating on "My life is completely integrated
toward a definite goal" (with "drifting" as the opposite pole).

Correlations of 1977 occupational satisfaction with 1940 parent and teacher
ratings on confidence and drive were near .15 among men and barely above zero
among women. There are correlations in the .08 to .15 range of work satisfaction
to positive relationships with a parent (rated retrospectively in 1940 and 1950). A
tendency for the relation with like-sex parent to correlate higher is unreliable.

The lower correlations among women were not clarified when we reanalyzed
within subgroups. Such minor variation across subgroups as appeared can be
attributed to chance. The following correlations are worth noting, however:

	Career workers		Income workers		Homemakers	
	r	N	r	N	r	N
Drive	.20	74	−.10	39	.12	42
Importance of schoolwork	.23	110	.08	40	−.05	65

R. Sears considered not only the variables we have used but a series of
indicators of work satisfaction and morale at successive ages. His concluding
paragraph on the findings fits our observations also, particularly for the men:

> So, the objective facts of life — the high level preparation, the success and status
> and financial rewards received — appear to have had negligible importance in deter-
> mining final satisfaction with the occupational side of life. Rather, it looks as if there
> were some continuing affective quality — an optimism about life, an enjoyment of
> occupational combat and a feeling of self-worth — that characterized the more satisfied
> of these men at age 30 and persisted through the next three decades of their lives.
> (R. Sears, 1977, p. 123).

Satisfaction with Present Marriage

Marital satisfaction has been explored rather thoroughly in Chapter 6, with
divorce as the primary dependent variable rather than a rating of satisfaction.
Marital satisfaction among our subjects was also explored by Holahan (1984),
who had a subsample of the later-maturity group fill out a questionnaire they had
originally responded to in 1940. She found that women's satisfaction scores
declined significantly between 1940 and 1981. A reanalysis considering only the
persons married in 1940 and 1981 (not necessarily to the same individual) did
not find a significant difference, however.

With two detailed reports available on marriage, there is no need here to
correlate the 1977 satisfaction measure with antecedents, as was done with work

satisfaction. Some items from the 1977 questionnaires do, however, have something more to tell us about happiness. Chapter 6 reported on how subjects, in 1972, rated the effect on the marriage of the wife's working. Ten percent of the men who responded, and 23 percent of the women, called the effect either mixed or negative. On a number of other variables regarding role relationships and allocation of responsibilities, Chapter 6 reported distributions of responses only. Here we relate those responses to expressed marital satisfaction.

Role Relationships

In 1977 Question 17 asked for statements about the wife's role in the male subject's career, or, in the women's blank, to her role in her husband's career. The husband was not asked about his role in his wife's career, and a question to the woman about her husband's role in her work proved unusable.*

To simplify, we label the response alternatives below. The phrasing of the woman's blank is bracketed.

Independent	She [I] had a career that was essentially independent of mine [his].
Collaboration	Her [My] work contributed directly to mine [his]. (Consider help in planning, collaboration, other regular interaction. Consider her [your] unpaid as well as paid work.)
Discussion	We discussed my [his] work frequently.
Social	She took interest in the social welfare of my associates and participated in other supporting activities. [I took substantial responsibility for the social welfare of his associates, built good will for his business, and other supporting activities.]
Knew little	She [I] knew very little about my [his] work activities.

The instructions were to check one or more statements out of the five offered. We treated each option as a separate binary variable. As a simple way of relating the responses to marital satisfaction, we report the percentage saying "Highly satisfying" among those who did and did not select a particular description. Then we take the difference. For example, with respect to the Social option, men's ratings of marital satisfaction were distributed as follows:

	Not at all satisfying				Highly satisfying	
	1	2	3	4	5	Total
Social checked		4		40	100 (69.4%)	144
Social not checked	4	18	12	69	140 (57.6%)	243
					(Difference = 11.8%)	

As no one such factor can have a consistently strong effect throughout the group, a difference of this size is worth taking seriously. The correlation, however, is only .13.

* The question about the husband's role with respect to the female subjects' career was not analyzed because the 1977 version invited multiple responses but the appropriate addend code was not applied.

TABLE 11.7

Differences in Marital and Work Satisfaction of Later-Maturity Group
Associated with Wife's Role in Husband's Work (1977)

Relationship of wife's activities to husband's work	Marital satisfaction		Work satisfaction	
	Men (wife's activities) (N = 389)	Women (own activities) (N = 310)	Men (wife's activities) (N = 389)	Women (own activities) (N = 242)
Collaboration	22	15	13	−2[a]
Social	12	15	11	−5[a]
Discussion	21	11	6	−3
Independent careers	0	−14	−9	20
Knew little	−31[a]	−19[b]	−9[a]	10[b]

SOURCE: 1977 questionnaire.

NOTE: The full response alternatives are given on p. 256. The figures are the differences in the percentage of those checking a particular option who reported they found their marriage or work "Highly satisfying" and the corresponding percentage among those who did not check this response. A minus sign indicates that the percentage among the noncheckers was higher than among the checkers. A positive difference indicates the reverse and points to greater satisfaction.

[a]Between 40 and 80 persons gave this response.

[b]Between 20 and 40 persons gave this response.

Table 11.7 summarizes findings not only on marital satisfaction but also on work satisfaction. The positive differences identify relationships associated with greater satisfaction; as usual, causality may run in either direction. For the wife to know nothing about the husband's work is a bad omen; involvement to any degree is a good omen. When the wife had an independent career, there was a negative relation with marital satisfaction of female subjects, not of males. This agrees with the finding in Chapter 6 cited above.

Relationships of these variables to work satisfaction were weak, and we leave interpretation to the reader.

Allocation of Responsibilities

In 1972 there was a 5-part question "To what extent did you [your husband] take responsibility for . . . ?", referring to particular tasks within the family. We report in terms of a scale from 5 (almost all husband's responsibility) to 1 (almost no participation by husband).

The correlations with marital satisfaction of male subjects were close to zero with the exception of "Managing family finances and major purchases" where r was $-.15$ ($+.12$ for women). The percentages rating the marriage "Highly satisfactory" related to husband's involvement as follows:

	Almost none 1	2	Equal share 3	4	Almost all 5
Men	80%	73%	74%	61%	54%
Women	40	56	54	64	68

The men evidently found it gratifying to delegate or share this responsibility; or perhaps the sharing was a symptom of harmony. The women, it appears, would have been somewhat happier without the sharing. When we average the percentages to strike a balance, columns 2 and 3 come out ahead by a tiny margin.

Sharing of household work may be a requisite for marital harmony in the 1990's, but it was not the norm for the marriages of our subjects. Half the male subjects and half the husbands of female subjects took no responsibility in this area; over 40 percent of males took some responsibility but less than their wives. The pattern of husband's responsibility for household work looks like this (with tiny cells ignored):

	Almost none 1	2	Equal share 3
Men	68	61	50
Women	52	63	80

The value of 80 came from only 20 women, but it suggests that the correlation might have been sizable if the range of male participation had not been so narrow. When we average the two rows, column 3 (equal shares) is the highest. For all save the "finances" item, frequencies were generally low in cells 1 and 5.

The two largest correlations were with women's responses regarding "care and training of children." The correlations of the husband's participation with the women's marital satisfaction are .19 and .27 (for ages before and after 16 respectively). The correlations for men were close to zero. (There may be some artifact in the correlations for the women. The question asked about present or most recent marriage. If the women's most recent marriage ended in divorce, this might account for the husband's minimal participation in the rearing of offspring. The males who remarried would not be reporting on a broken marriage.)

Turning Points in Life

As persons look over their past, particular events may stand out as shaping the course in their lives. In 1977 we asked the subjects to list five such events or "turning points," and to briefly explain why these particular events stand out. Table 11.8 summarizes the areas of life in which these events occurred. Individual cases add richness and a personal dimension to the quantitative data, and we will weave some case material from individuals we have described earlier in the book into the following discussion.

As we examine the responses of those subjects who completed this section, we find, not surprisingly, that family events and those relating to occupation and achievement were mentioned most frequently. However, the men and women differed in the overall significance of these two kinds of events. Men were somewhat more likely to see educational or occupational events as significant in shaping their lives, which is consistent with the gender differences in work histories. Women specified family events relatively more often than men. More

TABLE 11.8

Significant Events or Turning Points in Lives of
Later-Maturity Group (1977 Reports)

	Men (N = 335)		Women (N = 309)	
	No. mentioning	Pct. of N	No. mentioning	Pct. of N
Family events				
Marriage	214	63.9%	208	67.3%
Child-related	75	22.4	136	44.0
Death of child	8	2.4	18	5.8
Death of spouse	15	4.5	49	15.8
Divorce	19	5.7	37	12.0
Accident/illness	12	3.6	22	7.1
Spouse's retirement	1	0.3	21	6.8
Other	24	7.2	29	9.4
Total mentioning any of these	249	74.3	265	85.8
Achievement and occupation				
Education	131	39.1	107	34.6
New job	217	64.8	117	37.9
Promotion	41	12.2	12	3.9
Firing	12	3.6	3	1.0
Retirement	78	23.3	39	12.6
Other	43	12.8	39	12.6
Total mentioning any of these	295	88.1	214	69.3
Family of origin				
Father's death	18	5.4	28	9.1
Mother's death	13	3.9	32	10.4
Death of both father and mother	2	0.6	8	2.6
Parental divorce	3	0.9	2	0.6
Total mentioning any of these	33	9.9	62	20.1
Changes in physical environment				
Moves	40	11.9	70	22.7
Travel	19	5.7	49	15.9
Total mentioning either of these	58	17.3	106	34.3
Finances				
Reversals	3	0.9	6	1.9
Improvement	3	0.9	5	1.6
Depression	10	3.0	10	3.2
Total mentioning any of these	16	4.8	21	6.8
Own health	51	15.2	39	12.6
Growth				
Inner growth — satisfaction	8	2.4	19	6.1
Inner growth–pain	2	0.6	7	2.3
Total mentioning either of these	10	3.0	24	7.8
World War II	84	25.1	22	7.1
Other	47	14.0	58	18.8

SOURCE: 1977 questionnaire.

NOTE: Numbers add to more than "total mentioning," and percentages to over 100 because some respondents mentioned more than one event.

dramatic differences in men's and women's responses, however, were evident in the distributions of events within the two categories.

The most frequently listed achievement turning points were education and a new job, followed in importance by retirement and promotions. Educational and achievement events were viewed overwhelmingly as positive — so rated by 85 percent of the sample listing them. Although a nearly equal proportion of men and women saw education as a turning point in their lives, most of the other achievement events were chosen more frequently by men.

Looking back over the case histories presented earlier, we find that all three of the men described in Chapter 4 who had outstanding careers emphasized achievement in their listing of turning points. Harold, a physician, Walter, a scientist, and William, an investment analyst and banker, all mentioned educational and occupational milestones. In fact, William listed career-related events for all five of his turning points. The kinds of events noted by these men included initial training, as well as various kinds of advancement, and sometimes retirement. Such references were common among the majority of the men, who as we have found, were quite successful. However, not all men focused on these events. For example, Albert, the carpenter turned mountain climber, included no occupation-related events among his turning points.

Among the women, the career workers tended to mention one or more occupational events. The professors and teachers we have described in Chapter 5, such as Ruth, a zoologist, and Hope, who taught high school, listed such events as turning points. For Jean, the highly competent mathematics teacher who remained single, and whose life was described in Chapter 6, four out of five turning points were career-related. Others among the women also included occupational turning points. Susan, an income worker described in Chapter 5, did not work for most of her married life, and lists her return to work as a stenographer in mid life among her turning points. Among career changers, such as Edith who went from being a mathematics teacher to an aerodynamicist, career turning points were also important.

With respect to family events, men and women placed an equal emphasis on marriage as a significant event, about two-thirds of the sample mentioning it. However, women specified all of the other major family events more often than men. For example, women were twice as likely to specify child-related events and almost three times as likely to list death and divorce. The effects of family events typically were seen as positive, although women's characterization of the influence of family events was somewhat less positive than men's (72 percent of men who mentioned them viewed them positively, compared with 59 percent of women).

Some examples from the case histories illustrate the different salience of family events to the men and women. For example, both Harold, the physician, and Walter, the scientist, listed marriage among their turning points. However, although both reported high lifetime satisfaction from their children, neither mentioned having children as a turning point in their lives. Both of them had wives who were homemakers.

On the other hand, the women who had careers and families included their children among their turning points. For example, Hope, who spent 30 years in the classroom as a high school teacher, did not fail to mention her four children; Marilyn, who became a college professor in her 50's, also noted the raising of her children as among her important events. Homemakers, such as Linda, also tended to list children among their turning points.

As indicated above, family events were not always seen in as positive a light by the women as by the men. In some instances, for example, the negative impact of marriage on careers was mentioned. A case in point is Carla, whose life is described in Chapter 6. Her denial of admission at the institution where her husband taught resulted in divorce. References to widowhood, in addition to divorce, were often accompanied with comments on the pain involved and challenges encountered on the occasion of these events. Women tended to see deaths in their family of origin as a significant negative event more often than men, with almost twice as many women as men listing them as a turning point. This finding, along with those for marriage and family events, shows the greater salience of social networks to women. These results are consistent with those in Chapter 7 in suggesting that women's greater emphasis on relationships carries liabilities as well as benefits.

The impact of historical influences on the subjects' lives is reflected in their responses concerning financial turning points and World War II. Over half the financial events listed referred to the Depression. World War II was mentioned as a significant turning point by a quarter of the men, but only 7 percent of the women. Fifty-five percent of the men who referred to it saw the war as a positive event, and 9 percent saw it as mixed. Almost a quarter saw it as an uncompensated negative event, while for 13 percent the war's negative effects had some compensation. Some of the men were able to capitalize on their war experiences later (see Elder, Pavalko, & Hastings, 1991, for a discussion of the effect of cohort on war experiences). In William's case, the contacts he made during the war facilitated his shift from investments to banking.

Choices That Would Be Made Differently

Part of the self-assessment that occurs in aging is a realization that one might have done things differently, given the benefit of present knowledge of oneself and the world. In 1986, we invited the subjects, most of whom were in their mid-70's, to speculate about such alternative life choices. We asked: "Now looking back over your whole life, what choices would you make differently if you had the opportunity to live it again?"

Many of the subjects were quite satisfied with their life or had few regrets. It is noteworthy that one-third of the women and almost 40 percent of the men responded that there was nothing they would change. Some, such as Harold, the physician, and Hope, the high-school teacher with four children, gave simplereplies. He said, "None," and she stated, "None — I am satisfied and happy." Others, such as Albert, elaborated. He said, "None. Poor eyesight stopped my academic career, but I have had a good life — wonderful family, many friends, modest financial success. Now my old age mountaineering has made me a minor celebrity. My life has been a very interesting journey, especially after 70!" Gertrude, a homemaker we met in Chapter 5, says, "I would probably make all the same mistakes but also enjoy the many good and precious things that have been part of my blessed life."

Mirroring the diversity of our sample, we find a variety of concerns reflected in the responses of the remaining subjects. The things our subjects would change typically involved educational preparation, occupational life, some aspect of personality, and marriage. A summary of the major categories of responses is listed in Table 11.9.

Educational preparation, of course, is important in building a life structure, and educational choices were mentioned by one-fifth of the men and one-fourth of the women. Almost 8 percent of both men and women would have completed their education if given another chance. Several subjects would have delayed admission to high school or college until they were more mature. Choosing a different field or obtaining more education were frequent responses in this category, and were mentioned by more women than men. An example among the men is provided by Walter, the scientist. He said that he would take a lot more mathematics courses in college. However, Susan, who did not complete college because of financial circumstances and worked as a stenographer, stated, "While my education was adequate for what I needed it for, i.e., earning a living and helping my children, I think college or further musical education would have been very beneficial." She stated, further, that she felt that she had not used her gifts, and regretted it very much. Katherine, an active volunteer described in Chapter 5, relinquished her career aspirations after not finding opportunities in the foreign service, her chosen field. She said in 1986 that she probably would have obtained a Ph.D. after completing her master's degree.

Occupational choices were also salient to the subjects when they thought about what they might change about their lives. One-fifth of the subjects responded with some alteration of their occupational choices. The emphasis in these responses was somewhat different for the men and the women, however. Men tended to frame their response in terms of their chosen field, while women emphasized the level of occupation to a greater extent, stating that they would now seek a career or aim higher. The women's responses were consistent with their 1972 responses concerning their life time work patterns and their greater preferences for careers if they could live their lives again.

William, the investment analyst and banker, was an example of a man who would have chosen a different field. In his early case material he mentioned his teachers encouraging him to seek an academic career. His father, however, was

TABLE 11.9
*Percentage of Later-Maturity Group Mentioning Choices
They Would Make Differently (1986)*

	Men (N = 312)		Women (N = 280)	
	No. mentioning	Pct. of N	No. mentioning	Pct. of N
None	119	38.1%	91	32.5%
Education	58	18.6	69	24.6
Occupation	64	20.5	59	21.1
Marriage	24	7.7	46	16.4
Family	12	3.8	12	4.3
Finances	10	3.2	2	0.7
Aspects of personality	62	19.9	49	17.5
Other	16	5.1	12	4.3

SOURCE: 1986 questionnaire.
NOTE: Numbers add to more than total number of respondents, and percentages add to more than 100 because some respondents gave more than one response.

very much against this, and William ultimately went into business, very successfully. He obtained a Ph.D. and wrote a textbook along the way. He said, however, in 1986, that if he could do it again, he probably would not go into business, after all, but into a profession. Elizabeth, who had settled for part-time journalism, was one who would have chosen differently. She stated that she had planned after graduation from college to attend a noted school of journalism. She believed that had she gone ahead with this, she would have been "more career-minded rather than skittering about as I seem to have done!"

The choices that our subjects would have made differently indicate that marriage was more problematic for the women than for the men. Twice as many women as men referred to marriage in connection with different choices. An equal proportion of men and women felt that they had married the wrong person, but more women than men thought they had married too early. Forty-two percent of the single women responding in 1986 mentioned marriage as a possible choice if they could live their lives over, while none of the 11 single male respondents mentioned marriage. A variety of other choices were included in the remaining responses concerning marriage, including the decision to marry at all, remaining married, and divorcing.

Among the responses in the marriage category were the following. Judith, whose varied career in the arts and public health were described in Chapter 5, had some painful experiences in her marriages, and stated that she would now marry with great caution. Elton, whose several marriages were described in Chapter 6, stated that he would have attempted to learn earlier "the true facts of sexual relationships of marriage, as against the propaganda as taught to me as a child." Anne, the psychologist who became a successful administrator and remained single, and who was described in Chapter 5, had made peace with not having married, but clearly it was something she thought about. She said, "I might have tried harder to get married, but I'm not sure. Sometimes I feel I've missed an important part of life, but I don't brood about it, and am not even slightly unhappy."

Family issues in general were of about equal concern to men and women; however, specific areas of response differed by gender. Women's responses were spread over several areas, including the timing of parenthood, number of children, and child-rearing practices. For example, Beth, mentioned in Chapter 6, had a high school education, married soon after graduation, and soon had a child, only to divorce. She stated that, given a second chance, she would not have married so young and had a baby so soon. She would have liked further education. Men's responses, in contrast, were concentrated on concern that they had spent too little time on family relationships. The subjects also mentioned aspects of their personalities that they would change if they could. On the agentic, instrumental side these included working harder, being more assertive, having a goal, and being more self-confident. On the other hand, some would have liked to have been less self-centered, and more oriented toward others.

Summary

As we reflect on our subjects' reports on their life satisfactions, the most striking finding was their overall high level of satisfaction, further evidence that they were aging successfully. The subjects' satisfactions were particularly high in the central areas of work, family, children, and avocational experiences. These ratings do not appear to be reconstructions in aging, but to be rooted in their earlier life experiences. The ordering of areas of satisfaction is consistent with similar ratings at mid-life; and, as we have seen in earlier chapters, the group, on average, has been very successful in important life domains.

Those whose careers had been more successful rated their work satisfaction more highly. However, this satisfaction came from inner-directed sources of satisfaction, such as self-expression, personal sense of achievement, and interpersonal relations, more than from external sources, such as recognition and financial reward. Motivational variables such as ambition and self-confidence appear to have played an important role in the satisfaction achieved in work.

Among the men, professionals emphasized creativity and helping as sources of satisfaction in work, whereas men in the higher-business group emphasized administrative aspects of their work. For men in lower-level occupations the most satisfying aspect of work was friendly relations. Career women emphasized creativity, helping, and friendly relations as sources of satisfaction in work. Income workers emphasized friendly relations and financial rewards, while homemakers emphasized creativity and administration. Earned income in 1970 and 1971 correlated with retrospective satisfaction in 1977 among both men and women. Earlier motivational variables were more highly correlated with the retrospective work satisfaction of men than of women.

A wife's marital satisfaction was higher when she was involved in her husband's career. Perhaps such involvement indicated closeness in the marriage. Interestingly, a woman's having her own independent career was related to lower marital satisfaction of women, but not of men. This finding may reflect role strain on the part of the women in attempting to perform all their roles at a high level within the relatively traditional role divisions in marriage for this cohort. It is also possible that careers may have served as an alternative source of satisfaction for some of the women in unhappy marriages. Marital satisfaction for women was also related to greater responsibility by the husband for household work and for the care and training of children. The relation of the husband's taking responsibility for finances to marital satisfaction was negative for men and positive for women.

The events most often selected as turning points in our subjects' lives were in the central areas of family, and occupation and achievement. There was a stronger emphasis on achievement in the men's responses, and on family events in the women's responses. These differences corresponded to the different courses the men's and women's lives have taken and to the pressures of the gender roles of the times.

Perhaps the best test of the ultimate satisfaction of the group is what they would change about their lives. It is striking that after having lived over 70 years, a third of the women and 40 percent of the men found nothing that they would change if they could live their lives again. The areas specified by those who would have made changes were in the most basic life domains, which provide structure, opportunities, and relatedness. It is noteworthy that although achievement has been a central emphasis of the Terman Study, and although many of the members of the sample have achieved considerable success, the ranks of the well-satisfied are not confined to them. When some members of the group with modest achievements, who by choice or circumstance had placed greater emphasis on other aspects of life, looked back over their lives, they showed little tendency to wish their lives had been different.

Conclusions

In this chapter we consider the most salient findings concerning the Terman group in their later maturity. In general these individuals, so active and productive in their middle years, have approached aging with continuing mastery and competence. For some subjects, occupational achievement, which distinguished this group in their middle years, has continued into later maturity. Others have chosen to emphasize nonoccupational pursuits, typically rooted in earlier life choices.

Contemporary approaches to the study of aging emphasize the variability found in aging samples, and distinguish between normal, pathological, and optimal changes (Baltes & Baltes, 1990b; Rowe & Kahn, 1987). Findings showing variability with respect to physical, cognitive, and psychological functioning point to greater possibilities for the aging years than has heretofore been thought possible. The results of our study demonstrate the validity of the assumptions of this new, more positive approach. Many of the individuals in this group were "testing the limits" of successful aging (see Baltes & Baltes, 1990a). Comparisons of the group with others in the general population show more positive outcomes on a number of dimensions, including health and activity involvement in daily life.

Of course, even in this group of vital and active individuals, there were both qualitative and quantitative shifts in involvement and emphasis that were congruent with the physical and psychological realities of aging. Our subjects, while remaining active in later maturity, were showing shifts in their goals, as well as in their activities, toward those that are less demanding. The rate of the accommodations they were making as part of the aging process, however, appeared to be more directly under their control than is often the case in the general population. Their previous work histories had enabled many of them to retire gradually, and they indicated that the activities in which they engaged were mainly of their own choosing. Most of the subjects were experiencing aging within adequate financial circumstances, and most had maintained sufficient social resources. Their lives therefore showed the potential for the continuing achievement of meaning in the later years, when the necessary supports, both financial and social, are present.

We must remember that these individuals represent cohorts that experienced a major economic depression, two World Wars, and the extraordinary advances in science and technology in this century. The historical matrix in which they lived provided unique opportunities as well as limitations. The timing of the Depression and World War II in their lives influenced the level of education they achieved — securing high school or college degrees before the occurrence of these major events was more likely to lead to advanced degrees for both men and women. However, the occupational opportunity structure of the period was much more receptive to men than to women, and the men were in a better position to benefit occupationally from postwar prosperity. Improvements in public health practices and advances in medical treatment have extended the life expectancy of the group relative to their parents; medical procedures, such as coronary bypass surgery, have helped make their later years more productive and enjoyable.

The Subjects' Lives in Later Maturity

This account has documented the lives of the Terman group from their early 60's to their mid-70's. Despite the inevitable voluntary and involuntary losses of subjects in a study of over 60 years' duration, more than two-thirds of the original group contributed to our study of later maturity.

Health and Psychological Well-Being

Objective circumstances. The objective circumstances of the group's lives in later maturity were consistent with their relative advantage in family background and occupational achievement. In the most basic respect — survival — they appear to be significantly outliving others of their cohort. Moreover, they had reached their later years in financial circumstances that most consider adequate to their needs — an important fact because of the power of financial resources to mitigate some of the negative consequences of aging. At last report, most of the subjects were maintaining their independence, and were living in single-family housing of various types. By and large, they were satisfied with their living arrangements.

Perceived health. Most of the group considered their general health as quite good, despite various medical ailments — some quite serious. Most reported that they were in good or very good health from their early to mid-70's, and most reported that their energy and vitality were sufficient for a full program of activities. The most frequent health problems reported were cardiovascular illness, muscular-skeletal complaints, problems with vision, cancer, and general difficulties associated with aging, such as aches and pains, forgetfulness, and slowing down. They also reported a number of chronic concerns related to health, such as difficulties with hearing, muscular strength and control, and insufficient personal energy, but most indicated that they could manage these concerns successfully.

In general, few subjects indicated that they needed personal assistance. But predictably, older individuals reported poorer health, more need of assistance, and less satisfaction with their medical care than younger ones. However, while the group seemed to fall prey to the same types of physical decline in aging as the general population, their self-appraisals were noticeably more positive, suggesting less severe impairment, because of either preventive or treatment factors. These more positive self-ratings were consistent with the lower mortality rates of the group compared to the general population.

Perceived well-being. Our measures of anxious and depressed mood, as well as of happiness, indicated favorable overall levels of psychological well-being among the subjects in their seventies. In general, self-appraisals of psychological well-being were moderately positively related to self-appraisals of physical health. The subjects' reports of the recent range of their mood showed it to be fairly stable. Nevertheless, from their early to mid-70's, small declines were found in all the component variables in our self-report measure of psychological well-being of individuals responding at both times.

Antecedents. In our search for antecedents that might predict health and well-being in the group's mid-70's, we found the previous health and well-being of our subjects to be important determinants. Moreover, their positive expectancies about the later years, assessed in their early 60's, were positively related to feelings of psychological well-being fourteen years later in their mid-70's. For men, more normative marital history and having raised children showed small positive relations with good outcomes in aging. Previous marital and parenting experiences, however, did not appear to be related to health and psychological well-being of women.

Ambition and occupational achievement received particular emphasis in the Terman study because the group was gifted. Indices of ambition and involvement in work in the early years of later maturity were modestly related to the health and psychological well-being of our subjects. Type of previous occupation did not relate to health and psychological well-being in the men's mid-70's. There was, however, a small relationship among the women, with career women marginally higher on well-being than homemakers and income workers. The lifetime success ratings for men in 1960 related positively to their physical health in later maturity. Interestingly, high ambition from young adulthood to mid-life, although positively correlated with career success, was a negative predictor of men's psychological well-being in aging. Also, strikingly, one of the strongest antecedents of psychological well-being in aging for both men and women was an easygoing disposition (happiness of temperament and being easy to get along with), as measured by self-ratings in young adulthood. It appears that achievement attained in the presence of positive personality characteristics brings with it special rewards in terms of psychological outcomes in the later stages of life. In addition, previously active members of the sample were more likely to report greater psychological well-being in aging.

Correlates. A number of contemporaneous factors were related to psychological well-being in the group's mid-70's, physical health being the most important. There were additional factors, however, that appeared to have helped make the lives of the group both healthier and more satisfying. These included involvement and participation in life at many levels, including having more goals and ambitions, and participating in more activities. Religiosity, although not strong in the group as a whole, also showed modest positive relations to psychological well-being. Satisfaction in relationships was important to psychological well-being, particularly among women. Fortunately, few of the subjects lacked meaningful relationships. For men, the importance of dyadic relationships was apparent in the more positive well-being of married men. On the negative side, the experience of chronic stress, such as financial pressures, or difficulties of family members, was an important negative factor in our subjects' psychological well-being.

As we reflect on the many variables, both antecedent and contemporary, that were related to the successful aging of the group, we see that many are cognitive in nature (see also Rudinger & Thomae, 1990). These findings suggest that positive and hopeful approaches to life produce more positive outcomes. For example, optimistic expectations about aging are related to more positive psychological well-being in later maturity fourteen years later. Also, cognitive engagement in life in terms of goals and ambitions relates positively to the quality of life on many dimensions, including relationships, activities, and general health and psychological well-being.

In addition, in examining our subjects' lives at a case level, we were struck by the diversity of life patterns in the sample. For many of the subjects, life had by no means been smooth sailing. What seems to have made the difference in terms of their psychological well-being was the ability to cope with and create meaning from the challenges they faced. No doubt their high intelligence has been an asset in these respects, but other positive qualities of personality also appear to have been important.

Life-styles

When we examined the values, goals, and activities characterizing the group's life-styles in later maturity, we found evidence for both continuity and change in these domains. There was moderate stability in the level of endorsement of life goals of autonomy, involvement, achievement motivation, and acceptance between the group's early 70's and their mid-70's. Both men and women reduced their commitment to involvement and achievement goals over this period, but on average, they increased their commitment to acceptance goals. Moreover, the group's goals in later maturity were related to their earlier occupational patterns; for example, professionals tended to be more achievement-oriented than other occupational groups.

Our subjects' ambition in later maturity was related to their earlier ambition, particularly to their ambition in middle age. Also, they showed a slight tendency as they aged to see themselves as progressively more ambitious than others of their cohort. Apparently, while they may have been showing declines in achievement they perceived these as being smaller than those of the general population. However, our subjects' goal orientations over time reflected a relatively greater emphasis on personal, rather than achievement-related, forms of mastery and productivity.

Contrary to the prevailing myths and stereotypes at the time of our subjects' youth, these gifted individuals have lived multifaceted lives that were not limited to intellectual pursuits and accomplishments. They showed dynamic and diverse involvements during their young adult and middle years, and have carried many of these activities into later maturity. They participated more than members of other samples of older people in many kinds of activities — not just intellectual ones. The overall level of their participation remained impressively high in later maturity, though there was a trend toward withdrawal from activities that are physically, psychologically, and socially demanding.

The later-maturity group differed from the general population in their religious and political participation. Religion was not very important overall to either the men or the women and appears to have been less important to them than to others of their cohort. The women were, however, more religious than the men. The importance of religion in later maturity, as well as increases in religious interest, were related to earlier religious participation and interest, particularly to young adulthood and mid-life.

The subjects' level of voter participation was substantially greater than that of the general population throughout adulthood, and remained so in later maturity. They tended, on the whole, to be somewhat more politically conservative than others of their generation, the men being somewhat more conservative than the women. Occupational choices were related to political orientation; professionals were the most liberal among the men, and homemakers were the most conservative among the women.

The Terman men and women made many societal contributions in their earlier lives through their family and occupational involvements. In later maturity they maintained their contributions through memberships of organizations and through their individual efforts with relatives and friends and in volunteer work. There has been continuity in organizational membership, men being more likely to be affiliated with business or professional organizations, and women with educational, cultural, and community health organizations.

Lifetime Satisfactions

The retrospective lifetime satisfaction of the later-maturity group, at an average age of 67, were very positive. Most expressed considerable satisfaction concerning marriage, work, avocation, and children. Women's satisfactions from their children were particularly positive. Friendships and recreation were also highly satisfying for both men and women. These retrospective evaluations seemed to reflect lifelong patterns of affect and behavior; they were fairly stable when compared with those taken five years earlier, and consistent with the ordering of areas of satisfaction in mid-life.

The sources of occupational satisfaction differed across occupational groups. There was a strong retrospective preference for careers among the women, although a majority of the women had been homemakers or income workers. Career success was related to work satisfaction for men, and earlier motivational variables were more highly related to the work satisfaction of men than of women. Earned income in the early years of later maturity was related to retrospective satisfaction with work of both men and women.

In terms of marital satisfaction, a wife's involvement in her husband's career correlated with retrospective satisfaction of both men and women. However, having an independent career was negatively related to retrospective marital satisfaction of women. Marital satisfaction of women was positively related to the husband's sharing in household work and his involvement in the care and training of children.

Most strikingly, when the subjects were asked in later maturity if there was anything they would change about their lives if they had the opportunity to live their lives again, one-third of the women and two-fifths of the men found nothing they would change. The other subjects most often mentioned as candidates for change were alternative choices in level or content of education or occupation, the timing of marriage and choice of a marriage partner, and some aspect of personality, such as self-confidence or orientation toward others.

Gender and Aging

Sex Differences in Role Emphases

Occupational roles. Although experiences of the men and women in the sample were comparable in many areas, the striking sex differences in life orientation and experience cannot be ignored. In this cohort, role divisions between the sexes were sharp. Men were strongly oriented to occupational life, and were charged with providing financial support for their families. For women, the homemaking role was viewed as both normative and ideal, and career pursuit was typically seen as a threat to family life.

Throughout this account we have observed a strong emphasis on occupational achievement among the men. Almost all the men reached high levels of occupational status, and many made exceptional contributions in business or the professions. The societal mandate for occupational achievement was internalized by the men, and they were more likely than the women to see educational or occupational events as significant in shaping their lives. Similarly, occupational success was a greater factor in men's evaluations of their lifetime work satisfactions than in women's.

The proportion of women in the group who had careers was high for their generation. At the same time, a large majority of the women characterized their lifetime history as that of a homemaker or engagement in income work that they did not view as a career. The fact that there were twice as many single women as men, and that almost all these women had careers, testifies to the incompatibility between career and homemaking roles for this cohort. The highest achieving women were, in fact, those who did not marry or, if married, did not have children.

Responses in their mid-70's about ways in which they would live their lives over, if given the chance, suggest that many of the single women had chosen between careers and marriage. In 1986 over 40 percent of these women spontaneously mentioned marriage as a possible change they might make if they could live their lives again—at a time when combining careers and marriage was common for women. Contrary to the women's experience, a single life-style was not particularly conducive to the men's achievement. The single men showed no sign of regret about their decision not to marry.

In addition to the societal pressures on women toward homemaking, there was a very real lack of occupational opportunity for women of this cohort. A limited number of occupations were viewed as open to women, and women were rarely found in occupations other than those seen as traditionally feminine. Overall, few of the Terman women reached the same level of achievement as the men, despite the women's equally high intellectual ability.

Marital roles. Our subjects' role divisions in their marriages tended to be traditional, with women taking the major responsibility for household work and childrearing, and men the responsibility for financial support. However, more of the Terman women had careers independent of their husbands', and they were more involved in their husbands' work than the wives of the Terman men. The Terman women had appreciable support from their husbands for their own work and community service, particularly in regard to discussion of the wife's work. Career women reported slightly higher participation by their husbands in household work and childrearing than did the homemakers and income workers. A majority of the men and women said that a wife's working affected their marriage positively. However, the women were more likely than the men to say that the effect was mixed or negative.

The men and women who had multiple divorces shared a number of background and personality factors in comparison with those with intact marriages. These included a conflictual family background, stronger sexual interest in adolescence, and personality characteristics such as moodiness, impulsiveness, and a refusal to conform to authority. In contrast, there were both important similarities and marked differences between the never-married men and women. Neither sex differed from those in intact marriages in regard to family background, and both were less active sexually in adolescence. However, the single women were more successful than the single men, and ultimately showed more favorable levels of psychological adjustment.

Gender Differences in Life-style

In terms of the objective circumstances surrounding aging, a striking difference lies in the mortality figures. Throughout the study, we have lost men through death at a higher rate than women, but this sex difference has accelerated as the group grew older. The men and women reported different physical ailments, the women suffering from more chronic conditions, such as arthritis.

The men reached later maturity in a more advantaged financial position than the women. It was the married homemaker women, rather than the career women, whose financial situation most nearly matched that of the men. The most disadvantaged group financially was the unmarried women who were income workers.

Values and goals. Women endorsed autonomy goals more than men, particularly in regard to maintaining independence and health. Because many more of the women were living alone in later maturity, autonomy was a more salient issue for them. The women emphasized goals of involvement in relationships more than did the men. They also endorsed the acceptance goals of taking each day at a time and dying peacefully more than men did. In the early years of later maturity, the men were more likely to channel their ambition into employment-related pursuits, and the women were more likely to favor avocational pursuits as expressions of their ambition — results clearly related to normative occupational patterns. Although the Terman sample as a whole has not emphasized religion, religion was more important to the women than to the men in later maturity. The women, who were always somewhat more politically liberal than the men, showed a further slight shift in the liberal direction in later maturity.

Social relationships. Throughout the study there were differences in the men and women's orientations toward relationships. The women appeared to have broader friendship networks, and to emphasize interpersonal relationships more than the men did. In addition, the women placed greater emphasis on relationship goals, engaged in more social activities, and were more likely to help friends in later maturity than were the men. The women also reported more social interaction than men, and slightly more of them wanted more interaction. Similarly, satisfaction with the degree of companionship and intimacy was more highly related to women's health and psychological well-being in their mid-70's than to men's. Women also mentioned family events as turning points in their lives more frequently than men did.

These differences in relationship orientation and roles between men and women should not, however, obscure some other findings pointing to the importance of relationships to men's psychological well-being. The significance of primary relationships to men is underscored by the positive relationship of marriage and a normative marital history, as well as having had children, to their well-being in aging. In addition, fewer men never married, and few men lived alone in their later years because they were more likely than women to remarry after widowhood or divorce. Possibly these status variables were not as important to the women, many of whom were able to meet their relationship needs in other ways.

Although marital and parenting history in itself did not predict psychological well-being of women, those women who had children expressed high levels of satisfaction with the maternal experience. Many, however, would now choose what has become a normative lifestyle for educated women — the combination of a career with family life.

Commonalities Across Gender

The power of occupation in structuring both behavior and attitudes has been evident throughout this account. Repeatedly, we found differences within the sexes among those with different occupational orientations. Occasionally we found that occupational orientation was a greater determining factor than was gender. Moreover, there were important similarities in the values and behavior of professionals of both sexes. For example, the professional women expressed levels of ambition and achievement orientation in their later years comparable to those of the professional men. Other similarities between the professionals of both sexes included their intellectual and cultural activities, and a relatively more liberal political orientation.

Similarly, despite the differences in the levels of achievement of the men and women, we must note one area of striking similarity. Personality characteristics such as achievement motivation, self-esteem, purposiveness, and integration toward goals played an important role in the ultimate achievements of both sexes. Moreover, many of these personality characteristics were measured quite early in the subjects' lives. The significance of our findings with a gifted group, for whom achievement presented less challenge than for others, as well as the continued relation of these variables to achievement over the life cycle, underscores the more general importance of these personality strengths for lifetime achievement.

The Future

As we conclude our report on the Terman subjects in their mid-seventies, we do not leave the study of their lives, but only conclude this chapter in this landmark study of the human life cycle. The study of our gifted sample is far from over. At the time of this account, about 40 percent of this distinguished group remained alive. The archive is available to scholars, who will doubtless avail themselves of this rich resource. Also, although we have concentrated here on an aggregated account of our group, the intensive study of individual cases holds additional promise for understanding the interplay of unique factors in shaping the course of human lives.

We are now in the process of extending the study of the Terman subjects into later aging. These remarkable individuals offer promise of providing us with a model of optimal approaches to one of the greatest challenges that human beings face — bringing meaning and integrity to the final years of later maturity. In our study of the Terman subjects in this last phase of life, we shall focus on the ways in which they continue to create purpose in their lives, and the ways in which they cope with the inevitable losses and adaptive challenges of later aging. From what they have already taught us, we expect that they will provide continuing insights into the possibilities for enabling persons to live enriched and fuller lives in these later years.

Appendixes

Questionnaires, 1972–1986

The following pages reproduce the six questionnaires used in 1972 (separate forms for women and for men), 1977 (separate forms for women and for men), 1981–82, and 1986.

Terman Study of the Gifted
Stanford University, 1972

Date of filling out this blank ....
Please return by November 15, 1972, if possible.

INFORMATION BLANK FOR MEN

1. Full name .... Age at 1972 birthday ....

2. Address .... Telephone (............) ....-................
   Zip   A.C.

3. Name and address of someone through whom you could be reached if your address should change ....
   .... Relationship ....

4. Marital status at present (check) ...... Single ...... Married ...... Separated ...... Divorced ...... Widower
   If you have never married, check here ...... and skip to **A** on page 2.

5. Changes in your marital status, 1960–1972 (divorce, death of wife, remarriage, etc.). Give year of each change. Give
   name of new wife, if any. ....
   ....

6. Fill in one line for each of your children. Omit your adopted children or stepchildren, but do include deceased children.

Name; give married name for daughters. Child's address if different from yours.	Year of birth	M or F	If not living, year of death	No. of his (her) children (incl. deceased children)		
				Own	Adopt.	Stepchildren

How many children have you adopted? .... Over the course of your life, how many stepchildren have lived in your home
for a year or more? ....

Please answer questions 7–12 with regard to your present or most recent wife.

7. Wife's education (check)
   ...... High school or less ...... Some education beyond high school ...... College graduate ...... Postgraduate work

8. Place a check mark in each column to indicate which of the three alternative statements best applies to your wife's income-producing work during this time period. Please fill out as completely as possible even if you were not married to her
   at the time.

	1941–1945	1946–1950	1951–1955	1956–1960	1961–1965	1966–1972
She had steady, though not necessarily full-time, work (except for interruptions due to illness, pregnancy, involuntary unemployment, etc.).						
Her work was intermittent, irregular, and not a principal source of support or satisfaction.						
She rarely or never engaged in income-producing work.						

   Other (explain and date) ....
   ....

9. What was your wife's occupation during the largest part of her working life after age 30? (Title of job, and duties) ....
   ....
   Approximately what were her annual earnings, at the time when they were highest? $................................

10. Had she originally trained for, or prepared to engage in, an occupation that she did not actually practice after age 30?
    ...... Yes ...... No If yes, explain ....

[1]

11. Which of the following statements describes your wife's activities in relation to your career? Check more than one if applicable.

...... Her career was essentially independent of mine.
...... Her work contributed directly to mine. (Consider help in planning, collaboration, other regular interaction. Consider her unpaid as well as paid work.)
...... She took substantial responsibility for the social welfare of my associates, activities to build good will for my business, or other supporting activities.
...... We discussed my work frequently.
...... She knew very little about my work activities.

12. To what extent did you take responsibility in each of the areas listed at left? Place a check in each row.

	Almost none	Less than my wife's	About equal to wife's	Greater than my wife's	Almost entirely mine	Does not apply to my life
Care and training of our children, to age 16						
Care and training of our children after age 16						
Day-to-day household work						
Care of garden						
Managing family finances and major purchases						

A 1. My father: is living ...... died in the year .... at the age of ....

My mother: is living ...... died in the year .... at the age of ....

2. Please check to indicate your general health during 1970–1972:
...... Very good ...... Good ...... Fair ...... Poor ...... Very poor

Major changes in your physical or mental well-being since 1959, with date if applicable. ....

3. Your energy and vitality at this period in life (check one)
...... Vigorous; have considerable endurance
...... Adequate for a full program of activities
...... Have to limit myself somewhat
...... Lack of energy very much limits my activities

4. Your work in 1972. Give title of job or principal position, and exact nature of work ....

This work was (check) ...... Essentially full-time ...... Nearer to half-time ...... Much less than half-time

Other income-producing work receiving ten days or more per year of your time in 1972. ....

5. List, in chronological order, major changes you have made in your principal occupation since 1959. Give year of each change. ....

6. What aspects of your work have given you the greatest satisfaction in recent years? ....

In what ways, if any, does this answer differ from the answer you would have given to the same question ten years ago? ....

If you have completely withdrawn from income-producing work, skip to **B**.

[2]

7. On the whole, how do you feel about your work nowadays? (check)
...... It is exciting and rewarding.
...... It is rewarding most of the time.
...... There is not much satisfaction in it, but neither is it unpleasant.
...... Although the unpleasant aspects are tolerable, I shall be glad to escape from it.
...... I dislike it, and continue only out of necessity.

8. Compare your work activities in 1972 with those in 1960. On the whole, have your responsibilities increased or decreased? (check) ...... Increased ...... Decreased ...... About the same

In what ways have your responsibilities changed? ....
....
....

9. What major changes in your work do you plan to make during the next five years (1972–1977)? Include projects to be completed or initiated, shifts in amount or type of responsibility, partial or complete retirement. ....
....
....

10. Since retirement is a gradual process, we are taking retirement to mean reduction of work rather than cessation of work. Approximately when do you expect to reduce your work to quarter-time or less? (Check more than one if uncertain.) ...... 1987 or later ...... 1982–1986 ...... 1977–1981 ...... 1976 or before ...... Have already done so, in 19........

B 1. As you look ahead to the years when your age is 70–75, how do you feel about them?
...... Expect to enjoy those years thoroughly.
...... Expect to be contented enough.
...... Expect life to be rather unsatisfying.
...... Expect to dislike being retired.
...... Cannot say; have little idea what life will be like then.

2. For 1970 and 1971, please estimate the income figure requested to the nearest $1000 and enter in the appropriate space.
Enter X if the question does not apply.

What were your total earnings *from your work*? Do not include royalties, pensions, etc., from work in prior years.
What were the total earnings from *your wife's current work* (if you were married in the year indicated)?
What was your *total family income from all sources*? Include investments, pensions, earnings of yourself and your wife, etc.

In column (a), please give representative annual figures for the decade 1960–1969.

	1970	1971	(a)

3. How have you typically divided your time? Give approximate percentages for each period, and check to make sure that the total in each row is 100%.

	Income-producing work	Maintaining home and family	Volunteer public service, community service, church work	Participation in cultural activities	Recreation	Other
1960–1965	...............%	...............%	...............%	...............%	...............%	...............%
1966–1972	...............%	...............%	...............%	...............%	...............%	...............%

If entry in "Other" category exceeds 10%, describe general nature of the activities. ....
....

4. Since 1959, have you undertaken any training or education (other than independent reading)? ...... Yes ...... No
If yes, describe briefly. ....
....

[3]

5. In the period 1970–1972, what leisure-time activities (recreation, or unpaid service, or other responsibilities) have taken up substantial amounts of your time? ....
....
....

Consider your participation in organizations and community service today as compared with 1960. On the whole, have your responsibilities increased or decreased? (check) ...... Increased ...... Decreased ...... About the same
In what ways have your responsibilities changed? ....
....

6. How important was each of these goals in life, in the plans you made for yourself in early adulthood? Place a check in each column.

	Occupational success	Family life	Friendships	Richness of cultural life	Total service to society	Joy in living
Of prime importance to me; was prepared to sacrifice other things for this	....	....	....	....	....	....
Expected a good deal of myself in this respect	....	....	....	....	....	....
Looked forward to a normal amount of success in this respect	....	....	....	....	....	....
Less important to me than to most people	....	....	....	....	....	....

How satisfied are you with your experience in each of these respects? Check in each column.

	Occupational success	Family life	Friendships	Richness of cultural life	Total service to society	Joy in living
Had excellent fortune in this respect	....	....	....	....	....	....
Had a satisfactory degree of success	....	....	....	....	....	....
Had a mixed experience but am not discontented	....	....	....	....	....	....
On the whole, somewhat dissatisfied	....	....	....	....	....	....
Found little satisfaction in this area	....	....	....	....	....	....

7. List any special honors, awards, recognitions, biographical listings since 1959. ....
....
....

8. Identify briefly a few experiences, activities, or accomplishments that in retrospect give you the greatest feeling of accomplishment and pride. The activity may relate to your work, your family, your community, etc. Indicate your approximate ages when this was taking place. ....
....
....
....
....

9. Give any other significant information about yourself or your family that has not been covered in this questionnaire; e.g., any special good fortune, accomplishments, or change of status since 1959; any misfortunes or disappointments that have seriously affected your life. Also, list here any publications, patents, or other creative work since 1959. (If more space is needed, attach an additional sheet.) ....
....
....
....
....

[4]

Terman Study of the Gifted
Stanford University, 1972

Date of filling out this blank ....
Please return by November 15, 1972, if possible.

INFORMATION BLANK FOR WOMEN

1. Full name .... Age at 1972 birthday ....
   (include maiden name)

2. Address .... Telephone (............) ....-...............
   Zip   A.C.

3. Name and address of someone through whom you could be reached if your address should change ....
   .... Relationship ....

4. Marital status at present (check) ...... Single ...... Married ...... Separated ...... Divorced ...... Widow
   If you have never married, check here ...... and skip to **A** on page 2.

5. Changes in your marital status, 1960–1972 (divorce, death of husband, remarriage, etc.). Give year of each change. Give
   name of new husband, if any. ....
   ....

6. Fill in one line for each of your children. Omit your adopted children or stepchildren, but do include deceased children.

Name; give married name for daughters. Child's address if different from yours.	Year of birth	M or F	If not living, year of death	No. of his (her) children (incl. deceased children)		
				Own	Adopt.	Stepchildren

How many children have you adopted? ...... Over the course of your life, how many stepchildren have lived in your home
for a year or more? ......

Please answer questions 7–12 with regard to your present or most recent husband.

7. Husband's education (check)
   ...... High school or less ...... Some education beyond high school ...... College graduate ...... Postgraduate work

8. What was your husband's most recent principal occupation? Give title of his job, and exact nature of work. (If your marriage ended before 1959, give his principal occupation during the period of your marriage.) ....
   .... To what years does this answer apply? 19.......–.......

9. Since retirement is a gradual process, we are taking retirement to mean reduction of work rather than cessation of work.
   Approximately when does your husband expect to reduce his work to about quarter-time or less? (Check more than one
   if uncertain.)
   ...... 1987 or later ...... 1982–1986 ...... 1977–1981 ...... 1976 or before ...... He has already done so, in 19.........
   ...... Marriage ended during his working years

10. Which of the following statements describes your activities in relation to your husband's career? Check more than one
    if applicable.
    ...... I had a career that was essentially independent of his.
    ...... My work contributed directly to his. (Consider help in planning, collaboration, other regular interaction. Consider
    your unpaid as well as paid work.)
    ...... I took substantial responsibility for the social welfare of his associates, activities to build good will for his business,
    or other supporting activities.
    ...... We discussed his work frequently.
    ...... I knew very little about his work activities.

[1]

11. What role did your husband play in your career or your community service? (check)
    ...... I did not engage much in such activities during our marriage.
    ...... He knew very little about such activities of mine.
    ...... We discussed my work frequently.
    ...... He contributed directly to my activities.
    ...... In many of these activities we were full collaborators.

12. To what extent did your husband take responsibility in each of the areas listed at left? Place a check in each row.

	Almost entirely his	Greater than mine	About like mine	Less than mine	Almost none	Does not apply to my life
Care and training of our children, to age 16	....	....	....	....	....	....
Care and training of our children after age 16	....	....	....	....	....	....
Day-to-day household work	....	....	....	....	....	....
Care of garden	....	....	....	....	....	....
Managing family finances and major purchases	....	....	....	....	....	....

A 1. My father: is living ...... died in the year .... at the age of ....
   My mother: is living ...... died in the year .... at the age of ....

2. Please check to indicate your general health during 1970–1972:
   ...... Very good ...... Good ...... Fair ...... Poor ...... Very poor

   Major changes in your physical and/or mental well-being since 1959, with date, if applicable. ....
   ....
   ....

3. Your energy and vitality at this period in life. (check one)
   ...... Vigorous; have considerable endurance
   ...... Adequate for a full program of activities
   ...... Have to limit myself somewhat
   ...... Lack of energy very much limits my activities

4. Place a check mark in each column to indicate which of the three alternative statements best applies to your income-producing work during each time period.

	1941–1945	1946–1950	1951–1955	1956–1960	1961–1965	1966–1972
I had steady, though not necessarily full-time, work (except for interruptions due to illness, pregnancy, involuntary unemployment, etc.).	....	....	....	....	....	....
My work was intermittent, irregular, and not a principal source of support or satisfaction.	....	....	....	....	....	....
I rarely or never engaged in income-producing work.	....	....	....	....	....	....
Other (explain and date)						

....

If you have not worked since 1959, skip to **B**.

5. Your work in 1972. Give title of job or principal position, and exact nature of work (if working). ....
   ....

   This work was (check) ...... Essentially full-time ...... Nearer to half-time ...... Much less than half-time

   Other income-producing work receiving ten days or more per year of your time in 1972. ....
   ....

6. List, in chronological order, major changes you have made in your principal occupation since 1959. Give year of each change. ....
   ....
   ....

7. What aspects of your work have given you the greatest satisfaction in recent years? ....
   ....
   ....

[2]

In what ways, if any, does this answer differ from the answer you would have given to the same question ten years ago?

....

....

If you have completely withdrawn from income-producing work, skip to **B**.

8. On the whole, how do you feel about your work nowadays? (check)
...... It is exciting and rewarding.
...... It is rewarding most of the time.
...... There is not much satisfaction in it, but neither is it unpleasant.
...... Although the unpleasant aspects are tolerable, I shall be glad to escape from it.
...... I dislike it, and continue only out of necessity.

9. Compare your work activities in 1972 with those in 1960. On the whole, have your responsibilities increased or decreased? (check) ...... Increased ...... Decreased ...... About the same
In what ways have your responsibilities changed? ....
....
....

10. What major changes in your work do you plan to make during the next five years (1972–1977)? Include projects to be completed or initiated, shifts in amount or type of responsibility, partial or complete retirement. ....
....
....
....

Approximately when do you expect to reduce your work to about quarter-time or less? (Check more than one if uncertain.) ...... 1987 or later ...... 1982–1986 ...... 1977-1981 ...... 1976 or before ...... Have already done so, in 19........

B 1. As you look ahead to the years when your age is 70–75, how do you feel about them?
...... Expect to enjoy those years thoroughly.
...... Expect to be contented enough.
...... Expect life to be rather unsatisfying.
...... Expect to dislike being retired.
...... Cannot say; have little idea what life will be like then.

2. Had you originally trained for or prepared to engage in an occupation that you did not actually practice after age 30?
If yes, explain. ....
....

3. Below are descriptions of work patterns women follow. Please check in column (a) to indicate which best describes your history. Do not consider volunteer service or avocational activities.

	(a) As it was	(b) As I planned it	(c) As I now would choose
I have been primarily a homemaker.	....	....	....
I have pursued a career through most of my adult life.	....	....	....
I have pursued a career except during the period when I was raising a family.	....	....	....
I have done considerable work for needed income, but would not call it a career.	....	....	....
Other (explain)			

Now please indicate under (b) which of these patterns best describes the life you planned in early adulthood. Then indicate under (c) which of these categories you would prefer to have been in, as you look back now. You may, of course, give the same answer in two or three columns.

4. For 1970 and 1971, please estimate the income figure requested to the nearest $1000 and enter in the appropriate space. Enter X if the question does not apply.

	1970	1971	(a)
What were your total earnings *from your work*? Do not include royalties, pensions, etc., from work in prior years.	....	....	....
What were the total earnings from *your husband's current work* (if you were married in this year)?	....	....	....
What was your *total family income from all sources*? Include investments, pensions, earnings of yourself and your husband, etc.	....	....	....

In column (a), please give representative annual figures for the decade 1960–69.

[3]

5. How have you typically divided your time? Give approximate percentages for each period, and check to make sure that the total in each row is 100%.

	Income-producing work	Maintaining home and family	Volunteer public service, community service, church work	Participation in cultural activities	Recreation	Other
1960–1965	...............%	...............%	...............%	...............%	...............%	...............%
1966–1972	...............%	...............%	...............%	...............%	...............%	...............%

If entry in "Other" category exceeds 10%, describe the general nature of the activities. ....
....

6. Since 1959, have you undertaken any training or education (other than independent reading)? ...... Yes ...... No. If yes, describe briefly. ....

7. In the period 1970–1972, what leisure-time activities (recreation, unpaid service, or other responsibilities) have taken up substantial amounts of your time? ....
....

Consider your participation in organizations and community service today as compared with 1960. On the whole, have your responsibilities increased or decreased? (check) ...... Increased ...... Decreased ...... About the same
In what ways have your responsibilities changed? ....

8. How important was each of these goals in life, in the plans you made for yourself in early adulthood? Place a check in each column.

	Occupational success	Family life	Friendships	Richness of cultural life	Total service to society	Joy in living
Of prime importance to me; was prepared to sacrifice other things for this	....	....	....	....	....	....
Expected a good deal of myself in this respect	....	....	....	....	....	....
Looked forward to a normal amount of success in this respect	....	....	....	....	....	....
Less important to me than to most people	....	....	....	....	....	....

How satisfied are you with your experience in each of these respects? Check in each column.

	Occupational success	Family life	Friendships	Richness of cultural life	Total service to society	Joy in living
Had excellent fortune in this respect	....	....	....	....	....	....
Had a satisfactory degree of success	....	....	....	....	....	....
Had a mixed experience but am not discontented	....	....	....	....	....	....
On the whole, somewhat dissatisfied	....	....	....	....	....	....
Found little satisfaction in this area	....	....	....	....	....	....

9. List any special honors, awards, recognitions, biographical listings since 1959. ....
....

10. Identify briefly a few experiences, activities, or accomplishments that in retrospect give you the greatest feeling of accomplishment and pride. The activity may relate to your work, your family, your community, etc. Indicate your approximate ages when this was taking place. ....
....
....
....

11. Give any other significant information about yourself or your family that has not been covered in this questionnaire; e.g., any special good fortune, accomplishments, or change of status since 1959; any misfortunes or disappointments that have seriously affected your life. Also, list here any publications, patents, or other creative work since 1959. (If more space is needed, attach an additional sheet.) ....
....
....
....

[4]

Terman Study of the Gifted
Stanford University, 1977

Date of filling out this blank _____
Please return by December 10, 1977,
or as soon as possible.

INFORMATION BLANK FOR MEN

1. Full name _____ Age at 1977 birthday _____

2. Address _____
   _____ Telephone (_____) _____ - _____
   ZIP   A.C.

3. Marital status at present (circle one):   Single   Married   Separated   Divorced   Widower

4. Changes in your marital status, 1972–1977 (divorce, death of wife, remarriage, etc.). Give year of each change. Give name of
   new wife, if any. _____
   _____

5. List below the members of the household in which you are now living, giving their relation to you (e.g., spouse, brother,
   friend, roomer, etc.).

   If you are living alone, check here. ☐

Name	Relationship to you

6. How satisfied are you with your present living arrangements? (indicate by an X on the line)

   Highly   Generally   Somewhat   Not Very   Not At All

   Any Comments? _____

7. In what type of housing unit are you residing? (house, mobile home, condominium, apartment, etc.) _____
   _____

8. Do you plan to make any changes in your living arrangements in the near future? _____ If yes, what do you anticipate
   those changes might be? _____

9. How many living brothers and sisters do you have? _____

10. Of those brothers and sisters who *do not* live with you, *how many* do you (or your spouse)

    see or talk with on the telephone: write or receive letters from:

    Daily?   _____   Daily?   _____
    At least once a week?   _____   At least once a week?   _____
    At least once a month?   _____   At least once a month?   _____
    Less than once a month?   _____   Less than once a month?   _____
    Not at all?   _____   Not at all?   _____

— 1 —

11. My father is living at age _____; or, he died at age _____ when I was age _____.

My mother is living at age _____; or, she died at age _____ when I was age _____.

If you have always been single, please skip to question 18.

12. Fill in one line for each of your children. Include adopted and stepchildren who were raised in your home. If deceased, note year of death and cause in the last column.

Name	Sex	Year of Birth	Years of schooling completed	Occupation	Marital Status	Number of children	Location (City and State)

13. Of those children who *do not* live with you, *how many* do you (or your spouse)

see or talk with on the telephone:		write or receive letters from:	
Daily?	_____	Daily?	_____
At least once a week?	_____	At least once a week?	_____
At least once a month?	_____	At least once a month?	_____
Less than once a month?	_____	Less than once a month?	_____
Not at all?	_____	Not at all?	_____

Please answer questions 14 through 17 with regard to your present or most recent wife.

14. Women's work may take more varied forms than that of men, and may change with presence of children, moves to new locations, and other reasons. The question below is designed to show how your wife experienced this during her adult years. Place a check mark in each age column to indicate which of the 7 alternative statements best applies to your wife's work during that age period of her life. If two alternatives applied during a particular period, check both. If her status changed during any of the five-year periods, check the most representative one(s).

	Age 21–25	Age 26–30	Age 31–35	Age 36–40	Age 41–45	Age 46–50	Age 51–55	Age 56–60	Age 61–65	Age 66–70
Her work was primarily homemaking.	___	___	___	___	___	___	___	___	___	___
She had steady full-time work for income.	___	___	___	___	___	___	___	___	___	___
She had demanding volunteer work, half-time or more.	___	___	___	___	___	___	___	___	___	___
She had steady part-time work for income (about half-time).	___	___	___	___	___	___	___	___	___	___
She had volunteer work 1 or 2 days a week.	___	___	___	___	___	___	___	___	___	___
Her work was that of a student.	___	___	___	___	___	___	___	___	___	___
She had retired.	___	___	___	___	___	___	___	___	___	___

Other (explain and date) _____

— 2 —

15. What was your wife's occupation during the largest part of her working life? (Title of job, and duties) _____

_____

16. If your wife had income-producing work during most of your marriage, how has this affected your life together? _____

_____

_____

_____

17. Which of the following statements describes your wife's activities in relation to your career? Check more than one, if applicable.

_____ She had a career which was essentially independent of mine.

_____ Her work contributed directly to mine. (Consider help in planning, collaboration, other regular interaction. Consider her unpaid as well as paid work.)

_____ She took interest in the social welfare of my associates and participated in other supporting activities.

_____ We discussed my work frequently.

_____ She knew very little about my work activities.

18. Which of the following aspects of your work have given you greatest satisfaction in recent years? If retired, answer with reference to preretirement years. (Check once those you regard as important; double-check those most important.)

_____ A helping or teaching relationship with people in work.

_____ Friendly relationship with people in work.

_____ Financial gain.

_____ Administrative, organizational, pride in getting the work done.

_____ Creativity, learning, stimulation, personal growth.

_____ Recognition, competition.

_____ Other (please specify) _____

19. Amount of your work in 1977.

Income-Producing Work	*Unpaid Professional or Vocational Activities*
_____ None	_____ None
_____ Work much less than half-time	_____ Work much less than half-time
_____ Work about half-time	_____ Work about half-time
_____ Work somewhat less than full-time	_____ Work somewhat less than full-time
_____ Work essentially full-time	_____ Work essentially full-time

20. If you are not fully retired, give title of job or principal position and nature of work _____

_____

21. At any time since early adulthood, have you had a significant change in your occupation other than changes of duties with promotion? Please explain and give date. _____

_____

_____

22. If you are not fully retired, on the whole how do you feel about your work nowadays?

_____ It is exciting and rewarding.

_____ It is rewarding most of the time.

_____ There is not much satisfaction in it, but neither is it unpleasant.

_____ Although the unpleasant aspects are tolerable, I shall be glad to escape it.

_____ I dislike it, and continue only out of necessity.

23. In your main occupation, is/was retirement mandatory at some specific age?
    _____ No (if you check here, skip to question 25)
    _____ Yes. At what age?_____
    _____ Officially yes, but exceptions are made. Official age? _____
    _____ Officially no, but it is customary. Customary age? _____

24. In general, are there opportunities to continue the same occupation after mandatory retirement?
    _____ No   _____ Yes (if yes, check any of the following that apply.)
    _____ In other companies or institutions, with pay.
    _____ Under less advantageous employment circumstances.
    _____ As a consultant, free lance, etc.
    _____ Without institutional affiliation.
    _____ On a voluntary basis with my institution or company.
    _____ Other (please specify) _____

25. Which of the following arrangements would you personally prefer?
    _____ Retire even earlier at age _____.
    _____ Retire at regular time.
    _____ Continue to work full-time until about age_____.
    _____ Begin decreasing work or responsibility at age _____ and retire fully at about age _____.

26. Below is a time line in years since you were age 50. At what age did you drop down to *less* than full-time work (100%)? Enter an approximate percent under that year of age to show about how much time you worked. Continue giving percents for each subsequent year to your present age. *Work* may have been income-producing (e.g., law practice, business), or a continuation of previous work but without pay (e.g., research, writing), or volunteer service (e.g., politics, community organization work). You have to be the judge of what *full-time* meant to you, and also what *work* means! If in doubt, add a comment.

AGE	50	51	52	53	54	55	56	57	58	59	60	61	62	63	64	65	66	67	68	69	70	71	72	73	74	75
%																										

Comment: _____

27. For the year 1976, please enter approximate amount of annual income for each category which applies to you. Enter an "X" if the category does not apply, as, for example, if you had no wife in 1976. You don't need to belabor this to the last dollar.

    Your earned income $_____

    Your wife's earned income $_____

    Your social security payment $_____

    Your wife's social security payment $_____

    Other pension, yourself $_____

    Other pension, your wife $_____

    Your investment income $_____

    Your wife's investment income $_____

    Jointly owned investment income $_____

    Other (describe) _____ $_____

If the above figures do not reflect your approximate total family income, please describe the exceptions and give a total, or if your income for this one year was significantly unusual, please explain. _____

_____

_____

28. Please check to indicate your general health recently.

_____ Very good   _____ Fair   _____ Very poor

_____ Good   _____ __ Poor

Major changes in your physical or mental well-being since 1972, with date if applicable. _____

_____

29. Compared to other people of about your age, would you say that your health at present is:

_____ Better   _____ The same

_____ Worse   _____ Don't know

30. Your energy and vitality at this period of life (check one):

_____ Vigorous; have considerable endurance.   _____ Have to limit myself somewhat.

_____ Adequate for a full program of activities.   _____ Lack of energy very much limits my activities.

31. Taking things altogether, how would you describe yourself these days:

_____ Very happy   _____ Pretty happy   _____ Not too happy.

32. List below any organizations or institutions to which you have committed a substantial amount of time or interest.

Name of organization or institution	Compared with 5 years ago, my interest and participation has:		
	Increased	Remained the same	Decreased

33. How regularly do you vote? (check for each kind of election)

National election: _____ Always   _____ Usually   _____ Occasionally   _____ Rarely   _____ Never

State election: _____ Always   _____ Usually   _____ Occasionally   _____ Rarely   _____ Never

Local election: _____ Always   _____ Usually   _____ Occasionally   _____ Rarely   _____ Never

34. On national issues which political party most represents your leanings? _____

35. Rate yourself on the following scale as regards your political and economic viewpoint (Indicate by cross (X) on the line)

Radical	Very Liberal	Tend to be Liberal	Middle-of-the-road	Tend to be Conservative	Quite Conservative	Strongly Conservative

Comments _____

36. With respect to *religion*, since your middle years has there been any change in your:

Interest	*Formal Association*
_____ Increased	_____ Increased
_____ No change	_____ No change
_____ Decreased	_____ Decreased

Comments _____

— 5 —

37. Below is a list of activities. Please put a check in *one* of the first 4 columns which best describes your level of participation in each activity; then place a check in column 5 or column 6 if applicable.

Activity	At present, I do this:				(5) I used to do this in my middle years, but don't now	(6) I've taken this up recently
	(1) Fre- quently	(2) Occa- sionally	(3) Seldom	(4) Never		
Reading: newspapers, magazines						
Reading: books (fiction)						
Reading: books (nonfiction)						
Reading: professional publications						
Reading: avocational publications						
Watching TV: educational, cultural						
Watching TV: sporting events						
Watching TV: entertainment						
Attending movies						
Participating in competitive sports						
Noncompetitive physical activity						
Attending sporting events						
Listening to recorded music						
Playing or singing with a musical group						
Playing a musical instrument						
Creative writing, painting, sculpture, dramatics						
Competitive card or board games						
Solitary games or puzzles						
Playing with pets						
Traveling						
Going to concerts, plays, lectures, museums, etc.						
Working on hobbies, (collections, gardening, handicrafts)						
Home repairs and maintenance						
Visiting and communicating with relatives						
Informal visiting with friends and neighbors						
Entertaining						
Self-improvement—physical (exercise, diet)						
Continuing education (classes)						
Increasing knowledge or skill (independent study)						
Community service: helping friends or neighbors						
Community service: with a group						
Community service: work done at home						
Unpaid professional or technical work						
Other activities: please specify						

If you have begun retirement, please review the items you have checked under the first column ("frequently"), including any you may have added to the list. Has any *one* item replaced your main occupation as a principal focus for your efforts and energy? If so, double check that item.

— 6 —

38. For each of the following areas in life, indicate the overall level of satisfaction you have experienced. If you have had more than one marriage, and different experiences, check a column for each marriage, and circle the response that applies to your present or most recent spouse.

	Highly Satisfying	Generally Satisfying	Somewhat Satisfying	Not very Satisfying	Not at all Satisfying	Does not apply to my life
Income-producing work						
Your avocational activities or hobbies						
Your marriage						
Your children						
Friendships, social contacts						
Community service activities						
Participation in cultural activities						
Recreation						
Religion						
Other						

39. As compared to your friends or colleagues of the same sex and of about your age, how ambitious or aspiring do you consider yourself in regard to: (indicate by X on the line):

Excellence in your work   Much more   Somewhat more   Average   Somewhat less   Much less

Proficiency in avocational pursuits and hobbies   Much more   Somewhat more   Average   Somewhat less   Much less

Recognition by others of your accomplishments   Much more   Somewhat more   Average   Somewhat less   Much less

Maintaining an excellent standard of living   Much more   Somewhat more   Average   Somewhat less   Much less

40. During the last 10–15 years have you noticed any change in your ambition or aspiration to achieve the following: (indicate by X on line):

Excellence in your work   Increased Substantially   Increased Somewhat   Little Change   Decreased Somewhat   Decreased Substantially

Proficiency in avocational pursuits and hobbies   Increased Substantially   Increased Somewhat   Little Change   Decreased Somewhat   Decreased Substantially

Recognition by others of your accomplishments   Increased Substantially   Increased Somewhat   Little Change   Decreased Somewhat   Decreased Substantially

Maintaining an excellent standard of living   Increased Substantially   Increased Somewhat   Little Change   Decreased Somewhat   Decreased Substantially

41. As you look back over the course of your life, certain events may stand out as highly significant or turning points. List below five such events. Briefly explain why these particular events stand out.

Event	*Comment*
1.	
2.	
3.	
4.	
5.	

42. Give any other significant information about yourself or your family that has not been covered in this questionnaire; e.g., any special good fortune, accomplishments, or change of status since 1972; any misfortunes or disappointments that have seriously affected your life. Also, list here any publications, patents, or other creative work since 1972. If more space is needed, attach an additional sheet.

43. Name and address of someone through whom you could be reached if your address should change _____

_____ Relationship _____

Both Federal and University regulations require that we receive your formal consent to serve as a subject in such a research project as this. While we hope you have filled out most of the relevant items in the questionnaire, obviously you can answer or not as you choose. As always, the questionnaires will be kept in locked files and available only to our research staff members. For all research projects involving human subjects, the University requests that the following statement be signed:

I understand that if I am dissatisfied with any aspect of this program at any time, I may report grievances anonymously to the Sponsored Projects Office at Stanford (415) 497-2883.

Signature _____

— 8 —

Terman Study of the Gifted
Stanford University, 1977

Date of filling out this blank _____
Please return by December 10, 1977,
or as soon as possible.

INFORMATION BLANK FOR WOMEN

1. Full name _____ Age at 1977 birthday _____
   (include maiden name)

2. Address _____

   _____ Telephone (_____) _____-_____
   ZIP A.C.

3. Marital status at present (circle one):   Single   Married   Separated   Divorced   Widowed

4. Changes in your marital status, 1972–1977 (divorce, death of husband, remarriage, etc.). Give year of each change. Give name
   of new husband, if any. _____

   _____

5. List below the members of the household in which you are now living, giving their relation to you (e.g., spouse, sister, friend,
   roomer, etc.).

   If you are living alone, check here. ☐

Name	Relationship to you

6. How satisfied are you with your present living arrangements? (indicate by an X on the line)

   Highly   Generally   Somewhat   Not Very   Not At All

   Any Comments? _____

7. In what type of housing unit are you residing? (house, mobile home, condominium, apartment, etc.) _____

   _____

8. Do you plan to make any changes in your living arrangements in the near future? _____ If yes, what do you anticipate
   those changes might be? _____

9. How many living brothers and sisters do you have? _____

10. Of those brothers and sisters who *do not* live with you, *how many* do you (or your spouse)

    see or talk with on the telephone: write or receive letters from:

    Daily? _____   Daily? _____
    At least once a week? _____   At least once a week? _____
    At least once a month? _____   At least once a month? _____
    Less than once a month? _____   Less than once a month? _____
    Not at all? _____   Not at all? _____

— 1 —

11. My father is living at age _____; or, he died at age _____ when I was age _____.

My mother is living at age _____; or, she died at age _____ when I was age _____.

If you have always been single, please skip to question 18.

12. Fill in one line for each of your children. Include adopted and stepchildren who were raised in your home. If deceased, note year of death and cause in the last column.

Name	Sex	Year of Birth	Years of schooling completed	Occupation	Marital Status	Number of children	Location (City and State)

13. Of those children who *do not* live with you, *how many* do you (or your spouse)

see or talk with on the telephone:		write or receive letters from:	
Daily?	_____	Daily?	_____
At least once a week?	_____	At least once a week?	_____
At least once a month?	_____	At least once a month?	_____
Less than once a month?	_____	Less than once a month?	_____
Not at all?	_____	Not at all?	_____

Please answer questions 14 through 17 with regard to your present or most recent husband.

14. What was your husband's most recent principal occupation? Give title of his job and nature of work. _____

_____

15. In relation to income-producing work in 1977, is your husband:

         _____ Fully retired
         _____ Working much less than half-time
         _____ Working about half-time
         _____ Working somewhat less than full-time
         _____ Working essentially full-time

  a. Give year of your husband's retirement. Already retired, in 19_____.
                                      Expects to retire in 19_____

16. Which of the following statements describes your activities in relation to your husband's career? Check more than one if applicable.

       _____ I had a career that was essentially independent of his.
       _____ My work contributed directly to his. (Consider help in planning, collaboration, other regular interaction. Consider your unpaid as well as paid work.)
       _____ I took substantial responsibility for the social welfare of his associates, activities to build good will for his business, and other supporting activities.
       _____ We discussed his work frequently.
       _____ I knew very little about his work activities.

17. What role did your husband play in your career or your community service? (check more than one, if applicable.)

       _____ I did not engage much in such activities during our marriage.
       _____ He knew very little about such activities of mine.
       _____ We discussed my work frequently.
       _____ He contributed directly to my activities.
       _____ In many of these activities we were full collaborators.

— 2 —

18. Women's work may take more varied forms than that of men, and may change with presence of children, moves to new locations and other reasons. The question below is designed to show how you experienced this during your adult years. Place a check mark in each column to indicate which of the seven alternative statements best applies to your work during that age period of your life. If two alternatives applied during a particular period, check both. If your status changed during any of the five-year periods, check the most representative one(s).

	Age 21–25	Age 26–30	Age 31–35	Age 36–40	Age 41–45	Age 46–50	Age 51–55	Age 56–60	Age 61–65	Age 66–70
My work was primarily homemaking.	___	___	___	___	___	___	___	___	___	___
I had steady full-time work for income.	___	___	___	___	___	___	___	___	___	___
I had demanding volunteer work, half-time or more.	___	___	___	___	___	___	___	___	___	___
I had steady part-time work for income (about half-time).	___	___	___	___	___	___	___	___	___	___
I had volunteer work 1 or 2 days a week.	___	___	___	___	___	___	___	___	___	___
My work was that of a student.	___	___	___	___	___	___	___	___	___	___
I had retired.	___	___	___	___	___	___	___	___	___	___

Other (explain and date) _____

a. Which of the following aspects of your work have given you greatest satisfaction in recent years? (check once those you regard as important, double-check those most important):
___ A helping or teaching relationship with people in work.
___ Friendly relationship with people in work.
___ Financial gain.
___ Administrative, organizational, pride in getting the work done.
___ Creativity, learning, stimulation, personal growth.
___ Recognition, competition.
___ Other (please specify) _____

b. If you have had income-producing work during most of your marriage, how has this affected your life together? ___

_____

_____

_____

If you have not had income-producing work since age 50, please skip to question 27.

19. Amount of your work in 1977.

Income-Producing Work	Unpaid Professional or Vocational Activities
___ None	___ None
___ Work much less than half-time	___ Work much less than half-time
___ Work about half-time	___ Work about half-time
___ Work somewhat less than full-time	___ Work somewhat less than full-time
___ Work essentially full-time	___ Work essentially full-time

20. If you are not fully retired, give title of job or principal position and nature of work _____

_____

21. If you are not fully retired, on the whole how do you feel about your work nowadays?
___ It is exciting and rewarding.
___ It is rewarding most of the time.
___ There is not much satisfaction in it, but neither is it unpleasant.
___ Although the unpleasant aspects are tolerable, I shall be glad to escape it.
___ I dislike it, and continue only out of necessity.

22. At any time since early adulthood, have you had a significant change in your occupation other than changes of duties with promotion? Please explain and give date. _____

_____ _____

23. In your main occupation, is/was retirement mandatory at some specific age?
_____ No (if you check here, skip to question 25)
_____ Yes. At what age?_____
_____ Officially yes, but exceptions are made. Official age? _____
_____ Officially no, but it is customary. Customary age? _____

24. In general, are there opportunities to continue the same occupation after mandatory retirement?
_____ No _____ Yes (if yes, check any of the following that apply.)
_____ In other companies or institutions, with pay.
_____ Under less advantageous employment circumstances.
_____ As a consultant, free lance, etc.
_____ Without institutional affiliation.
_____ On a voluntary basis with my institution or company.
_____ Other (please specify) _____

25. Which of the following arrangements would you personally prefer?
_____ Retire even earlier at age _____.
_____ Retire at regular time.
_____ Continue to work full-time until about age_____.
_____ Begin decreasing work or responsibility at age _____ and retire fully at about age _____.

26. Below is a time line in years since you were age 50. At what age did you drop down to *less* than full-time work (100%)? Enter an approximate percent under that year of age to show about how much time you worked. Continue giving percents for each subsequent year to your present age. *Work* may have been income-producing (e.g., law practice, business), or a continuation of previous work but without pay (e.g., research, writing), or volunteer service (e.g., politics, community organization work). You have to be the judge of what *full-time* meant to you, and also what *work* means! If in doubt, add a comment.

AGE	50	51	52	53	54	55	56	57	58	59	60	61	62	63	64	65	66	67	68	69	70	71	72	73	74	75
%																										

Comment: _____

27. For the year 1976, please enter approximate amount of annual income for each category which applies to you. Enter an "X" if the category does not apply, as, for example, if you had no husband in 1976. You don't need to belabor this to the last dollar.

Your earned income $_____
Your husband's earned income $_____
Your social security payment $_____
Your husband's social security payment $_____
Other pension, yourself $_____
Other pension, your husband $_____
Your investment income $_____
Your husband's investment income $_____
Jointly owned investment income $_____
Other (describe) _____ $_____

If the above figures do not reflect your approximate total family income, please describe the exceptions and give a total, or if your income for this one year was significantly unusual, please explain. _____

_____

_____

— 4 —

28. Please check to indicate your general health recently.
_____ Very good   _____ Fair   _____ Very poor
_____ Good   _____ Poor
Major changes in your physical or mental well-being since 1972, with date if applicable. _____
_____

29. Compared to other people of about your age, would you say that your health at present is:
_____ Better   _____ The same
_____ Worse   _____ Don't know

30. Your energy and vitality at this period of life (check one):
_____ Vigorous; have considerable endurance.   _____ Have to limit myself somewhat.
_____ Adequate for a full program of activities.   _____ Lack of energy very much limits my activities.

31. Taking things altogether, how would you describe yourself these days:
_____ Very happy   _____ Pretty happy   _____ Not too happy.

32. List below any organizations or institutions to which you have committed a substantial amount of time or interest.

Name of organization or institution	Compared with 5 years ago, my interest and participation has:		
	Increased	Remained the same	Decreased

33. How regularly do you vote? (check for each kind of election).
National election: _____ Always   _____ Usually   _____ Occasionally   _____ Rarely   _____ Never
State election: _____ Always   _____ Usually   _____ Occasionally   _____ Rarely   _____ Never
Local election: _____ Always   _____ Usually   _____ Occasionally   _____ Rarely   _____ Never

34. On national issues which political party most represents your leanings? _____

35. Rate yourself on the following scale as regards your political and economic viewpoint (Indicate by cross (X) on the line)

| Radical | Very Liberal | Tend to be Liberal | Middle-of-the-road | Tend to be Conservative | Quite Conservative | Strongly Conservative |

Comments _____

36. With respect to *religion*, since your middle years has there been any change in your:

Interest   *Formal Association*
_____ Increased   _____ Increased
_____ No change   _____ No change
_____ Decreased   _____ Decreased

Comments _____

— 5 —

37. Below is a list of activities. Please put a check in *one* of the first 4 columns which best describes your level of participation in each activity; then place a check in column 5 or column 6 if applicable.

Activity	At present, I do this:				(5) I used to do this in my middle years, but don't now	(6) I've taken this up recently
	(1) Fre-quently	(2) Occa-sionally	(3) Seldom	(4) Never		
Reading: newspapers, magazines						
Reading: books (fiction)						
Reading: books (nonfiction)						
Reading: professional publications						
Reading: avocational publications						
Watching TV: educational, cultural						
Watching TV: sporting events						
Watching TV: entertainment						
Attending movies						
Participating in competitive sports						
Noncompetitive physical activity						
Attending sporting events						
Listening to recorded music						
Playing or singing with a musical group						
Playing a musical instrument						
Creative writing, painting, sculpture, dramatics						
Competitive card or board games						
Solitary games or puzzles						
Playing with pets						
Traveling						
Going to concerts, plays, lectures, museums, etc.						
Working on hobbies, (collections, gardening, handicrafts)						
Home repairs and maintenance						
Visiting and communicating with relatives						
Informal visiting with friends and neighbors						
Entertaining						
Self-improvement—physical (exercise, diet)						
Continuing education (classes)						
Increasing knowledge or skill (independent study)						
Community service: helping friends or neighbors						
Community service: with a group						
Community service: work done at home						
Unpaid professional or technical work						
Other activities: please specify						

If you have begun retirement, please review the items you have checked under the first column ("frequently"), including any you may have added to the list. Has any *one* item replaced your main occupation as a principal focus for your efforts and energy? If so, double check that item.

— 6 —

38. For each of the following areas in life, indicate the overall level of satisfaction you have experienced. If you have had more than one marriage, and different experiences, check a column for each marriage, and circle the response that applies to your present or most recent spouse.

	Highly Satisfying	Generally Satisfying	Somewhat Satisfying	Not very Satisfying	Not at all Satisfying	Does not apply to my life
Income-producing work						
Your avocational activities or hobbies						
Your marriage						
Your children						
Friendships, social contacts						
Community service activities						
Participation in cultural activities						
Recreation						
Religion						
Other						

39. As compared to your friends or colleagues of the same sex and of about your age, how ambitious or aspiring do you consider yourself in regard to: (indicate by X on the line):

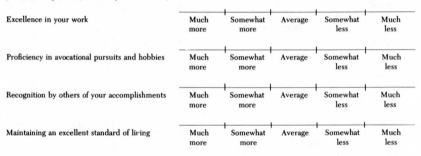

Excellence in your work

Much more   Somewhat more   Average   Somewhat less   Much less

Proficiency in avocational pursuits and hobbies

Much more   Somewhat more   Average   Somewhat less   Much less

Recognition by others of your accomplishments

Much more   Somewhat more   Average   Somewhat less   Much less

Maintaining an excellent standard of living

Much more   Somewhat more   Average   Somewhat less   Much less

40. During the last 10–15 years have you noticed any change in your ambition or aspiration to achieve the following: (indicate by X on line):

Excellence in your work

Increased Substantially   Increased Somewhat   Little Change   Decreased Somewhat   Decreased Substantially

Proficiency in avocational pursuits and hobbies

Increased Substantially   Increased Somewhat   Little Change   Decreased Somewhat   Decreased Substantially

Recognition by others of your accomplishments

Increased Substantially   Increased Somewhat   Little Change   Decreased Somewhat   Decreased Substantially

Maintaining an excellent standard of living

Increased Substantially   Increased Somewhat   Little Change   Decreased Somewhat   Decreased Substantially

41. As you look back over the course of your life, certain events may stand out as highly significant or turning points. List below five such events. Briefly explain why these particular events stand out.

Event	Comment
1.	
2.	
3.	
4.	
5.	

42. Give any other significant information about yourself or your family that has not been covered in this questionnaire; e.g., any special good fortune, accomplishments, or change of status since 1972; any misfortunes or disappointments that have seriously affected your life. Also, list here any publications, patents, or other creative work since 1972. If more space is needed, attach an additional sheet.

43. Name and address of someone through whom you could be reached if your address should change _____

_____Relationship_____

Both Federal and University regulations require that we receive your formal consent to serve as a subject in such a research project as this. While we hope you have filled out most of the relevant items in the questionnaire, obviously you can answer or not as you choose. As always, the questionnaires will be kept in locked files and available only to our research staff members. For all research projects involving human subjects, the University requests that the following statement be signed:

I understand that if I am dissatisfied with any aspect of this program at any time, I may report grievances anonymously to the Sponsored Projects Office at Stanford (415) 497-2883.

Signature _____

— 8 —

Terman Study of the Gifted
Stanford University, 1981-82   Date of filling out this blank _____

1. Full name _____Age at 1981 birthday _____

2. Address _____

    _____Telephone (____) _____
                                       zip   A.C.

3. Marital status at present (Circle one):   Single   Married   Separated

                                              Divorced   Widowed

4. Changes in your marital status, 1977-1981 (Divorce, Death of Spouse, Remarriage,etc.)
    Give year of each change. Give name of new spouse, if any _____
    _____

5. List below the members of the household in which you are now living, giving their
    relation to you (e.g., spouse, brother, daughter, friend, roomer, etc.)
    [ ]   Check here if living alone.

1. Name	2. Relationship to you	3. Approximate age

6. Have you made any changes in your living arrangements since 1977? _____
    Describe the changes, indicating reasons _____
    _____

7. How satisfied are you with your present living arrangements? (Indicate by an X)

    Highly   Generally   Somewhat   Not very   Not at all

8. Are there likely to be any changes in your living arrangements in the next
    few years? _____.   If yes, what might these changes be? _____
    _____

9a. To what extent do you interact with others on a close personal basis?

    Much of the   Several hours   Rarely
       time   in most weeks

9b. How satisfied are you with this amount?

    Would like   Fully   Would like
    much more   satisfied   much less

10a. Do you provide the personal care or assistance that some friend or relative needs?

    Explain _____

10b. To what extent do you need personal care or assistance?

    Must have   Have some   Need little
    considerable help   recurrent needs   or no help

    Explain _____

2.

11. Compared with five years ago, how much time do you devote to homemaking, house-care and other private living activities?

| Much less time | A little less | About the same | A little more | Much more time |

12. Below is a time line in years. Enter an approximate percent under each year to show about how much time you worked. Work may have been income-producing (e.g., law practice, business), or a continuation of previous work but without pay (e.g., research, writing), or volunteer service (e.g., politics, community organization work). You have to be the judge of what full-time meant to you, and also what work means! If in doubt, add a comment.

Year	1975	1976	1977	1978	1979	1980	1981
%							

Comment _____

13. Do you anticipate any changes in the amount or kind of your work activities during the next three years? No_____ Yes _____, as follows:

_____ Expect responsibilities to increase

_____ Considering a change in type of work

_____ Expect to reduce amount and/or responsibility

14. In the following list, check to indicate categories of activities that occupy you occasionally during the year, and double check those that occupy you frequently.

_____ Reading books: Fiction

_____ Reading: Non-fiction or professional or avocational publications

_____ Watching TV: Entertainment

_____ Watching TV: Educational, cultural

_____ Working on hobbies (collections, gardening, handicrafts, ...)

_____ Going to concerts, plays, lectures, museums, ...)

_____ Serious practice on arts (music, art, writing, dramatics, ...)

_____ Meetings of social groups, clubs

_____ Managing personal property and finance

_____ Informal visiting with friends, neighbors, children

_____ Physical self improvement (exercise, diet)

_____ Continuing education, increasing knowledge or skills

_____ Community service with organizations

_____ Helping others (friends, neighbors, children)

_____ Competitive activities (bridge, golf, ...)

_____ Other: _____

3.

15. To what extent does this pattern of activities represent your own choice?

Entirely   Moderately   Hardly
                                                          at all

Check any of the following factors that make your pattern different from what you would prefer.

_____ Limited health and energy.
_____ Lack of opportunities for older persons.
_____ Sense of responsibility for an activity or organization.
_____ Wishes and needs of spouse or children.
_____ Limited financial resources.
_____ Other. What?_____

16. Have any disappointments, failures, deaths of friends or family, uncongenial relationships with others, etc., exerted an influence upon you? Describe ___
_____
_____

17. What factors do you think have contributed most to your happiness in recent years?
_____
_____

18. Your general health since 1976: (circle) Very good; Good; Fair; Poor; Very poor.

19. Major changes in your physical or mental well-being since 1977, with date if applicable. _____
_____

20. Are there any aspects of your health that give you cause to worry about your well-being over the next few years? Please explain _____
_____

21. Has there been any tendency toward nervousness, worry, special anxieties or nervous breakdown in recent years? _____ Nature of such difficulties _____
_____

22. Your energy and vitality at this period of life (check one):

_____ Vigorous, have considerable endurance.
_____ Adequate for a full program of activities.
_____ Have to limit myself somewhat.
_____ Lack of energy very much limits my activities.

23. Make two X-marks on the line below to show the range within which your mood has fluctuated during the last month or two.

Very cheerful; elated	Fairly cheerful	Matter of-fact	Fairly depressed	Very depressed; gloomy

24. Make two X-marks on the line below to show the range of your feelings during the last month or two.

Very relaxed calm	Fairly relaxed	Half-way between extremes	Fairly tense; anxious	Very worried; tense; anxious

4.

25. Taking things altogether, how would you describe yourself these days:

    _____ Very happy   _____ Pretty happy   _____ Not too happy

26. Which of the following describe goals or purposes you have for your life. Check twice the three that are most important.

    _____ To remain as independent as I am at present.
    _____ To be financially secure.
    _____ To remain healthy.
    _____ To take each day as it comes.
    _____ To die peacefully.
    _____ To continue to make a contribution to society.
    _____ To continue to make a contribution to children.
    _____ To continue to make a contribution to spouse.
    _____ To continue to work.
    _____ To have many pleasant personal relationships.
    _____ To enjoy intimacy with others.
    _____ To enjoy hobbies and other activities.
    _____ To continue to grow personally, be creative and productive.
    _____ To produce social change.
    _____ To have opportunities for achievement or competition.
    _____ Other: _____

27. If, since 1976, you have had honors, noteworthy assignments or appointments, or special accomplishments, note them here. _____

    _____
    _____
    _____

28. Name and address of someone through whom you could be reached if your address should change. _____

    _____
    _____ Relationship _____

                              ****

Both Federal and University regulations require that we receive your formal consent to serve as a subject in such a research project as this. While we hope you have filled out most of the relevant items in the questionnaire, obviously you can answer or not as you choose. As always, the questionnaires will be kept in locked files and available only to our research staff members. For all research projects involving human subjects, the University requests that the following statement be signed:

> I understand that if I am dissatisfied with any aspect of this program at any time, I may report grievances anonymously to the Sponsored Projects Office at Stanford (415) 497-2883.

                              Signature _____

TERMAN STUDY OF THE GIFTED   STANFORD UNIVERSITY, 1986

Both Federal and University regulations require your formal consent to serve as a subject in such a research project as this. While we hope you fill out most of the relevant items in the questionnaire, obviously you can answer or not as you choose. As always the questionnaires will be kept in locked files and available only to accredited research workers. For all research projects involving human subjects, the University requests that the following statement be signed:

> I understand that if I am dissatisfied with any aspect of this program at any time, I may report grievances anonymously to the Sponsored Projects Office at Stanford. Phone (415) 497-2883.

Signature_____

Date of filling out this blank_____, 198__   Age at 1985 birthday_____

1   Full name_____

2   Address_____

_____ Telephone (_____)_____
                                         ZIP   A.C.

3   Marital status at present: (circle one)

     Single   Married   Separated   Divorced   Widowed   Other:_____

4   Any change in marital status since 1981?_____

_____

5   Which of the following best describes your present living arrangements?

     ____ Single family house; duplex   ____ Nursing home; hospital
     ____ Mobile home   ____ Rooming house
     ____ Apartment; residential hotel   ____ Convent; monastery
     ____ Retirement complex   ____ Other:_____

6   If you are living alone, check here: ____

     Otherwise, list below the members of the household in which you are now living, giving their relation to you (e.g., spouse, daughter, friend, etc.).

NAME	RELATIONSHIP TO YOU	APPROXIMATE AGE

7   Consider your 10 best friends (excluding family and close relatives). How many of them would you place in each of the following categories?

     ____ Intimate; we share most of our joys and sorrows.
     ____ Companionship; frequent interaction arising out of shared interests.
     ____ Casual; we don't seek each other out.

8   How satisfied are you with this amount of intimacy and companionship?

Would like	Fully	Would like
much more	satisfied	much less

9   Among the members of your immediate family and close relatives, with about how many do you have each of the following relationships?

_____ Intimate; we share most of our joys and sorrows.
_____ Companionship; frequent interaction arising out of shared interests.
_____ Casual; we don't seek each other out.
_____ Indifference or hostility; we actively avoid one another, or
　　　　make no effort to be friendly.

10   How satisfied are you with this amount of intimacy and companionship?

Would like	Fully	Would like
much more	satisfied	much less

11   Your health since 1981: (circle)　　Very good　　Good　　Fair　　Poor　　Very poor

12   Major changes in your physical or mental well-being since 1981, with date if applicable.

_____

_____

13   Are there any aspects of your health that give you cause to worry about your well-being

over the next few years? Please explain. _____

_____

14   How satisfied are you with the quality and availability of your health care?

Highly	Generally	Somewhat	Not very	Not at all
satisfied	satisfied	satisfied	satisfied	satisfied

15   Your energy and vitality in this period of life: (check one)

_____ Vigorous, have considerable endurance.
_____ Adequate for a full program of activities.
_____ Have to limit myself.
_____ Lack of energy very much limits my activities.

16   To what extent do you need personal care or assistance?

Must have con-	Have some	Need little
siderable help	recurrent needs	or no help

17   Do you provide personal care or assistance that some friend or relative needs?

Yes _____ No _____ If Yes, describe _____

- 2 -

18 In the last few years, have any disappointments, failures, deaths of friends or family, uncongenial relationships with others, etc., exerted an influence upon you?

Describe_____

_____

19 Make two **X** marks on the line below to show the range within which your mood has fluctuated during the last month or two.

|_____|_____|_____|_____|

| Very cheer-
ful; elated | Fairly
cheerful | Matter-
of-fact | Fairly
depressed | Very depressed;
gloomy |

20 Make two **X** marks on the line below to show the range of your feelings during the last month or two.

|_____|_____|_____|_____|

| Very relaxed;
calm | Fairly
relaxed | Half-way
between
extremes | Fairly
tense | Very tense,
worried; anxious |

21 Which statement below would best characterize your use of alcohol in recent years? Check one.

A____ I never take a drink, or only on rare occasions.

B____ I am a moderate drinker. I have seldom or never been intoxicated.

C____ I consider myself between ratings **B** and D in the use of liquor.

D____ I am a fairly heavy drinker; I drink to excess rather frequently but do not feel that it has interfered seriously with my work or relationships with others.

E____ Alcohol is a serious problem. I am frequently drunk and attempts to stop drinking have been unsuccessful.

If alcohol has been a serious problem, what steps have been taken?

_____

22 Taking things altogether, how would you describe yourself these days: (check one)

____Very happy   ____Pretty happy   ____Not too happy

23 As compared to your friends or colleagues of the same sex and of about your age, how ambitious or aspiring do you consider yourself with regard to excellence in whatever projects you now engage in?

|_____|_____|_____|_____|

| Much more | Somewhat more | Average | Somewhat less | Much less |

24 Everyone has his/her own level of financial need -- how much money it takes to be quite comfortable. How are your financial resources? (check one)

____ More than
enough   ____ Quite
adequate   ____ Barely adequate
with care   ____ Really
insufficient

25 In the following list, check **once** any category of activities that occupies you
    occasionally during the year. Check **twice** those that occupy you frequently.

       A ____ Reading books: Fiction
       B ____ Reading: Non-fiction or professional or avocational publications
       C ____ Watching TV: Entertainment
       D ____ Watching TV: Educational, cultural
       E ____ Working on hobbies (collections, gardening, handicrafts, etc.)
       F ____ Going to concerts, plays, lectures, museums, etc.
       G ____ Serious practice on arts (music, art, writing, dramatics, etc.)
       H ____ Meetings of social groups, clubs, playing cards
       I ____ Managing personal property and finance
       J ____ Informal visiting with friends, neighbors, children
       K ____ Physical self-improvement (exercise, diet)
       L ____ Continuing education, increasing knowledge or skills
       M ____ Community service with organizations
       N ____ Helping others (friends, neighbors, children)
       O ____ Competitive activities (golf, bridge, etc.)
       P ____ Other: _____

26 Thinking more specifically of how you spend a typical week, give the percentage of
    time devoted to the following. (Use an 8-hour day; should add to 100%.)

       A ____% Occupational work for pay
       B ____% Occupational work without pay (e.g., writing, designing, etc.)
       C ____% Community volunteer work
       D ____% Physical recreation (e.g., walking, gardening)
       E ____% Sedentary recreation (e.g., reading, TV)
       F ____% Housekeeping; errands; chores; shopping
       G ____% Meeting health needs (e.g., going to doctor, dentist, etc.)
       H ____% Other:_____

27 Compared with five years ago, how much time do you devote to homemaking, housecare,
    and other private living activities?

    |_____|_____|_____|_____|
    Much less   A little less   About the same   A little more   Much more

28 Here is a list of experiences that many elderly people find troubling. Some of them can be
    real hassles. Check **once** those that have troubled you recently, but that in one way or
    another you are able to handle without too much stress. Check **twice** those that
    you cannot handle very well and that are causing you fairly severe stress.

       A Declining physical abilities:
           1 ____ hearing
           2 ____ vision
           3 ____ health
           4 ____ muscular strength or control
       B ____ Care of family member
       C ____ Not seeing enough people

D ____ Rising prices of common goods and services
E ____ Local transportation; getting around town
F ____ Children's/grandchildren's difficulties
G ____ Too many things to do -- chores, etc.
H ____ Not enough personal energy
I ____ Managing property and accounts
J ____ Misplaced or lost things; poor memory
K ____ Other _____
L ____ Another _____
M ____ Still another _____

29   Which of the following describe goals or purposes you have for your life?
Check **once**, and then check **twice** the three that are most important.

A____ To remain as independent as I can be
B____ To be financially secure
C____ To be as healthy as possible
D____ To take each day as it comes
E____ To die peacefully
F____ To make a contribution to society
G____ To make a contribution to my children
H____ To make a contribution to my spouse
I____ To continue to work
J____ To have many pleasant personal relationships
K____ To enjoy intimacy with others
L____ To enjoy a hobby or other activities
M____ To continue to grow personally, be creative and productive
N____ To produce social change
O____ To have opportunities for achievement or competition
P____ Other: _____

30   How important to you are the following aspects of religion and church?

VERY	MODERATELY	NOT AT ALL	
____	____	____	A Worship and prayer
____	____	____	B Spiritual reading, or radio/TV
____	____	____	C Trying to understand religious truths more deeply
____	____	____	D Going to church as a social activity
____	____	____	E Participating in church pageants, socials and the like
____	____	____	F Participating in church governance, committees
____	____	____	G Supporting social betterment causes
____	____	____	H Welfare activities
____	____	____	I Other:_____

Which of these have increased in importance in recent years? (circle)

A   B   C   D   E   F   G   H   I

Which of these have decreased in importance in recent years? (circle)

A   B   C   D   E   F   G   H   I

31 Note here any honors, noteworthy assignments or appointments, special accomplish-
    ments or interesting activities since 1981. Check **X** the one most important to you.

    _____

    _____

    _____

    _____

32 As you look back over your life, what factors would you say have contributed to your life
    accomplishments?   Check **once** all of the following that have had a definitely
    helpful effect.   Check **twice** those that have been most helpful.

    A____ Superior mental ability   G____ Persistence in working toward a goal
    B____ Adequate education   H____ Excellent health
    C____ Good social adjustment   I ____ Lucky "chance" factors
    D____ Good personality   J____ Help or support from other people (e.g.,
    E____ Good mental stability   spouse, children, friends, employer, etc.)
    F____ Good habits of work

33 On the other hand, what factors would you say have hindered your life accomplishments?
    Check **once** each thing that has had a definitely hindering effect.
    Check **twice** those that have hindered most.

    A____ Inadequate mental ability   G____ Lack of persistence in working toward a goal
    B____ Inadequate education   H____ Poor health
    C____ Poor social adjustment   I ____ Unlucky "chance" factors
    D____ Poor personality   J____ Hindering by other people (e.g., spouse,
    E____ Mental instability   children, friends, employer, etc.)
    F____ Poor work habits

34 Now, looking back over your whole life, what choices would you make differently if
    you had the opportunity to live it again?

    _____

    _____

    _____

    _____

35 Name and address of someone through whom you can be reached if your
    address should change.

    _____

    _____

    Telephone (_____)_____   Relationship _____
                    A.C.

The following questions, for both men and women, are about your experiences during World War II. The first 10 concern military service; if you were not in military service, check here_____ and go to Question 46.

36 When did you enter and leave military service?

    A Entered: Year 19____ Month____ Rank (or pay-grade)_____

    B Discharged: Year 19____ Month____ Rank (or pay-grade)_____

37 Were you drafted into the Armed Forces or did you enlist? (check one)

    A ____ Drafted   C ____ Entered from ROTC

    B ____ Enlisted   D ____ Entered from reserve

38 Over how long a period did you serve under combat conditions or subject to enemy action?

    A____ Never subject to enemy action   B____ weeks; or, ____ months

39 Did you enter the reserve after you left military service?

    ____ No   ____ Yes   For how long? _____

40 Were your military training experiences helpful in your subsequent career?   ____ No

    ____ Not applicable   ____ Yes; if Yes, how? _____

    _____

41 Over the years, have you received any G.I. financial benefits?

    A ____ No   Why not?_____

    B ____ Yes, for education

    C ____ Yes, for housing or other loan

42 Considering the best and worst periods of your life, where would you place "military service?" Circle appropriate number.

    Worst   1 2 3 4 5 6 7 8 9 10   Best

43 Upon re-entering civilian life, which of the following conditions describe your situation at the time? Check the appropriate items.

    A ____ I returned to an old job that was   D ____ I lived with my parents for a while

            waiting for me   E ____ I lived independently with my spouse

    B ____ I sought employment   F ____ I took some time off

    C ____ I went back to school   G ____ Other:_____

44 Have your personal views of military service become more negative or more positive since your discharge?

    A ____ More negative. Why?_____

    B ____ No change.

    C ____ More positive. Why?_____

45 Considering the most influential events in your life, where would you place "military service" on the scale below?

    Least   1 2 3 4 5 6 7 8 9 10   Most

    influential   influential

46 If you were married at the time of your wartime experiences, were you separated from your family? ____ For how long? _____

47 Did your spouse enter military service during World War II?
_____ Not married   _____ No   _____ Yes   Entered 19_____   Discharged 19_____

48 What effects did any separations have on you? _____
_____

On your family?_____
_____

49 As a result of your wartime experience, did your relations with parents, spouse, and children change in any noteworthy way? or did they remain the same? Check the appropriate spaces in the columns that apply to you:

MOTHER   FATHER   SPOUSE   CHILDREN

_____	_____	_____	_____	A Became closer
_____	_____	_____	_____	B Became more distant
_____	_____	_____	_____	C Gained respect
_____	_____	_____	_____	D More discord in relationship
_____	_____	_____	_____	E Acquired more independence
_____	_____	_____	_____	F Felt more dependent
_____	_____	_____	_____	G Showed more respect for me
_____	_____	_____	_____	H Became more accepting of me
_____	_____	_____	_____	I I became more understanding
_____	_____	_____	_____	J No change
_____	_____	_____	_____	K Other changes:_____

50 You may have been faced with certain major life decisions during World War II. Did **wartime** conditions influence the timing of these decisions in any way? Check **once** those decisions you had to face then. Check **twice** those that were highly significant to you.
In each case, say what your decision was.

A_____ Choosing a career _____
_____

B_____ When to begin full-time work _____
_____

C_____ When to enter or to complete higher education_____
_____

D_____ When to leave parental home _____
_____

E_____ When to marry _____
_____

F_____ When to have children _____
_____

51 Life experiences, as in wartime, often have some mixture of the good and the bad.
What were the most desirable and undesirable experiences of World War II in your life?
Desirable?_____
_____

Undesirable?_____
_____

Attrition: Causes and Consequences

Definitions and Issues Investigated

This Appendix is provided for readers interested in the details of attrition in the sample. Because this study has been carried out over such an extended period of time, we have had the opportunity to explore thoroughly the patterns and correlates of attrition in the sample over the life course. The analyses presented here provide the bases for the conclusions concerning attrition summarized in Chapter 3.

We shall use the same three categories to classify attriters as those delineated in Chapter 3: death, choice, and loss. Their definitions are repeated below. To reduce repetition of phrases and to compress headings in tables, we shall sometimes abbreviate to D (death), Q (quit), and L (involuntary loss) in our discussion.

Death (D group). If a subject died after he or she last returned a questionnaire and before we mailed the next one, the attrition is charged to death. If a questionnaire went unanswered prior to death — the subject answered in 1955, missed in 1960, died in 1964 — this is counted as choice. Subjects who became incapacitated were also placed in the D group. Because the incapacitated were so few, we shall speak of the group simply as persons who died.

Choice (Q group). During the 65 years of the study, 15 men and 21 women asked that their names be removed from the mailing list. Nonresponders make up the rest of the "choice" category.

Loss (L group). The "loss" group is distinguished from the "choice" group because we doubt that these subjects received our mailings. Some of them probably were silent withdrawals like most cases labeled attrition by choice. No doubt, however, many in the lost group were lost merely because of moves or name changes.

Persons whose last return was prior to 1940, or who never responded, are omitted from the attrition analyses, except for Tables 3.1 and 3.2. The following temporal subdivisions provide the framework for most of the analyses in this chapter:

1: Last return in 1940, 1945, or 1950 (Q1 or D1 group)
2: Last return in 1955 or 1960 (Q2 or D2 group)
3: Last return in 1972 or 1977 (Q3 or D3 group)
4: Responded in 1982 (R group)

Thus a D3 case died between 1972 and 1982, and a Q2 case has not responded since 1955 or 1960. In the tables, "all choice withdrawals," "all deaths," and "all attriters" will refer to a pooling of the first three rubrics (unless it is indicated that a particular line of a table refers to a narrower time slice).

In some subgroups, the numbers of cases in later tables are inconsistent with corresponding numbers in Tables 3.1 and 3.2, which represent our best present evaluation of the status of subjects at the end of 1986. In most subcategories, the inconsistencies between the numbers in Tables 3.1 and 3.2 and later tables are too small to merit discussion.

The most important difference is that a fraction of those who had not responded since 1955 or 1960 (Group Q2) "came back" in 1986. Since they had not responded from 1972 through 1982, they acted like attriters by choice. They are counted as attriters in the analytic tables. Many of these were persons for whom new addresses were obtained through a painstaking search by the staff; in some instances, telephone contacts were also made. Without that search, most or all of these subjects would have remained attriters; hence we do not think that coding them as choice withdrawals has distorted our description of attriters. These persons, though counted as attriters in Table B.1 and subsequently, are included in the later-maturity group, which includes all subjects who answered any of the 1972 to 1986 questionnaires, whether or not they were treated here as cases of attrition. The details of this selection were presented in Chapter 2.

Those who had not responded since 1972 or 1977 (the Q3 cases) but responded in 1986 also posed a problem. About half of them are called attriters in the analytic tables only because they failed to return the 1982 questionnaire. They are not like the Q2 attriters who failed repeatedly to respond. We shall see that on many variables the Q3 subgroup differs little from those responding in 1982, whom we call the "remainder," or "R" group. All Q3 cases were retained in the later-maturity sample.

Precursors of Attrition

In the analyses of attrition that follow, we consider three questions: (1) How did withdrawals by choice differ from 1982 respondents? (2) How did those who died or became disabled differ from 1982 respondents? (3) How did the attriters as a group differ from those who continued through 1982? We do not compare the relatively small group of lost subjects with nonattriters, nor do we subdivide

TABLE B.I

Percentage of Questionnaires Returned by Attriters by Choice
Before Dropout and by Remainder Group

		Year of last response			
Period	No. of questionnaires distributed	1940, 1945, or 1950 (group Q1)	1955 or 1960 (group Q2)	1972 or 1977 (group Q3)	1982 Remainder (group R)
		MEN			
N		25	79	55	418
Pre-1940	5	44%[a]	52%	58%	57%
1940–50	5		73[a]	86	92
1955–60	2			89	94
		WOMEN			
N		13	57	48	399
Pre-1940	5	49%	50%	61%	56%
1940–50	5		79[a]	85	91
1955–60	2			84[a]	94

SOURCE: Questionnaires in years indicated.
NOTE: For explanation of Q1, Q2, Q3, and R, see p. 317.
[a]For contrast of number of questionnaires returned with group R, $p < .01$ by t-test.

them, except where they are counted in overall figures along with subjects in the choice and death attrition groups.

Frequency of Returns. Withdrawal by the individual (apart from sudden death) is a gradual process, evidenced by each subject's rate of returning questionnaires in three time periods: 1922 to 1936, 1940 to 1950, and 1955 to 1960. Many questionnaires and other measuring instruments were used to collect data between 1921 and 1960, but our analysis of attrition is limited to twelve questionnaires, five in each of the first two periods, and two in the last. (These cover more than half the variables measured directly from the subjects during that time and provide an adequate sample for our purposes.)

To compare the rate of return just before withdrawal with that at earlier times, subjects were classified into four groups by date of last return, as described above. Table B.1 shows the percentage of questionnaires returned by attriters by choice and by the remainder group. The dates of questionnaires appear in the left-hand column. Comparison of the 1972/77 column in Table B.1 with that for 1982 shows rather small differences, but those leaving the study earlier (the Q1s and Q2s) were consistently less responsive than the 1982 respondents (the remainder, R). In each of the rows giving values for two or three subgroups of attriters by choice, their response rates are ordered from left to right; those most nearly ready to drop out returned, on average, somewhat fewer questionnaires.

Table B.2 summarizes rates of response from subjects prior to death. The differences across rows are small and none approaches nominal significance. No down-the-column trend appears in the ratios. In short, with respect to number

of questionnaires returned, those subjects who died while still actively participating in the research differed very little from those who lived and continued to
participate.

The responses from lost subjects (not shown in the table) were not much
below the rate of the 1982 respondents before 1940, but thereafter their rate of
response was markedly below the rate of 1982 respondents. The fact that the lost
cases are so similar to attriters by choice in this respect reinforces the suspicion
that some of the lost were in fact silent withdrawals. In sum, those who withdrew
by choice or were lost cases before 1972 contributed significantly fewer responses, even when responding between 1928 and 1950, than those who would
remain until 1982 or later.

Nonresponsiveness and Delay. We investigated two other possible indices
of early reluctance to respond and both support the notion that reluctance reveals
itself in subtle ways. One is the frequency of unanswered questions in the returned questionnaires. We looked at the number of missing responses in the
1936, 1940, and 1955 questionnaires, choosing them because they had relatively
high rates of return. Eight comparisons of means were available for each sex. In
thirteen of the sixteen, those classed as attriters by choice left more questions
unanswered than 1982 respondents; eight of the differences were nominally
significant ($p < .05$).

The second index measured delay in responding by the number of days
intervening between the mailing of the questionnaire and its return. These data
(somewhat incomplete) were available from the 1936 and 1940 follow-ups. Data
for women whose last response was in the decade 1940–1950 were too in-

TABLE B.2

Percentage of Questionnaires Returned by Attriters by Death
Before Dropout and by Remainder Group

Period	No. of questionnaires distributed	1940, 1945, or 1950 (group D1)	1955 or 1960 (group D2)	1972 or 1977 (group D3)	1982 Remainder (group R)
			Year of last response		
		MEN			
N		25	90	76	418
Pre-1940	5	54%	56%	56%	57%
1940–50	5		89	92	92
1955–60	2			96	94
		WOMEN			
N		13	37	33	399
Pre-1940	5	55%	56%	61%	56%
1940–50	5		89	94	91
1955–60	2			98	94

SOURCE: Questionnaires in years indicated.
NOTE: For explanation of D1, D2, D3, and R, see p. 317.

complete to be used; for each of the other choice attrition groups two comparisons with the remainder group could be made. With one exception, the attriters by choice had a longer response time than the subjects who responded in 1982. The differences were generally small, but two attriter subgroups lagged on average by 50 days and those differences were nominally significant. There was no sex difference in delay or in missing responses.

Voluntary withdrawal is, therefore, a gradual process. Well before a subject lapses finally into nonresponse, he or she responds to fewer requests; attrition is already beginning. The questionnaires that are returned tend to be less completely answered and the return tends to be slow. Such forms of noncooperation are more subtle than the coarse ones of simply ignoring a request, or refusing a request for information, or asking to be dropped from the mailing list.

We shall examine further the ways in which the attriters differ from the remainder. But at this point we can already say that the subjects missing from the final later-maturity group tend to be the more reluctant and less cooperative members of the original sample. More important, data from the early years of the study were disproportionately supplied by the nonreluctant participants.

Correlates of Attrition

How do the attriters differ from the remaining participants? Some attrition subgroups are too small for separate analysis. In particular, cases of attrition prior to 1940 were few and we have little information on them.

Most of our analyses will compare subgroups of attriters by choice (Groups Q1–Q3) and subgroups of attriters by death (Groups D1–D3) with the subjects responding in 1982, the remainder (Group R). (As noted, the choice and death subgroups are those who left the study [1] after 1940 to 1950 inclusive, [2] after 1955 or 1960, and [3] after 1972 or 1977.) For testing the statistical significance of differences on ordered variables across groups, we use one-way analysis of variance, with t-tests when these are needed for more precise evaluation of differences in a specific pair of groups. For a categorical variable, chi-square is used. Some analyses will contrast attriters by choice or death as a whole with those responding in 1982, with analysis of variance, using a t-test, or chi-square as the significance test.

The choice of dependent variables poses a problem. With about 3,000 variables available from the first forty years of this study, some guiding notion as to possible fruitfulness was required if we were not to be swamped with random comparisons and meaningless significance values. Of course, certain obvious psychological and demographic variables required testing, but beyond those our guiding notion has been whether the subjects displayed a not-too-well-defined blend of drive, health, competence, and success. Imprecise though it was, the notion has proved useful, and as results are compiled, this general notion will take on a firm character.

Age and Intelligence. Neither age nor IQ was found to be a correlate of attrition. On age when selected, which ranged from under six to over sixteen,

TABLE B.3

Educational Levels of Attriters and Remainder Group

	Men Year of last response				Women Year of last response			
Educational level	1940, 1945, or 1950	1955 or 1960	1972 or 1977	1982	1940, 1945, or 1950	1955 or 1960	1972 or 1977	1982
Percentage attriters by choice compared with remainder groups								
Group[a]	Q1	Q2	Q3	R	Q1	Q2	Q3	R
N	25	79	55	418	13	57	48	399
Graduate degree	28%	30%	36%	50%	0%	23%	17%	27%
Some graduate work	44	40	43	57	30	46	36	43
A.B. or B.S.	56	62	63	80	31	68	62	71
Percentage attriters by death compared with remainder groups								
Group[a]	D1	D2	D3	R	D1	D2	D3	R
N	25	90	76	418	13	37	33	399
Graduate degree	16%	42%	37%	50%	23%	30%	46%	27%
Some graduate work	24	50	44	57	31	57	55	43
A.B. or B.S.	36	72	69	80	62	73	70	71

SOURCE: Cumulative education data.
NOTE: For explanation of groups Q1, Q2, Q3, D1, D2, D3, and R, see p. 317.
[a]For contrast with Group R, $p < .01$ by median test.

distributions in the choice and death attrition groups resemble that of the remainder. Also, those with 1936 as last year of response did not differ from the remainder group in 1936 age. Nor was there any difference in IQ, early school achievement, or Concept Mastery score in middle age.

Socioeconomic Status of Family. For some children, the status of the family of origin is an important support to self-esteem. It seemed likely that higher levels of parental education and occupation might be associated with the greater drive and intellectual interest that might induce subjects to remain participants. However, we found no difference among our groups in quality of the parental home or of its neighborhood. These variables were measured years before they came into common use as a measure of socioeconomic status. It appears that in the Terman group the socioeconomic status of the family of origin was unrelated to attrition. (Data on the incomes of the families of origin were not available.)

Subjects' Education. Educational level was, however, related to attrition. Those who finished college were much less likely to drop out than those whose education stopped short of a bachelor's degree. The numbers in the third row of Table B.3 show a marked difference between choice and remainder columns for males. (Subtraction from 100 shows what percentage of each group did not finish college.) Male attrition by death shows somewhat the same pattern. Women in the earliest choice and death attrition groups (Q1 and D1) attained less education than women in the remainder, but this cannot be said of post-1950 female attriters. Lost subjects (not shown in the table) had a similar pattern to attrition by choice.

This table is confined to subjects who had reached adulthood; nearly all provided information after the age of 25. Even so, a possible bias is present. A person who did not report to us after (say) 1945 cannot be credited with education completed after 1945. Many subjects continued in higher education after that date; one bachelor's degree, in fact, was completed in 1980. Impressive though these cases are, they are not large proportionately. A check on bias was made by determining how much education each subject had completed by 1940. It was not possible to form groups identical to those of Table B.3, but the reanalysis establishes that any bias in the comparisons of Table B.3 is small indeed.*

Occupational Success. Among the women, neither extent of employment nor their retrospective 1972 rating of lifetime occupational satisfaction distinguished withdrawals by choice from the remainder group. Among the men, neither the type of occupation (business or professional) nor the 1972 lifetime satisfaction rating distinguishes withdrawals by choice or death from the remainder. Attrition was, however, associated with men's level of occupational achievement. Those who had highly successful careers and those whose achievements were more modest had different response rates.

After the 1940 follow-up, Terman and Oden (1947) selected 150 "most" and "least successful" men — the "A" and "C" groups. A "B" rating was assigned to all others. (No such rating was made for women.) The criteria for selection were: "(a) nature of work, importance of position, and professional output; (b) qualities of leadership, influence, and initiative; (c) recognition and honors (scientific, civic, professional), awards, biographical listings, election to learned societies, etc.; and (d) earned income. For most occupations, except business, income received the least weight" (Oden, 1968, p. 53).

In 1940 perhaps a quarter of the group was too young to be well evaluated. But two decades later their ages were fully suitable, and Oden and Dr. Helen Marshall repeated the evaluation. In 1960 they selected only 100 A cases and 100 C cases, again assigning a B rating to all others. (There were not 150 who could be called C's.) There was considerable overlap of the two ratings (Oden, 1968), but there was enough shuffling of position to make it useful to examine both sets of ratings with respect to attrition.

Table B.4 makes possible several comparisons. Although at the time of ratings, A's and C's were equally numerous. C's were more numerous than A's among those who would later be classified as "choice" withdrawals. Those classified as withdrawals by death showed a small difference of the same sort, in the 1940 ratings only. In the remainder, the pattern was reversed; A's appreciably outnumbered C's. Death was not consistently associated with A/C status,

* The figures across the bottom of the attrition by choice section of Table B.3 are, in order, 56, 62, 63, 80; 31, 68, 62, 71. The corresponding figures based on education to 1940 are 62, 63, 62, 79; 33, 68, 62, 70. Only the first entry shows a nontrivial discrepancy, and it comes from a tiny group. A tally on postgraduate education shows substantially smaller proportions in the 1940 data than the "lifetime" record of Table B.3; but the patterning across subgroups is consistent between the two.

TABLE B.4
*Staff Ratings of Occupational Success of Men
in Attriter and Remainder Groups (Percentages)*

Rating	Choice[a]	Death[b]	Remainder	Base rate[c]
1940	N = 154	N = 188	N = 416	
A	12%	19%	21%	19%
B	64	56	66	63
C	23	24	13	18
1960	N = 94	N = 142	N = 400	
A	13%	16%	16%	16%
B	60	70	74	71
C	28	14	10	13

SOURCE: Ratings by research staff of degree of occupational success; "A" being highest, and "C" lowest.
[a]Contrast with remainder group: $p < .01$.
[b]Contrast with remainder group: $p < .05$.
[c]Weighted average of other columns.

whereas subsequent attrition by choice was comparatively frequent among C's. The men who remained for study in later maturity tended to have been more successful in their careers than the total sample.

Health. Chronic ill-health seems a likely cause of withdrawal by choice. This is an uncommon problem in the early years of life, but after middle age increasing numbers of people feel — and often are — more or less continuously affected by physical disorders. Self-estimates of health status were collected during the half-century from 1928 to 1977. The phrasing varied; for example, one survey asked about general health in the preceding six years, and one asked about general health "recently." All surveys after 1928 employed this 5-point scale: "Very good," "Good," "Fair," "Poor," "Very poor."

Our first comparison examines self-ratings by attriters in their last year of response. Table B.5 summarizes reports in the period 1955 to 1977, ignoring the early years, when there were few attriters. In the columns for attriters, each entry comes from a new sample. The remainder group, on the contrary, remains essentially fixed; numbers of cases fluctuate only because some persons failed to respond in each round of questioning.

Those who would shortly leave the study consistently rated their health lower than those who responded in 1982 (the remainder group, R). The differences were about the same size for men and women. Among males, withdrawals by death gave lower self-ratings than withdrawals by choice. This was not true of women.

The question naturally arises whether attriters had been reporting less-than-excellent health in surveys long before they left the study. Considering not only last-year response as in Table B.5 but also the response in the two prior surveys

TABLE B.5

*Self-Ratings of Health in Year of Last Response in Attriter Groups
and in Same Year for Remainder Group*

Year of attriters' last response	Men				Women			
	Attriters		Remainder		Attriters		Remainder	
	N	Mean	Mean	Diff.	N	Mean	Mean	Diff.
Attriters by choice compared with remainder group								
1955	41	3.98	4.44	−.47[a]	20	4.05	4.36	−.31[a]
1960	27	4.37	4.46	−.09	26	4.15	4.36	−.21
1972	24	3.79	4.42	−.63[b]	16	3.38	4.25	−.88[a]
1977	11	4.18	4.34	−.16	17	3.76	4.29	−.53[a]
Attriters by death compared with remainder group								
1955	22	3.73	4.44	−.72[a]	4	3.00	4.36	−1.36
1960	68	4.12	4.46	−.34[a]	32	4.06	4.36	−.30
1972	37	3.62	4.42	−.80[a]	14	3.57	4.25	−.68
1977	37	3.89	4.34	−.45[b]	18	3.89	4.29	−.40

SOURCE: Questionnaires in years indicated.

NOTE: N's for the remainder group were 373–434 (men) and 345–398 (women). The remainder group entry in each row is from the report for the year shown at left. Differences were computed prior to rounding.

[a]By t test, $p < .01$.   [b]$p < .05$.

("Lag 1," "Lag 2"), subgroup means differ from the corresponding means in the remainder as follows (on the average, over the years):

Difference in mean self-ratings of health	Choice		Death	
	Men	Women	Men	Women
Last-year difference	−.37	−.44	−.72	−.47
Lag-1 difference	−.13	−.22	−.13	−.22
Lag-2 difference	−.08	−.27	−.13	−.09

The Lag-1 response for a person whose last year was 1955 came from the 1950 survey, from 1960 for a person whose last year was 1972, and so on. The consistent negative averaged lagged differences suggest some small tendency for prospective attriters to report poorer health in surveys ten or more years prior to their last response. Emphasis should, however, be placed on the difference between the final year and prior years. Attrition associated with declining health casts its shadow a long time before in some cases, but most attriters reported health similar to that of the remainder group in all surveys save that of their last response.*

The preceding findings led us to wonder about the mortality rate in the "choice" withdrawal group. To the best of our knowledge they were still alive

* In the analysis just summarized for choice and death cases the last year of response was 1955–1977. Persons who failed to respond in 1977 and 1982, but who did respond in 1986, are counted in the remainder group. (They are counted in Group Q3 in other analyses for this appendix.) Full data were not available, so the three means for a subgroup are based on slightly different sets of persons. Having formed a mean for a group such as "Q [or D] male, last year 1955," we subtracted it from the corresponding R mean, then weighted by the number of Q [or D] cases to form the mean difference reported above. Prior to averaging, the means in the various small subsets of cases fluctuated irregularly; therefore, our overall summary seems to say as much as the data warrant.

when they withdrew, but if they reported deteriorated health, their lives may have been at risk. The issue can be resolved by comparing the proportion of all attriters by choice still alive at the end of 1982 with survival in the rest of the sample. (A 1982 search via family and friends provided us with information on the living-or-dead status of a substantial number of cases in the choice withdrawal group.)

If we exclude persons of unknown vital status at the time of analysis, we get the following percentages:

| | Men | | | | Women | | | |
| | Group Q | | Groups R & D | | Group Q | | Groups R & D | |
	N	Pct.	N	Pct.	N	Pct.	N	Pct.
Alive in 1982	87	58%	429	69%	72	66%	402	82%
Dead in 1982	62	42	192	31	37	34	88	18
p by chi-square			<.05				<.01	

In both sexes, withdrawals by choice had a higher mortality rate than those who responded through 1982 or until time of death. We suggest that poorer health, as judged by the subjects themselves, was a factor in producing attrition by choice. Conversely, attrition by choice, appearing as a prognostic sign of impending death, warned of a more serious fate ahead.

Marital History. The hypothesis that persons with atypical marital histories would be more likely to leave the study is confirmed by Table B.6. Men who never married are much overrepresented in both the choice and death groups. Combining choice, death, and remainder subjects, 72 men out of a total of 804 in the table were single (9 percent), but such men constituted only 3 percent of the remainder group. Among women also, the proportion of always-single was appreciably greater in the choice and death groups than in the remainder, though the contrast was not so marked as among men. (This analysis, confined to attriters after 1940, does not include persons who left the study before they were old enough to marry.)

TABLE B.6
Marital Status of Attriters and Remainder Group

| | Men | | | | | Women | | | | |
| | Attriters | | Remainder | | | Attriters | | Remainder | | |
Marital status	N	Pct.	N	Pct.	Ratio	N	Pct.	N	Pct.	Ratio
Attriters by choice compared with remainder group										
Always single	21	12.5%	11	2.6%	4.8	19	15.2%	29	7.3%	2.1
Married at some time	147	87.5	407	97.4	0.9	106	84.8	370	92.7	0.9
Attriters by death compared with remainder group										
Always single	40	18.3	11	2.6	7.0	24	23.3	29	7.3	3.2
Married at some time	178	81.7	407	97.4	0.8	79	76.7	370	92.7	0.8

SOURCE: Cumulative marriage data.
NOTE: Ratio is the percent in the attrition by choice or death group divided by the percent in the remainder group in each row. For all four contrasts, $p < .01$ by chi-square.

TABLE B.7

Marital Histories of Ever-Married Attriters and Remainder Group

	Men					Women				
	Attriters		Remainder			Attriters		Remainder		
Marital history	N	Pct.	N	Pct.	Ratio	N	Pct.	N	Pct.	Ratio
Attriters by choice compared with remainder group										
Intact marriage	98	67%	266	65%	1.0	63	59%	185	50%	1.2
Divorced	40	27	83	20	1.4	27	26	67	18	1.4
Divorced and widowed	4	3	11	3	1.0	6	6	23	6	1.0
Widowed without divorce	5	3	47	12	0.3	10	9	95	26	0.4
Attriters by death compared with remainder group										
Intact marriage	112	63	266	65	1.0	41	52	185	50	1.0
Divorced	57	32	83	20	1.6	25	32	67	18	1.8
Divorced and widowed	3	2	11	3	0.7	11	14	23	6	2.3
Widowed without divorce	6	3	47	12	0.3	2	3	95	26	0.1

SOURCE: Cumulative marital data.
NOTE: Ratio is the percent in the attrition by choice or death group divided by the percent in the remainder group in each row.

Table B.7 contrasts persons whose first marriages worked out in various ways. There is an evident tendency for those who married only once and lost that spouse to death to remain in the study. The number of cases distributed across the "widowed" rows is small, but the differences are consistent. One can readily understand that a subject who has lost a spouse would wish to "keep up contacts" as part of a search for stability in life; that would reduce attrition by choice in this group. (The tiny groups who had both death of spouse and divorce in their histories are included in the table for completeness, but no contrast is worthy of mention.)

When persons with an uninterrupted single marriage and those who had one or more divorces were compared, there was a weak association between attrition and divorce. It is somewhat illegitimate to make a significance test on selected rows, but we have made such a gesture. Pooling the sexes, the association of the choice/remainder contrast with divorce is not significant, whereas the death/remainder contrast is nominally significant ($p < .01$). It would be improper to infer, however, that in replications of the study one of these associations would have been stronger than the other.

One other aspect of marital history — relative immaturity at the time of first marriage — is informative. The age at which persons married — if they married at all — does not differentiate the choice, death, and remainder groups; all three groups married at an average age of 26–27 years. Nor does age at puberty as such differentiate the groups. The time elapsed between puberty and marriage — which we take as an indicator of maturity at the time of marriage* — does show a

* We are indebted to Drs. John and Beatrice Whiting for suggesting this ingenious index of immaturity at the time of marriage. Its value is not limited to this contribution to the study of attrition; it is also used in Chapter 6.

marked association with attrition. The percentages of men who married within ten years of puberty are as follows:

Choice attriters	47% (N = 85)
Death attriters	45% (N = 109)
Remainder	30% (N = 218)

(These numbers are far below the usual sizes of these groups because data on puberty were incomplete and because the always-single are omitted.) Unusually early marriage by men can probably best be viewed in the same light as not marrying and marrying-and-divorcing. All three histories represent deviations from the norms of the time.

The finding applies only to men. Females reach puberty about a year earlier than males, on average. Early marriage was more usual for women than for men when our subjects were young. Marriage would have been less likely to interfere with a woman's educational plans than a man's.

Mental Disturbance. From the file up to 1928, Oden made a clinical evaluation of each subject's general adjustment. Few of them showed any difficulties. By 1940, more indications of mild maladjustment had emerged, but information was insufficient for rating some subjects. The ratings were repeated after the 1950 and 1960 follow-ups. This was Oden's scale:

0: Satisfactory; minor and realistic anxieties only
1: Some difficulty; psychiatric or other help sought
2: Considerable difficulty, interference with marriage, occupation, or social relationships, or hospitalization

These ratings reflected apparent adjustment in the past as well as at the time of the latest evidence. Thus a subject once rated as "1" could become a "2" but not a "0." If therapy or other circumstances enabled him or her to adjust satisfactorily, the subject nonetheless would be classified as a "1" from decade to decade. In effect, this cumulative rating evaluated how much psychopathology the person had shown over the years. Those not reporting in 1940 were not given a 1940 rating, and anyone who died was dropped from later ratings even though most of the life history was known.

Of the 763 men rated in 1940, 20 percent were judged to show some or considerable difficulty; the corresponding figure for the women was 18 percent (of 605). Ratings of "2" increased from 1940 to 1960 by 4 percent among men and by 1 percent among women.

The ratings before 1940 showed no difference between the groups. Means of later ratings of attriters and the remainder appear in Table B.8. Ratings of male withdrawals by choice were higher (less favorable) than ratings of the remainder. Only one of the differences between attriters by choice and attriters by death approached significance, but they were all higher for choice withdrawals. The differences among women were smaller than those among men, but the pattern is similar. Comparing all attriters (after 1940, choice, death, and lost subjects pooled) with the remainder group suggests that our later-maturity sample under-represents the poorly adjusted males. It is reasonably representative, with regard to mental health, of the original group of females.

Details of change in mental health from one decade to the next had been recorded. These answers to specific questions in 1940, 1950, and 1960 did not reveal any correlates of attrition. Review of individual cases suggests that the behaviors covered in the specific questions tended to be transitory.

One other finding is of some interest. In 1955, a question was asked about tendencies toward nervousness, special anxieties, emotional difficulties, or nervous breakdown. The self-reports were coded in considerable detail — 19 categories — all representative of either anxiety or depression. Among the 1955 respondents, anxiety was more commonly reported (men, 23 percent, women, 29 percent) than depression (men, 2 percent, women, 6 percent). Those who would later be attriters by choice reported anxiety significantly more often than did the remainder group. Depression was also reported more frequently by male withdrawals by choice than by males in the remainder. These differences are in line with our previous conclusion about the representatives of the remainder group in terms of mental health. They add the suggestion that, when entering later maturity, our subjects were substantially more prone to anxiety than to depression as a form of mental distress.

Self-Esteem. It seemed possible that subjects would have lower self-esteem if their education, occupational status, and (if male) occupational success were relatively limited, or if they had histories of poor health, poor social adjustment, or nonnormative marital histories. If so, attriters would be expected to express less self-esteem than others.

Data from childhood and young adulthood do not support this expectation. In 1922, 1928, and 1940, a parent (usually the mother) rated the subject on many

TABLE B.8

Ratings on Mental Disturbance in Attriters and Remainder Group

Year of rating	Choice		Death		All attriters		Remainder	
	N	Mean	N	Mean	N	Mean	N	Mean
				MEN				
1940	143	0.36[a]	180	0.28[a]	358	0.30[a]	405	0.19
1950	143	0.57[a]	171	0.43[a]	347	0.49[a]	411	0.28
1960	105	0.65[a]	144	0.43	273	0.51[a]	396	0.32
				WOMEN				
1940	109	0.33[b]	82	0.20	216	0.27	389	0.20
1950	114	0.52[b]	76	0.45	214	0.49[b]	394	0.37
1960	75	0.56	65	0.42	156	0.51	368	0.41

SOURCE: Ratings by research staff on a scale of increasing mental disturbance from 0 to 2.
[a]For contrast with the remainder group, by one-way analysis of variance, $p < .01$.
[b]For contrast with the remainder group, by one-way analysis of variance, $p < .05$.

TABLE B.9

Six Indicators of Male Attriters' Self-Esteem Relative to Remainder Group

	Attriters by choice								
	Year of last response								
	1940–50 Q1		1955–60 Q2		1972–77 Q3		Total		All attriters	
Indicator of self-esteem	N	M[a]	N	M[a]	N	M[a]	N	M[a]	N	M[a]
"Feeling of inferiority" (1940)[b]	19	88	66	109	46	102	131	103	320	103
"Self-esteem" (1950)	9	69[d]	40	80[c]	43	108	92	92	254	92[d]
"Self-satisfaction" (1950)	9	82	41	76[c]	43	102	93	88[d]	259	92
"Lived up to intellectual abilities" (1950)	9	96	42	92[c]	43	96	94	94[c]	260	95[c]
"Lived up to intellectual abilities" (1960)			27	90[c]	47	88[c]	74	89[c]	229	93[c]
"Occupational satisfaction" (1972)					50	84[c]	50	84[c]	123	92

SOURCE: Questionnaires by years indicated.

NOTE: "Feeling of inferiority" is a self-rating by the subject. "Self-esteem" is a self-rating on qualities such as social adjustment, personality, and others listed in the text. "Self-satisfaction" is a self-rating on items from which the subject gained life satisfaction, such as work, recognition, income, and others mentioned in the text. "Lived up to intellectual abilities" is a self-rating of how well the subject thought he had done this. "Occupational satisfaction" is a self-rating of occupational success, weighted by subject's retrospective judgment of importance of success to him in mid-life.

[a]Each entry expresses the mean for the attriters as a percentage of the mean for the remainder group. The means for that group are, in order, 5.99, 5.93, 5.55, 4.64, 3.70, and 12.86.

[b]Ratio inverted; a number below 100 represents greater feelings of inferiority than in the remainder group.

[c]For contrast with mean in the remainder group, $p < .01$ by one-way analysis of variance.

[d]$p < .05$ by one-way analysis of variance.

personality traits. Two were self-confidence and feelings of inferiority. In 1922 and 1928, their teachers and, in 1940, their spouses rated them on the same scales. The choice and death attrition groups and the remainder did not differ significantly on these variables.

In 1940, for the first time, the subjects were asked to appraise themselves on such scales. Self-evaluations in the attrition subgroups of women did not differ from each other, on average, nor from those in the remainder group. However, male attriters by choice differed from the remainder, as detailed in Table B.9. (The table does not show data for the death group because their self-evaluations were similar to those of the remainder.) In order to measure the variable on somewhat comparable scales, the table reports means relative to those of the remainder (Group R).* In the extreme right-hand column, five of the six entries are below 100, the mean of the attrition group being lower than that of the remainder group. This implies less favorable self-images among attriters by choice than among the remainder, on average.

Patterning in Table B.9 suggests that recency of self-descriptions before attrition is relevant, as it was in the self-rating of health. The lowest ratings appear toward the left in the first three rows. The small Ns in the extreme left-hand

* Readers will recognize that such ratings would be altered by movement of the "zero point" of a scale. Any plausible change of this type should not affect the conclusions drawn here. The raw-score means can be recaptured by a simple multiplication.

column should be noted, however. The 1940 question asked how much the respondent had suffered from a feeling of inferiority. There was no noteworthy difference between groups.

Another question from 1940 asked "How well do you consider your early mental superiority is being maintained?" Possible answers were "more marked," "no change," "less marked." The findings from this question are better summarized by percentages than by means and so do not appear in the table. Again the early male withdrawals by choice differed from the remainder; 62.5 percent of male early attriters by choice (Groups Q1 and Q2) chose "less marked" compared with 32.5 percent of the remainder.

In 1950 subjects checked a list of "Factors which have contributed to your life accomplishments to date," double-checking especially important factors. The factors were as follows: "superior mental ability, adequate education, good social adjustment, good personality, good mental stability, persistence in working towards a goal, good habits of work, excellent health, and lucky 'chance' factors." A measure of "self-esteem" was obtained by counting checkmarks. The Q1 and Q2 subgroups clearly made fewer of these responses than other attriters or the remainder.

The 1950 survey also asked, "From what aspects of your life do you gain the greatest satisfaction?" The subject checked or double-checked items on the following list: "work itself, recognition for accomplishments, income, avocational activities or hobbies, marriage, children, religion, social contacts, community service, other." A measure of "self-satisfaction" was constructed by counting checkmarks. The results show a considerable shortfall in Groups Q1 and Q2 compared with the remainder.

In 1950, subjects were also asked: "On the whole, how well do you think you have lived up to your intellectual abilities? (Don't limit your answer to economic or vocational success only.)" The six answer choices offered ranged from "fully" to "total failure." The question was repeated in 1960 with a 5-point response scale. It is interesting that the 1972/77 dropouts were much further from the remainder in 1960 than in 1950. Withdrawal from this study seems to be somewhat associated with a sense of not being worthy of it.

The last row in Table B.9 refers to an indicator of lifetime occupational satisfaction reported in detail by Sears (1977). The measure took into account a self-rating on amount of success, weighted by a retrospective judgment on how important gaining such success had been to the subject in early mid-life. The choice withdrawal group's score was lower than that of the remainder. None of the other ratings on sources of satisfaction — marriage, friendship, community service — displayed any such difference.

The foregoing results on self-esteem refer to the men only. The self-esteem of women attriters differed negligibly from that of the remainder group. We can only speculate about the reasons, but it is worth noting that many of the qualities in the 1950 scales and the basic thrust of the scale on "lived up to intellectual abilities" carried an implication of success at work. In the period of this study, work was more central to men than to most women. Questions emphasizing values other than achievement might have shown differences in self-esteem between women who did and did not leave the study.

Noncorrelates of Attrition. Not all of the variables that seemed promising, in terms of our initial expectations, differentiated among groups. Alcoholism did not show differences where we expected them, but it is difficult to assess from our data. Subjects did report in 1940, 1950, and 1960 on their use of alcohol, and we have combined these reports. None of the choice subgroups differed appreciably or consistently from the remainder group.

A second noncorrelate was achievement motivation. The many measures available fall into two classes: those that reflect achieving behavior, and those that report on motivation (Sears, 1977). It has already been seen that the behavior variables (education, occupational success) were related to attrition by choice. The attitude measures were not. Self-ratings on ambition in the middle years and seemingly relevant ratings by parents and teachers in the school years yielded no significant differences between choice withdrawals and the remainder.

Summary

Despite the fact that this study has now been in progress for over 66 years, more than two-thirds of the subjects responded to at least one of the four questionnaires in later maturity. An analysis of the frequency of earlier returns of those who would leave the study before 1982, our comparison year for attrition, showed that those who withdrew by choice or were lost cases before 1972 contributed significantly fewer responses, even when responding between 1928 and 1950, than those who would remain until 1982 or later. They also had a higher frequency of unanswered questions and a greater delay in responding. Attriters were not different from nonattriters in IQ or socioeconomic status of the family of origin. Those who remained in the study became somewhat better educated, and the occupational success of the men who remained was also higher, as was their self-confidence and self-esteem. Those who left the study had poorer health than those who remained. The remaining subjects tended to have more normative marital histories; there are relatively more individuals who had intact marriages or who were widowed in the remainder group as compared with the attriters, while the opposite is true for the divorced and always-single.

Reference Matter

Works Cited

Abelson, R. P. (1981). Psychological status of the script concept. *American Psychologist* 36, 715–29.

Abramson, P. R. (1983). *Political attitudes in America: Formation and change.* San Francisco: W. H. Freeman.

Adams, R., & Blieszner, R. (1989). *Older adult friendships: Structure and process.* Newbury Park, Calif.: Sage.

Albert, R. S., & Runco, M. A. (1986). The achievement of eminence: A model based on a longitudinal study of exceptionally gifted boys and their families. In R. J. Sternberg & J. E. Davidson, eds., *Conceptions of giftedness* (pp. 332–57). New York: Cambridge University Press.

Aldwin, C. M., Spiro, A., Levensen, M. R., & Bossé, R. (1989). Longitudinal findings from the normative aging study: 1. Does mental health change with age? *Psychology and Aging* 4: 295–306.

Alexander, K. L., Eckland, B. K., & Griffin, L. J. (1975). The Wisconsin model of socioeconomic achievement: A replication. *American Journal of Sociology* 81: 324–42.

Almquist, E. M., & Angrist, S. S. (1971). Role model influences on college women's career aspirations. *Merrill-Palmer Quarterly* 17: 263–79.

Anderson, K. H., Burkhauser, R. B., & Quinn, J. F. (1986). Do retirement dreams come true? The effect of unanticipated events on retirement plans. *Industrial and Labor Relations Review* 39: 518–26.

Antonucci, T. C. (1990). Social supports and social relationships. In R. H. Binstock & L. K. George, eds., *Handbook of aging and the social sciences*, 3rd ed. (pp. 205–26). San Diego: Academic Press.

Antonucci, T., & Akiyama, H. (1987). An examination of sex differences in social support among older men and women. *Sex Roles* 17: 737–49.

———. (1988). *The negative effects of intimate social networks among older women as compared with men*. Paper presented at the Gerontological Society of America Meeting, San Francisco, Nov.

Antonucci, T. C., & Jackson, J. S. (1987). Social support, interpersonal efficacy, and health. In L. Carstensen & B. A. Edelstein, eds., *Handbook of clinical gerontology* (pp. 291–311). New York: Pergamon Press.

Atchley, R. C. (1988). *Social forces and aging*. Belmont, Calif.: Wadsworth.

Atkinson, J. W. (1978). The mainsprings of achievement-oriented activity. In J. W. Atkinson & J. O. Raynor, eds., *Personality, motivation and achievement* (pp. 11–39). New York: Halsted.

Atkinson, J. W., Lens, W., & O'Malley, P. M. (1976). Motivation and ability: Interactive psychological determinants of intellective performance, educational achievement, and each other. In W. H. Sewell, R. M. Hauser, & D. L. Featherman, eds., *Schooling and achievement in American society* (pp. 29–60). New York: Academic Press.

Austrom, D. R. (1984). *The consequences of being single*. New York: P. Lang.

Babchuk, N. (1978–79). Aging and primary relations. *International Journal of Aging and Human Development* 9: 137–51.

Bailyn, L., & Schein, E. H. (1976). Life/career considerations as indicators of quality of employment. In A. D. Biderman & T. F. Drury, eds., *Measuring work quality for social reporting* (pp. 151–68). New York: Sage.

Baltes, P. B. (1989). The many faces of human aging: Toward a psychological culture of old age. Keynote lecture of the Annual Meeting of the Max Planck Society for the Advancement of Sciences, Wiesbaden, June.

Baltes, P. B., & Baltes, M. M. (1990a). Psychological perspectives on successful aging: The model of selective optimization with compensation. In Baltes & Baltes, 1990b: 1–34.

———, eds. (1990b). *Successful aging: Perspectives from the behavioral sciences*. Cambridge, Eng.: Cambridge University Press.

Baltes, P. B., Dittmann-Kohli, F., & Dixon, R. A. (1984). New perspectives on the development of intelligence in adulthood: Toward a dual-process conception and a model of selective optimization and compensation. In P. B. Baltes & O. G. Brim, Jr., eds., *Life-span development and behavior* (vol. 6, pp. 33–76). Orlando, Fla.: Academic Press.

Baltes, P. B., Smith, J., Staudinger, U., & Sowarka, D. (1990). Wisdom: One facet of successful aging? In M. Perlmutter, ed., 1990: 63–81.

Banner, L. W. (1974). *Women in modern America: A brief history*. New York: Harcourt Brace Jovanovich.

Barker, D. T., & Clark, R. L. (1980). Mandatory retirement and labor force participation of respondents in the Retirement History Study. *Social Security Bulletin* 43: 20–29, 55.

Baruch, G. K. (1976). Girls who perceive themselves as competent: Some antecedents and correlates. *Psychology of Women Quarterly* 1: 38–49.

Bayer, L. M., Whissell-Buechy, D., & Honzik, M. P. (1981). Health in the middle years. In D. H. Eichorn, J. A. Clausen, N. Haan, M. P. Honzik, & P. H. Mussen, eds., *Present and past in middle life* (pp. 55–88). New York: Academic Press.

Bayley, N., & Oden, M. H. (1955). The maintenance of intellectual ability in gifted adults. *Journal of Gerontology* 10: 91–107.

Bengtson, V., Rosenthal, C., & Burton, L. (1990). Families and aging: Diversity and heterogeneity. In R. H. Binstock & L. K. George, eds., *Handbook of aging and the social sciences*, 3rd ed. (pp. 263–87). San Diego: Academic Press.

Bentler, P. M., & Newcomb, M. D. (1978). Longitudinal study of marital success and failure. *Journal of Consulting and Clinical Psychology* 46: 1053–70.

Bernard, J. (1942). *American family behavior*. New York: Harper.

——. (1964). *Academic women*. University Park: Pennsylvania State University Press.

——. (1981). The good-provider role: Its rise and fall. *American Psychologist* 36: 1–12.

Betz, N. E., & Fitzgerald, L. F. (1987). *The career psychology of women*. Orlando, Fla.: Academic Press.

Betz, N. E., & Hackett, G. (1981). The relationship of career-related self-efficacy expectations to perceived career options in college women and men. *Journal of Counseling Psychology* 28: 399–410.

Blazer, D., & Palmore, E. B. (1976). Religion and aging in a longitudinal panel. *The Gerontologist* 16: 82–85.

Block, J. (1971). *Lives through time*. Berkeley, Calif.: Basic Books.

Blood, R. O., & Wolfe, D. M. (1960). *Husbands and wives*. Glencoe, Ill.: Free Press.

Bossé, R., & Ekerdt, D. J. (1981). Change in self-perception of leisure activities with retirement. *The Gerontologist* 21: 650–54.

Braito, R., & Anderson, D. (1983). The ever-single elderly woman. In E. W. Markson, ed., *Older women* (pp. 195–225). Lexington, Mass.: Lexington Books.

Brandtstadter, J., & Baltes-Gotz, B. (1990). Personal control over development and quality of life perspectives in adulthood. In Baltes & Baltes, 1990b: 197–224.

Brandtstadter, J., & Renner, G. (1990). Tenacious goal pursuit and flexible goal adjustment: Explication and age-related analysis of assimilative and accommodative strategies of coping. *Psychology and Aging* 5: 58–67.

Brody, E. M., & Kleban, M. H. (1983). Day-to-day mental and physical health symptoms of older people: A report on health logs. *Gerontologist* 23: 75–85.

Brody, E. M., Kleban, M. H., Johnsen, P. T., Hoffman, C., & Schoonover, C. B. (1987). Work status and parent care: A comparison of four groups of women. *Gerontologist* 27: 201–8.

Bryant, F. B., & Veroff, J. (1982). The structure of psychological well-being: A sociohistorical analysis. *Journal of Personality and Social Psychology* 43: 653–73.

Burgess, E. W., & Cottrell, L. S. (1938). The prediction of adjustment in marriage. *American Sociological Review* 1: 737–51.

Burgess, E. W., & Wallin, P. (1953). *Engagement and marriage*. Chicago: J. B. Lippincott.

Burks, B. S., Jensen, D. W., & Terman, L. M. (1930). *The promise of youth: Follow-up studies of a thousand gifted children. Vol. 3. Genetic studies of genius*. Stanford, Calif.: Stanford University Press.

Burlin, F. (1976). The relationship of parental education and maternal work and occupational status to occupational aspiration in adolescent females. *Journal of Vocational Behavior* 9: 99–104.

Burrus-Bammel, L. L., & Bammel, G. (1985). Leisure and recreation. In J. E. Birren & K. W. Schaie, eds., *Handbook of the psychology of aging*, 2nd ed. (pp. 848–63). New York: Van Nostrand Reinhold.

Butler, R. N. (1963). The life review: An interpretation of reminiscence in the aged. *Psychiatry* 26: 65–76.

Campbell, A., Converse, P. E., & Rogers, W. I. (1976). *The quality of American life*. New York: Russell Sage Foundation.

Card, J. J., Steel, L., & Abeles, R. P. (1980). Sex differences in realization of individual potential for achievement. *Journal of Vocational Behavior* 17: 1–21.

Carstensen, L. L. (1987). Age-related changes in social activity. In L. L. Carstensen & B. A. Edelstein, eds., *Handbook of clinical gerontology* (pp. 222–37). New York: Pergamon Press.

Chafe, W. H. (1972). *The American woman: Her changing social, economic, and political roles, 1920–1970.* New York: Oxford University Press.

Chappell, N. L., & Badger, M. (1989). Social isolation and well-being. *Journal of Gerontology* 44: 169–76.

Chiriboga, D. A., & Cutler, L. (1980). Stress and adaptation: Life span perspectives. In L. W. Poon, ed., *Aging in the 1980s* (pp. 347–62). Washington, D.C.: American Psychological Association.

Cicirelli, V. G. (1989). Feelings of attachment to siblings and well-being in later life. *Psychology and Aging* 4: 211–16.

Clark, M., & Anderson, B. G. (1967). *Culture and aging.* Springfield, Ill.: Charles C. Thomas.

Clausen, J. A. (1981). Men's occupational careers in the middle years. In D. H. Eichorn, J. A. Clausen, N. Haan, M. P. Honzik, & P. H. Mussen, eds., *Present and past in middle life* (pp. 321–51). New York: Academic Press.

Clausen, J. A., & Gilens, M. (1990). Personality and labor force participation across the life course: A longitudinal study of women's careers. *Sociological Forum* 5: 595–618.

Cohen, J., & Cohen, P. (1975). *Applied multiple regression/correlation analysis for the behavioral sciences.* Hillsdale, N.J.: Lawrence Erlbaum Associates.

Cole, C. L., Cole, A. L., & Dean, D. G. (1980). Emotional maturity and marital adjustment: A decade replication. *Journal of Marriage and the Family* 42: 533–39.

Connidis, I. A., & Davies, L. (1990). Confidants and companions in later life: The place of family and friends. *Journal of Gerontology* 45: 141–49.

Costa, P. T., Jr., McCrae, R. R., & Norris, A. H. (1981). Personal adjustment to aging: Longitudinal prediction from neuroticism and extraversion. *Journal of Gerontology* 36: 78–85.

Costa, P. T., Jr., Zonderman, A. B., & McCrae, R. R. (1985). Longitudinal course of social support among men in the Baltimore longitudinal study of aging. In I. Sarason & B. R. Sarason, eds., *Social support: Theory, research, and applications* (pp. 137–54). The Hague: Nijhoff.

Crandall, V., & Battle, E. (1970). The antecedents and adult correlates of academic and intellectual achievement effort. In J. Hill, ed., *Minnesota Symposia on Child Psychology* (vol. 4, pp. 36–93). Minneapolis: University of Minnesota Press.

Cutler, S. J. (1985). Aging and voluntary association participation. In E. Palmore & E. W. Busse, eds., *Normal Aging III* (pp. 415–28). Durham, N.C.: Duke University Press.

Cutler, S. J., & Hendricks, J. (1990). Leisure and time use across the life cycle. In R. H. Binstock and L. K. George, eds., *Handbook of aging and the social sciences*, 3rd ed. (pp. 169–85). San Diego: Academic Press.

Cutrona, C., Russell, D., & Rose, J. (1986). Social support and adaptation to stress by the elderly. *Psychology and Aging* 1: 47–54.

DeCarlo, T. J. (1974). Recreation participation patterns and successful aging. *Journal of Gerontology* 29: 416–22.

Depner, C. E., & Ingersoll-Dayton, B. (1988). Supportive relationships in later life. *Psychology and Aging* 3: 348–57.

Dickinson, R. L., & Beam, L. (1931). *A thousand marriages.* Baltimore: William & Wilkins.

Diener, E. (1984). Subjective well-being. *Psychological Bulletin* 95: 542–75.

Dittmann-Kohli, F. (1990). Possibilities and constraints for the construction of meaning in old age. *Ageing and Society* 10: 279–94.

Duncan, O. D., Featherman, D. L., & Duncan, B. (1972). *Socioeconomic background and achievement*. New York: Seminar Press.

Dworkin, R. H., & Widom, C. S. (1977). Undergraduate MMPI profiles and the longitudinal prediction of adult social outcome. *Journal of Consulting and Clinical Psychology* 45: 620–24.

Eccles, J., Adler, T., & Meece, J. L. (1984). Sex differences in achievement: A test of alternate theories. *Journal of Personality and Social Psychology* 46: 26–43.

Elder, G. H., Jr. (1969). Occupational mobility, life patterns, and personality. *Journal of Health and Social Behavior* 10: 308–23.

———. (1974). *Children of the great depression*. Chicago: University of Chicago Press.

Elder, G. H., Jr., Pavalko, E. K., & Hastings, T. J. (1991). Talent, history, and the fulfillment of promise. *Psychiatry* 54: 251–67.

Erickson, R. C., Post, R. D., & Paige, A. B. (1975). Hope as a psychiatric variable. *Journal of Clinical Psychology* 32: 324–30.

Ericsson, K. A. (1990). Peak performance and age: An examination of peak performance in sports. In Baltes & Baltes, 1990b: 164–96.

Erikson, E. H. (1959). Identity and the life cycle: Selected papers. *Psychological Issues* 1.

Erikson, E. H., Erikson, J. M., & Kivnick, H. Q. (1986). *Vital involvement in old age*. New York: Norton.

Erikson, R. S., Luttbeg, N. R., & Tedin, K. L. (1988). *American public opinion: Its origins, content, and impact*, 3rd ed. New York: Macmillan.

Evans, M. D., & Laumann, E. O. (1983). Professional commitment: Myth or reality? In D. J. Treiman & R. V. Robinson, eds., *Research in Social Stratification and Mobility: A research annual* (vol. 2, pp. 3–40). Greenwich, Conn.: JAI Press.

Falk, W. W., & Cosby, A. G. (1978). Women's marital-familial statuses and work histories: Some conceptual considerations. *Journal of Vocational Behavior* 13: 126–40.

Farmer, H. S. (1985). Model of career and achievement motivation for women and men. *Journal of Counseling Psychology* 32: 363–90.

Fassinger, R. E. (1985). A causal model of college women's career choice. *Journal of Vocational Behavior* 27: 123–53.

Featherman, D. L. (1980). Schooling and occupational careers: Constancy and change in worldly success. In O. G. Brim & J. Kagan, eds., *Constancy and change in human development* (pp. 675–738). Cambridge, Mass.: Harvard University Press.

Featherman, D. L., & Hauser, R. M. (1978). *Opportunity and change*. New York: Academic Press.

Fennema, E., & Sherman, J. (1977). Sex-related differences in mathematics achievement, spatial visualization and affective factors. *American Educational Research Journal* 14: 51–71.

Field, D., & Minkler, M. (1988). Continuity and change in social support between young-old and old-old or very-old age. *Journal of Gerontology* 43: 100–106.

Fiske, M. (1980). Changing hierarchies of commitment in adulthood. N. Smelser & E. H. Erikson, eds., *Themes of work and love in adulthood* (pp. 238–64). Cambridge, Mass.: Harvard University Press.

Fiske, M., & Chiriboga, D. A. (1990). *Change and continuity in adult life*. San Francisco: Jossey-Bass.

Folkman, S., Lazarus, R. S., Pimley, S., & Novacek, J. (1987). Age differences in stress and coping processes. *Psychology and Aging* 2: 171–84.

Fredrickson, B. L., & Carstensen, L. L. (1990). Choosing social partners: How old age and anticipated endings make people more selective. *Psychology and Aging* 5: 335–47.

Fries, J. F. (1990). Medical perspectives upon successful aging. In Baltes & Baltes, 1990b: 35–49.

George, L. K. (1978). The impact of personality and social status upon activity and psychological well-being. *Journal of Gerontology* 33: 840–47.

———. (1981). Subjective well-being: Conceptual and methodological issues. In C. Eisdorfer, ed., *Annual Review of Gerontology and Geriatrics* 2: 344–82. New York: Springer.

———. (1990). Social structure, social processes, and social-psychological states. In R. H. Binstock & L. K. George, eds., *Handbook of aging and the social sciences* (3d ed., pp. 186–204). San Diego: Academic Press.

George, L. K., & Clipp, E. C. (1991). Subjective components of aging well. *Generations* 15: 57–60.

George, L. K., & Landerman, R. (1984). Health and subjective well-being: A replicated secondary data analysis. *International Journal of Aging and Human Development* 19: 133–56.

Glick, P. C. (1975). A demographer looks at American families. *Journal of Marriage and the Family* 37: 15–26.

Gordon, C., Gaitz, C. M., & Scott, J. (1976). Leisure and lives: Personal expressivity across the life span. In R. H. Binstock & E. Shanas, eds., *Handbook of aging and the social sciences* (pp. 310–41). New York: Van Nostrand Reinhold.

Gottfredson, L. S. (1981). Circumscription and compromise: A developmental theory of occupational aspirations. *Journal of Counseling Psychology Monograph* 28: 545–79.

Grambs, J. D. (1989). *Women over forty: Visions and realities.* New York: Springer Publishing Company.

Gratton, B., & Haug, M. (1983). Decision and adaptation: Research on female retirement. *Research on Aging* 5: 59–76.

Greenfield, S., Greiner, L., & Wood, M. M. (1980). The "feminine mystique" in male-dominated jobs: A comparison of attitudes and background factors of women in male-dominated versus female-dominated jobs. *Journal of Vocational Behavior* 17: 291–309.

Gurin, G., Veroff, J., & Feld, S. (1960). *Americans view their mental health.* New York: Basic Books.

Hamilton, G. V. (1929). *A research in marriage.* New York: Albert & Charles Boni.

Harris, Louis, & Associates. (1975). *The myth and reality of aging in America.* Washington, D.C.: The National Council on Aging, Inc.

———. (1981). *Aging in the eighties: America in transition.* Washington, D.C.: National Council on Aging, Inc.

Hauser, P. M. (1964). Labor force. In R. Faris, ed., *Handbook of modern sociology* (pp. 161–91). Chicago: Rand McNally.

Heckhausen, J., Dixon, R. A., & Baltes, P. B. (1989). Gains and losses in development throughout adulthood as perceived by different adult age groups. *Developmental Psychology* 25: 109–21.

Helmreich, R. L., Spence, J. T., Beane, W. E., Lucker, G. W., & Matthews, K. A. (1980). Making it in academic psychology: Demographic and personality correlates of attainment. *Journal of Personality and Social Psychology* 39: 896–908.

Helson, R., Mitchell, V., & Moane, G. (1984). Personality and patterns of adherence and nonadherence to the social clock. *Journal of Personality and Social Psychology* 46: 1079–96.

Henderson, R. W. (1981). Home environment and intellectual performance. In R. W. Henderson, ed., *Parent-child interaction: Theory, research, and prospects* (pp. 1–32). New York: Academic Press.

Hendricks, J., & Hendricks, C. D. (1986). *Aging in mass society: Myths and realities.* Boston: Little, Brown.

Holahan, C. K. (1981). Lifetime achievement patterns, retirement and life satisfaction of gifted aged women. *Journal of Gerontology* 36: 741–49.

——. (1984). Marital attitudes over forty years: A longitudinal and cohort analysis. *Journal of Gerontology* 39: 49–57.

——. (1984–85). The relationship between life goals at thirty and perceptions of goal attainment and life satisfaction at seventy for gifted men and women. *International Journal of Aging and Human Development* 20: 21–31.

——. (1988). Relation of life goals at age 70 to activity participation and health and psychological well-being among Terman's gifted men and women. *Psychology and Aging* 3: 286–91.

Holahan, C. K., & Gilbert, L. A. (1979). Conflict between major life roles: The men and women in dual career couples. *Human Relations* 32: 451–67.

Holahan, C. K., & Holahan, C. J. (1987). Self-efficacy, social support, and depression in aging: A longitudinal analysis. *Journal of Gerontology* 42: 65–68.

Holahan, C. K., Holahan, C. J., & Belk, S. S. (1984). Adjustment in aging: The roles of life stress, hassles, and self-efficacy. *Health Psychology* 3: 315–28.

Honig, M. (1985). Partial retirement among women. *Journal of Human Resources* 20: 613–21.

House, J. S., Landis, K. R., & Umberson, D. (1988). Social relationships and health. *Science* 241: 540–45.

Howe, C. Z. (1988). Selected social gerontology theories and older adult leisure involvement: A review of the literature. *Journal of Applied Gerontology* 6: 448–63.

Husberger, B. (1985). Religion, age, life satisfaction, and perceived sources of religiousness: A study of older persons. *Journal of Gerontology* 40: 615–20.

Huyck, M. H. (1990). Gender differences in aging. In J. E. Birren & K. W. Schaie, eds., *Handbook of the psychology of aging*, 3rd ed. (pp. 124–32). San Diego: Academic Press.

Idler, E. L. (1987). Religious involvement and the health of the elderly: Some hypotheses and an initial test. *Social Forces* 66: 226–38.

Idler, E. L., & Kasl, S. (1991). Health perceptions and survival: Do global evaluations of health status really predict mortality? *Journal of Gerontology* 46: 55–65.

Irelan, L. M. (1972). Retirement history study: Introduction. *Social Security Bulletin* 35: 3–8.

Janos, P. M., & Robinson, N. M. (1985). Psychosocial development in intellectually gifted children. In F. D. Horowitz & M. O'Brien, eds., *The gifted and talented: Developmental perspectives* (pp. 149–96). Washington, D.C.: American Psychological Association.

Johnson, J. H., & Harris, W. G. (1980). Personality and behavioral characteristics related to divorce in a population of male applicants for psychiatric evaluation. *Journal of Abnormal Psychology* 89: 510–13.

Jondrow, J., Breckling, F., & Marcus, A. (1987). Older workers in the market for part-time employment. In S. H. Sandell, ed., *The problem isn't age: Work and older Americans* (pp. 84–99). New York: Praeger.

Jung, C. G. (1993). *Modern man in search of a soul.* New York: Harcourt Brace and World.

Kaplan, G., Barell, V., & Lusky, A. (1988). Subjective state of health and survival in elderly adults. *Journal of Gerontology* 43: 114–20.

Keith, P. M. (1989). *The unmarried in later life.* New York: Praeger.

Kelly, J. R. (1974). Socialization toward leisure: A developmental approach. *Journal of Leisure Research* 6: 181–93.

———. (1977). Leisure socialization: Replication and extension. *Journal of Leisure Research* 9: 121–32.

Kelly, J. R., Steinkamp, M. W., & Kelly, J. R. (1987). Later-life satisfaction: Does leisure contribute? *Leisure Sciences* 9: 189–200.

Kessler, R. C., McLeod, J. D., & Wethington, E. (1985). The costs of caring: A perspective on the relationship between sex and psychological distress. In I. G. Sarason & B. R. Sarason, eds., *Social support: Theory, research, and applications* (pp. 491–506). The Hague: Nijhoff.

Klinger, E. (1977). *Meaning and void: Inner experience and the incentives in people's lives.* Minneapolis: University of Minnesota Press.

Koenig, H. G., Kvale, J. N., & Ferrel, C. (1988). Religion and well-being in later life. *The Gerontologist* 28: 18–20.

Kohen, J. (1983). Old but not alone: Informal social supports among the elderly by marital status and sex. *The Gerontologist* 23: 57–63.

Kohn, M. L., & Schooler, C. (1973). Occupational experience and psychological functioning: An assessment of reciprocal effects. *American Sociological Review* 38: 97–118.

———. (1978). The reciprocal effects of the substantive complexity of work and intellectual flexibility: A longitudinal assessment. *American Journal of Sociology* 84: 24–52.

Kozma, A., & Stones, M. J. (1990). Decrements in habitual and maximal physical performance with age. In M. Perlmutter, ed., 1990: 1–23.

Krause, N. (1986a). Social support, stress, and well-being among older adults. *Journal of Gerontology* 41: 512–19.

———. (1986b). Stress and sex differences in depressive symptoms among older adults. *Journal of Gerontology* 41: 727–31.

Krause, N., Liang, J., & Yatomi, N. (1989). Satisfaction with social support and depressive symptoms: A panel analysis. *Psychology and Aging* 4: 88–97.

Kriger, S. F. (1972). n Ach and perceived parental child-rearing attitudes of career women and homemakers. *Journal of Vocational Behavior* 2: 419–32.

Labouvie-Vief, G. (1985). Intelligence and cognition. In J. E. Birren & K. W. Schaie, eds., *Handbook of the psychology of aging*, 2nd ed. (pp. 500–530). New York: Van Nostrand Reinhold.

Larson, R. (1978). Thirty years of research on the subjective well-being of older Americans. *Journal of Gerontology* 33: 109–25.

Larson, R., Mannell, R., & Zuzanek, J. (1986). Daily well-being of older adults with friends and family. *Psychology and Aging* 1: 117–26.

LaRue, A., Bank, L., Jarvik, L., & Hetland, M. (1979). Health in old age: How do physicians' ratings and self-ratings compare? *Journal of Gerontology* 34: 687–91.

LaRue, A., Dessonville, C., & Jarvik, L. F. (1985). Aging and mental disorders. In J. E.

Birren & K. W. Shaie, eds., *Handbook of the psychology of aging*, 2d ed. (pp. 664–702). New York: Van Nostrand Reinhold.

Lawton, M. P. (1985). Activities and leisure. In M. P. Lawton & G. L. Maddox, eds., *Annual Review of Gerontology and Geriatrics* 5: 127–64. New York: Springer.

Lawton, M. P., Kleban, M. H., & diCarlo, E. (1984). Psychological well-being in the aged: Factorial and conceptual dimensions. *Research on Aging* 6: 67–97.

Lawton, M. P., Moss, M., & Fulcomer, M. (1986–87). Objective and subjective uses of time by older people. *International Journal of Aging and Human Development* 24: 171–88.

Lazarus, R. S., & DeLongis, A. (1983). Psychological stress and coping in aging. *American Psychologist* 38: 245–54.

Lemkau, J. P. (1983). Women in male-dominated professions: Distinguishing personality and background characteristics. *Psychology of Women Quarterly* 8: 144–65.

Levinson, D. J., Darrow, C. N., Klein, E. B., Levinson, M. H., & McKee, B. (1978). *The seasons of a man's life*. New York: Knopf.

Liang, J., Dvorkin, L., Kahana, E., & Mazian, F. (1980). Social integration and morale: A reexamination. *Journal of Gerontology* 35: 746–57.

Locke, E. A. (1976). The nature and causes of of job satisfaction. In M. D. Dunnette, ed., *Handbook of industrial and organizational psychology* (pp. 1297–1349). Chicago: Rand McNally.

Longino, C. F., & Lipman, A. (1981). Married and spouseless men and women in planned retirement communities: Support network differentials. *Journal of Marriage and the Family* 43: 169–77.

Longino, C. F., Jr., Warheit, G. J., & Green, J. A. (1989). Class, aging, and health. In K. S. Markides, ed., *Aging and health: Perspectives on gender, race, ethnicity, and class* (pp. 79–109). Newbury Park, Calif.: Sage.

Lowenthal, M. F., & Haven, C. (1968). Interaction and adaptation: Intimacy as a critical variable. *American Sociological Review* 33: 20–30.

Lowenthal, M. F., & Robinson, B. (1976). Social networks and isolation. In R. H. Binstock & E. Shanas, eds., *Handbook of aging and the social sciences* (pp. 432–56). New York: Van Nostrand Reinhold.

Lynd, R. S., & Lynd, H. M. (1937). *Middletown in transition: A study in cultural conflicts*. New York: Harcourt Brace.

Maddox, G. L., & Douglass, E. B. (1973). Self-assessment of health: A longitudinal study of elderly subjects. *Journal of Health and Social Behavior* 14: 87–93.

Marshall, H., & Oden, M. H. (1962). The status of the mature gifted individual as a basis for evaluation of the aging process. *Gerontologist* 2: 201–6.

Marshall, S. J., & Wijting, J. P. (1980). Relationships of achievement motivation and sex-role identity to college women's career orientation. *Journal of Vocational Behavior* 16: 299–311.

Matthews, E., & Tiedeman, D. V. (1964). Attitudes toward career and marriage and the development of life style in young women. *Journal of Counseling Psychology* 11: 375–84.

McAvoy, L. H. (1979). The leisure preferences, problems, and needs of the elderly. *Journal of Leisure Research* 11: 40–47.

McClelland, D. (1971). *Assessing human motivation*. Morristown, N.J.: General Learning Press.

McCranie, E. W., & Kahan, J. (1986). Personality and multiple divorce: A prospective study. *Journal of Nervous and Mental Disease* 174: 161–64.

Moberg, D. O. (1970). Religion in the later years. In A. M. Hoffman, ed., *The daily needs and interests of older persons* (pp. 175–91). Springfield, Ill.: Charles C. Thomas.

———. (1990). Religion and aging. In Ferraro, K. F., ed., *Gerontology: Perspectives and issues* (pp. 179–205). New York: Springer.

Morgan, W. R., Parnes, H. S., & Less, L. J. (1985). Leisure activities and social networks. In Parnes et al., 1985: 119–45.

Murstein, B. I., & Glaudin, V. (1968). The use of the MMPI in the determination of marital maladjustment. *Journal of Marriage and the Family* 28: 651–55.

Mussen, P. H., & Haan, N. (1981). A longitudinal study of patterns of personality and political ideologies. In D. H. Eichorn, J. A. Clausen, N. Haan, M. P. Honzik, & P. H. Mussen, eds., *Present and past in middle life* (pp. 3391–3409). New York: Academic Press.

Mussen, P., Honzik, M. P., & Eichorn, D. H. (1982). Early adult antecedents of life satisfaction at age 70. *Journal of Gerontology* 37: 316–22.

National Center for Health Statistics (1987). Current estimates from the National Interview Survey, United States, 1986. *Vital and Health Statistics*, Series 10, No. 164.

———. (1989). *Vital statistics of the United States, 1987.* Hyattsville, Md.: U.S. Department of Health and Human Services.

Neugarten, B. L., Havighurst, R. J., & Tobin, S. S. (1961). The measurement of life satisfaction. *Journal of Gerontology* 16: 134–43.

Niemi, R. G., Mueller, J., & Smith, T. W. (1989). *Trends in public opinion: A compendium of survey data.* New York: Greenwood.

Norris, F. H., & Murrell, S. A. (1990). Social support, life events, and stress as modifiers of adjustment to bereavement by older adults. *Psychology and Aging* 5: 429–36.

Nowlin, J. B. (1985). Successful aging. In E. Palmore, E. W. Busse, G. L. Maddox, J. B. Nowlin, & I. C. Siegler, eds., *Normal Aging III: Reports from the Duke Longitudinal Studies, 1975–1984* (pp. 36–43). Durham, N.C.: Duke University Press.

Oden, M. H. (1968). The fulfillment of promise: 40-year follow-up of the Terman gifted group. *Genetic Psychology Monographs* 77: 3–93.

Okun, M. A., Stock, W. A., Haring, M. J., & Witter, R. A. (1984). Health and subjective well-being: A meta-analysis. *International Journal of Aging and Human Development* 19: 111–31.

Orlofsky, J. L., & Stake, J. E. (1981). Psychological masculinity and femininity: Relationship to striving and self-concept in the achievement and interpersonal domains. *Psychology of Women Quarterly* 6: 218–33.

Palmore, E. (1979). Predictors of successful aging. *Gerontologist* 19: 427–31.

———. (1981). *Social patterns in normal aging: Findings from the Duke Longitudinal Study.* Durham, N.C.: Duke University Press.

Palmore, E. B., Burchett, B. M., Fillenbaum, G. G., George, L. K., & Wallman, L. M. (1985). *Retirement: Causes and consequences.* New York: Springer.

Parnes, H. S., Crowley, J. E., Haurin, R. J., Less, L. J., Morgan, W. R., Mott, F. L., & Nestel, G. (1985). *Retirement among American men.* Lexington, Mass.: Lexington Books.

Parnes, H. S., & Less, L. J. (1985). Introduction and overview. In Parnes et al., 1985: 1–29.

Pedro, J. D., Wolleat, P., Fennema, E., & Becker, A. D. (1981). Election of high school mathematics by females and males: Attributions and attitudes. *American Educational Research Journal* 18: 207–18.

Peppers, L. G. (1976). Patterns of leisure and adjustment to retirement. *Gerontologist* 16: 441–46.

Perlmutter, M., ed. (1990). *Late life potential*. Washington, D.C.: Gerontological Society of America.

Pleck, J. H. (1985). *Working wives/working husbands*. Beverly Hills, Calif.: Sage Publications.

Preston, S. H., & McDonald, J. (1979). The incidence of divorce within cohorts of American marriages contracted since the Civil War. *Demography* 16: 1–25.

Price-Bonham, S. & Johnson, C. K. (1982). Attitudes toward retirement: A comparison of professional and nonprofessional married women. In M. Szinovacz, ed., *Women's retirement: Policy implications of recent research* (pp. 123–38). Beverly Hills, Calif.: Sage.

Princeton Religion Research Center (1982). *Religion in America*. Princeton, N.J.: The Gallup Poll.

Quinn, J. F. (1981). The extent and correlates of partial retirement. *Gerontologist* 21: 634–43.

Quinn, J. F., & Burkhauser, R. B. (1990). Work and retirement. In R. H. Binstock & L. K. George, eds., *Handbook of aging and the social sciences*, 3d ed. (pp. 307–27). San Diego: Academic Press.

Quinn, J. F., Burkhauser, R. V., & Myers, D. C. (1990). *Passing the torch: The influence of economic incentives on work and retirement*. Kalamazoo, Mich.: Upjohn Institute for Employment Research.

Rapoport, R., & Rapoport, R. N. (1980). Balancing work, family, and leisure: A triple helix model. In C. B. Derr, ed., *Work, family, and the career* (pp. 318–28). New York: Praeger.

Reisman, J. M. (1988). An indirect measure of the value of friendship for aging men. *Journal of Gerontology* 43: 109–10.

Reker, G. T., Peacock, E. J., & Wong, P. T. P. (1987). Meaning and purpose in life and well-being: A life-span perspective. *Journal of Gerontology* 42: 44–49.

Reker, G. T., & Wong, P. T. P. (1985). Personal optimism, physical and mental health: The triumph of successful aging. In J. E. Birren & J. Livingston, eds., *Cognition, stress, and aging* (pp. 134–73). Englewood Cliffs, N.J.: Prentice-Hall.

———. (1988). Aging as an individual process: Toward a theory of personal meaning. In J. E. Birren & V. L. Bengtson, eds., *Emergent theories of aging* (pp. 214–46). New York: Springer.

Roadburg, A. (1981). Perceptions of work and leisure among the elderly. *Gerontologist* 21: 142–45.

Robinson, P. K., Coberly, S., & Paul, C. E. (1985). Work and retirement. In R. H. Binstock & E. Shanas, eds., *Handbook of aging and the social sciences*, 2d ed. (pp. 503–27). New York: Van Nostrand Reinhold.

Rokeach, M. (1973). *The nature of human values*. New York: Free Press.

Rosenfeld, R. A. (1979). Women's occupational careers: Individual and structural explanations. *Sociology of Work and Occupations* 6: 283–311.

Rossi, A. S., ed. (1985). *Gender and the life course*. New York: Aldine.

Rowe, J. W., & Kahn, R. L. (1987). Human aging: Usual and successful. *Science* 237: 143–49.

Rudinger, Georg, & Thomae, H. (1990). The Bonn Longitudinal Study of Aging: Coping, life adjustment, and life satisfaction. In Baltes & Baltes, 1990b: 265–95.

Russell, D. W., & Cutrona, C. E. (1991). Social support, stress, and depressive symptoms among the elderly: Test of a process model. *Psychology and Aging* 6: 190–201.

Russo, N. F., & O'Connell, A. N. (1980). Models from our past: Psychology's fore-mothers. *Psychology of Women Quarterly* 5: 11–54.

Ryff, C. D. (1989a). Happiness is everything, or is it? Explorations on the meaning of psychological well-being. *Journal of Personality and Social Psychology* 57: 1069–81.

———. (1989b). In the eye of the beholder: Views of psychological well-being among middle-aged and older adults. *Psychology and Aging* 4: 195–210.

———. (1991). Possible selves in adulthood and old age: A tale of shifting horizons. *Psychology and Aging* 6: 286–95.

Salthouse, T. A. (1991). Cognitive facets of aging well. *Generations* 15: 35–38.

Sammartino, F. J. (1987). The effect of health on retirement. *Social Security Bulletin* 50: 31–47.

Schaie, K. W. (1990). The optimization of cognitive functioning in old age: Predictions based on cohort-sequential and longitudinal data. In Baltes & Baltes, 1990b: 94–117.

Schiedel, D. G., & Marcia, J. E. (1985). Ego identity, intimacy, sex role orientation, and gender. *Developmental Psychology* 21: 149–60.

Schiffler, R. J. (1975). Demographic and social factors in women's work lives. In S. H. Osipow, ed., *Emerging woman: Career analysis and outlooks* (pp. 10–22). Columbus, Ohio: Charles E. Merrill.

Schmitz-Scherzer, R. (1976). Longitudinal change in leisure behavior of the elderly. In H. Thomae, ed., *Patterns of Aging: Findings from the Bonn Longitudinal Study of Aging, Contributions to Human Development*, vol. 3 (pp. 127–36). Basel, Switzerland: Karger.

———. (1979). Ageing and leisure. *Society and Leisure* 2: 377–96.

Sears, P. S. (1977). Life satisfaction of Terman's gifted women, 1922–72: Comparisons with the gifted men and with normative samples. Paper presented at the 5th annual Spring conference, School of Education, University of Wisconsin, Madison, March.

Sears, P. S., & Barbee, A. H. (1977). Career and life satisfactions among Terman's gifted women. In J. C. Stanley, W. C. George, & C. H. Solano, eds., *The gifted and the creative: A fifty-year perspective* (pp. 28–65). Baltimore: Johns Hopkins University Press.

Sears, P. S., & Sears, R. R. (1978). From childhood to middle age to later maturity. Paper presented at the American Psychological Association Meeting, Toronto, August.

Sears, R. R. (1977). Sources of life satisfactions of the Terman gifted men. *American Psychologist* 32: 119–28.

———. (1981). The role of expectancy in adaptation to aging. In S. B. Kiesler, J. N. Morgan, & V. K. Oppenheimer, eds., *Aging: Social change* (pp. 407–30). New York: Academic Press.

———. (1984). The Terman Gifted Children Study (TGC). In S. A. Mednick, M. Harway, & K. M. Finello, eds., *Handbook of longitudinal research* (pp. 398–414). New York: Praeger.

Sewell, W. H., & Hauser, R. M. (1975). *Education, occupation, and earnings: Achievement in the early career.* New York: Academic Press.

Sewell, W. H., Hauser, R. M., & Wolf, W. C. (1980). Sex, schooling, and occupational status. *American Journal of Sociology* 86: 551–83.

Shanas, E., & Maddox, G. L. (1985). Health, health resources, and the utilization of care. In R. H. Binstock & E. Shanas, eds., *Handbook of aging and the social sciences*, 2d ed. (pp. 696–726). New York: Van Nostrand Reinhold.

Shavelson, R. J., Hubner, J. J., & Stanton, G. C. (1976). Self-concept: Validation of construct interpretations. *Review of Educational Research* 46: 407–41.

Shaw, L. B. (1984). Retirement plans of middle-aged married women. *Gerontologist* 24: 154–59.

Sherman, J. (1982). Continuing in mathematics: A longitudinal study of the attitudes of high school girls. *Psychology of Women Quarterly* 7: 132–40.

Shneidman, E. S. (1973). Suicide notes reconsidered. *Psychiatry* 36: 379–94.

Simonton, D. K. (1990). Does creativity decline in the later years? Definition, data, and theory. In M. Perlmutter, 1990: 83–112.

Simpson, I. H., Back, K. W., & McKinney, J. C. (1966). Continuity of work and retirement activities and self-evaluation. In I. H. Simpson & J. C. McKinney, eds., *Social aspects of aging* (pp. 106–19). Durham, N.C.: Duke University Press.

Skolnick, A. (1981). Married lives: Longitudinal perspectives on marriage. In D. H. Eichorn, J. A. Clausen, N. Haan, M. P. Honzik, & P. H. Mussen, eds., *Present and past in middle life* (pp. 269–98). New York: Academic Press.

Spaeth, J. L. (1976). Cognitive complexity: A dimension underlying the socioeconomic achievement process. In W. H. Sewell, R. M. Hauser, & D. L. Featherman, eds., *Schooling and achievement in American society* (pp. 103–37). New York: Academic Press.

Spreitzer, E., & Riley, L. E. (1974). Factors associated with singlehood. *Journal of Marriage and the Family* 36: 533–42.

Stake, J. E. (1979). The ability/performance dimension of self-esteem: Implications for women's achievement behavior. *Psychology of Women Quarterly* 3: 365–77.

Stephan, C. W., & Corder, J. (1985). The effects of dual-career families on adolescents' sex-role attitudes, work and family plans, and choices of important others. *Journal of Marriage and the Family* 47: 921–29.

Stewart, A. J. (1980). Personality and situation in the prediction of women's life patterns. *Psychology of Women Quarterly* 5: 195–206.

Stock, W. A., Okun, M. A., & Benin, M. (1986). Structure of subjective well-being among the elderly. *Psychology and Aging* 1: 91–102.

Strain, L. A., & Chappell, N. L. (1982). Confidants — Do they make a difference in the quality of life? *Research on Aging* 4: 479–502.

Stroud, J. (1981). Women's careers: Work, family, and personality. In D. H. Eichorn, J. A. Clausen, N. Haan, M. P. Honzik, & P. H. Mussen, eds., *Present and past in middle life* (pp. 353–90). New York: Academic Press.

Szinovacz, M., ed., (1982). *Women's retirement: Policy implications of recent research.* Beverly Hills, Calif.: Sage.

Tangri, S. S. (1972). Determinants of occupational role innovation among college women. *Journal of Social Issues* 28: 177–99.

Terman, L. M. (1938). *Psychological factors in marital happiness.* New York: McGraw-Hill.

———. (1947; Rev. ed. 1955). Marital adjustment and its prediction. In M. Fishbein and E. W. Burgess, eds., *Successful marriage* (pp. 113–26). New York: Doubleday.

Terman, L. M., assisted by B. T. Baldwin, E. Bronson, J. C. DeVoss, F. Fuller, F. L. Goodenough, T. L. Kelley, M. Lima, H. Marshall, A. H. Moore, A. S. Raubenheimer, G. M. Ruch, R. L. Willoughby, J. B. Wyman, & D. H. Yates (1925). *Mental and physical traits of a thousand gifted children. Vol. 1. Genetic studies of genius.* Stanford, Calif.: Stanford University Press.

Terman, L. M., & Oden, M. H. (1940). II. Status of the California gifted group at the end of sixteen years. III. Correlates of adult achievement in the California gifted group. In *Yearbook of the National Society for the Study of Education*, 39: pt. 1, 67–89.

———. (1947). *The gifted child grows up. Vol. IV. Genetic studies of genius.* Stanford, Calif.: Stanford University Press.

———. (1959). *The gifted group at mid-life. Vol. V. Genetic studies of genius.* Stanford, Calif.: Stanford University Press.

Thurnher, M. (1975). Continuities and discontinuities in value orientation. In M. F. Lowenthal, M. Thurnher, D. Chiriboga, & Associates, eds., *Four stages of life*: *A comparative study of women and men facing transitions* (pp. 176–200). San Francisco: Jossey-Bass.

Tinsley, D. J., & Faunce, P. S. (1980). Enabling, facilitating, and precipitating factors associated with women's career orientation. *Journal of Vocational Behavior* 17: 183–94.

Tinsley, H. E. A., Colbs, S. L., Teaff, J. D., & Kaufman, N. (1987). The relationship of age, gender, health and economic status to the psychological benefits older persons report from participation in leisure activities. *Leisure Sciences* 9: 53–65.

Tomlinson-Keasey, C., Warren, L. W., & Elliott, J. E. (1986). Suicide among gifted women: A prospective study. *Journal of Abnormal Psychology* 95: 123–30.

Treiman, D. J. (1985). The work histories of women and men: What we know and what we need to find out. In Rossi, 1985: 213–31.

Troll, L. E. (1982). *Continuations*: *Adult development and aging.* Monterey, Calif.: Brooks/Cole.

Troll, L. E., & Bengtson, V. (1979). Generations in the family. In W. Burr, R. Hill, F. Nye, & I. Reiss, eds., *Contemporary theories about the family* (pp. 126–61). New York: Free Press.

U.S. Bureau of the Census (1988). *Statistical Abstract of the United States 1988* (108th ed.). Washington, D.C.: U.S. Government Printing Office.

U.S. Senate Special Committee on Aging (1987–88). *Aging America*: *Trends and projections.* Washington, D.C.: U.S. Department of Health and Human Services.

Vaillant, G. E. (1977). *Adaptation to life.* Boston: Little, Brown.

Vaillant, G. E. (1990). Avoiding negative life outcomes: Evidence from a forty-five year study. In Baltes & Baltes, 1990b: 332–58.

Vaillant, G. E., & Vaillant, C. O. (1990). Determinants and consequences of creativity in a cohort of gifted women. *Psychology of Women Quarterly* 14: 607–16.

Verbrugge, L. M. (1989). Gender, aging, and health. In K. S. Markides, ed., *Aging and health*: *Perspectives on gender, race, ethnicity, and class* (pp. 23–73). Newbury Park, Calif.: Sage.

Veroff, J. E., Douvan, E., & Kulka, R. (1981). *The inner American.* New York: Basic Books.

Walker, S. N. (1990). Promoting healthy aging. In K. F. Ferraro, ed., *Gerontology*: *Perspectives and issues* (pp. 266–82). New York: Springer.

Ward, R. A. (1979). The never-married in later life. *Journal of Gerontology* 34: 861–69.

Ward, R. A., Sherman, S. R., & LaGory, M. (1984). Subjective network assessments and subjective well-being. *Journal of Gerontology* 39: 93–101.

Wellman, B., & Hall, A. (1986). Social networks and social support: Implications for later life. In V. Marshall, ed., *Later life*: *The social psychology of aging* (pp. 191–231). Beverly Hills, Calif.: Sage.

Williams, T. (1976). Abilities and environments. In W. H. Sewell, R. M. Hauser, & D. L. Featherman, eds., *Schooling and achievement in American society* (pp. 61–101). New York: Academic Press.

Willis, S. L. (1990). Contributions of cognitive training research to understanding late life potential. In Perlmutter, 1990: 25–42.

Wolfson, K. P. (1976). Career development patterns of college women. *Journal of Counseling Psychology* 23: 119–25.

Wright, P. H. (1989). Gender differences in adults' same and cross-gender friendships. In Adams & Blieszner, 1989: 197–221.

Yalom, I. D. (1980). *Existential psychotherapy*. New York: Basic Books.

Yoesting, D. R., & Christensen, J. E. (1978). Re-examining the significance of childhood recreation patterns on adult leisure behavior. *Leisure Sciences* 1: 219–29.

Index

In this index an "f" after a number indicates a separate reference on the next page, and an "ff" indicates separate references on the next two pages. A continuous discussion over two or more pages is indicated by a span of page numbers, e.g., "pp. 57–58." *Passim* is used for a cluster of references in close but not consecutive sequence.

Diener, E., 218
Disappointments, 168–71, 172
Discriminant analysis, 55, 107, 143f, 152f
Dittman-Kohli, F., 192, 194, 214
Divorce: of subjects' parents, 14, 37, 104, 125–26, 138, 259; through mid-life, 21; and attrition in survey responses, 35–39 *passim*, 326, 331; and occupational experience, 88ff, 103, 109, 119, 135, 143; and multi-divorced persons, 123f, 135–43 *passim*, 156–57, 273; and once-divorced persons, 123f, 135–42 *passim*, 156–57; and gender differences, 126f, 131f, 137–44 *passim*, 159f, 171; median age at, 131; and presence of offspring, 131; and remarriage, 131–32; as deviation from cultural norm, 132–33; and mental health, 132, 141–43, 144, 157; and Marital Aptitude Test scores, 134–35; and adolescent sex behavior, 135, 138–39, 144, 156, 273; and age at first marriage, 135, 144, 156; and family background, 135, 136–37, 144, 156; and intellectual performance, 135f; and personality traits, 135, 139–40, 141, 144, 156–57, 273; and childhood happiness, 137–38, 144, 157; and alcohol use, 141f; and educational attainment, 143; and social interaction, 165–68 *passim*, 196; and intimacy, 167–68, 172
Dixon, R. A., 192
Domestic responsibility, 127–30
Douglass, E. B., 224
Drug use, 31
Duke Longitudinal Studies, 181, 201, 229f, 238
Duncan, B., 51
Duncan, O. D., 51
Dvorkin, L., 166
Dworkin, R. H., 135
Dyadic relationships, 134, 158f, 270

Easygoing personality: and divorce rates, 140, 149f, 153; and health/well-being, 237, 242, 270
Eccles, J., 104
Eckland, B. K., 51
Economic conditions, 1, 12, 27–32 *passim*, 39, 261
Educational attainment: of parents, 13, 104; through mid-life, 17, 20, 45–46; of men, 44–46, 53, 77, 79, 268; Great Depression's effect on, 45–46, 79, 118, 268;

World War II's effect on, 45f, 79, 118, 268; and occupational levels, 53, 55f, 80, 107f, 119; and retirement patterns, 77, 79; of women, 84–85, 107f, 152, 268; and divorce rates, 143; and marital history, 143, 151; and life satisfactions, 248; as turning point in life, 258–60; and attrition in survey responses, 321–22, 331. *See also* Academic degrees; Academic performance
Educational choices, retrospective assessment of, 262f, 272
Eichorn, D. H., 238
Ekerdt, D. J., 175, 187
Elder, G. H., Jr., 27, 53, 61, 261
Elliott, J. E., 123
Emotionality: and divorce, 140f, 144, 157; and health/well-being, 237f, 242
Erickson, R. C., 191
Ericsson, K. A., 3
Erikson, E. H., 3, 61, 192, 214, 243
Erikson, J. M., 3, 192
Erikson, R. S., 206f
Ethnicity, *see* Racial and ethnic background
Evans, M. D., 49
Extracurricular activities, 2, 15, 54f, 188

Falk, W. W., 106
Family background: of original Terman sample, 12–14, 15; and men's occupational levels, 51–52, 55f, 80; and women's occupational levels, 103f; and divorce rates, 135, 136–37, 144, 156; and never-divorced persons, 136–38, 148; and never-married persons, 148; and longevity, 268
Family composition, 14
Family relations: balanced with career pursuits, 43–44, 60–62, 83ff; and women's goal orientation, 43–44, 98–102, 107, 193f; women's role in, 43–44; and men's goal orientation, 60–62, 80, 193f; and life satisfactions, 62, 78f, 245–47; men's role in, 62; and men's retirement patterns, 78f; Great Depression's effect on, 83; and women's occupational levels, 102–7 *passim*; and women's career interruptions, 108–10, 119; and intimacy, 166–68, 171; and social activities, 177–81 *passim*, 187; and turning points in life, 258–61, 265; retrospective assessment of, 263f. *See also* Offspring; Parents; Siblings
Family size, 124–25
Farmer, H. S., 51, 104

Library of Congress Cataloging-in-Publication Data

Holahan, Carole K.
  The gifted group in later maturity / Carole K. Holahan and Robert
R. Sears in association with Lee J. Cronbach.
    p.   cm.
Includes bibliographical references and index.
ISBN 0-8047-2407-5 (alk. paper)
1. Gifted aged — United States — Longitudinal studies.   2. Gifted
children — United States — Longitudinal studies.   3. Terman, Lewis
Madison, 1877–1956.   I. Sears, Robert R. (Robert Richardson)
II. Cronbach, Lee J. (Lee Joseph).
BF724.85.G54H65   1995
155.67'087'9 — dc20
94-4819   CIP

⊗This book is printed on acid-free paper. It was
typeset in 10/12 Times by Keystone Typesetting, Inc.